12

Love & Lies

LOVE and LIES by MUSAWO

The Lilina Ending

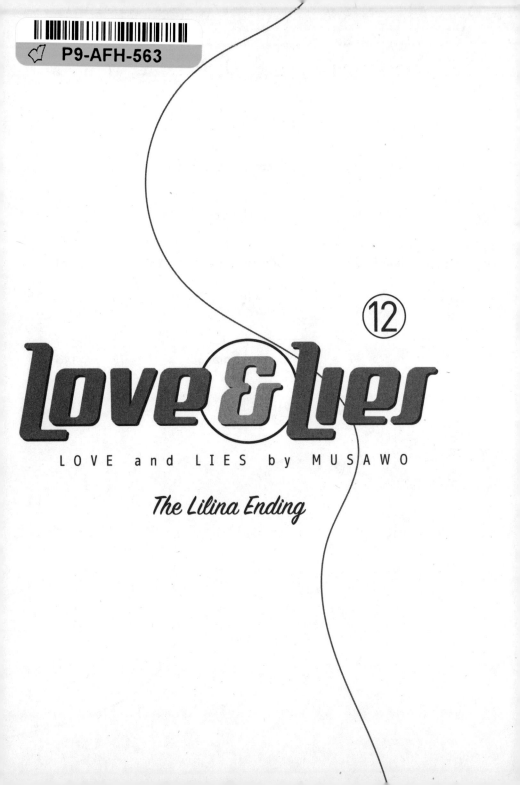

CONTENTS

Chapter 45   Protected by a Lie   3

Chapter 46   Given by Love   41

Chapter 47   Accepting Love and Lies   61

Chapter 48   Thank You   101

Chapter 49   Special Someone   143

Final Chapter   At the End of the Red String   165

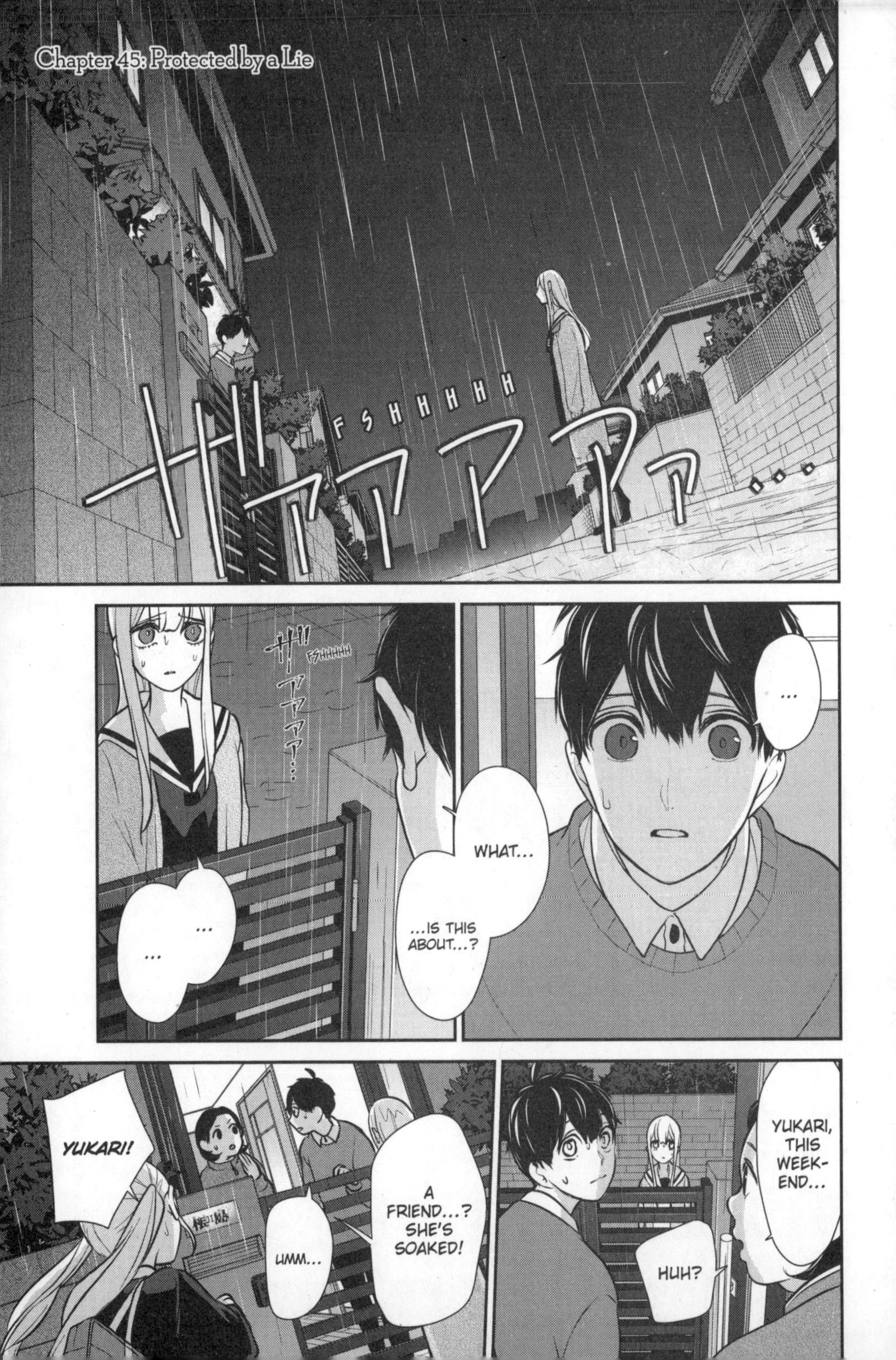
Chapter 45: Protected by a Lie
ザァァァァ…
FSHHHHHH
...
WHAT...
...IS THIS ABOUT...?
ザァァァ…
FSHHHHH
...
...
YUKARI, THIS WEEK-END...
HUH?
A FRIEND...? SHE'S SOAKED!
UMM...
YUKARI!

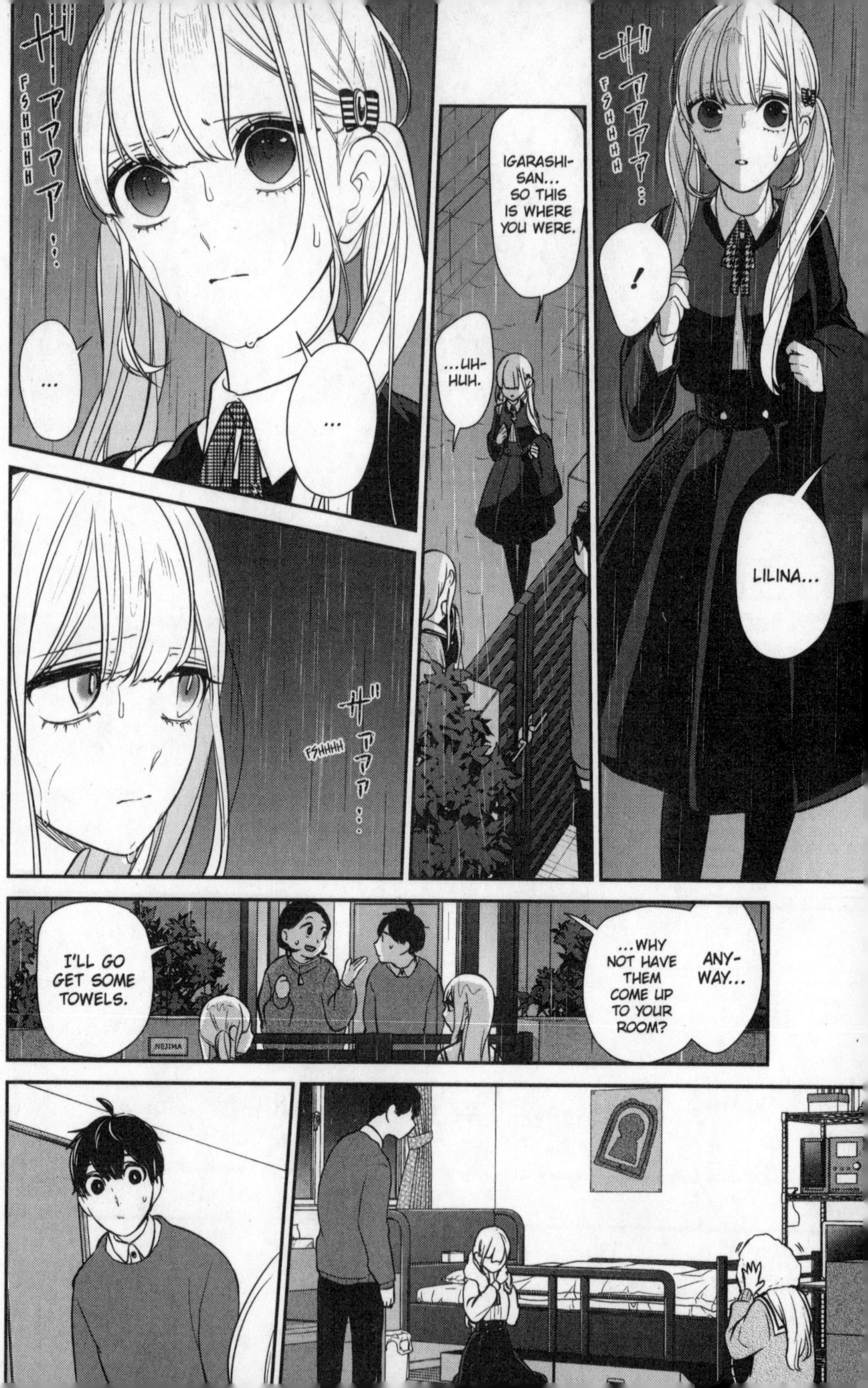
FSHHHHH
!
LILINA...
IGARASHI-SAN... SO THIS IS WHERE YOU WERE.
...UH-HUH.
FSHHHHH
...
...
FSHHHH
ANY-WAY...
...WHY NOT HAVE THEM COME UP TO YOUR ROOM?
I'LL GO GET SOME TOWELS.
NEJIMA

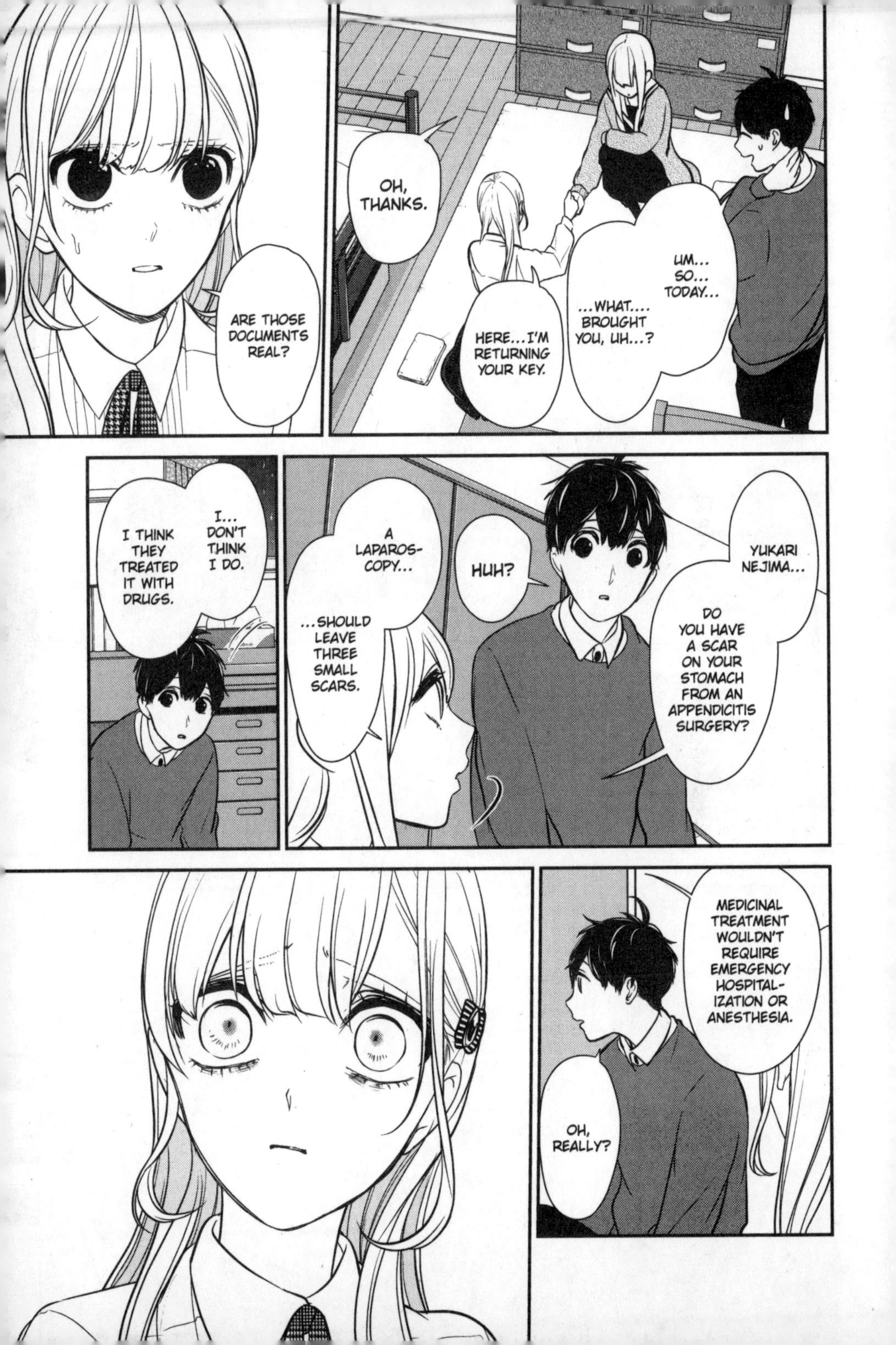
UM... SO... TODAY...
...WHAT.... BROUGHT YOU, UH...?
HERE...I'M RETURNING YOUR KEY.
OH, THANKS.
ARE THOSE DOCUMENTS REAL?
YUKARI NEJIMA...
DO YOU HAVE A SCAR ON YOUR STOMACH FROM AN APPENDICITIS SURGERY?
HUH?
A LAPAROS-COPY...
...SHOULD LEAVE THREE SMALL SCARS.
I... DON'T THINK I DO.
I THINK THEY TREATED IT WITH DRUGS.
MEDICINAL TREATMENT WOULDN'T REQUIRE EMERGENCY HOSPITAL-IZATION OR ANESTHESIA.
OH, REALLY?

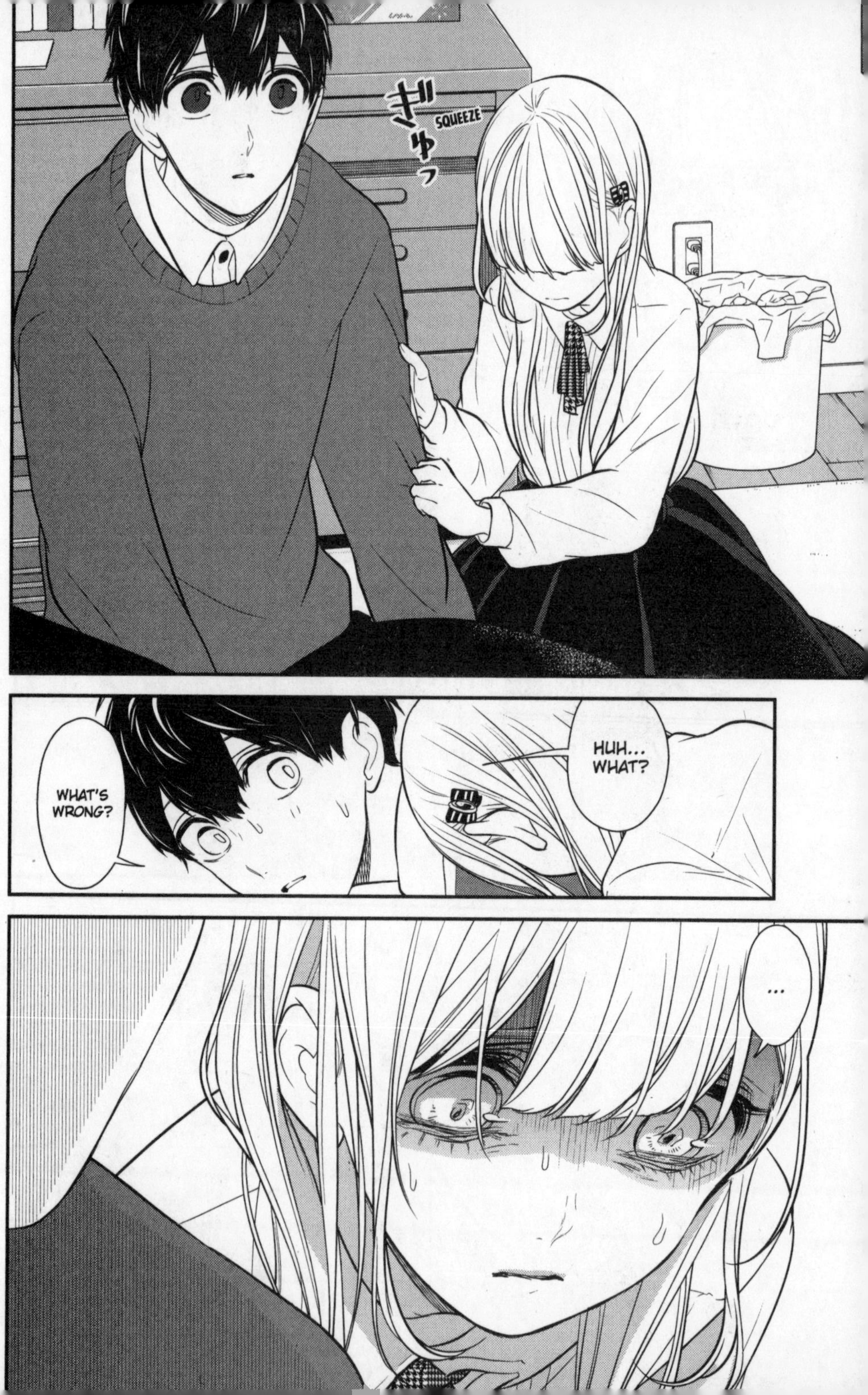
ギュッ
SQUEEZE
HUH... WHAT?
WHAT'S WRONG?
...

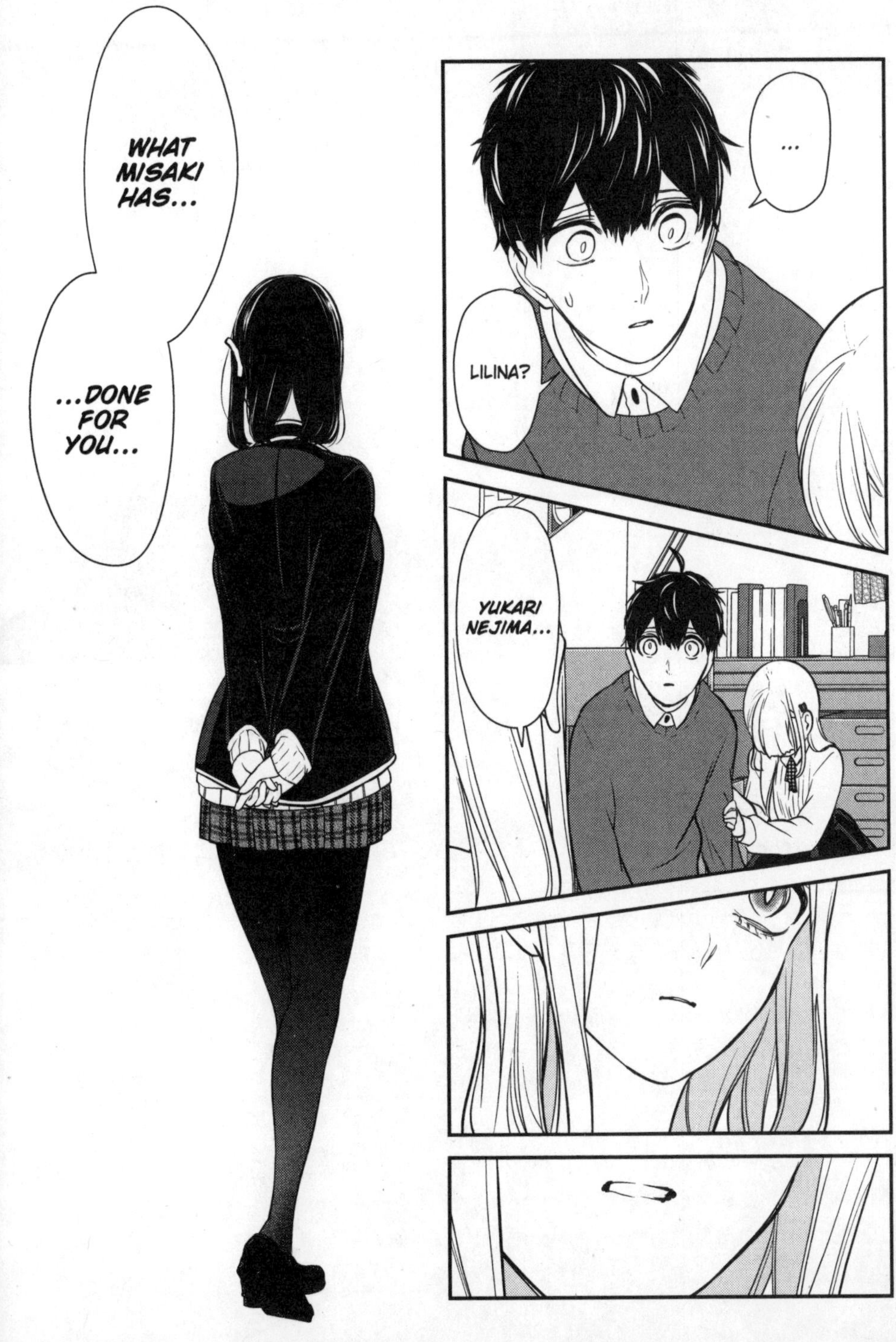
...
LILINA?
YUKARI NEJIMA...
WHAT MISAKI HAS...
...DONE FOR YOU...

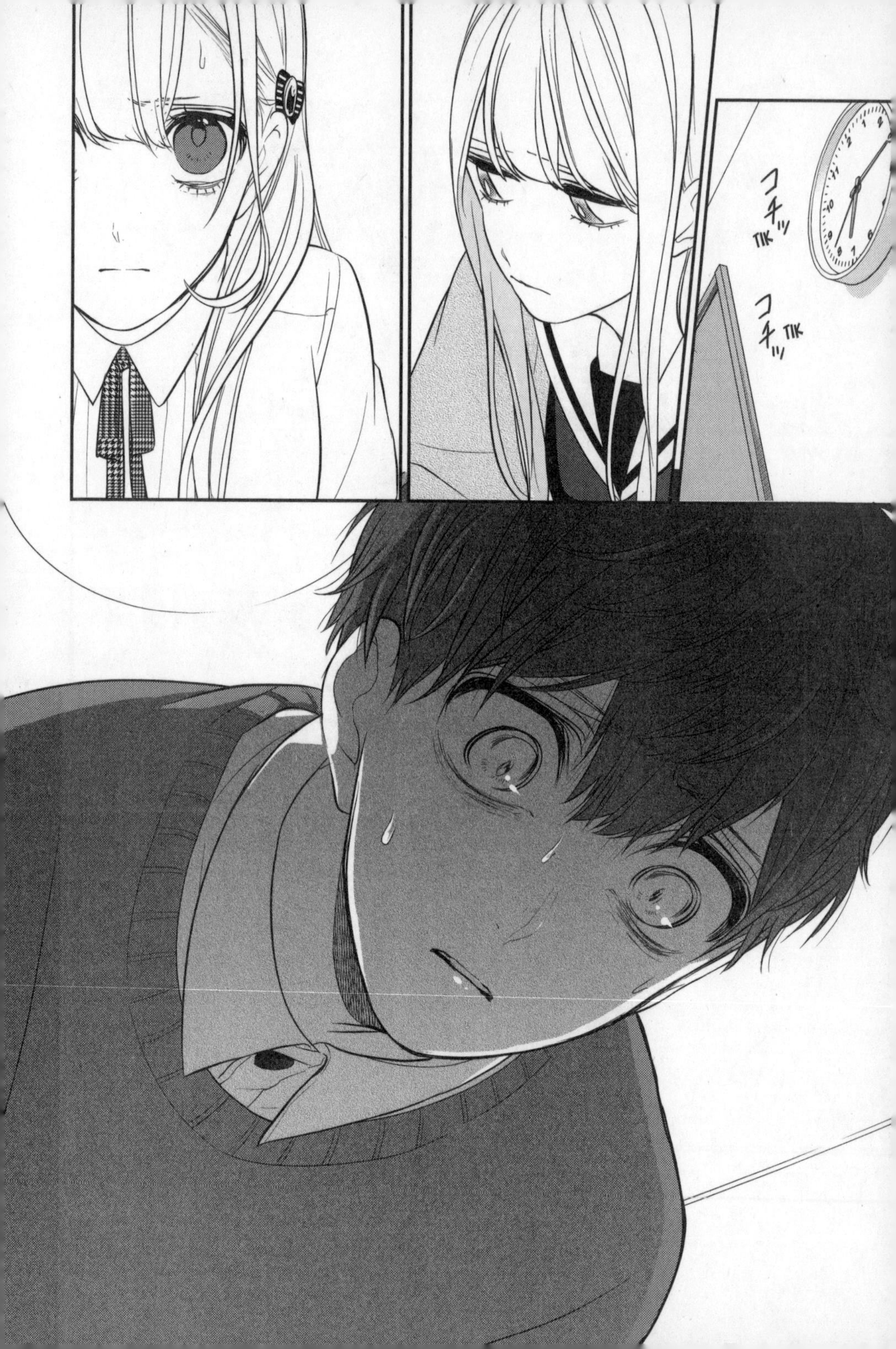

コチッ
TIK
コチッ
TIK

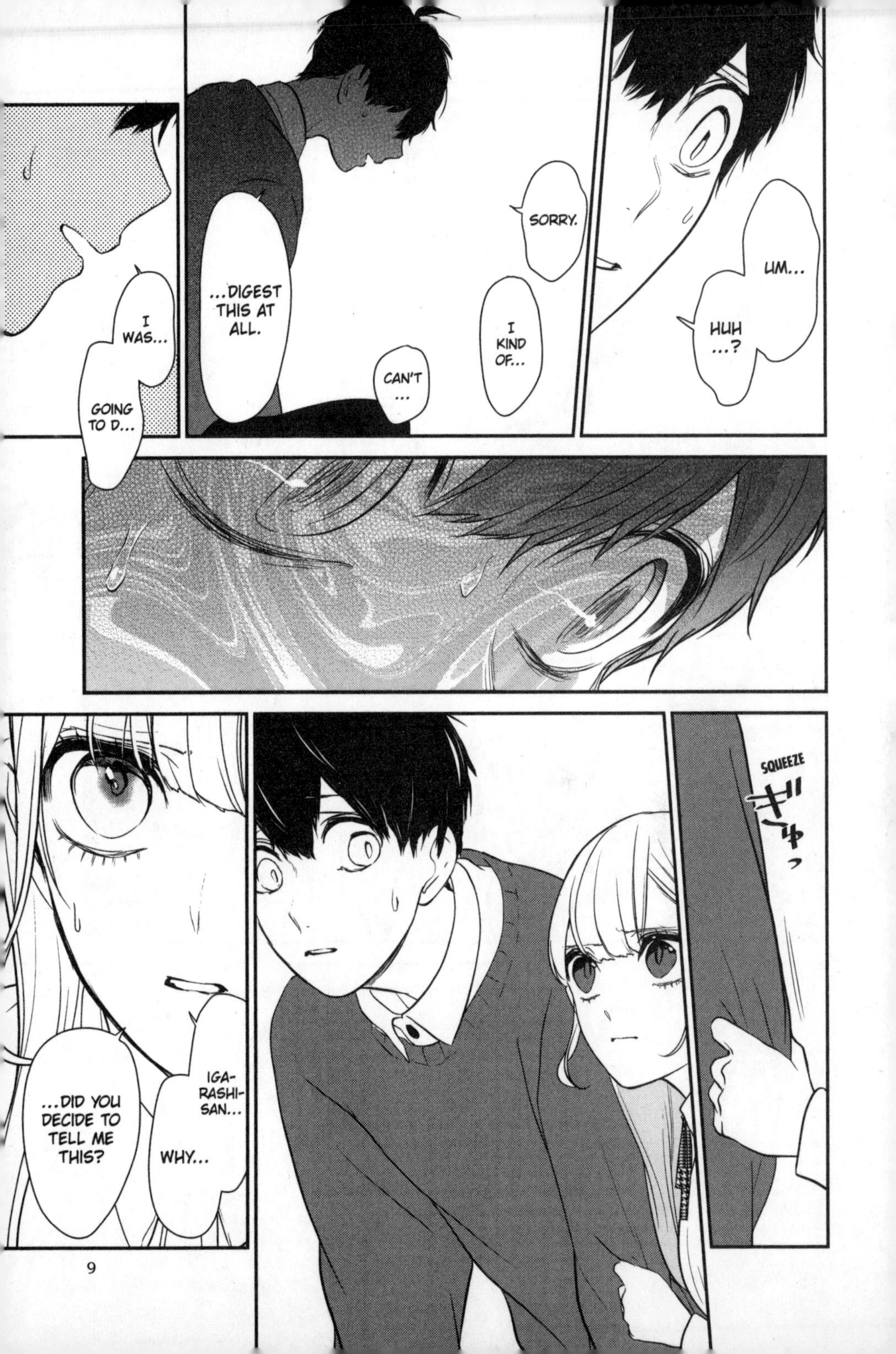
UM...
HUH ...?
SORRY.
I KIND OF...
CAN'T ...
...DIGEST THIS AT ALL.
I WAS...
GOING TO D...
SQUEEZE
IGA-RASHI-SAN...
WHY...
...DID YOU DECIDE TO TELL ME THIS?

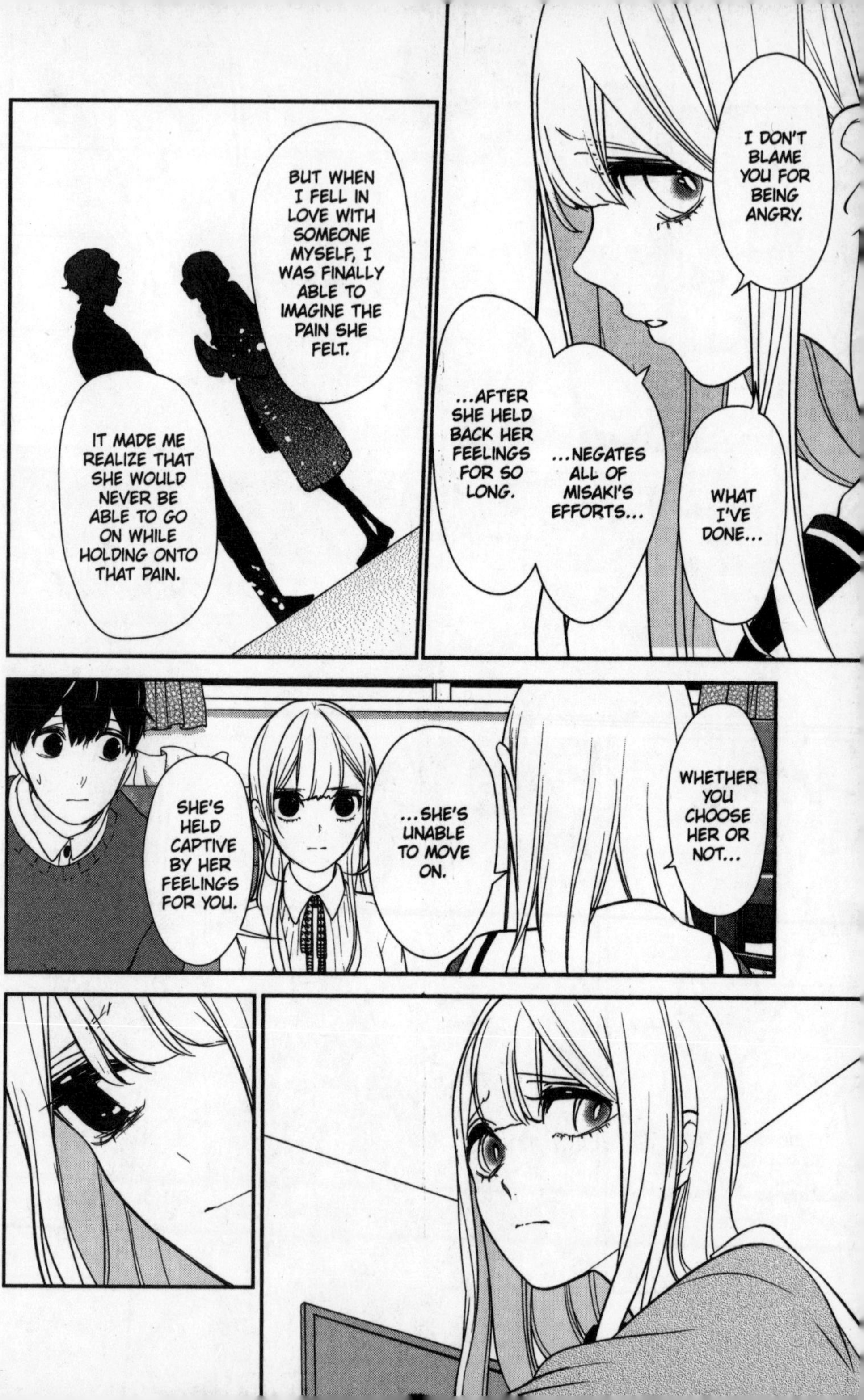
I DON'T BLAME YOU FOR BEING ANGRY.
WHAT I'VE DONE...
...NEGATES ALL OF MISAKI'S EFFORTS...
...AFTER SHE HELD BACK HER FEELINGS FOR SO LONG.
BUT WHEN I FELL IN LOVE WITH SOMEONE MYSELF, I WAS FINALLY ABLE TO IMAGINE THE PAIN SHE FELT.
IT MADE ME REALIZE THAT SHE WOULD NEVER BE ABLE TO GO ON WHILE HOLDING ONTO THAT PAIN.
WHETHER YOU CHOOSE HER OR NOT...
...SHE'S UNABLE TO MOVE ON.
SHE'S HELD CAPTIVE BY HER FEELINGS FOR YOU.

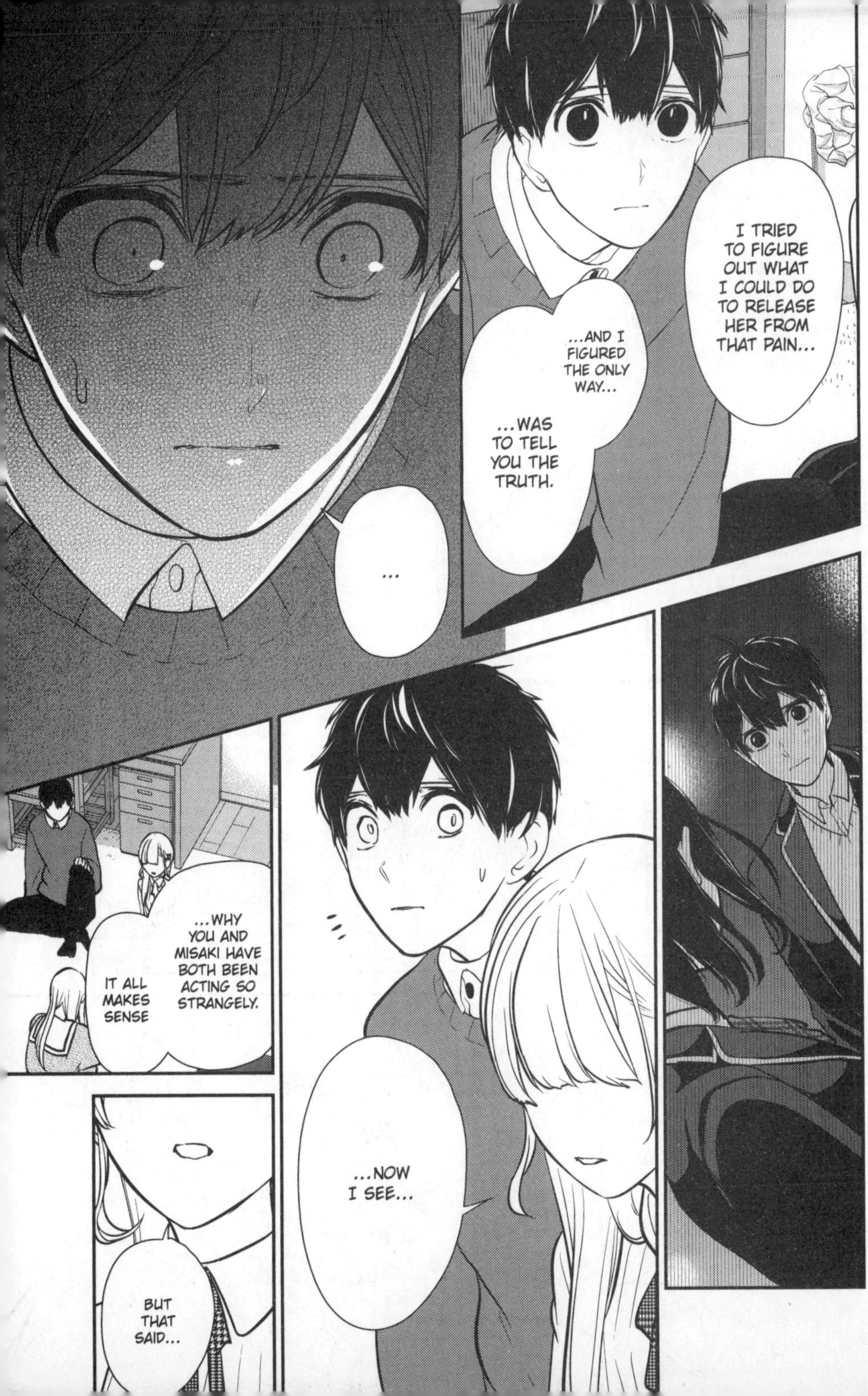
I TRIED TO FIGURE OUT WHAT I COULD DO TO RELEASE HER FROM THAT PAIN...
...AND I FIGURED THE ONLY WAY...
...WAS TO TELL YOU THE TRUTH.
...
...NOW I SEE...
...WHY YOU AND MISAKI HAVE BOTH BEEN ACTING SO STRANGELY.
IT ALL MAKES SENSE
BUT THAT SAID...

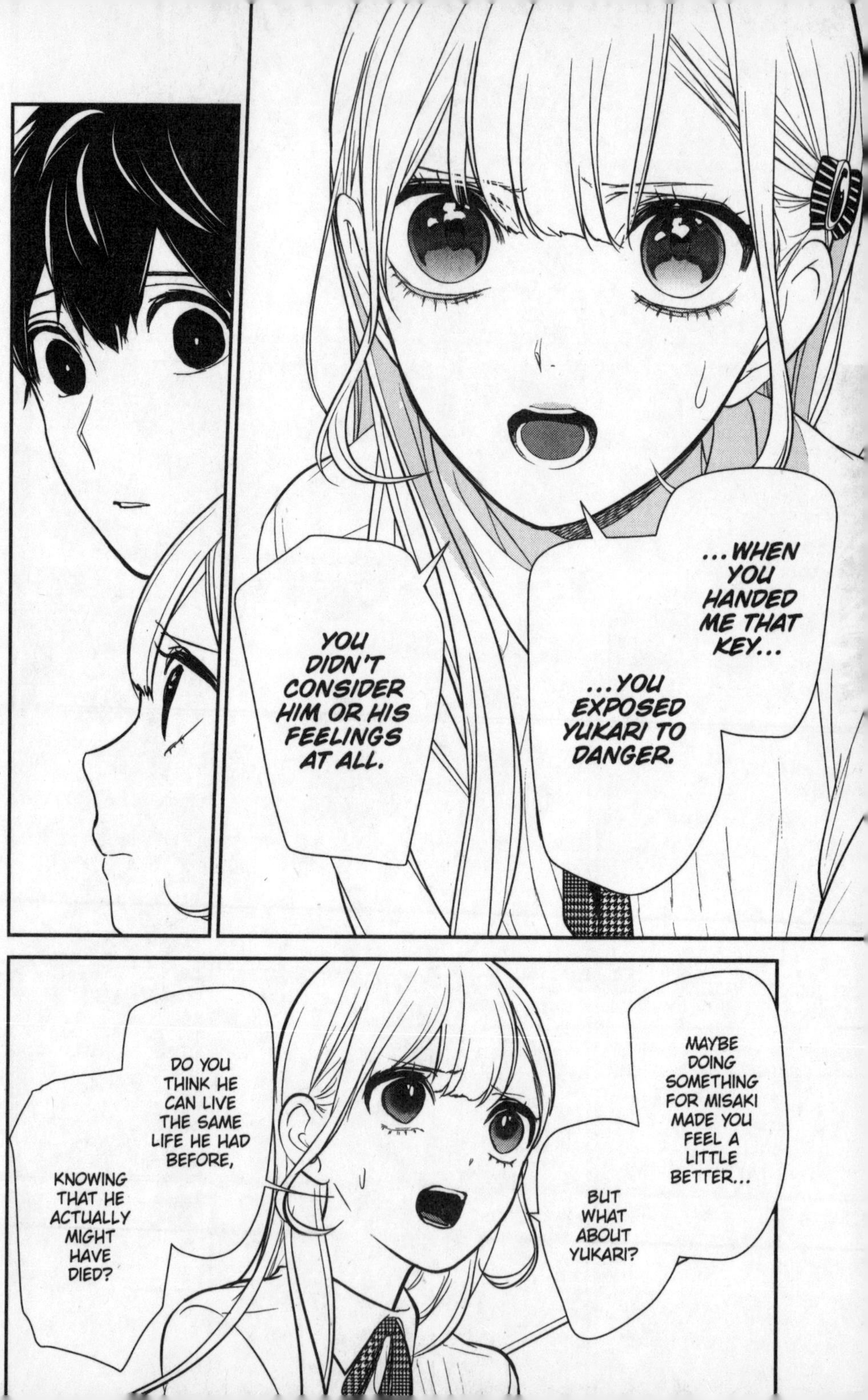
...WHEN YOU HANDED ME THAT KEY...
...YOU EXPOSED YUKARI TO DANGER.
YOU DIDN'T CONSIDER HIM OR HIS FEELINGS AT ALL.
MAYBE DOING SOMETHING FOR MISAKI MADE YOU FEEL A LITTLE BETTER...
BUT WHAT ABOUT YUKARI?
DO YOU THINK HE CAN LIVE THE SAME LIFE HE HAD BEFORE,
KNOWING THAT HE ACTUALLY MIGHT HAVE DIED?

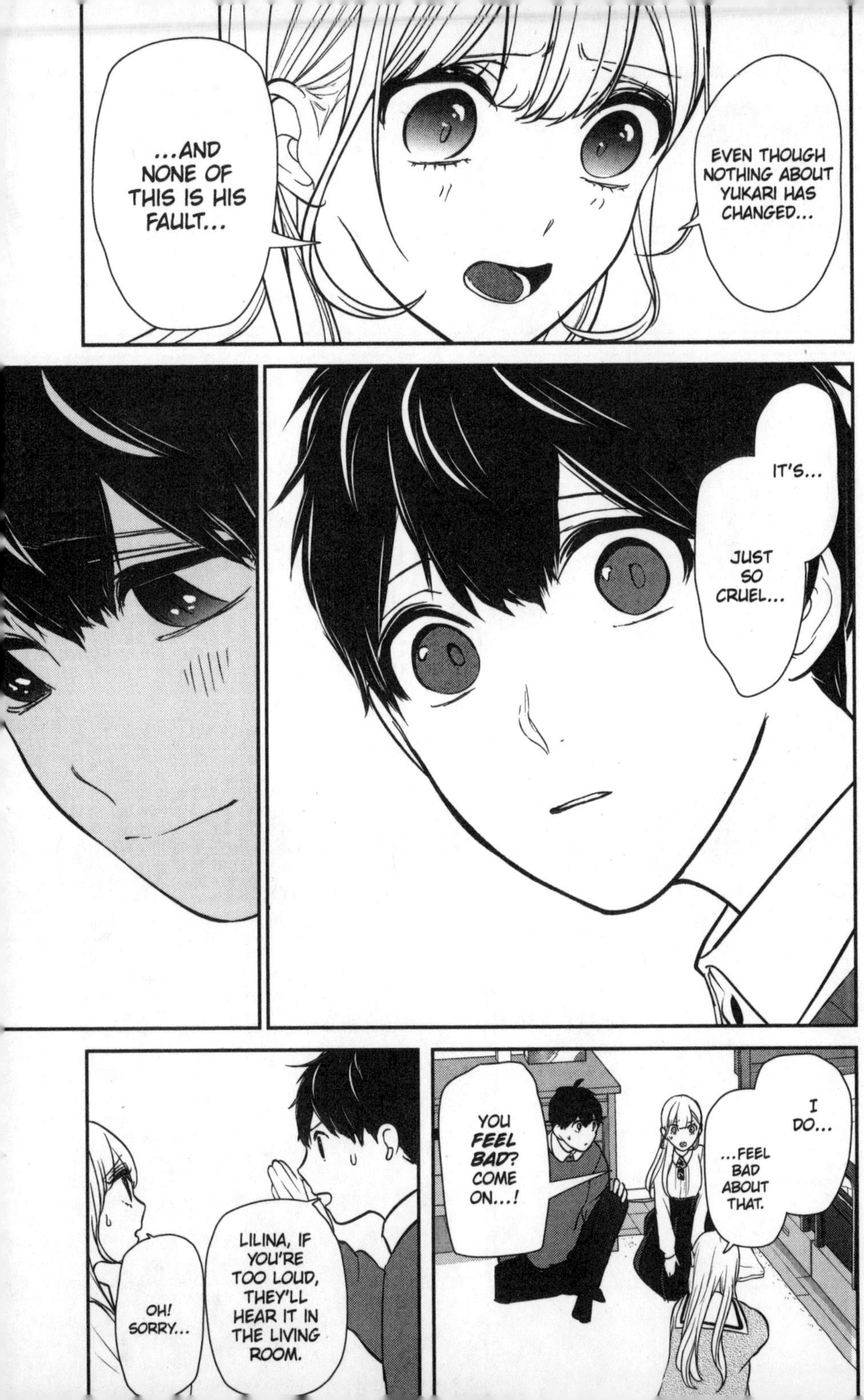
EVEN THOUGH NOTHING ABOUT YUKARI HAS CHANGED...
...AND NONE OF THIS IS HIS FAULT...
IT'S...
JUST SO CRUEL...
I DO...
...FEEL BAD ABOUT THAT.
YOU *FEEL BAD*? COME ON...!
LILINA, IF YOU'RE TOO LOUD, THEY'LL HEAR IT IN THE LIVING ROOM.
OH! SORRY...

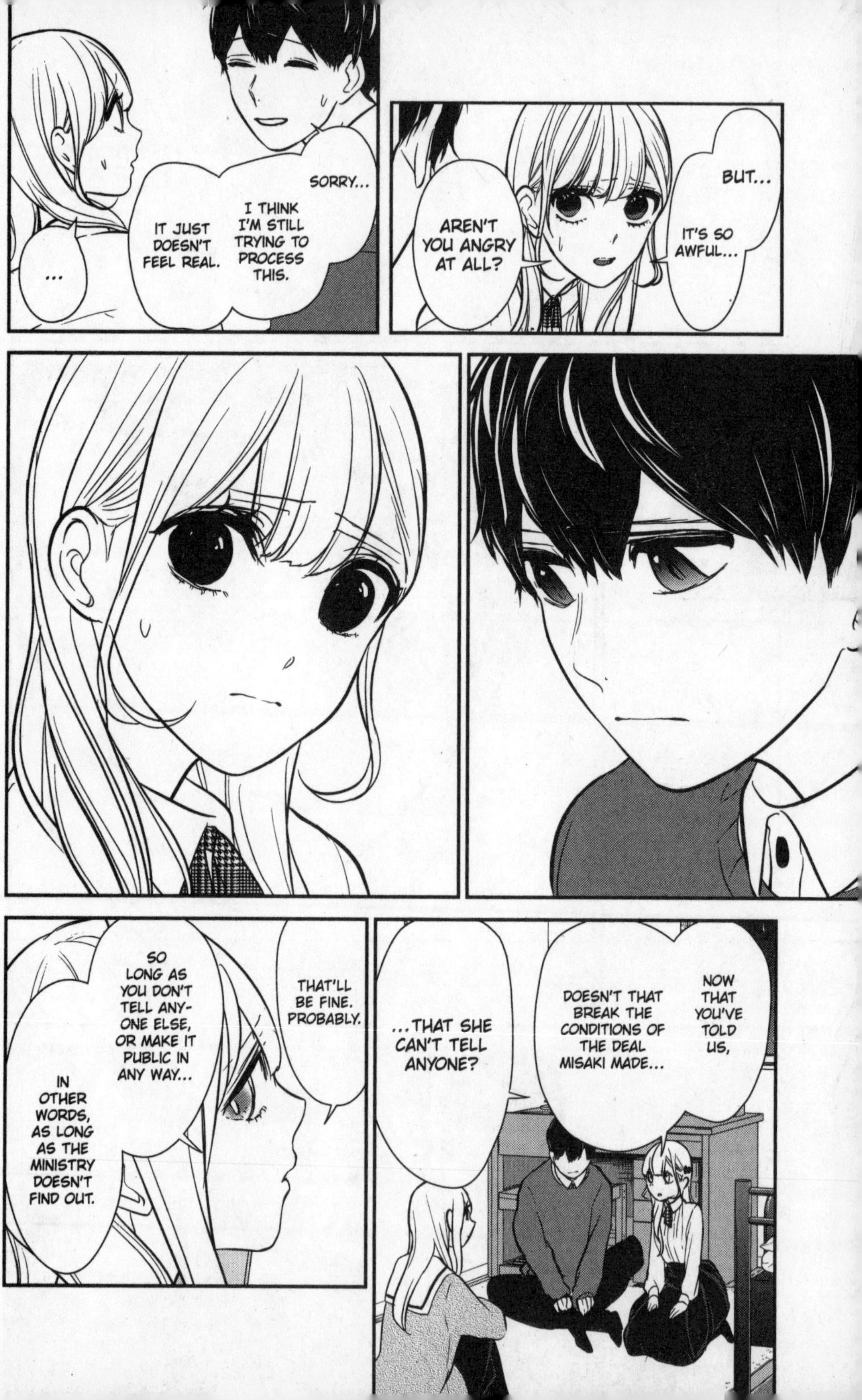
BUT...
IT'S SO AWFUL...
AREN'T YOU ANGRY AT ALL?
SORRY...
I THINK I'M STILL TRYING TO PROCESS THIS.
IT JUST DOESN'T FEEL REAL.
...
NOW THAT YOU'VE TOLD US,
DOESN'T THAT BREAK THE CONDITIONS OF THE DEAL MISAKI MADE...
...THAT SHE CAN'T TELL ANYONE?
THAT'LL BE FINE. PROBABLY.
SO LONG AS YOU DON'T TELL ANY-ONE ELSE, OR MAKE IT PUBLIC IN ANY WAY...
IN OTHER WORDS, AS LONG AS THE MINISTRY DOESN'T FIND OUT.

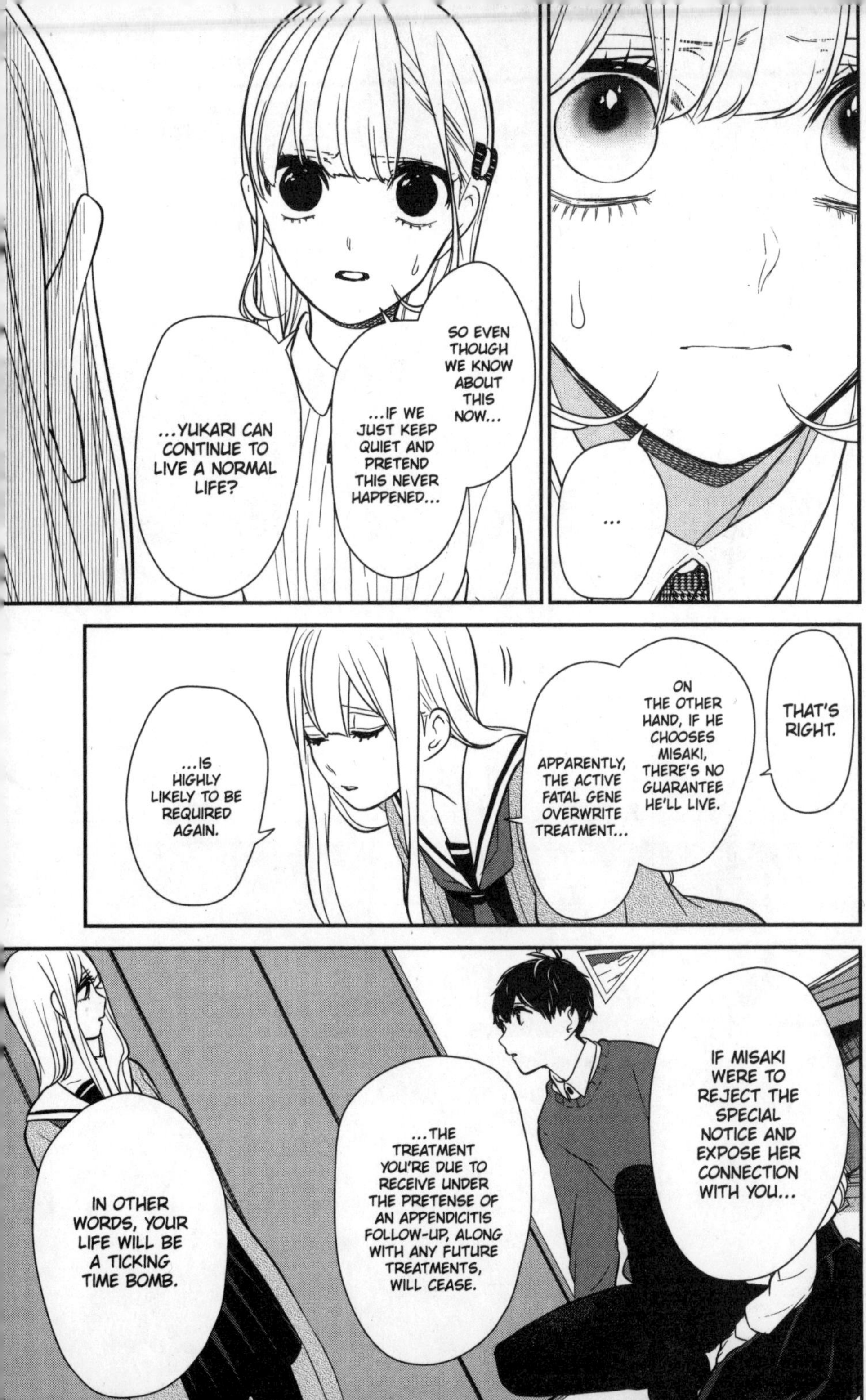
...
SO EVEN THOUGH WE KNOW ABOUT THIS NOW...
...IF WE JUST KEEP QUIET AND PRETEND THIS NEVER HAPPENED...
...YUKARI CAN CONTINUE TO LIVE A NORMAL LIFE?
THAT'S RIGHT.
ON THE OTHER HAND, IF HE CHOOSES MISAKI, THERE'S NO GUARANTEE HE'LL LIVE.
APPARENTLY, THE ACTIVE FATAL GENE OVERWRITE TREATMENT...
...IS HIGHLY LIKELY TO BE REQUIRED AGAIN.
IF MISAKI WERE TO REJECT THE SPECIAL NOTICE AND EXPOSE HER CONNECTION WITH YOU...
...THE TREATMENT YOU'RE DUE TO RECEIVE UNDER THE PRETENSE OF AN APPENDICITIS FOLLOW-UP, ALONG WITH ANY FUTURE TREATMENTS, WILL CEASE.
IN OTHER WORDS, YOUR LIFE WILL BE A TICKING TIME BOMB.

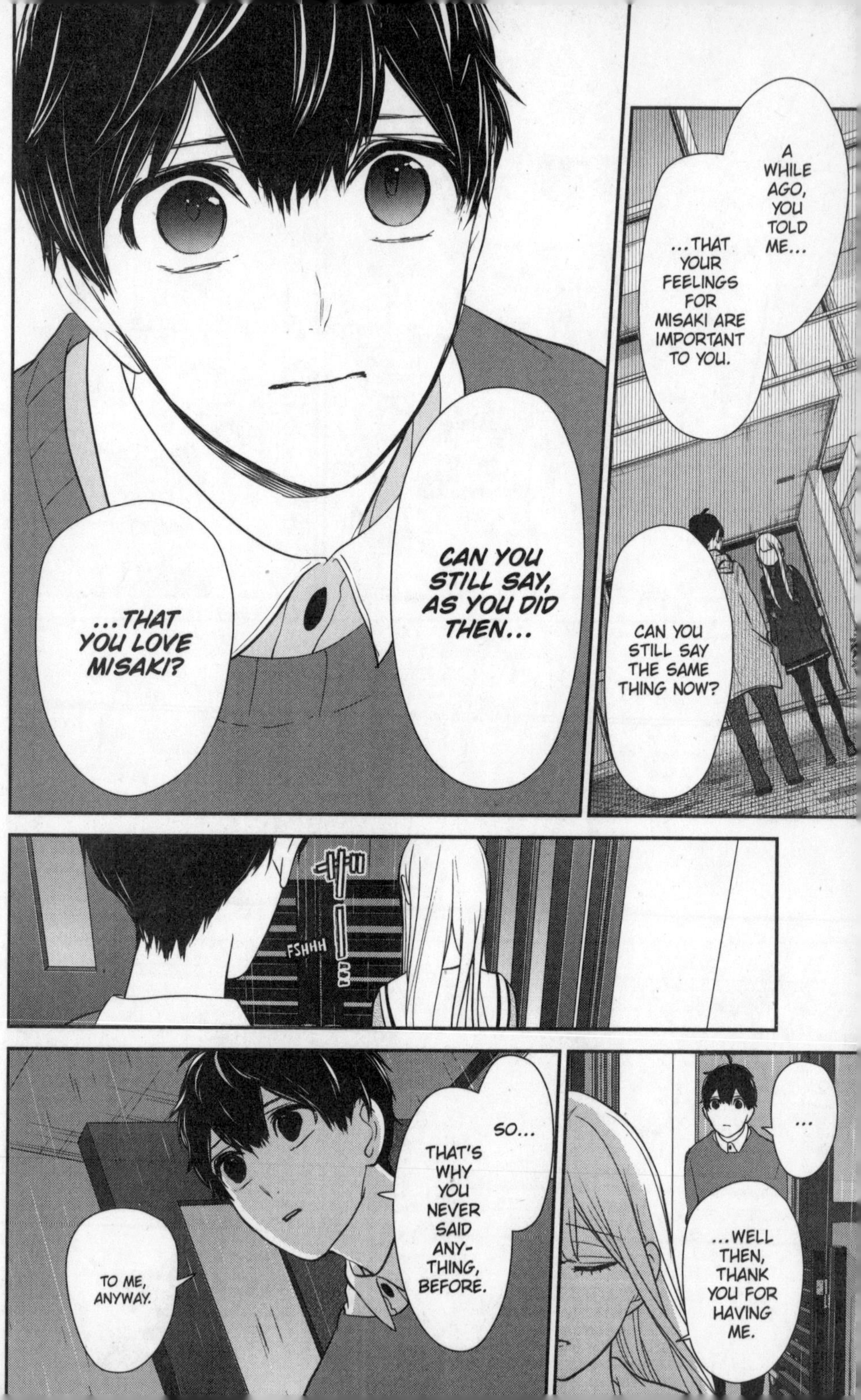
A WHILE AGO, YOU TOLD ME...
...THAT YOUR FEELINGS FOR MISAKI ARE IMPORTANT TO YOU.
CAN YOU STILL SAY THE SAME THING NOW?
CAN YOU STILL SAY, AS YOU DID THEN...
...THAT YOU LOVE MISAKI?
FSHHH
...
...WELL THEN, THANK YOU FOR HAVING ME.
SO...
THAT'S WHY YOU NEVER SAID ANY-THING, BEFORE.
TO ME, ANYWAY.

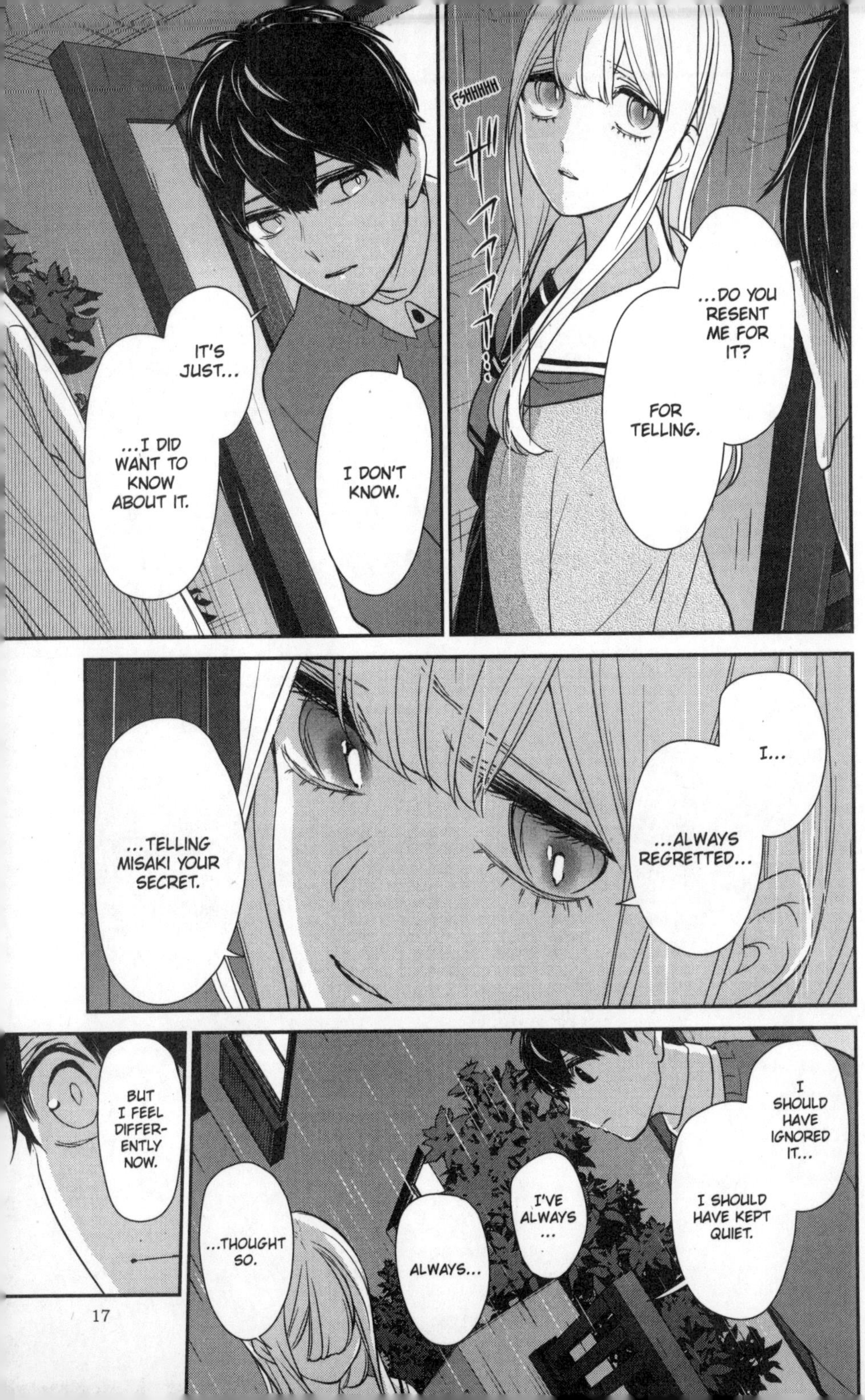
FSHHHHH
...DO YOU RESENT ME FOR IT?
FOR TELLING.
I DON'T KNOW.
IT'S JUST...
...I DID WANT TO KNOW ABOUT IT.
I...
...ALWAYS REGRETTED...
...TELLING MISAKI YOUR SECRET.
I SHOULD HAVE IGNORED IT...
I SHOULD HAVE KEPT QUIET.
I'VE ALWAYS ...
ALWAYS...
...THOUGHT SO.
BUT I FEEL DIFFER-ENTLY NOW.

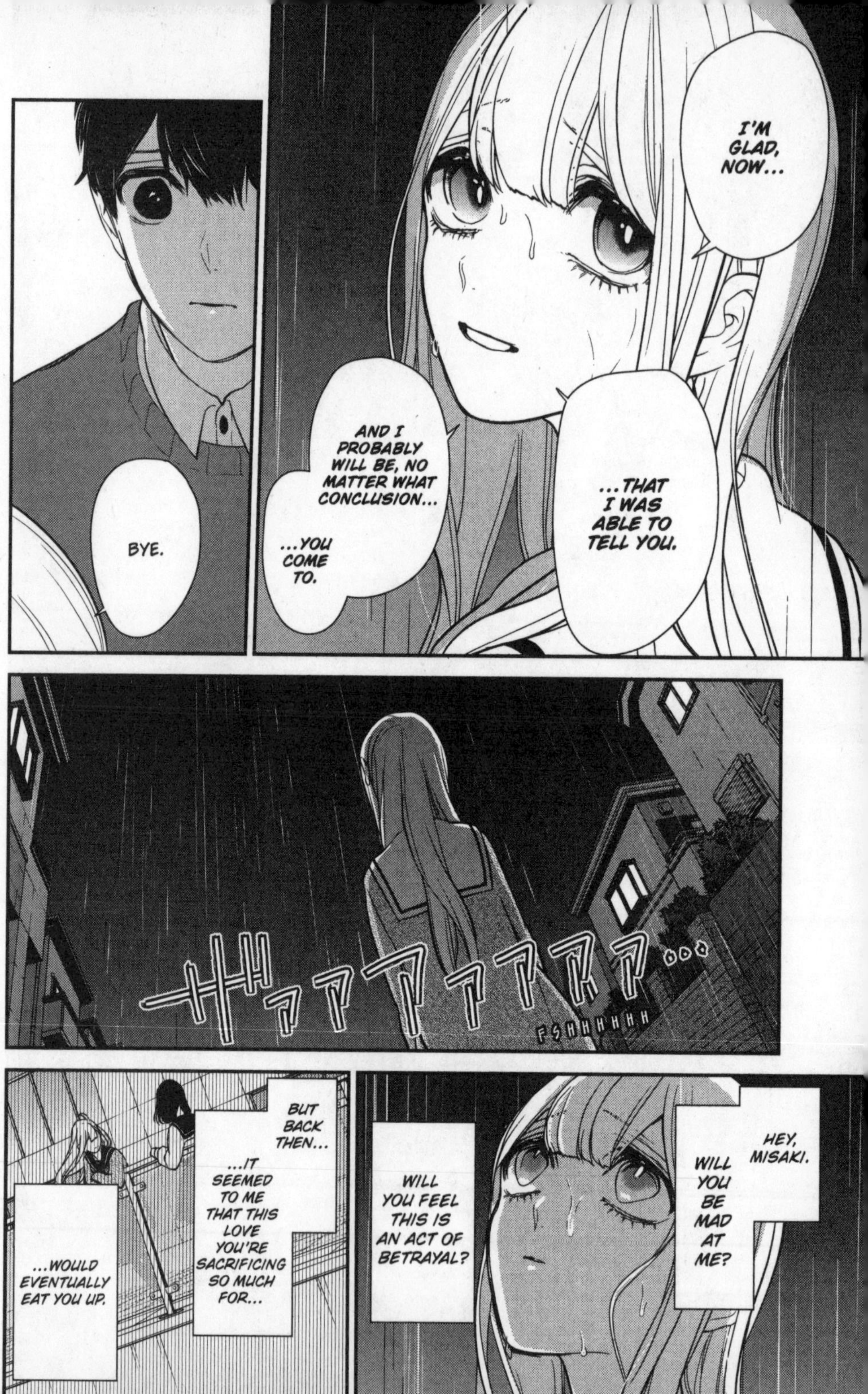
I'M GLAD, NOW...
...THAT I WAS ABLE TO TELL YOU.
AND I PROBABLY WILL BE, NO MATTER WHAT CONCLUSION...
...YOU COME TO.
BYE.
FSHHHHHHH
HEY, MISAKI.
WILL YOU BE MAD AT ME?
WILL YOU FEEL THIS IS AN ACT OF BETRAYAL?
BUT BACK THEN...
...IT SEEMED TO ME THAT THIS LOVE YOU'RE SACRIFICING SO MUCH FOR...
...WOULD EVENTUALLY EAT YOU UP.

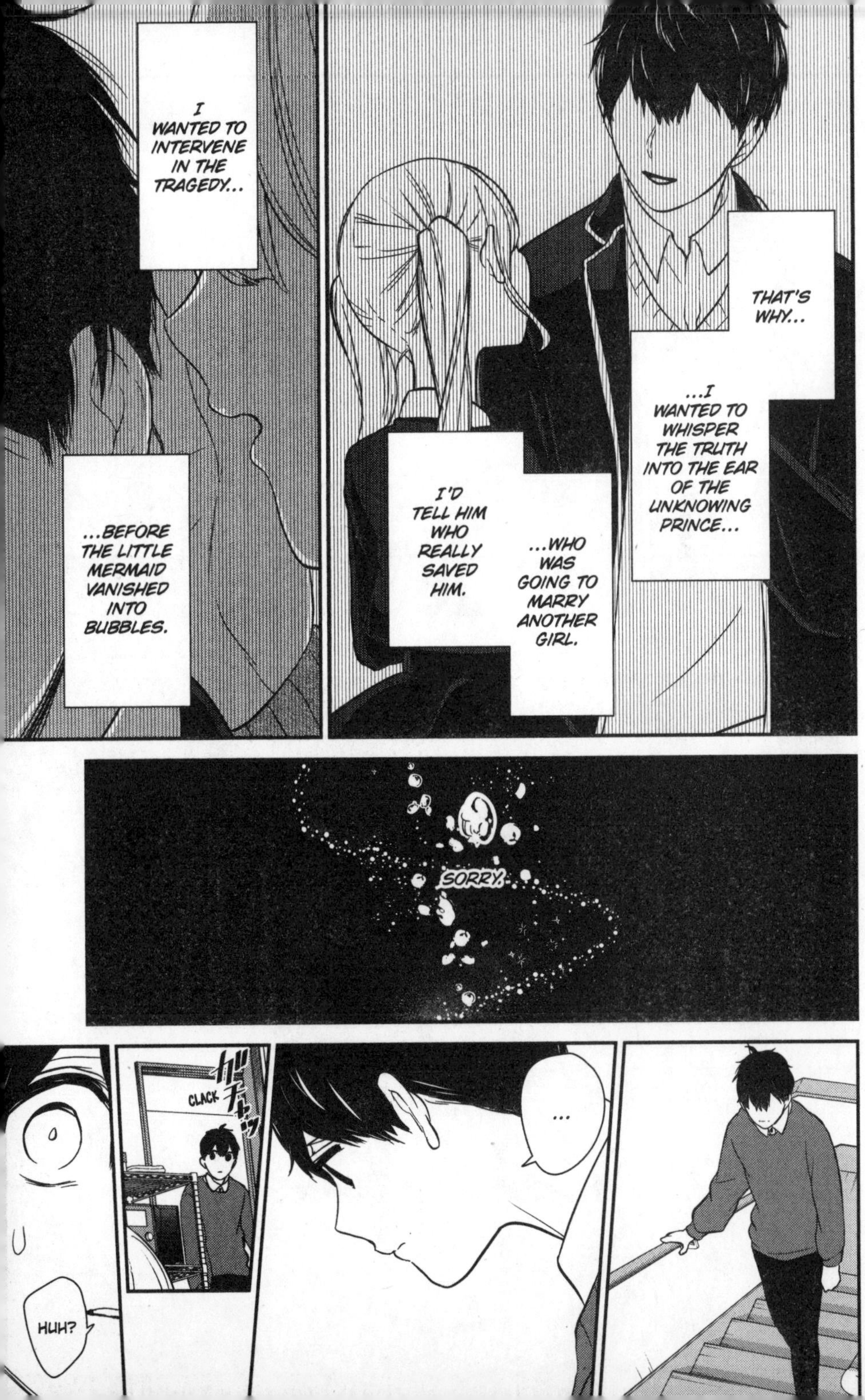
THAT'S WHY...
...I WANTED TO WHISPER THE TRUTH INTO THE EAR OF THE UNKNOWING PRINCE...
...WHO WAS GOING TO MARRY ANOTHER GIRL.
I'D TELL HIM WHO REALLY SAVED HIM.
I WANTED TO INTERVENE IN THE TRAGEDY...
...BEFORE THE LITTLE MERMAID VANISHED INTO BUBBLES.
SORRY.
...
CLACK
HUH?

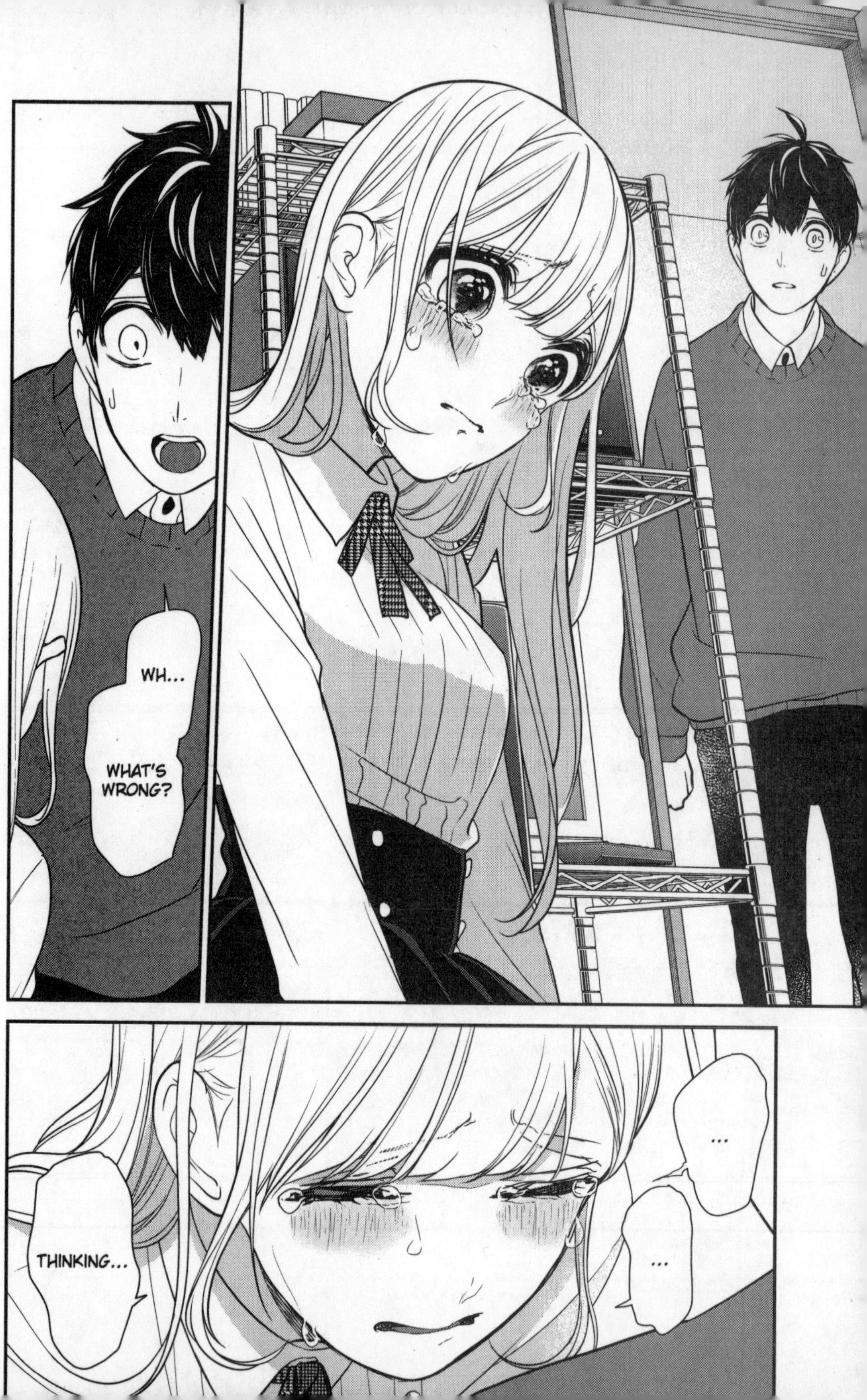
WH...
WHAT'S WRONG?
...
...
THINKING...

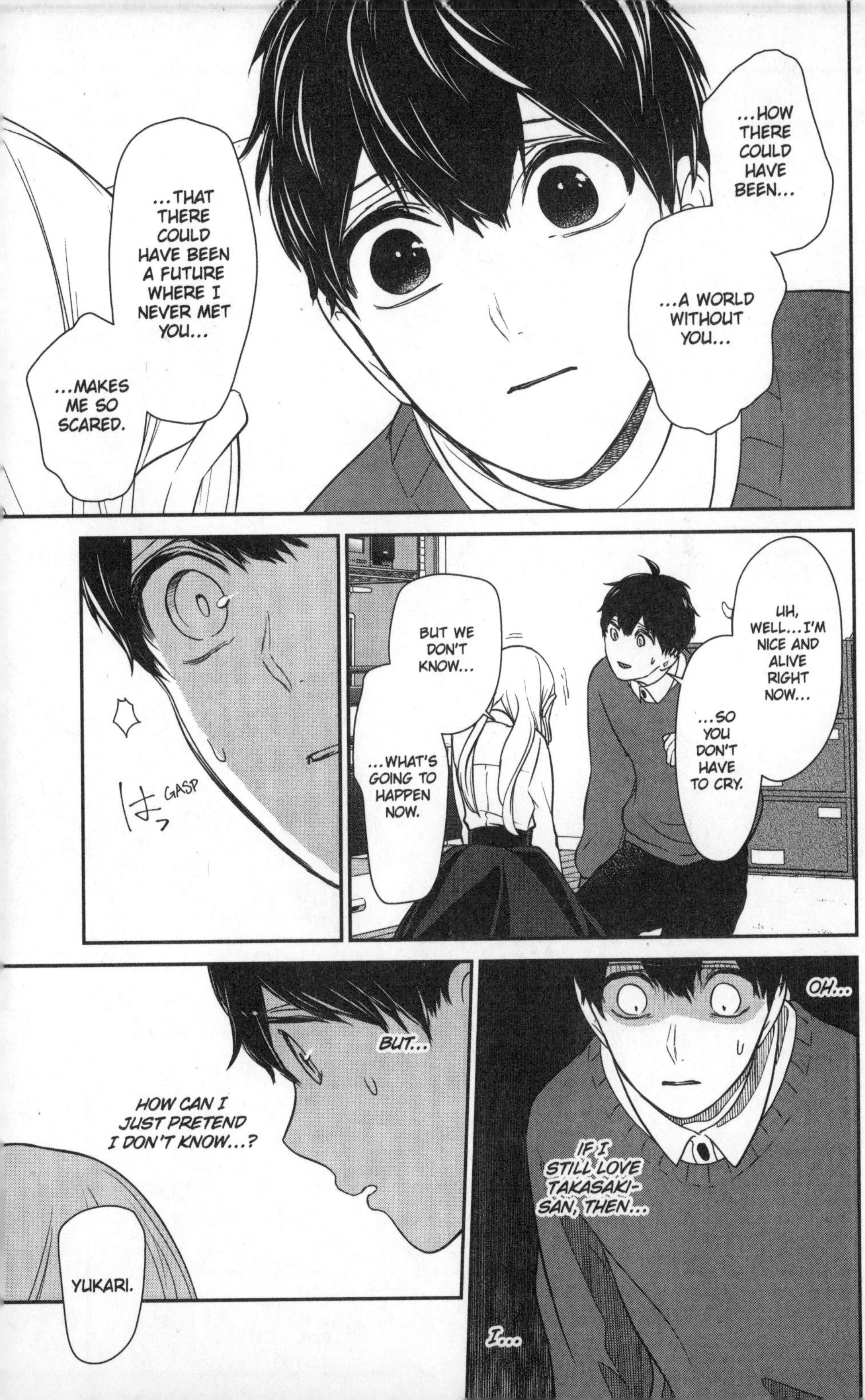
...HOW THERE COULD HAVE BEEN...
...A WORLD WITHOUT YOU...
...THAT THERE COULD HAVE BEEN A FUTURE WHERE I NEVER MET YOU...
...MAKES ME SO SCARED.
UH, WELL...I'M NICE AND ALIVE RIGHT NOW...
...SO YOU DON'T HAVE TO CRY.
BUT WE DON'T KNOW...
...WHAT'S GOING TO HAPPEN NOW.
は GASP
OH...
IF I STILL LOVE TAKASAKI-SAN, THEN...
I...
BUT...
HOW CAN I JUST PRETEND I DON'T KNOW...?
YUKARI.

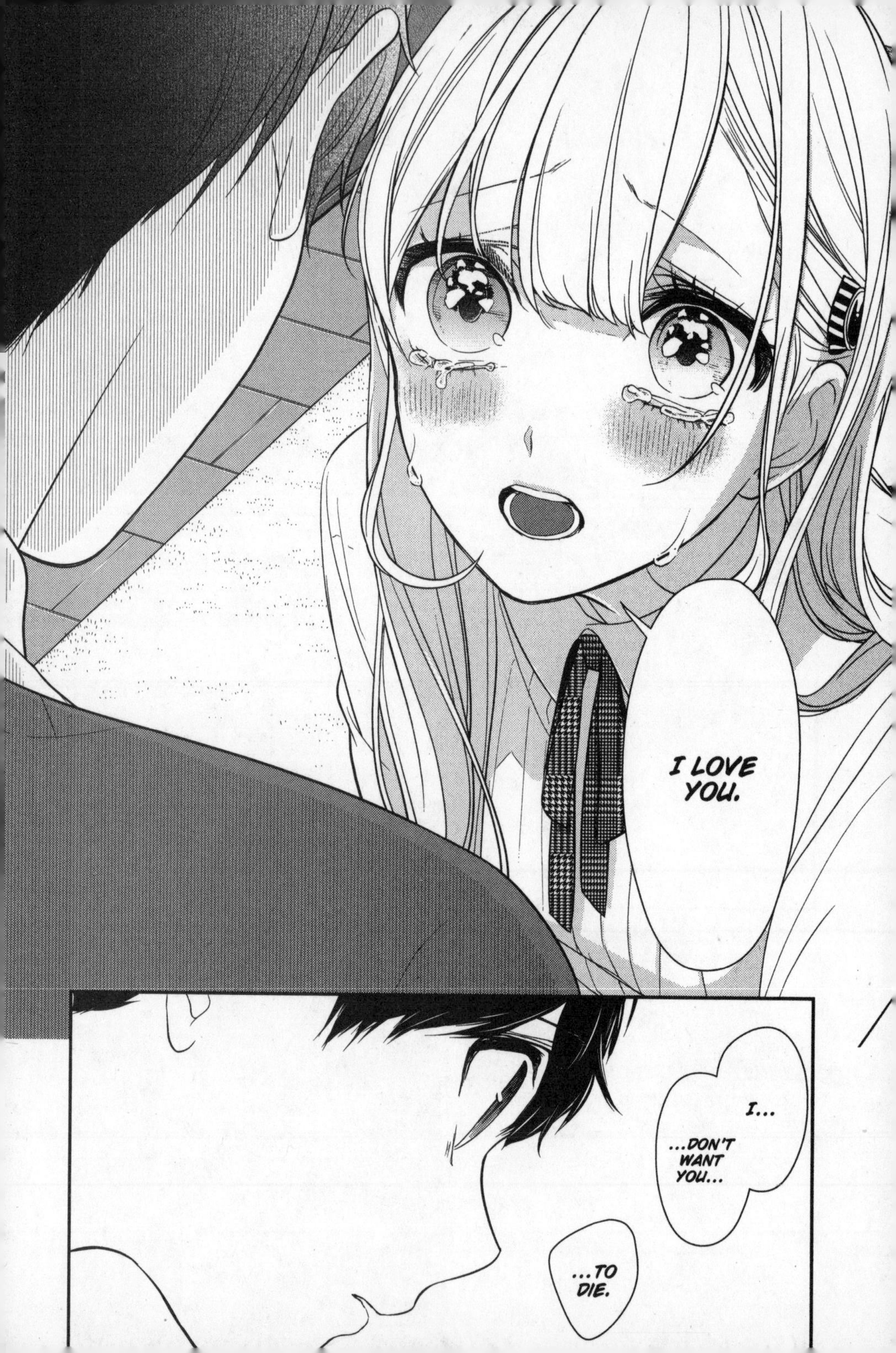
I LOVE YOU.
I...
...DON'T WANT YOU...
...TO DIE.

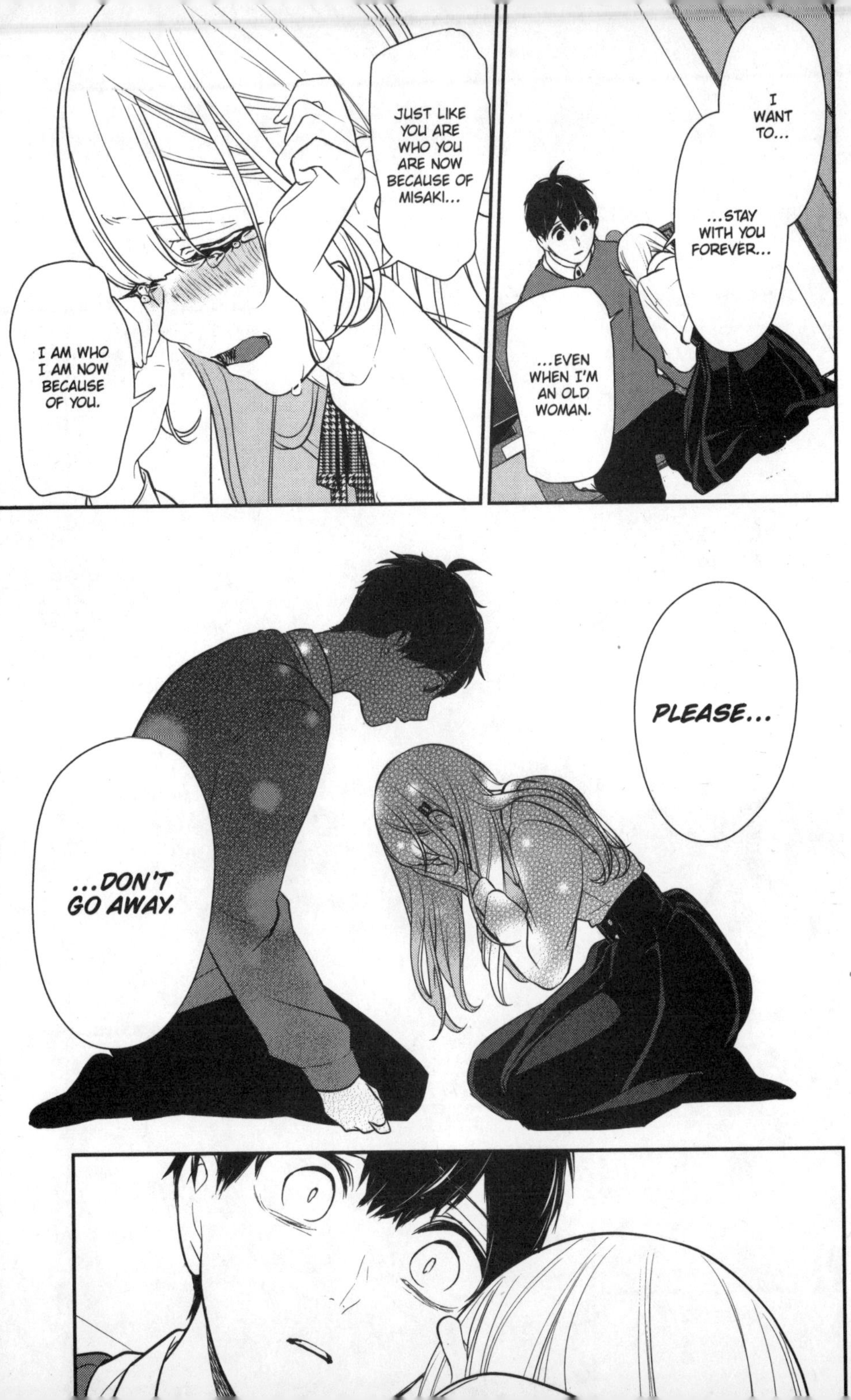
I WANT TO...
...STAY WITH YOU FOREVER...
...EVEN WHEN I'M AN OLD WOMAN.
JUST LIKE YOU ARE WHO YOU ARE NOW BECAUSE OF MISAKI...
I AM WHO I AM NOW BECAUSE OF YOU.
PLEASE...
...DON'T GO AWAY.

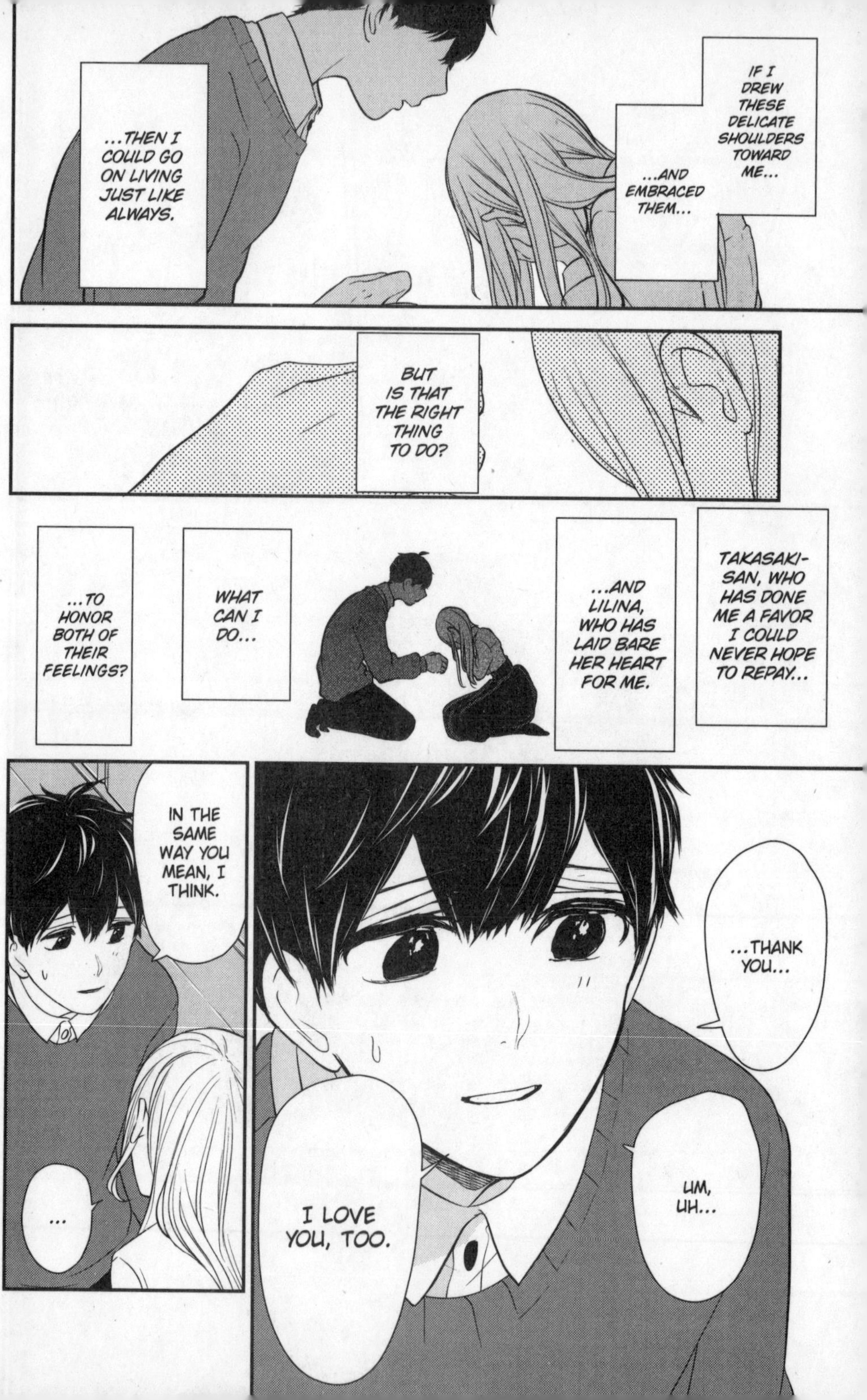
IF I DREW THESE DELICATE SHOULDERS TOWARD ME...
...AND EMBRACED THEM...
...THEN I COULD GO ON LIVING JUST LIKE ALWAYS.
BUT IS THAT THE RIGHT THING TO DO?
TAKASAKI-SAN, WHO HAS DONE ME A FAVOR I COULD NEVER HOPE TO REPAY...
...AND LILINA, WHO HAS LAID BARE HER HEART FOR ME.
WHAT CAN I DO...
...TO HONOR BOTH OF THEIR FEELINGS?
...THANK YOU...
UM, UH...
I LOVE YOU, TOO.
IN THE SAME WAY YOU MEAN, I THINK.
...

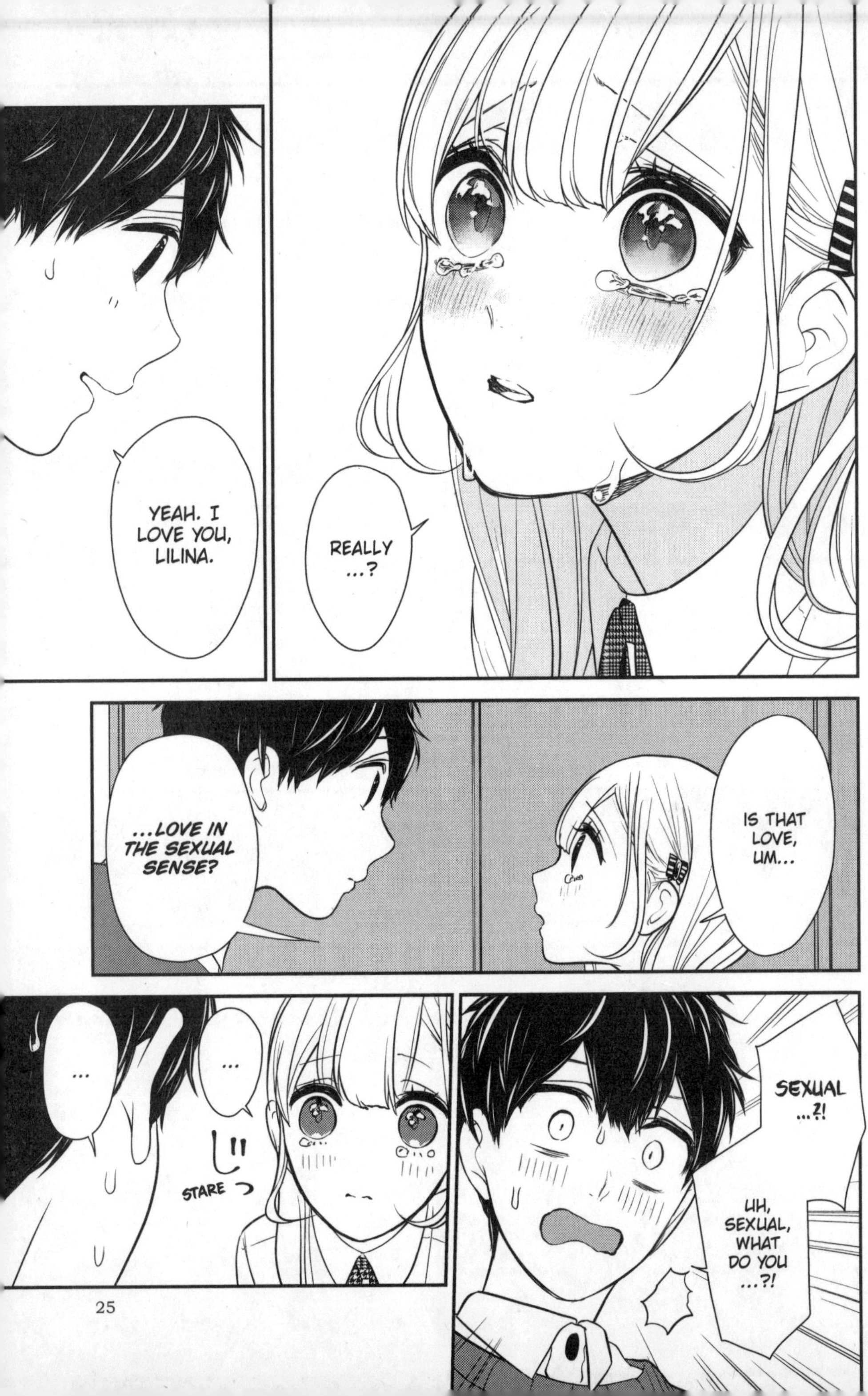
REALLY ...?
YEAH. I LOVE YOU, LILINA.
IS THAT LOVE, UM...
...LOVE IN THE SEXUAL SENSE?
SEXUAL ...?!
UH, SEXUAL, WHAT DO YOU ...?!
...
...
STARE

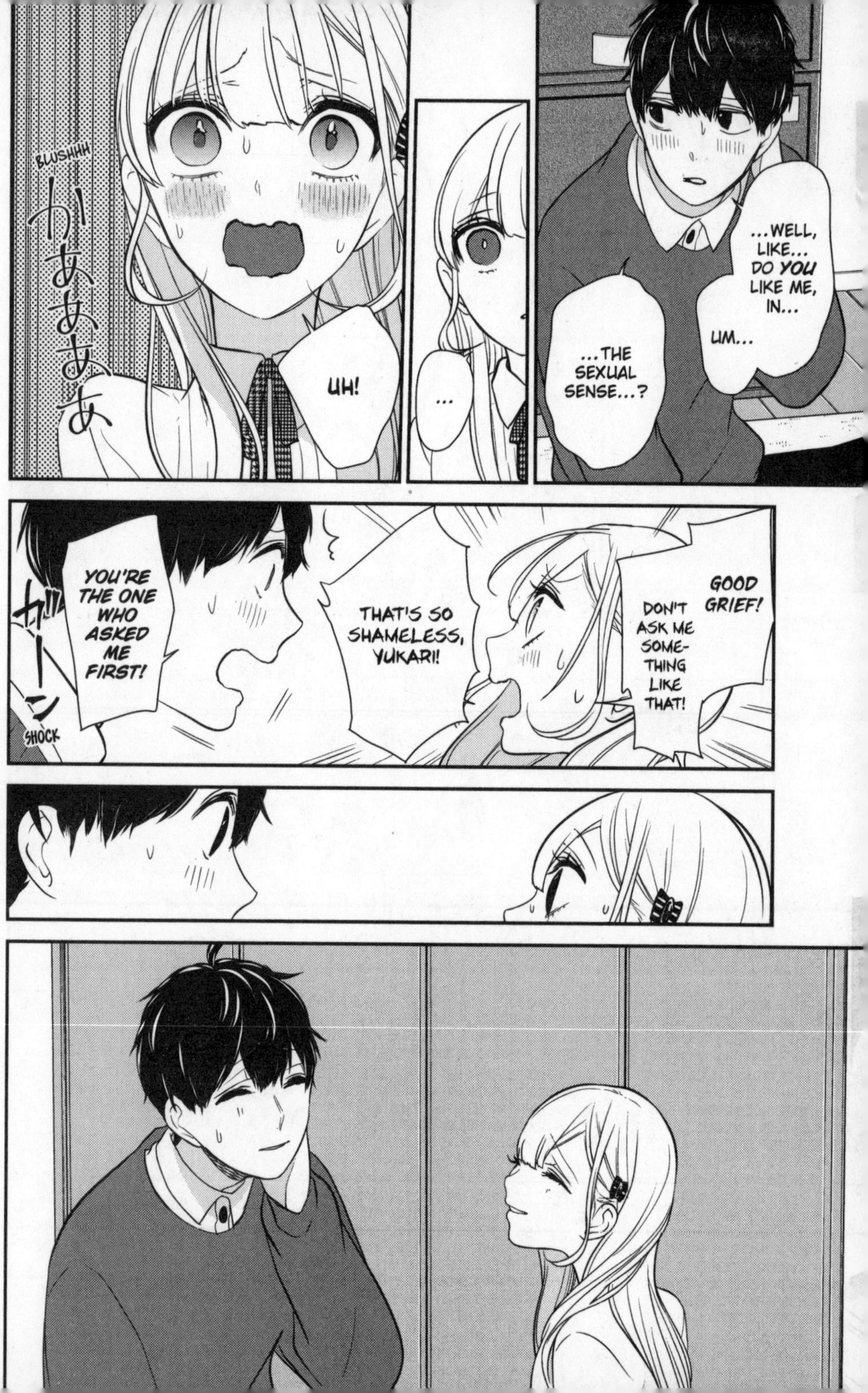
...WELL, LIKE... DO *YOU* LIKE ME, IN...
UM...
...THE SEXUAL SENSE...?
...
UH!
BLUSHHH
GOOD GRIEF!
DON'T ASK ME SOME-THING LIKE THAT!
THAT'S SO SHAMELESS, YUKARI!
YOU'RE THE ONE WHO ASKED ME FIRST!
SHOCK

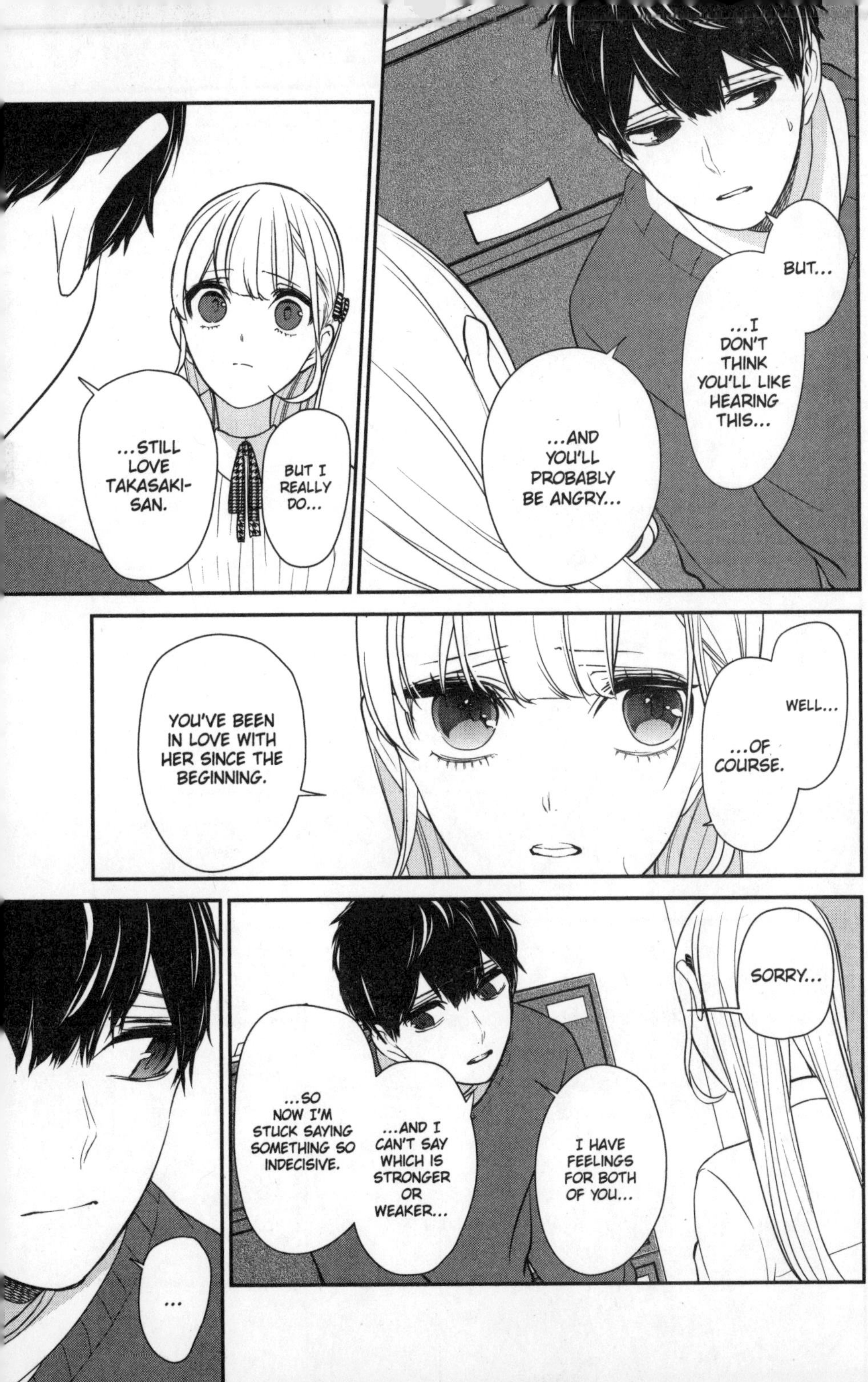
BUT...
...I DON'T THINK YOU'LL LIKE HEARING THIS...
...AND YOU'LL PROBABLY BE ANGRY...
BUT I REALLY DO...
...STILL LOVE TAKASAKI-SAN.
WELL...
...OF COURSE.
YOU'VE BEEN IN LOVE WITH HER SINCE THE BEGINNING.
SORRY...
I HAVE FEELINGS FOR BOTH OF YOU...
...AND I CAN'T SAY WHICH IS STRONGER OR WEAKER...
...SO NOW I'M STUCK SAYING SOMETHING SO INDECISIVE.
...

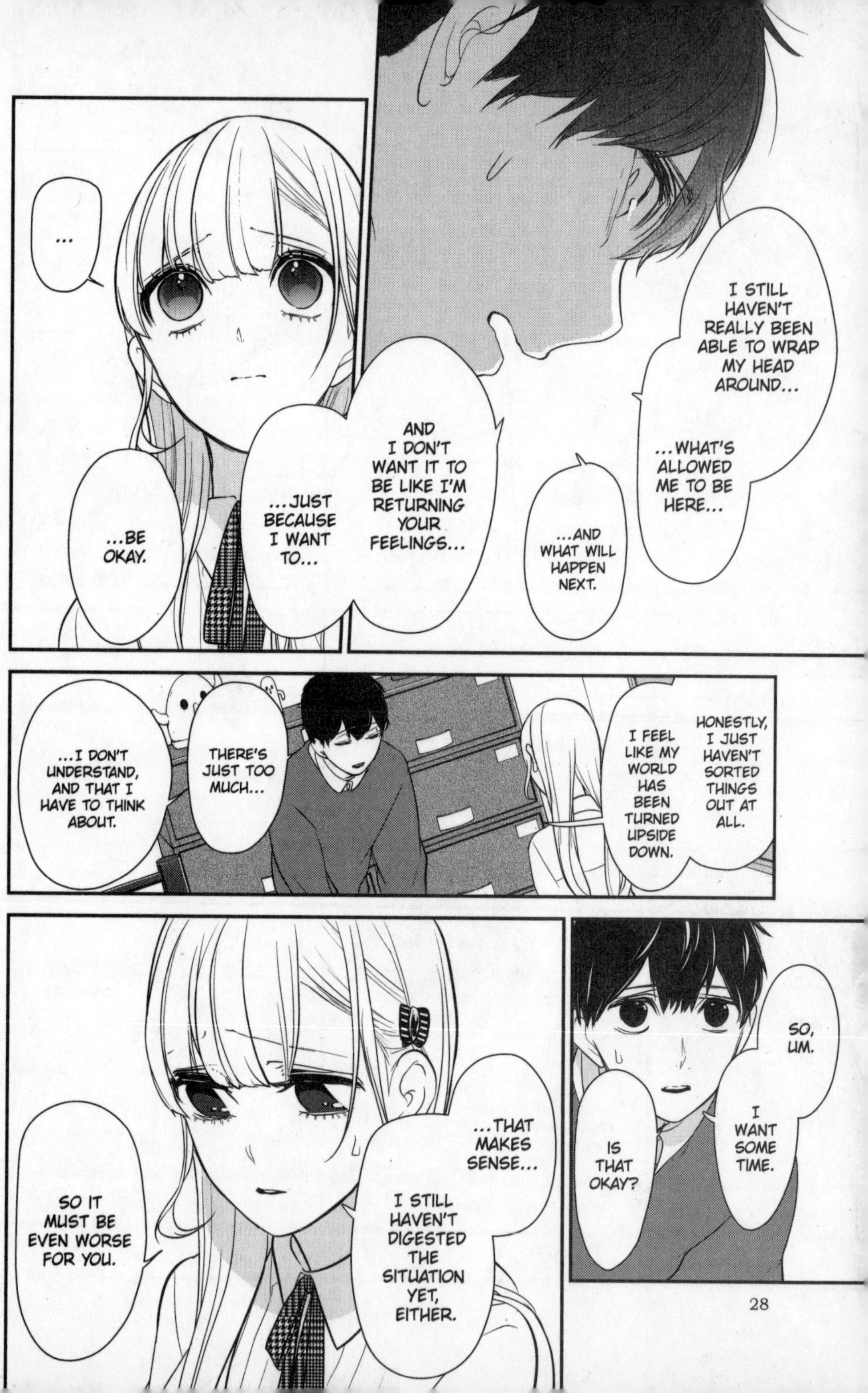
I STILL HAVEN'T REALLY BEEN ABLE TO WRAP MY HEAD AROUND...
...WHAT'S ALLOWED ME TO BE HERE...
...AND WHAT WILL HAPPEN NEXT.
AND I DON'T WANT IT TO BE LIKE I'M RETURNING YOUR FEELINGS...
...
...JUST BECAUSE I WANT TO...
...BE OKAY.
HONESTLY, I JUST HAVEN'T SORTED THINGS OUT AT ALL.
I FEEL LIKE MY WORLD HAS BEEN TURNED UPSIDE DOWN.
THERE'S JUST TOO MUCH...
...I DON'T UNDERSTAND, AND THAT I HAVE TO THINK ABOUT.
SO, UM.
I WANT SOME TIME.
IS THAT OKAY?
...THAT MAKES SENSE...
I STILL HAVEN'T DIGESTED THE SITUATION YET, EITHER.
SO IT MUST BE EVEN WORSE FOR YOU.

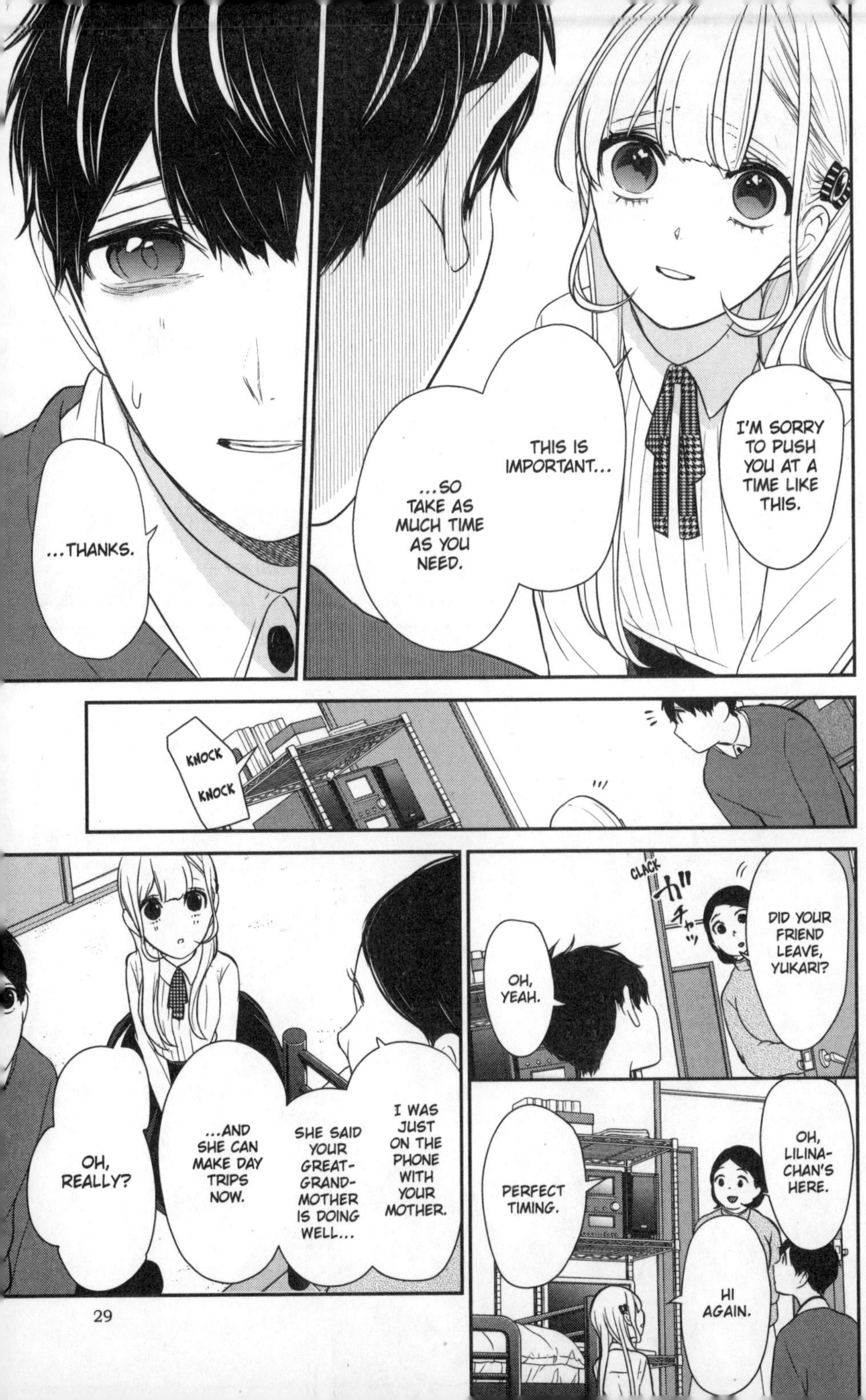
I'M SORRY TO PUSH YOU AT A TIME LIKE THIS.
THIS IS IMPORTANT...
...SO TAKE AS MUCH TIME AS YOU NEED.
...THANKS.
KNOCK
KNOCK
CLACK
DID YOUR FRIEND LEAVE, YUKARI?
OH, YEAH.
OH, LILINA-CHAN'S HERE.
PERFECT TIMING.
HI AGAIN.
I WAS JUST ON THE PHONE WITH YOUR MOTHER.
SHE SAID YOUR GREAT-GRANDMOTHER IS DOING WELL...
...AND SHE CAN MAKE DAY TRIPS NOW.
OH, REALLY?

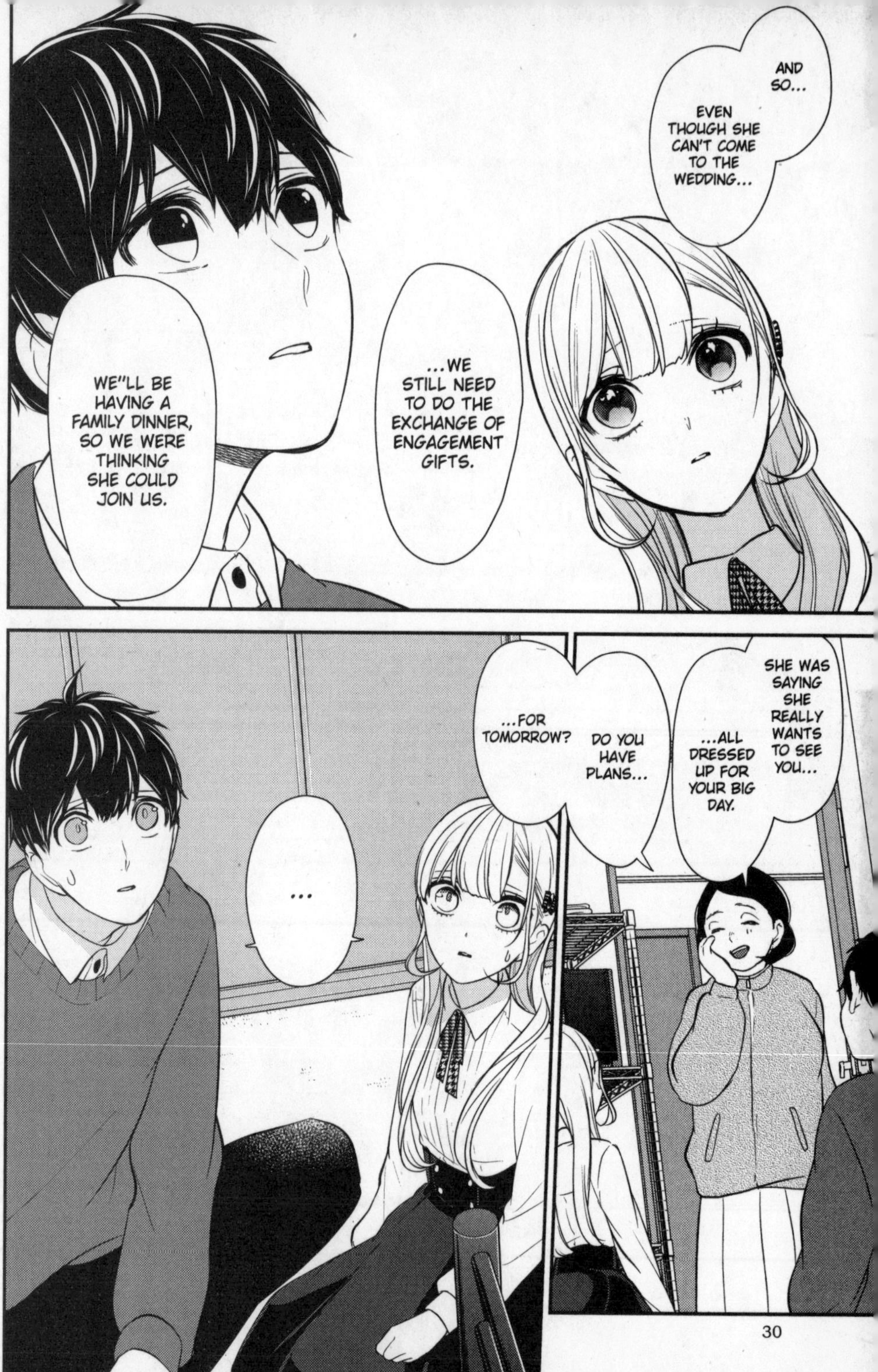
AND SO...
EVEN THOUGH SHE CAN'T COME TO THE WEDDING...
...WE STILL NEED TO DO THE EXCHANGE OF ENGAGEMENT GIFTS.
WE"LL BE HAVING A FAMILY DINNER, SO WE WERE THINKING SHE COULD JOIN US.
SHE WAS SAYING SHE REALLY WANTS TO SEE YOU...
...ALL DRESSED UP FOR YOUR BIG DAY.
DO YOU HAVE PLANS...
...FOR TOMORROW?
...

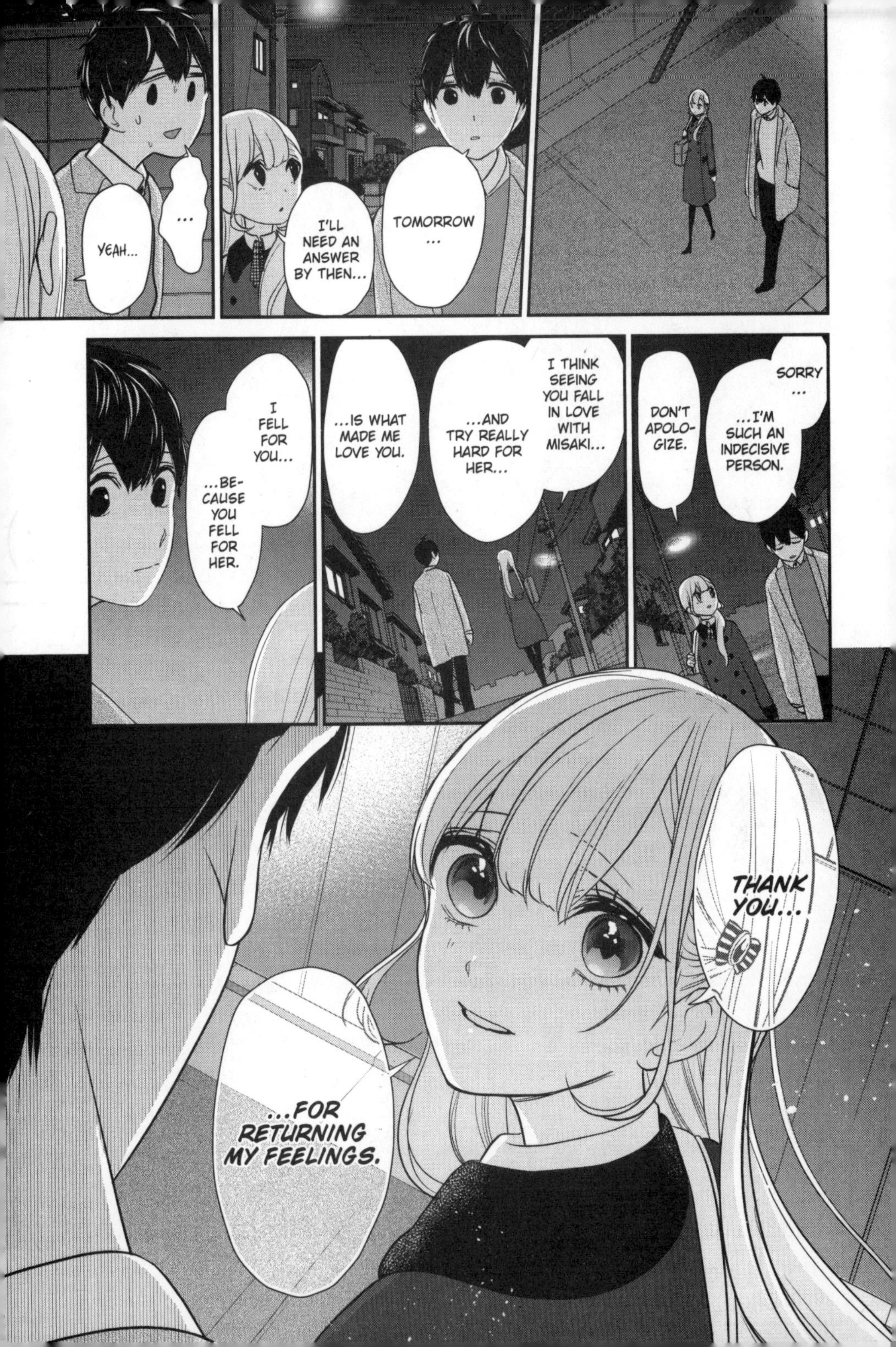
TOMORROW ...
I'LL NEED AN ANSWER BY THEN...
...
YEAH...
SORRY ...
...I'M SUCH AN INDECISIVE PERSON.
DON'T APOLO-GIZE.
I THINK SEEING YOU FALL IN LOVE WITH MISAKI...
...AND TRY REALLY HARD FOR HER...
...IS WHAT MADE ME LOVE YOU.
I FELL FOR YOU...
...BE-CAUSE YOU FELL FOR HER.
THANK YOU...
...FOR RETURNING MY FEELINGS.

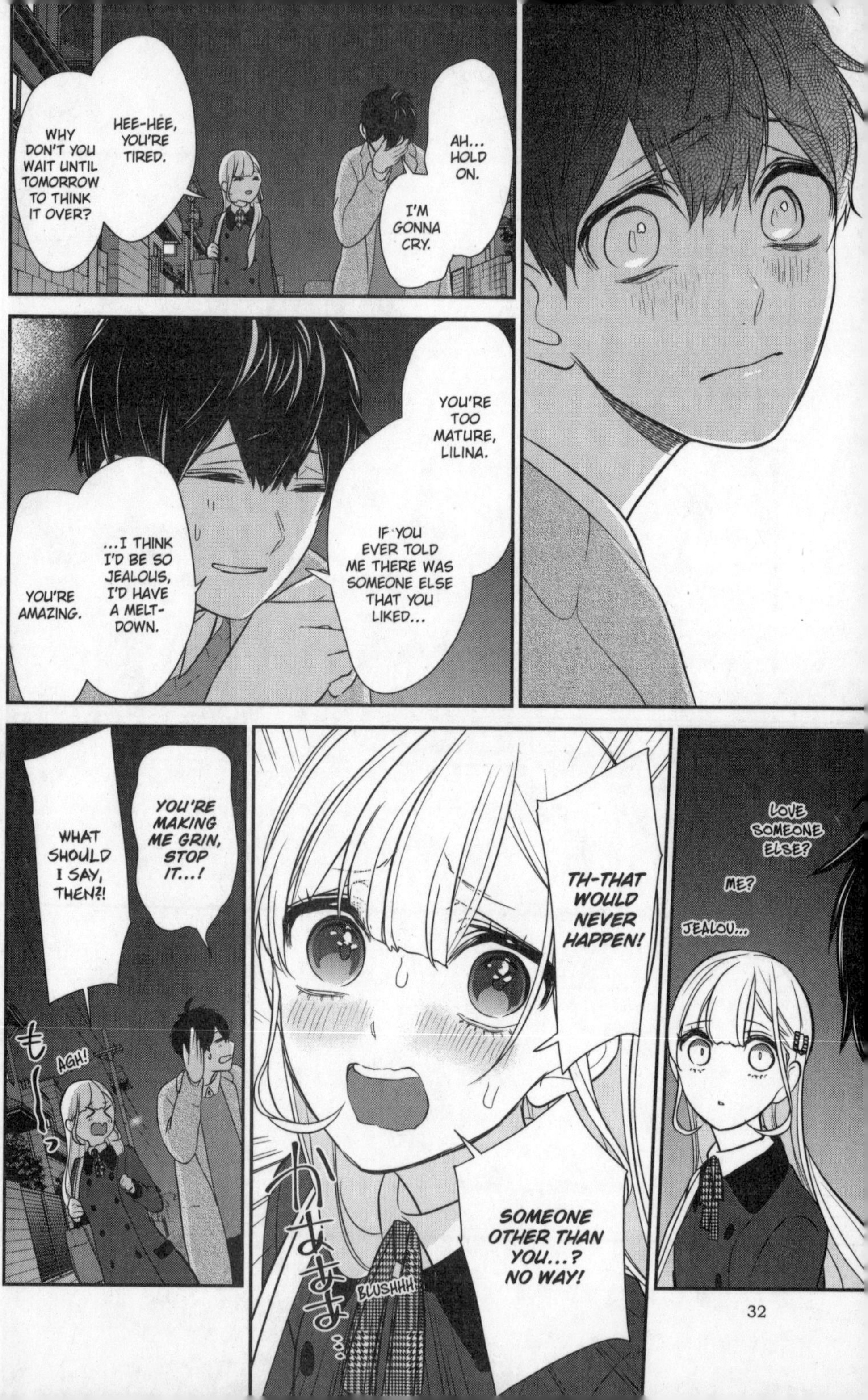
AH... HOLD ON.
I'M GONNA CRY.
HEE-HEE, YOU'RE TIRED.
WHY DON'T YOU WAIT UNTIL TOMORROW TO THINK IT OVER?
YOU'RE TOO MATURE, LILINA.
IF YOU EVER TOLD ME THERE WAS SOMEONE ELSE THAT YOU LIKED...
...I THINK I'D BE SO JEALOUS, I'D HAVE A MELT-DOWN.
YOU'RE AMAZING.
LOVE SOMEONE ELSE?
ME?
JEALOU...
TH-THAT WOULD NEVER HAPPEN!
SOMEONE OTHER THAN YOU...? NO WAY!
BLUSHHH
YOU'RE MAKING ME GRIN, STOP IT...!
WHAT SHOULD I SAY, THEN?!
AGH!

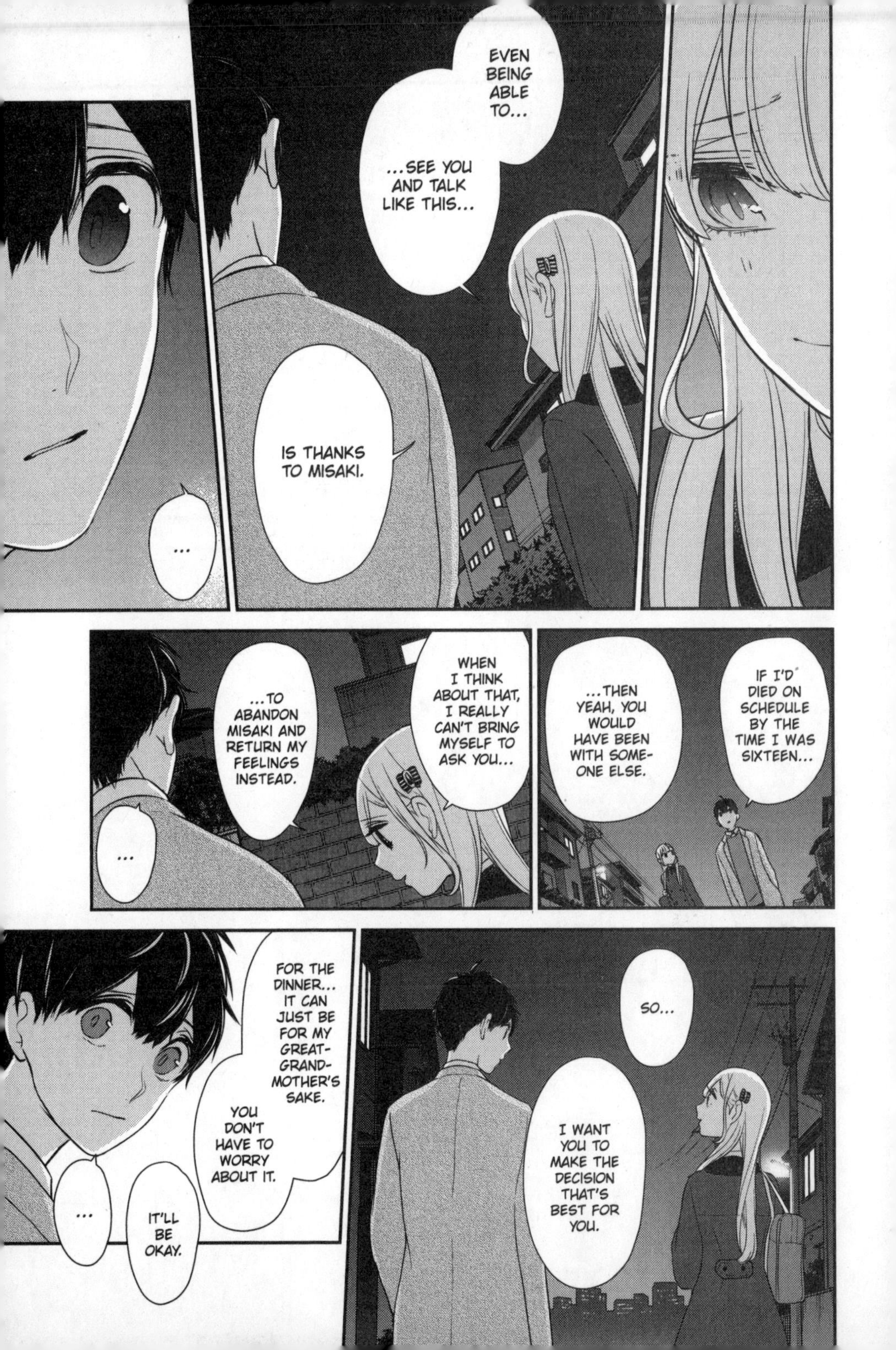
EVEN BEING ABLE TO...
...SEE YOU AND TALK LIKE THIS...
IS THANKS TO MISAKI.
...
IF I'D DIED ON SCHEDULE BY THE TIME I WAS SIXTEEN...
...THEN YEAH, YOU WOULD HAVE BEEN WITH SOMEONE ELSE.
WHEN I THINK ABOUT THAT, I REALLY CAN'T BRING MYSELF TO ASK YOU...
...TO ABANDON MISAKI AND RETURN MY FEELINGS INSTEAD.
...
SO...
I WANT YOU TO MAKE THE DECISION THAT'S BEST FOR YOU.
FOR THE DINNER... IT CAN JUST BE FOR MY GREAT-GRANDMOTHER'S SAKE.
YOU DON'T HAVE TO WORRY ABOUT IT.
IT'LL BE OKAY.
...

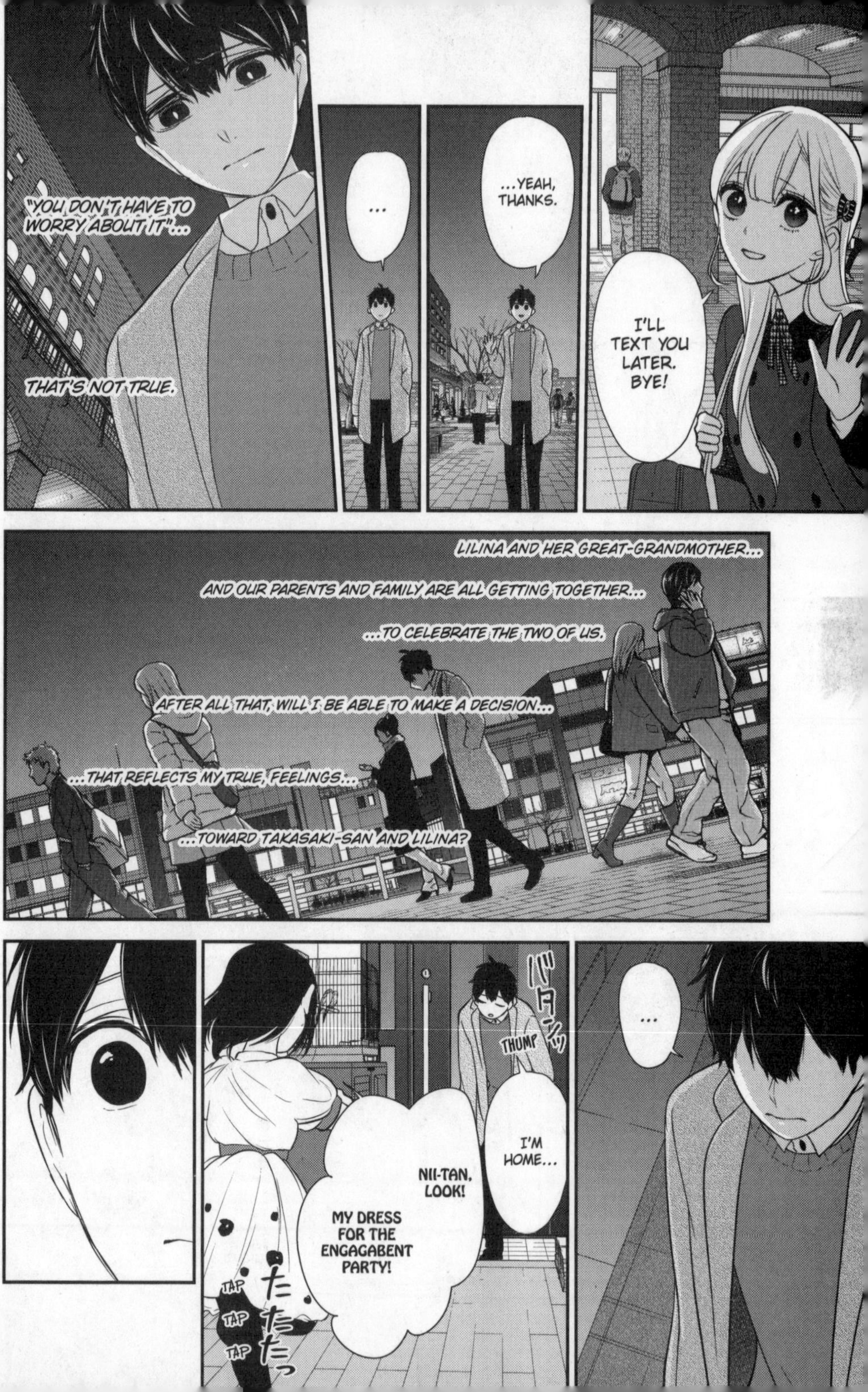
I'LL TEXT YOU LATER. BYE!
...YEAH, THANKS.
...
"YOU DON'T HAVE TO WORRY ABOUT IT"...
THAT'S NOT TRUE.
LILINA AND HER GREAT-GRANDMOTHER...
AND OUR PARENTS AND FAMILY ARE ALL GETTING TOGETHER...
...TO CELEBRATE THE TWO OF US.
AFTER ALL THAT, WILL I BE ABLE TO MAKE A DECISION...
...THAT REFLECTS MY TRUE, FEELINGS...
...TOWARD TAKASAKI-SAN AND LILINA?
...
バタン
THUMP
I'M HOME...
NII-TAN, LOOK!
MY DRESS FOR THE ENGAGABENT PARTY!
たたたっ
TAP
TAP
TAP

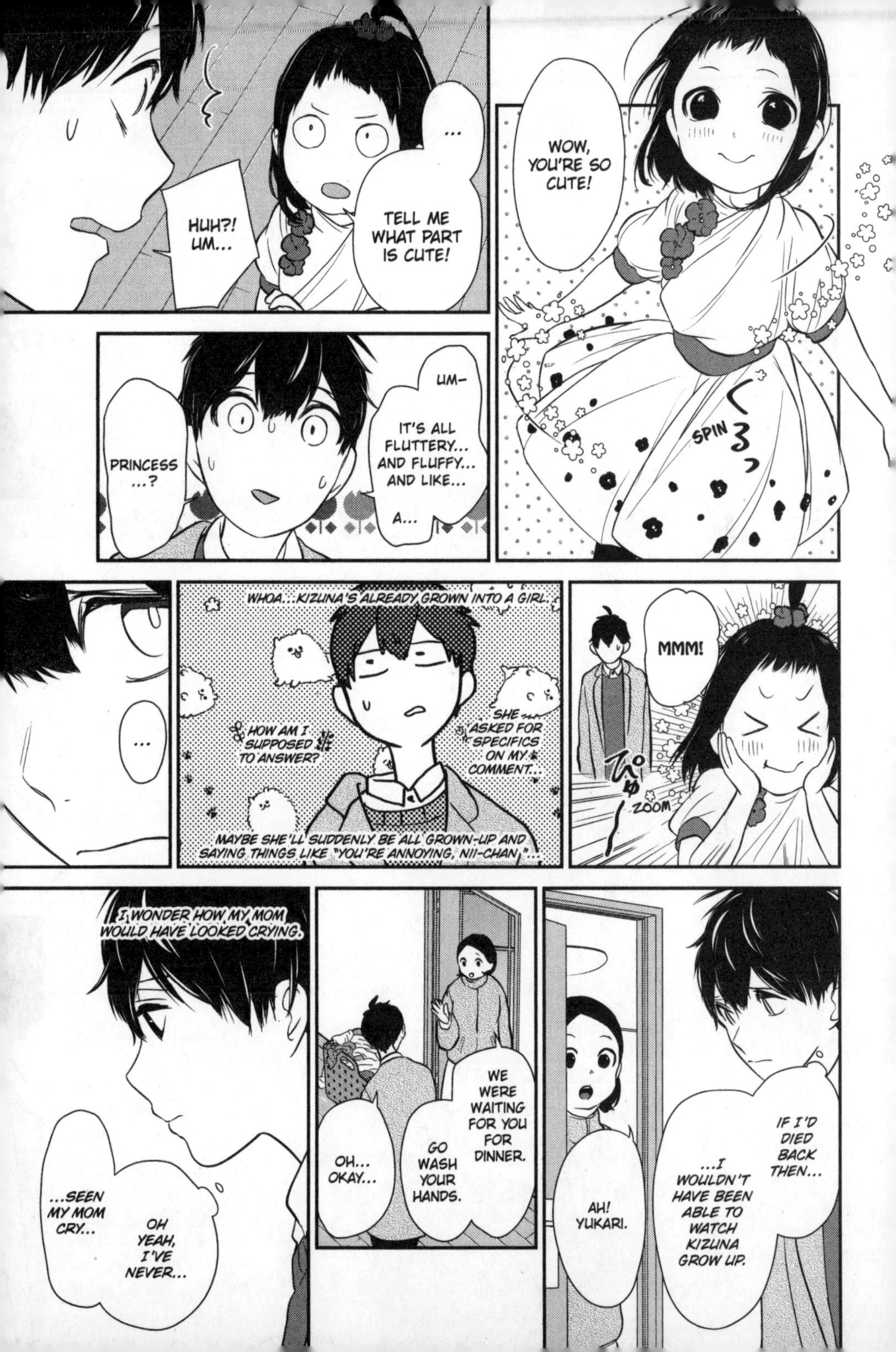
WOW, YOU'RE SO CUTE!
SPIN
...
TELL ME WHAT PART IS CUTE!
HUH?! UM...
UM-
IT'S ALL FLUTTERY... AND FLUFFY... AND LIKE...
A...
PRINCESS ...?
MMM!
ZOOM
WHOA...KIZUNA'S ALREADY GROWN INTO A GIRL.
SHE ASKED FOR SPECIFICS ON MY COMMENT...
HOW AM I SUPPOSED TO ANSWER?
MAYBE SHE'LL SUDDENLY BE ALL GROWN-UP AND SAYING THINGS LIKE "YOU'RE ANNOYING, NII-CHAN."...
...
IF I'D DIED BACK THEN...
...I WOULDN'T HAVE BEEN ABLE TO WATCH KIZUNA GROW UP.
AH! YUKARI.
WE WERE WAITING FOR YOU FOR DINNER.
GO WASH YOUR HANDS.
OH... OKAY...
I WONDER HOW MY MOM WOULD HAVE LOOKED CRYING.
OH YEAH, I'VE NEVER...
...SEEN MY MOM CRY...

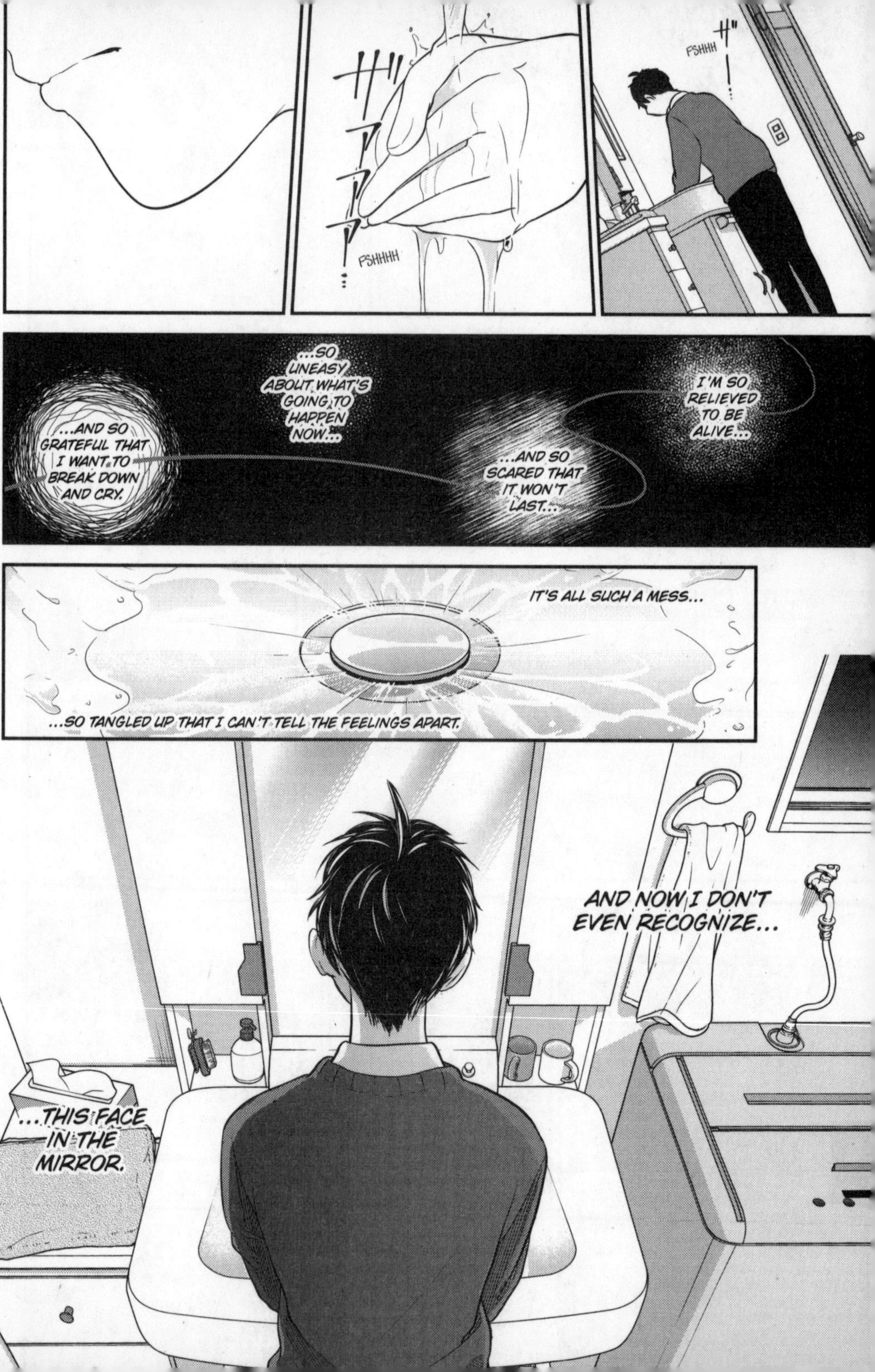
FSHHH
FSHHHH
I'M SO RELIEVED TO BE ALIVE...
...AND SO SCARED THAT IT WON'T LAST...
...SO UNEASY ABOUT WHAT'S GOING TO HAPPEN NOW...
...AND SO GRATEFUL THAT I WANT TO BREAK DOWN AND CRY.
IT'S ALL SUCH A MESS...
...SO TANGLED UP THAT I CAN'T TELL THE FEELINGS APART.
AND NOW I DON'T EVEN RECOGNIZE...
...THIS FACE IN THE MIRROR.

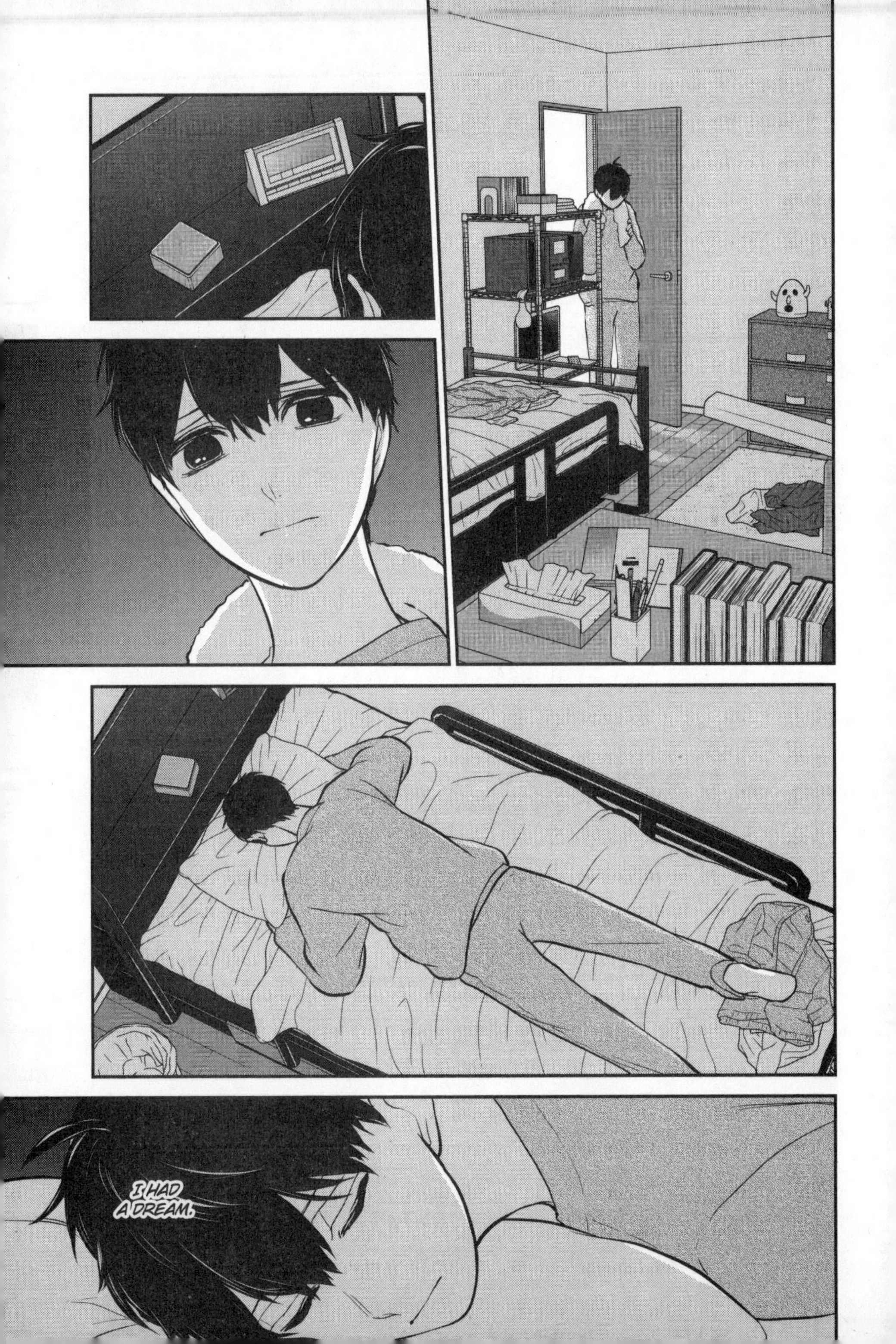
I HAD A DREAM.

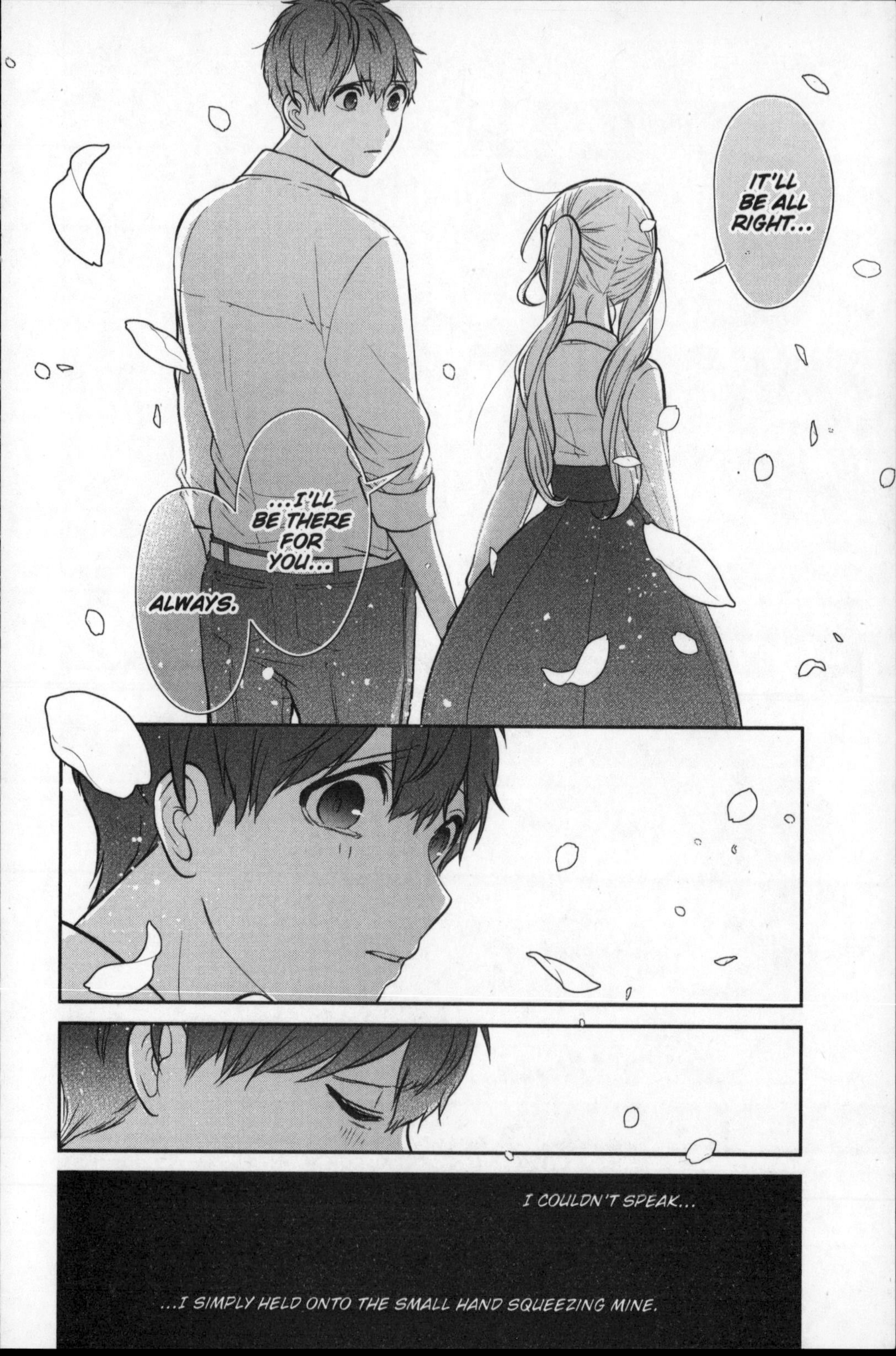
IT'LL BE ALL RIGHT...
...I'LL BE THERE FOR YOU...
ALWAYS.
I COULDN'T SPEAK...
...I SIMPLY HELD ONTO THE SMALL HAND SQUEEZING MINE.

Love & Lies

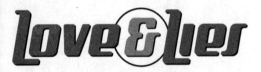

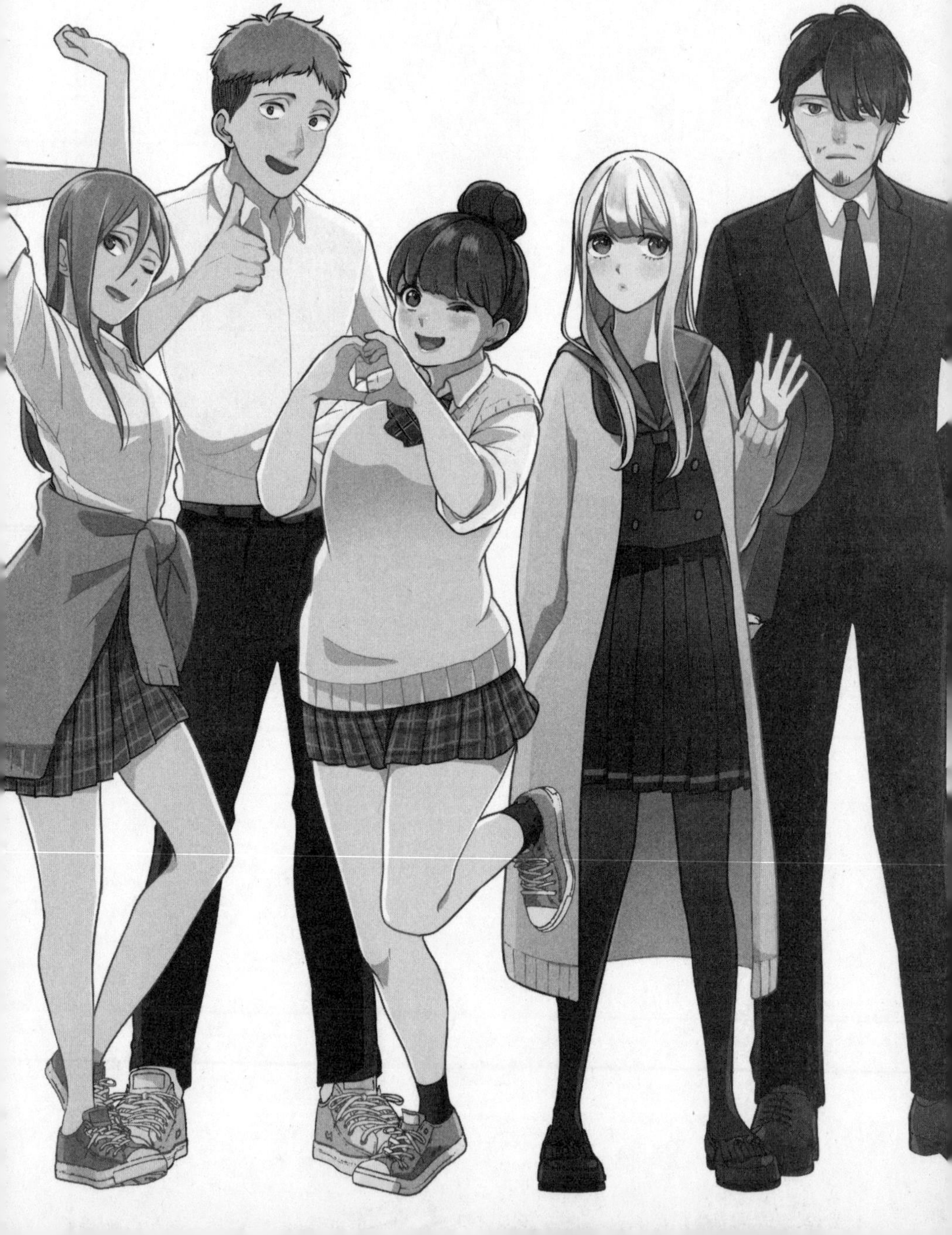

Chapter 46: Given by Love

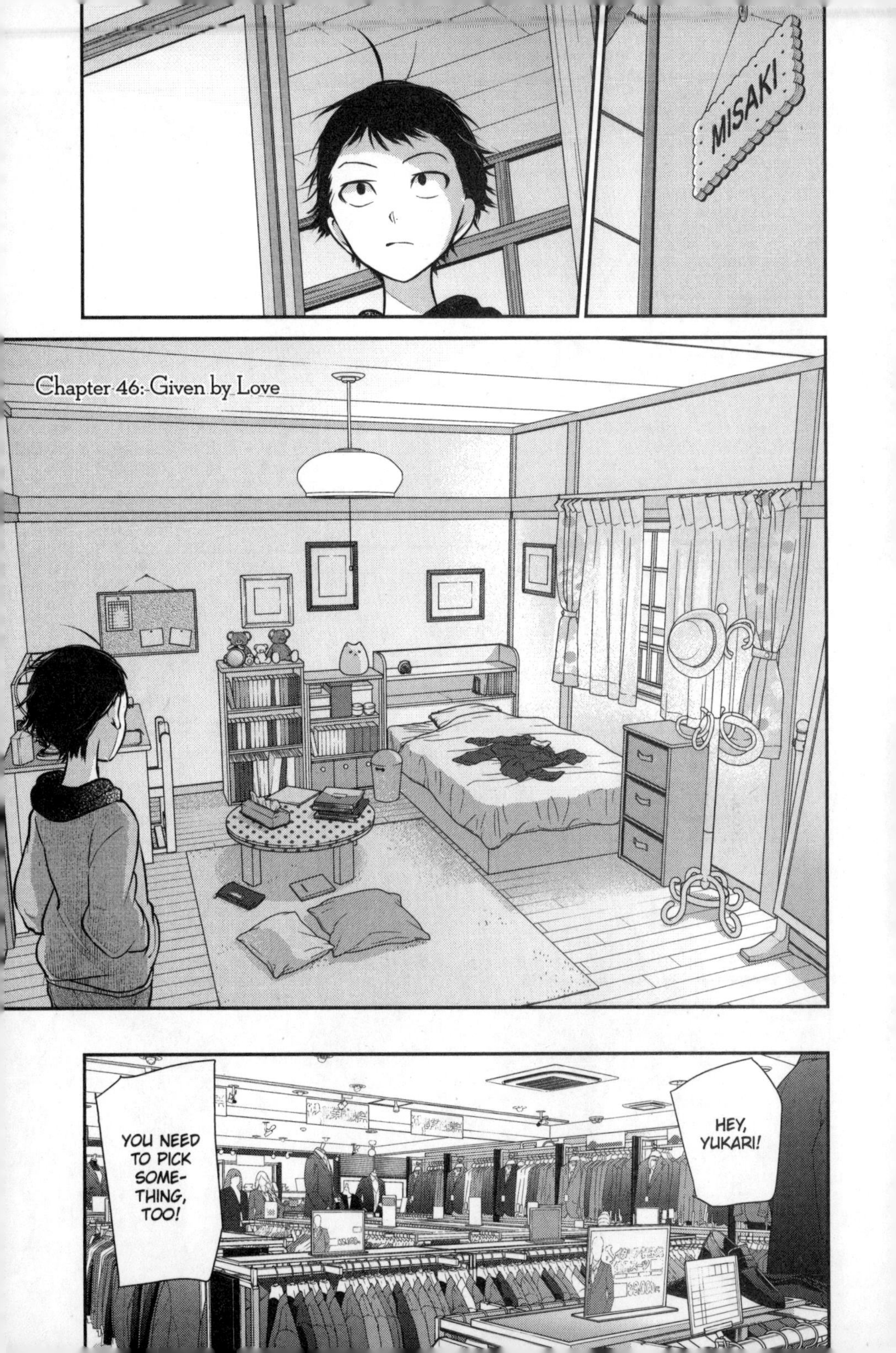
MISAKI
HEY, YUKARI!
YOU NEED TO PICK SOME-THING, TOO!

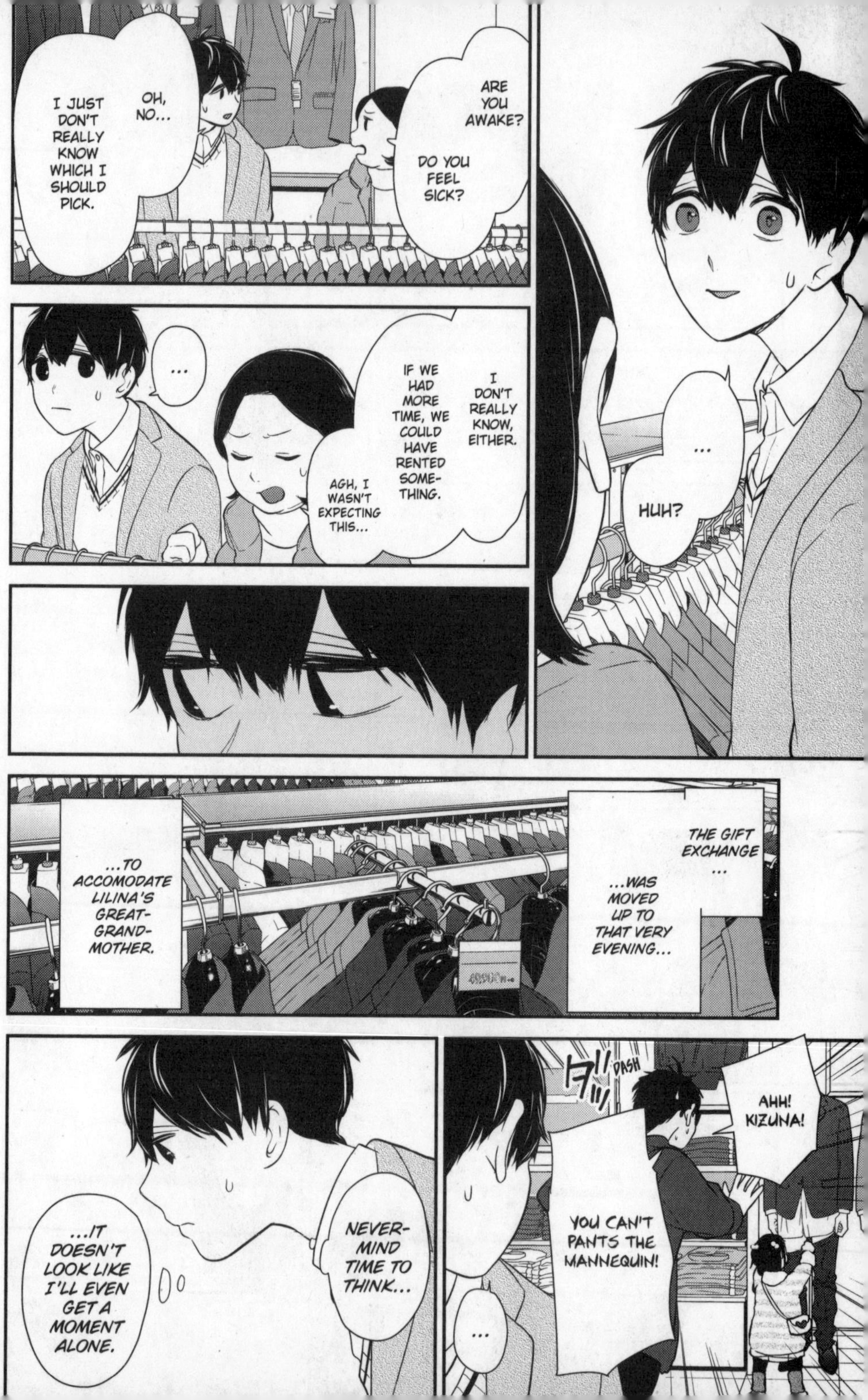
...
HUH?
ARE YOU AWAKE?
DO YOU FEEL SICK?
OH, NO...
I JUST DON'T REALLY KNOW WHICH I SHOULD PICK.
I DON'T REALLY KNOW, EITHER.
IF WE HAD MORE TIME, WE COULD HAVE RENTED SOME-THING.
AGH, I WASN'T EXPECTING THIS...
...
THE GIFT EXCHANGE...
...WAS MOVED UP TO THAT VERY EVENING...
...TO ACCOMODATE LILINA'S GREAT-GRAND-MOTHER.
AHH! KIZUNA!
DASH
YOU CAN'T PANTS THE MANNEQUIN!
...
NEVER-MIND TIME TO THINK...
...IT DOESN'T LOOK LIKE I'LL EVEN GET A MOMENT ALONE.

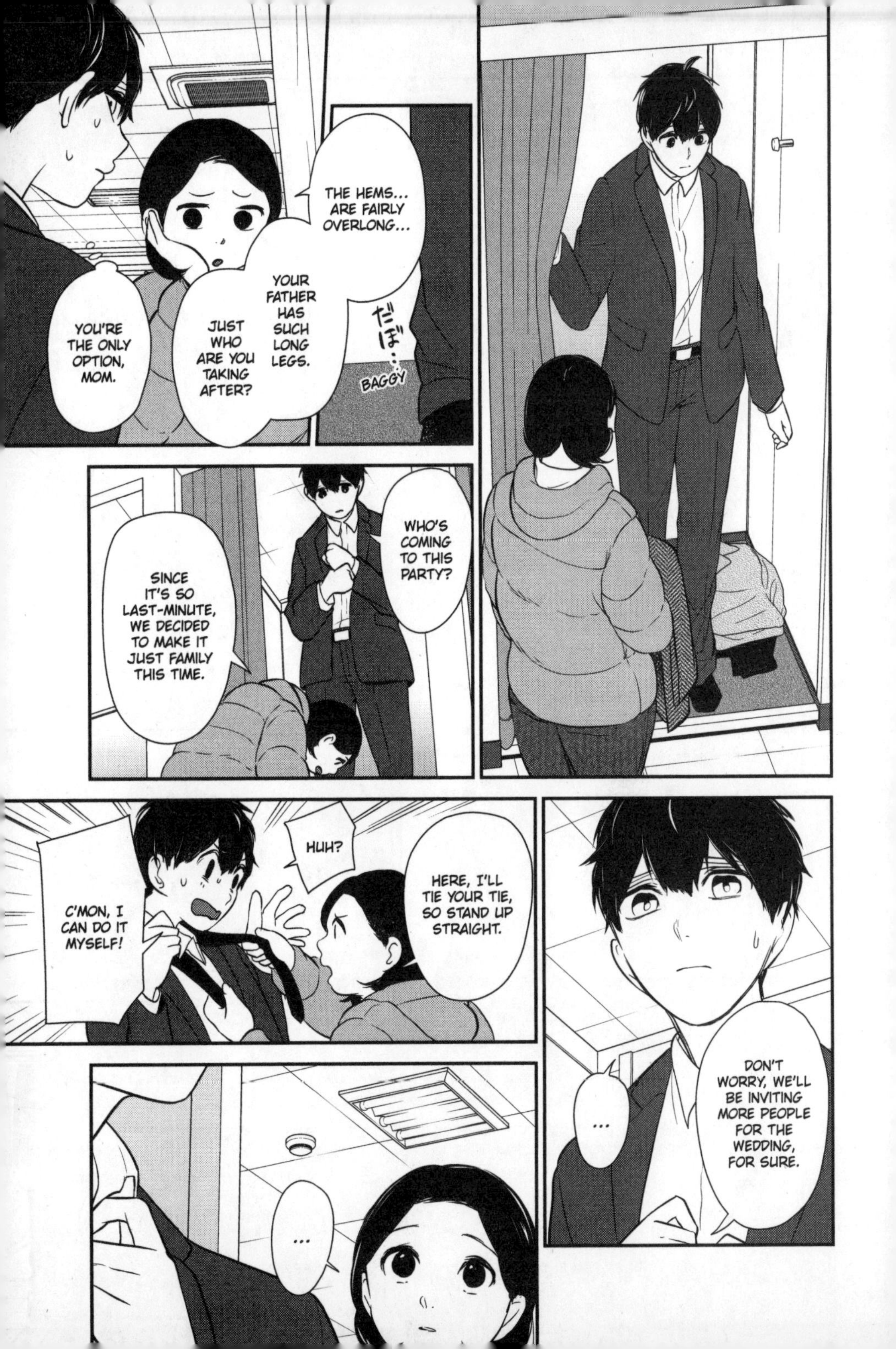
THE HEMS... ARE FAIRLY OVERLONG...
だぼ…
BAGGY
YOUR FATHER HAS SUCH LONG LEGS.
JUST WHO ARE YOU TAKING AFTER?
YOU'RE THE ONLY OPTION, MOM.
WHO'S COMING TO THIS PARTY?
SINCE IT'S SO LAST-MINUTE, WE DECIDED TO MAKE IT JUST FAMILY THIS TIME.
DON'T WORRY, WE'LL BE INVITING MORE PEOPLE FOR THE WEDDING, FOR SURE.
...
HERE, I'LL TIE YOUR TIE, SO STAND UP STRAIGHT.
HUH?
C'MON, I CAN DO IT MYSELF!
...

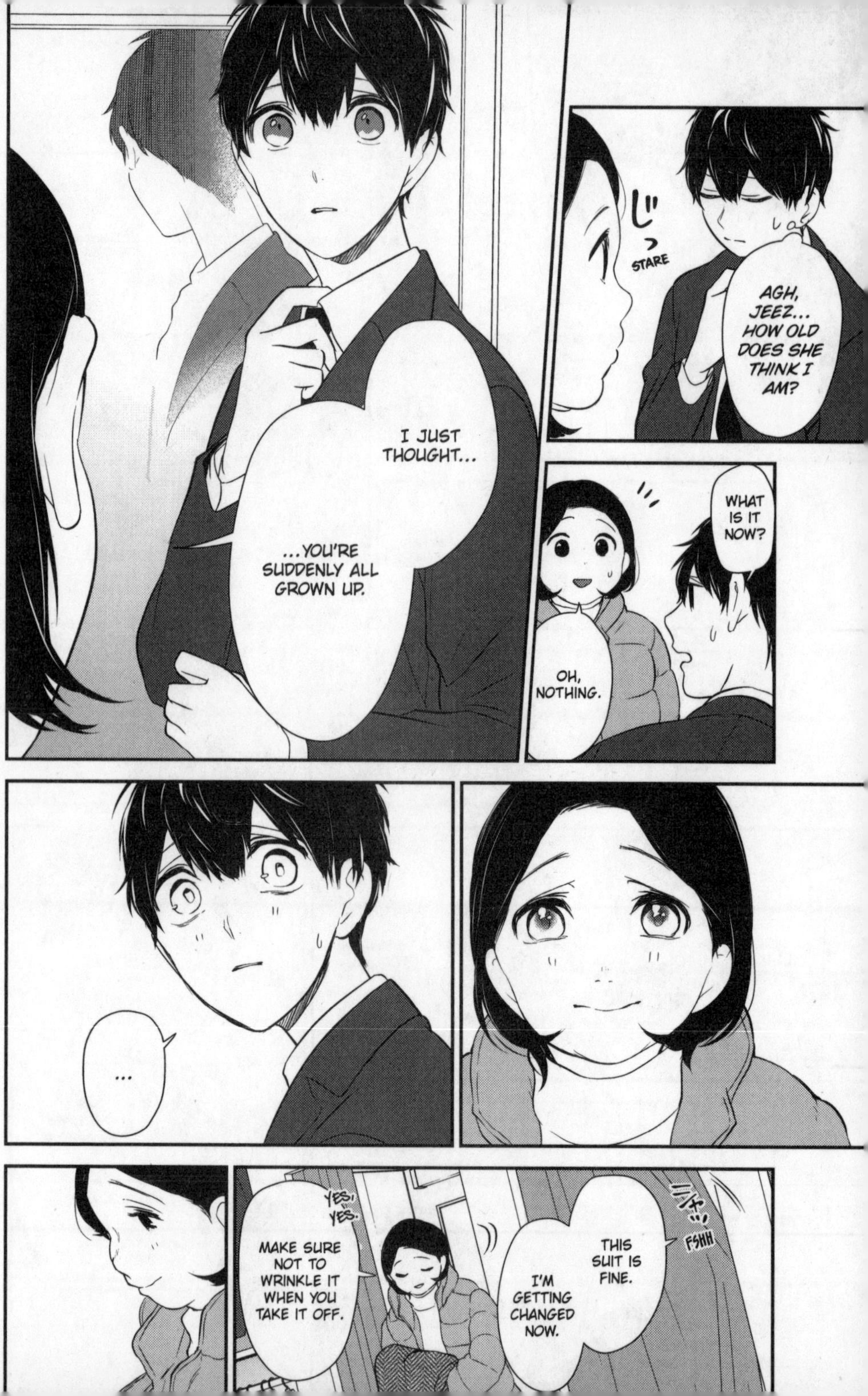
じっ
STARE
AGH, JEEZ... HOW OLD DOES SHE THINK I AM?
WHAT IS IT NOW?
OH, NOTHING.
I JUST THOUGHT...
...YOU'RE SUDDENLY ALL GROWN UP.
...
FSHH
THIS SUIT IS FINE.
I'M GETTING CHANGED NOW.
YES, YES.
MAKE SURE NOT TO WRINKLE IT WHEN YOU TAKE IT OFF.

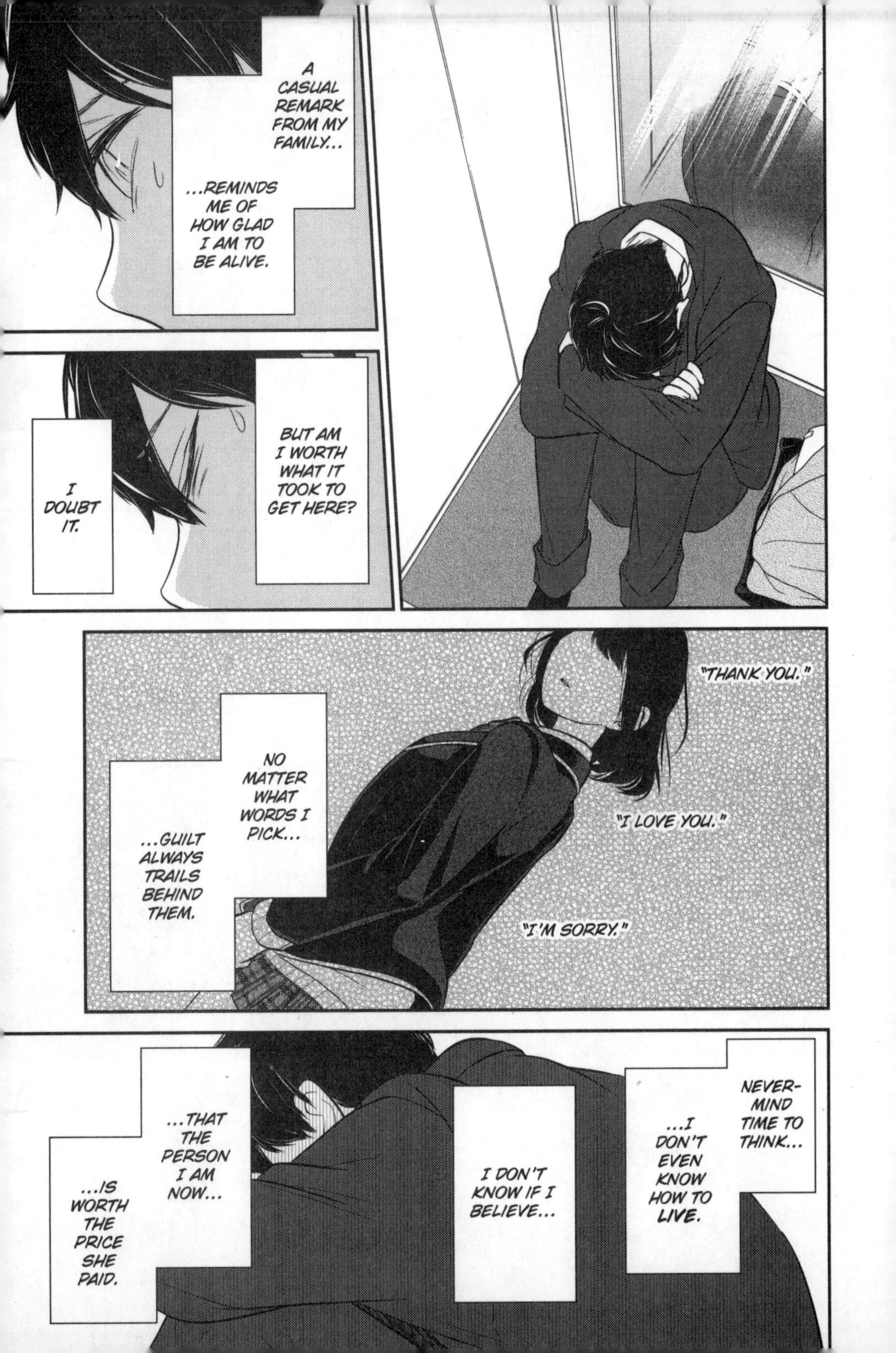
A CASUAL REMARK FROM MY FAMILY...
...REMINDS ME OF HOW GLAD I AM TO BE ALIVE.
BUT AM I WORTH WHAT IT TOOK TO GET HERE?
I DOUBT IT.
"THANK YOU."
"I LOVE YOU."
"I'M SORRY."
NO MATTER WHAT WORDS I PICK...
...GUILT ALWAYS TRAILS BEHIND THEM.
NEVER-MIND TIME TO THINK...
...I DON'T EVEN KNOW HOW TO LIVE.
I DON'T KNOW IF I BELIEVE...
...THAT THE PERSON I AM NOW...
...IS WORTH THE PRICE SHE PAID.

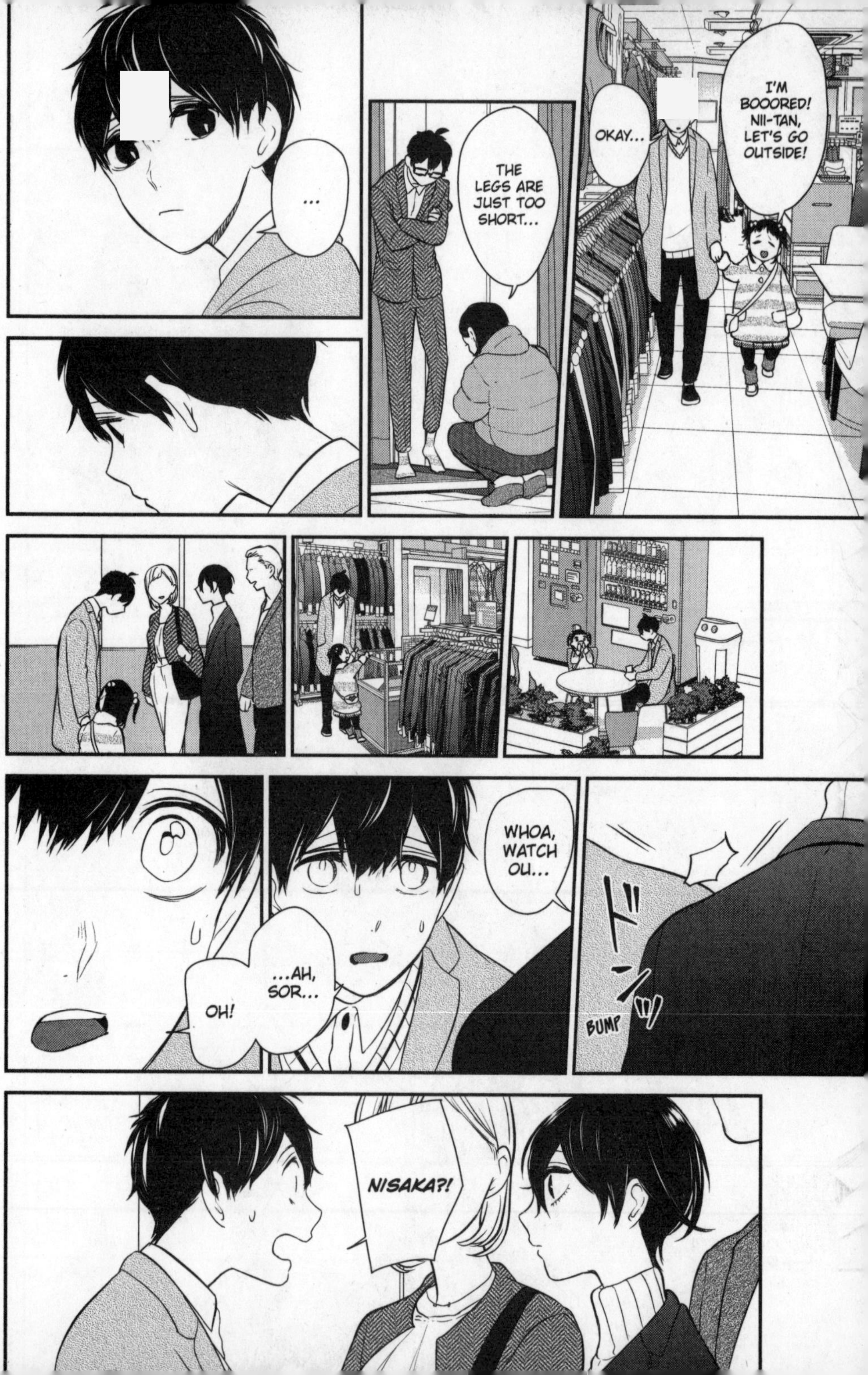
I'M BOOORED! NII-TAN, LET'S GO OUTSIDE!
OKAY...
THE LEGS ARE JUST TOO SHORT...
...
ドン
BUMP
WHOA, WATCH OU...
...AH, SOR...
OH!
NISAKA?!

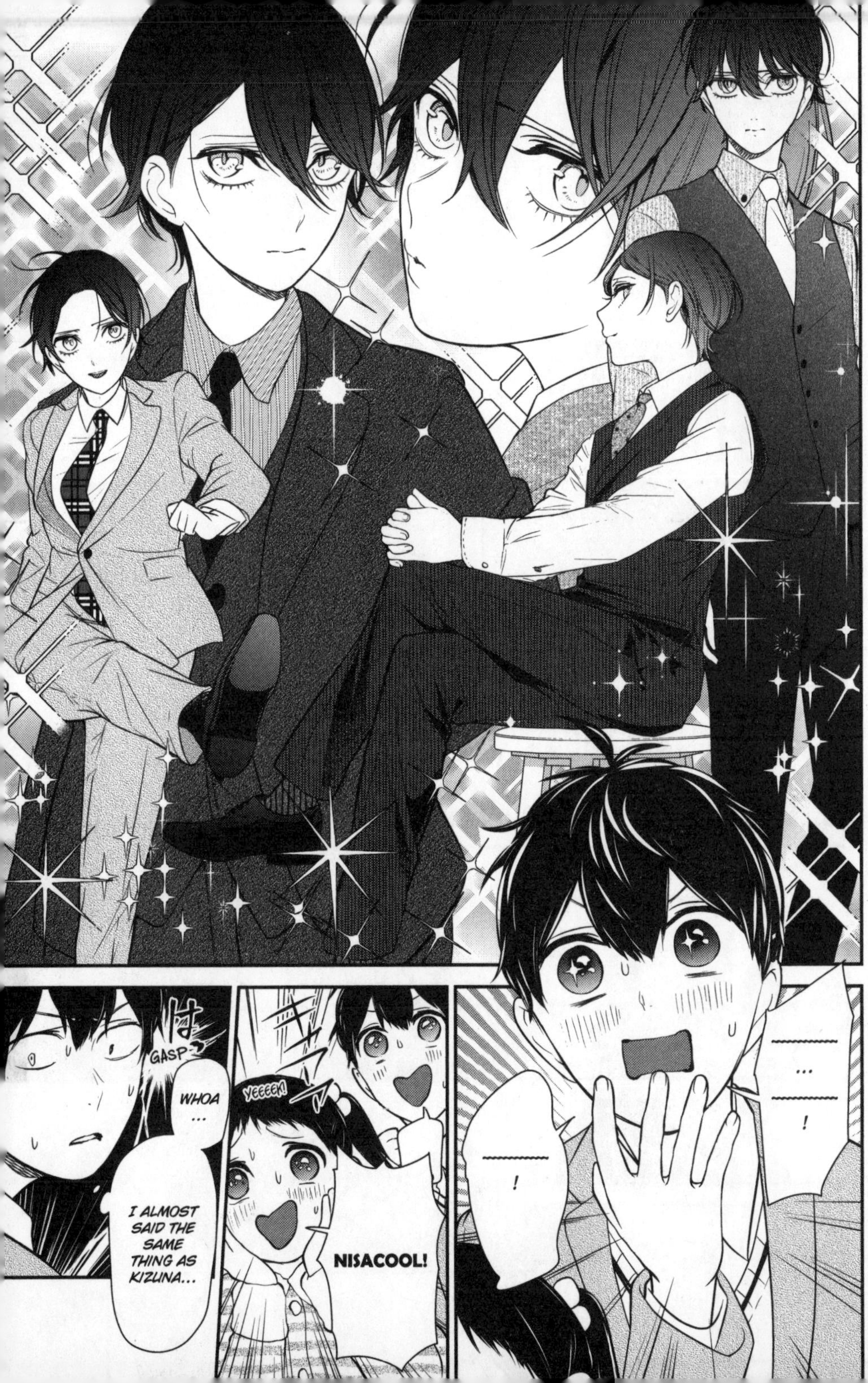

———
...
———
!
———
!
YEEEEK!
NISACOOL!
は
GASP
WHOA
...
I ALMOST SAID THE SAME THING AS KIZUNA...

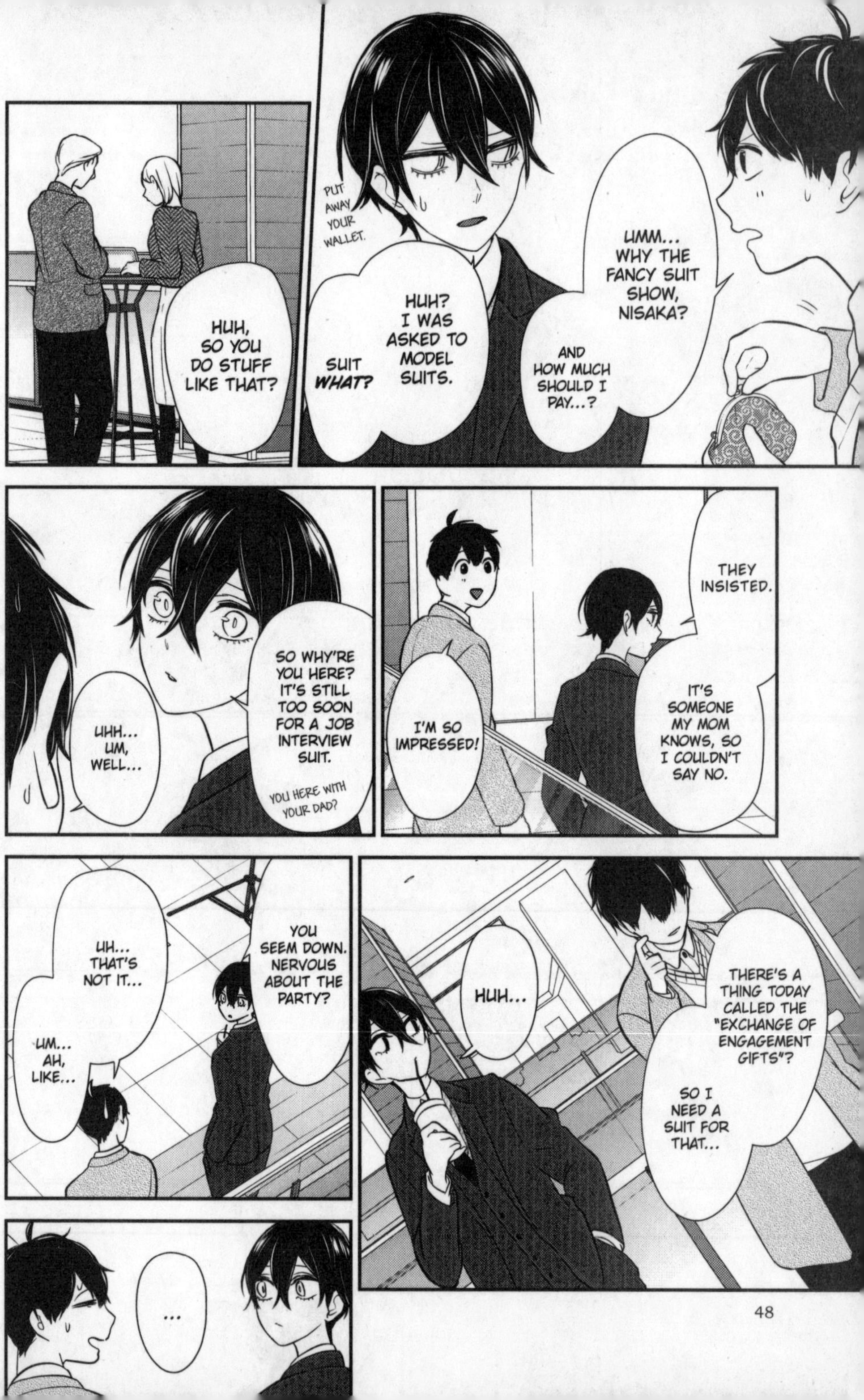
UMM... WHY THE FANCY SUIT SHOW, NISAKA?
AND HOW MUCH SHOULD I PAY...?
PUT AWAY YOUR WALLET.
HUH? I WAS ASKED TO MODEL SUITS.
SUIT *WHAT?*
HUH, SO YOU DO STUFF LIKE THAT?
THEY INSISTED.
IT'S SOMEONE MY MOM KNOWS, SO I COULDN'T SAY NO.
I'M SO IMPRESSED!
SO WHY'RE YOU HERE? IT'S STILL TOO SOON FOR A JOB INTERVIEW SUIT.
YOU HERE WITH YOUR DAD?
UHH... UM, WELL...
THERE'S A THING TODAY CALLED THE "EXCHANGE OF ENGAGEMENT GIFTS"?
SO I NEED A SUIT FOR THAT...
HUH...
YOU SEEM DOWN. NERVOUS ABOUT THE PARTY?
UH... THAT'S NOT IT...
UM... AH, LIKE...
...

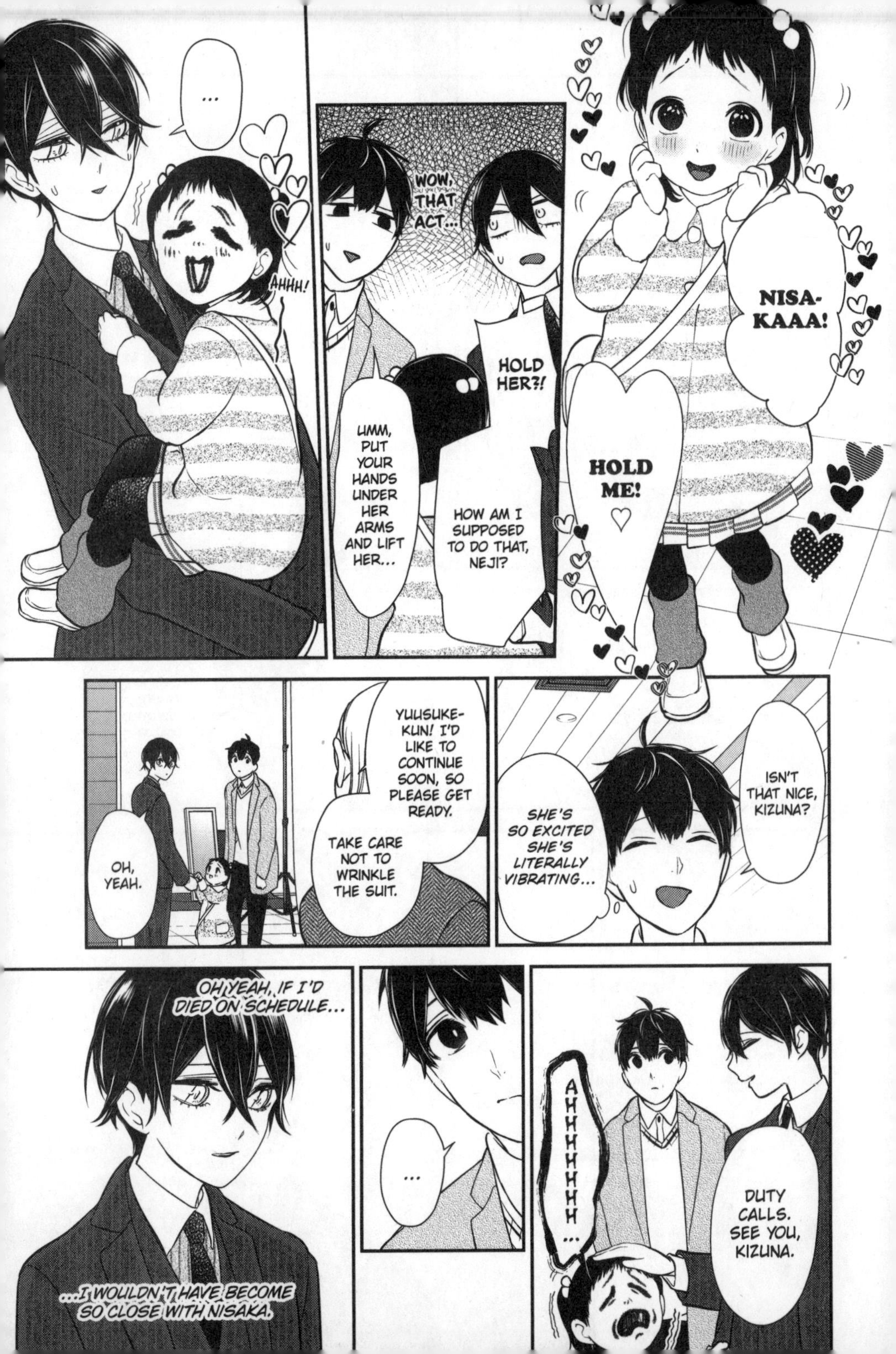
NISA-KAAA!
HOLD ME! ♡
WOW, THAT ACT...
HOLD HER?!
HOW AM I SUPPOSED TO DO THAT, NEJI?
UMM, PUT YOUR HANDS UNDER HER ARMS AND LIFT HER...
...
AHHH!
ISN'T THAT NICE, KIZUNA?
SHE'S SO EXCITED SHE'S LITERALLY VIBRATING...
YUUSUKE-KUN! I'D LIKE TO CONTINUE SOON, SO PLEASE GET READY.
TAKE CARE NOT TO WRINKLE THE SUIT.
OH, YEAH.
DUTY CALLS. SEE YOU, KIZUNA.
AHHHHHHHH...
...
OH YEAH, IF I'D DIED ON SCHEDULE...
...I WOULDN'T HAVE BECOME SO CLOSE WITH NISAKA.

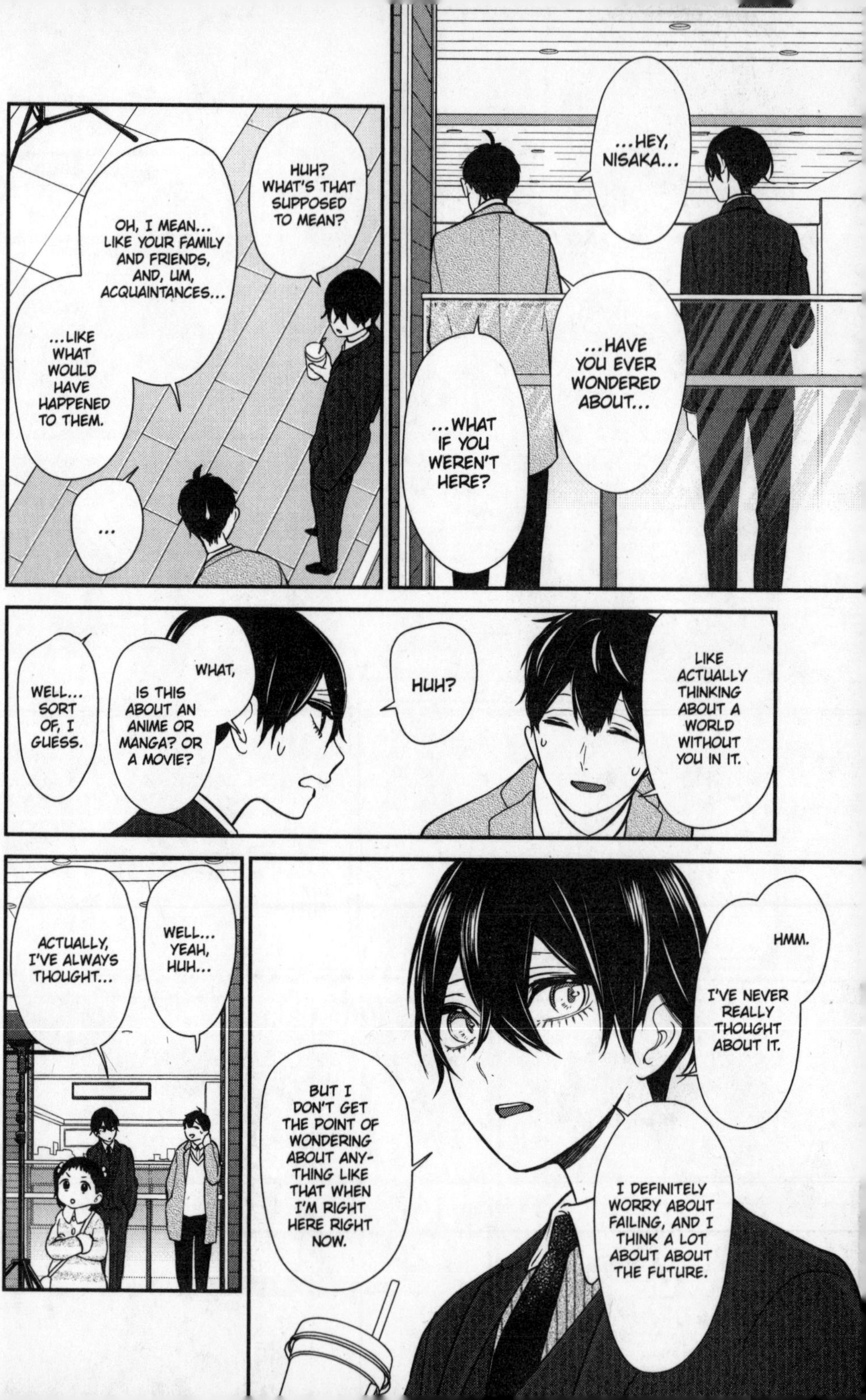
...HEY, NISAKA...
...HAVE YOU EVER WONDERED ABOUT...
...WHAT IF YOU WEREN'T HERE?
HUH? WHAT'S THAT SUPPOSED TO MEAN?
OH, I MEAN... LIKE YOUR FAMILY AND FRIENDS, AND, UM, ACQUAINTANCES...
...LIKE WHAT WOULD HAVE HAPPENED TO THEM.
...
LIKE ACTUALLY THINKING ABOUT A WORLD WITHOUT YOU IN IT.
HUH?
WHAT, IS THIS ABOUT AN ANIME OR MANGA? OR A MOVIE?
WELL... SORT OF, I GUESS.
HMM.
I'VE NEVER REALLY THOUGHT ABOUT IT.
I DEFINITELY WORRY ABOUT FAILING, AND I THINK A LOT ABOUT ABOUT THE FUTURE.
BUT I DON'T GET THE POINT OF WONDERING ABOUT ANY-THING LIKE THAT WHEN I'M RIGHT HERE RIGHT NOW.
WELL... YEAH, HUH...
ACTUALLY, I'VE ALWAYS THOUGHT...

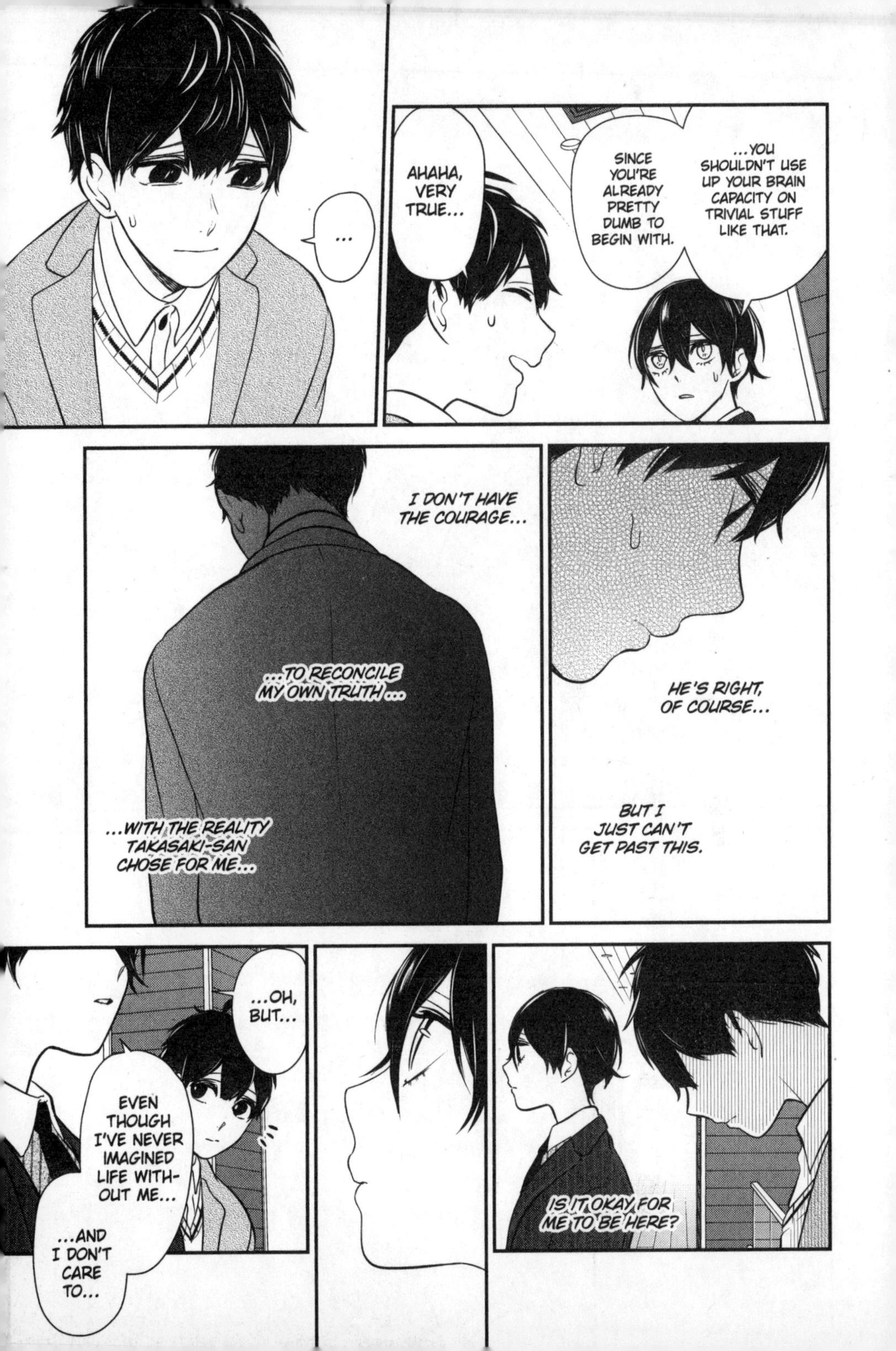
...YOU SHOULDN'T USE UP YOUR BRAIN CAPACITY ON TRIVIAL STUFF LIKE THAT.
SINCE YOU'RE ALREADY PRETTY DUMB TO BEGIN WITH.
AHAHA, VERY TRUE...
...
HE'S RIGHT, OF COURSE...
BUT I JUST CAN'T GET PAST THIS.
I DON'T HAVE THE COURAGE...
...TO RECONCILE MY OWN TRUTH...
...WITH THE REALITY TAKASAKI-SAN CHOSE FOR ME...
IS IT OKAY, FOR ME TO BE HERE?
...OH, BUT...
EVEN THOUGH I'VE NEVER IMAGINED LIFE WITH-OUT ME...
...AND I DON'T CARE TO...

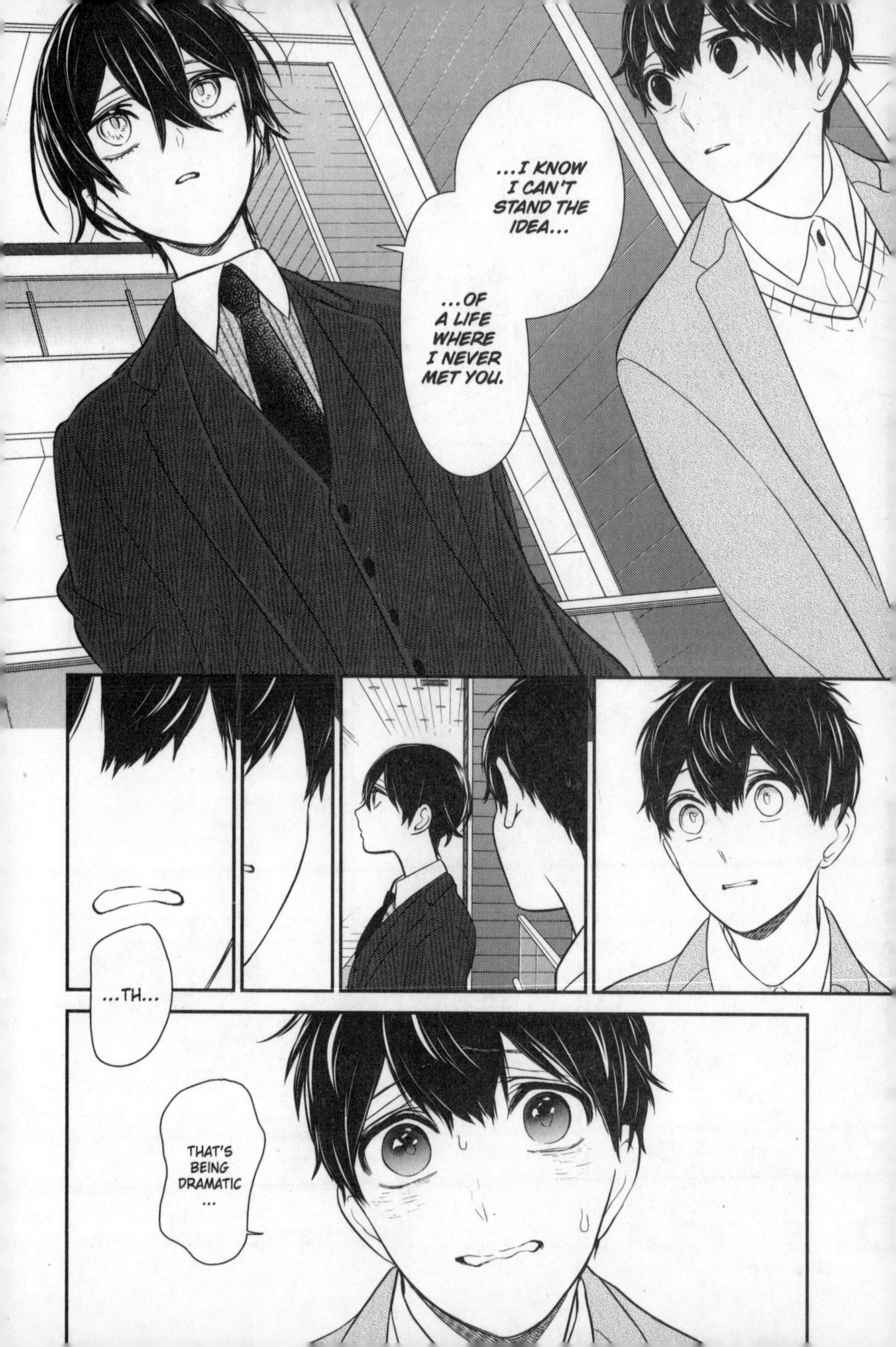
...I KNOW I CAN'T STAND THE IDEA...
...OF A LIFE WHERE I NEVER MET YOU.
...TH...
THAT'S BEING DRAMATIC ...

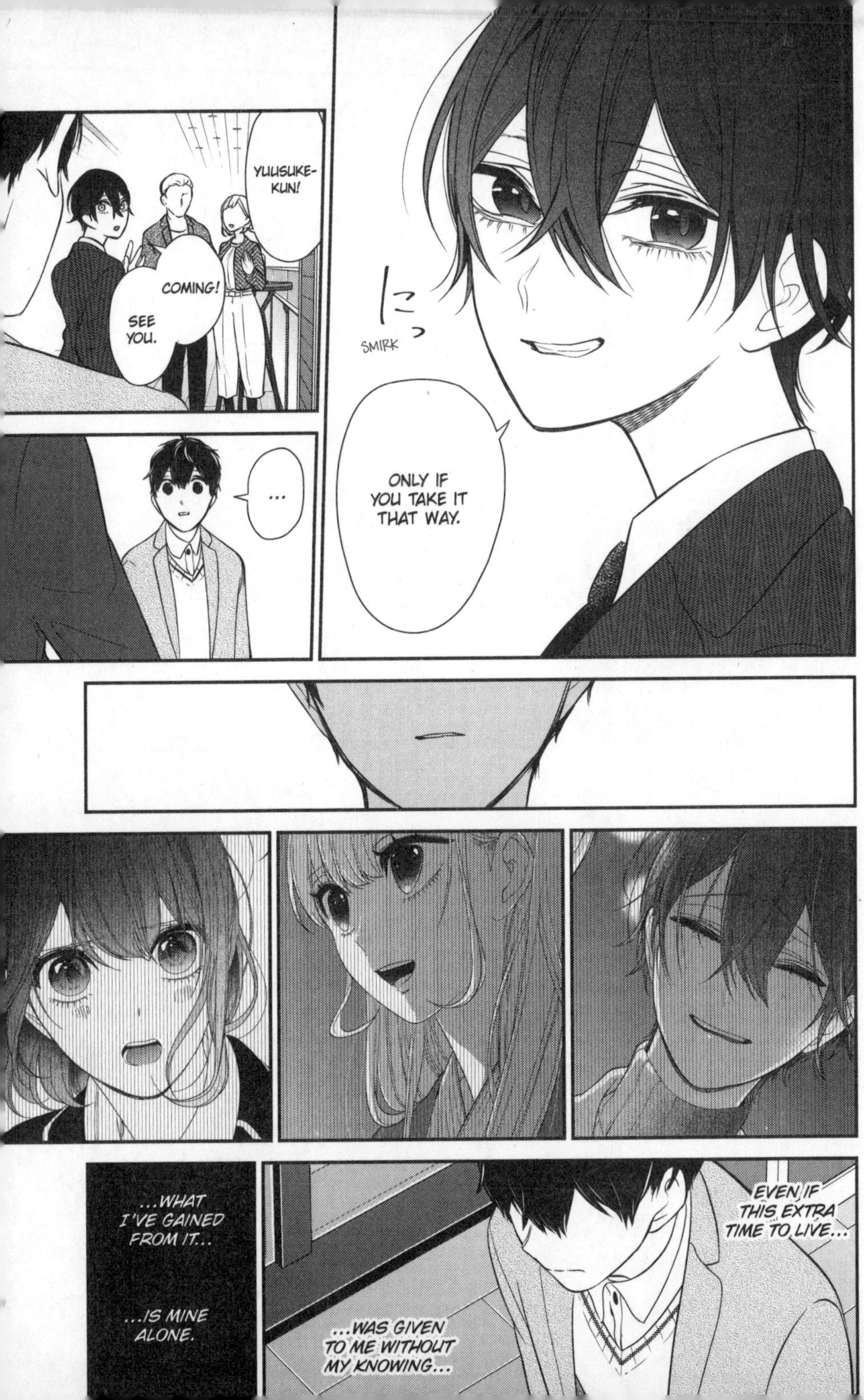
にっ
SMIRK
ONLY IF YOU TAKE IT THAT WAY.
YUUSUKE-KUN!
COMING!
SEE YOU.
...
EVEN IF THIS EXTRA TIME TO LIVE...
...WAS GIVEN TO ME WITHOUT MY KNOWING...
...WHAT I'VE GAINED FROM IT...
...IS MINE ALONE.

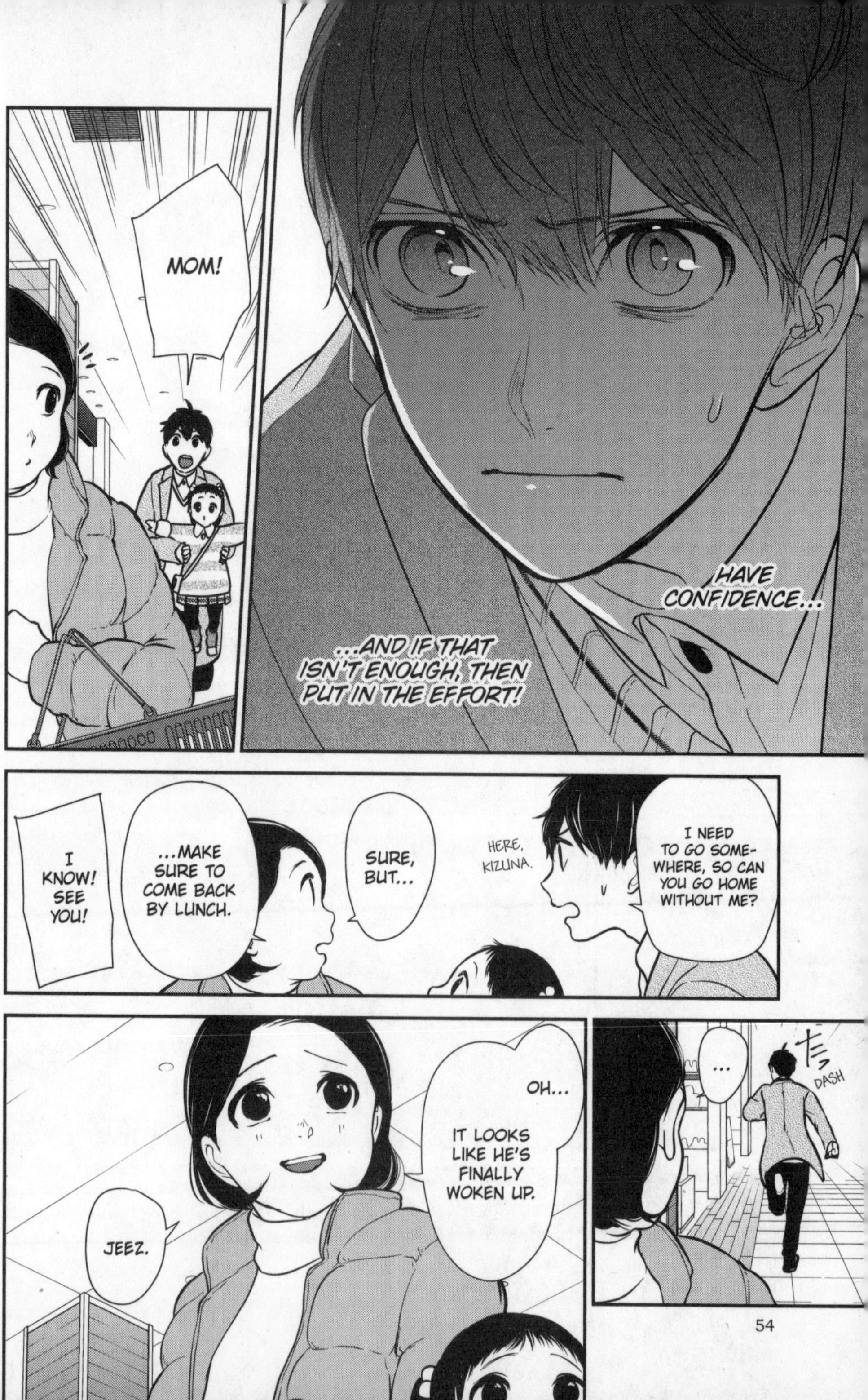
HAVE CONFIDENCE...
...AND IF THAT ISN'T ENOUGH, THEN PUT IN THE EFFORT!
MOM!
I NEED TO GO SOME-WHERE, SO CAN YOU GO HOME WITHOUT ME?
HERE, KIZUNA.
SURE, BUT...
...MAKE SURE TO COME BACK BY LUNCH.
I KNOW! SEE YOU!
...
DASH
OH...
IT LOOKS LIKE HE'S FINALLY WOKEN UP.
JEEZ.

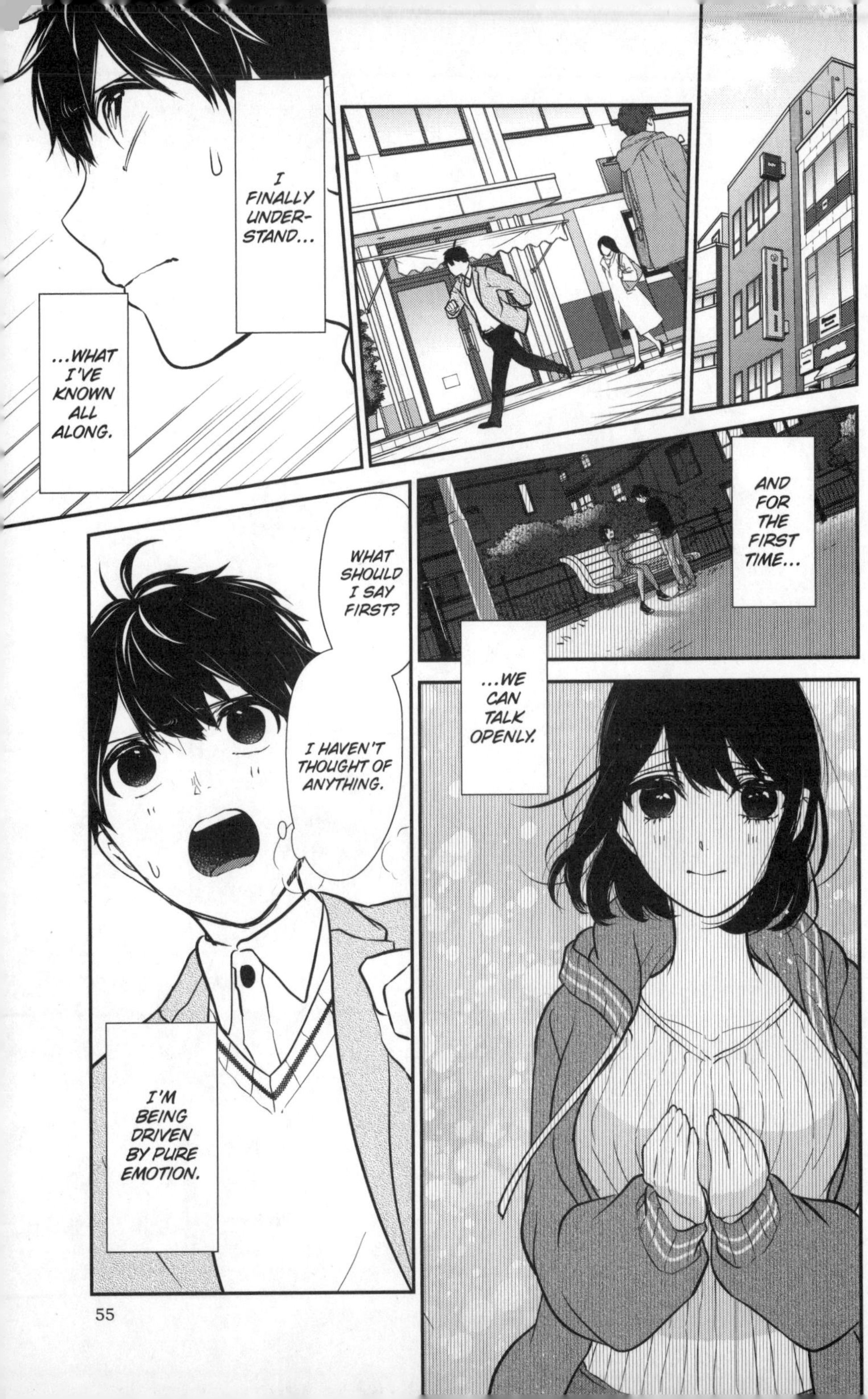
I FINALLY UNDER-STAND...
...WHAT I'VE KNOWN ALL ALONG.
AND FOR THE FIRST TIME...
...WE CAN TALK OPENLY.
WHAT SHOULD I SAY FIRST?
I HAVEN'T THOUGHT OF ANYTHING.
I'M BEING DRIVEN BY PURE EMOTION.

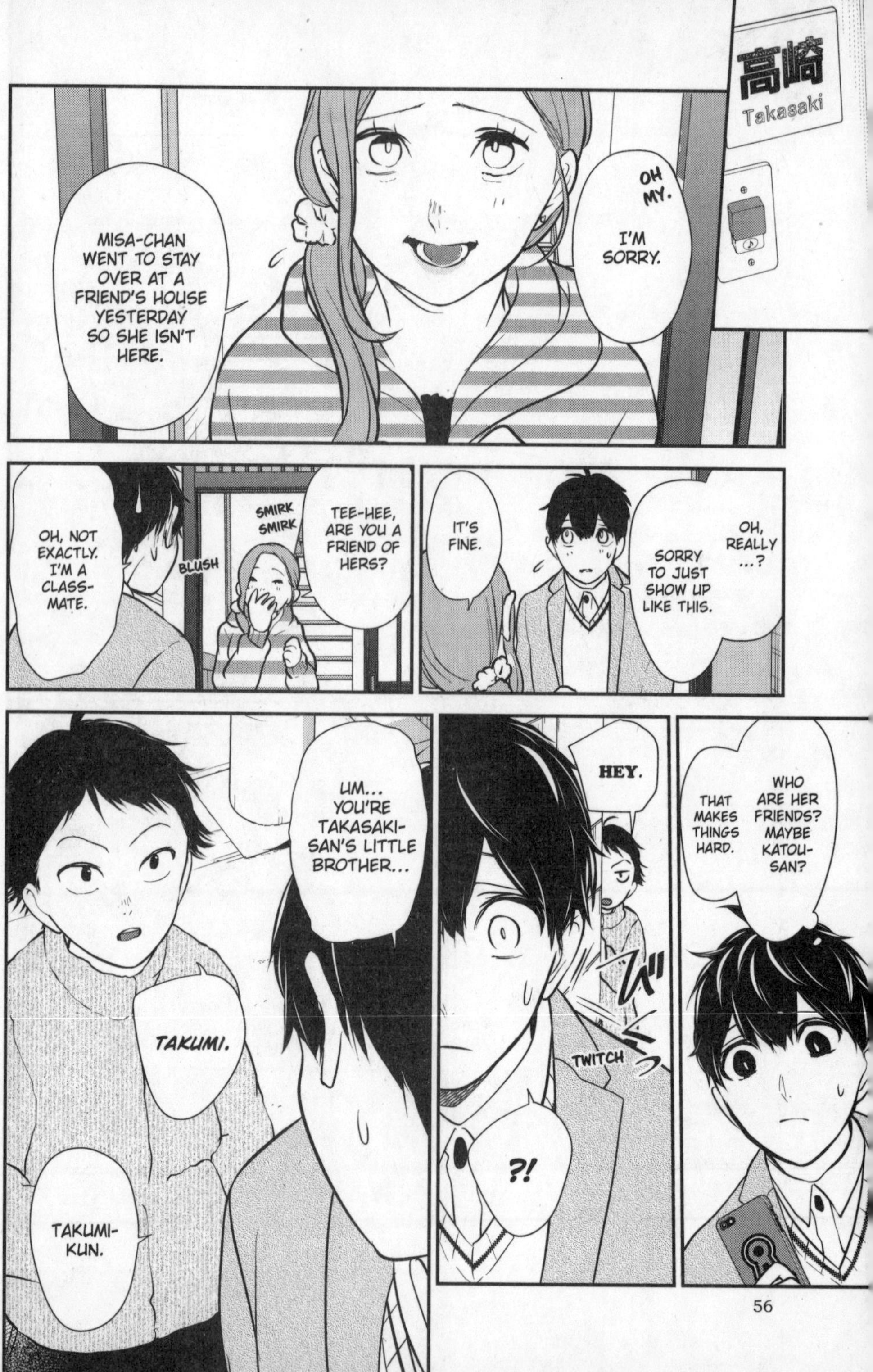
高崎
Takasaki
OH MY.
I'M SORRY.
MISA-CHAN WENT TO STAY OVER AT A FRIEND'S HOUSE YESTERDAY SO SHE ISN'T HERE.
OH, REALLY ...?
SORRY TO JUST SHOW UP LIKE THIS.
IT'S FINE.
TEE-HEE, ARE YOU A FRIEND OF HERS?
SMIRK SMIRK
BLUSH
OH, NOT EXACTLY. I'M A CLASSMATE.
WHO ARE HER FRIENDS? MAYBE KATOU-SAN?
THAT MAKES THINGS HARD.
HEY.
TWITCH
?!
UM... YOU'RE TAKASAKI-SAN'S LITTLE BROTHER...
TAKUMI.
TAKUMI-KUN.

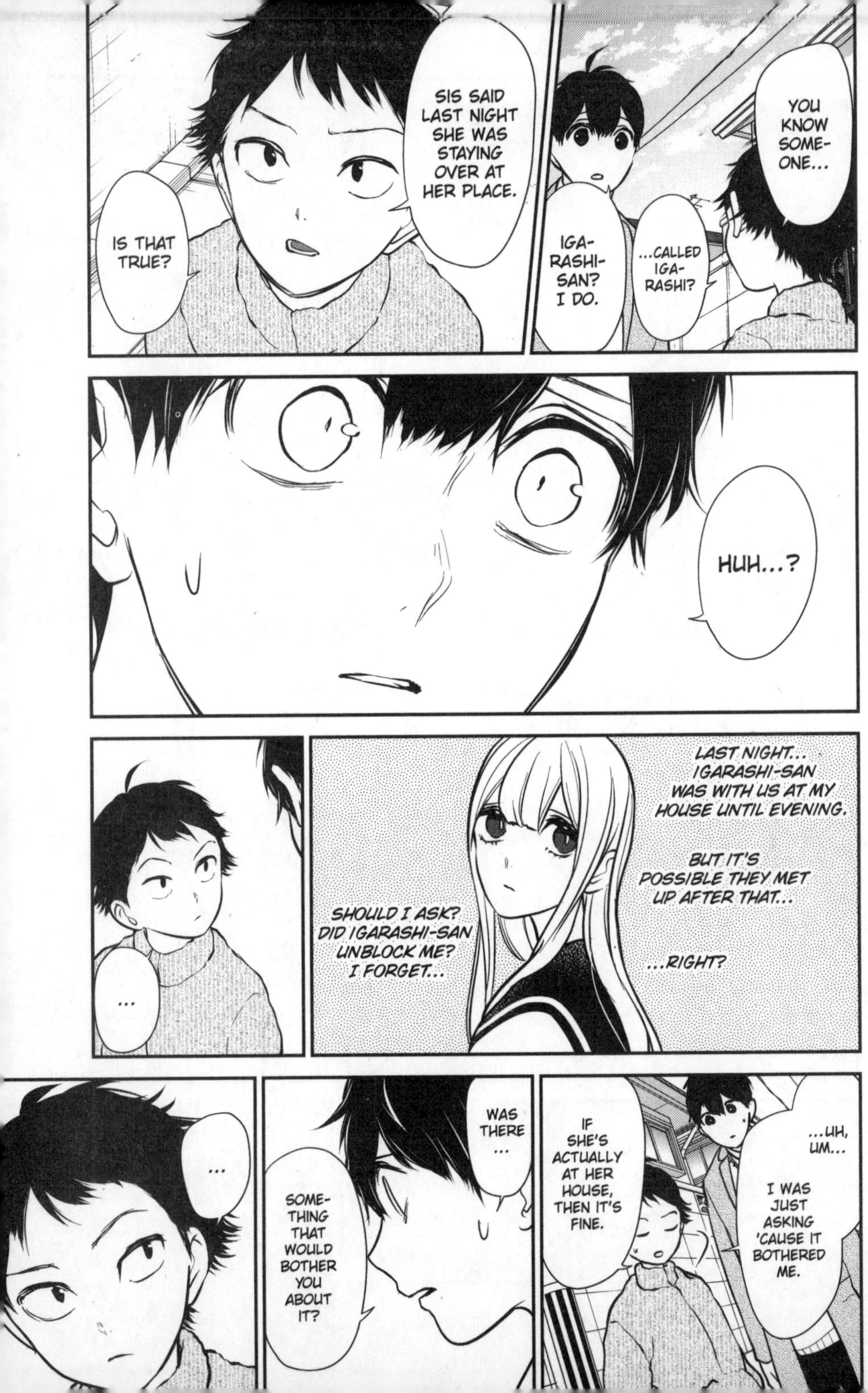
YOU KNOW SOME-ONE...
...CALLED IGA-RASHI?
IGA-RASHI-SAN? I DO.
SIS SAID LAST NIGHT SHE WAS STAYING OVER AT HER PLACE.
IS THAT TRUE?
HUH...?
LAST NIGHT... IGARASHI-SAN WAS WITH US AT MY HOUSE UNTIL EVENING.
BUT IT'S POSSIBLE THEY MET UP AFTER THAT...
...RIGHT?
SHOULD I ASK? DID IGARASHI-SAN UNBLOCK ME? I FORGET...
...
...UH, UM...
I WAS JUST ASKING 'CAUSE IT BOTHERED ME.
IF SHE'S ACTUALLY AT HER HOUSE, THEN IT'S FINE.
WAS THERE...
SOME-THING THAT WOULD BOTHER YOU ABOUT IT?
...

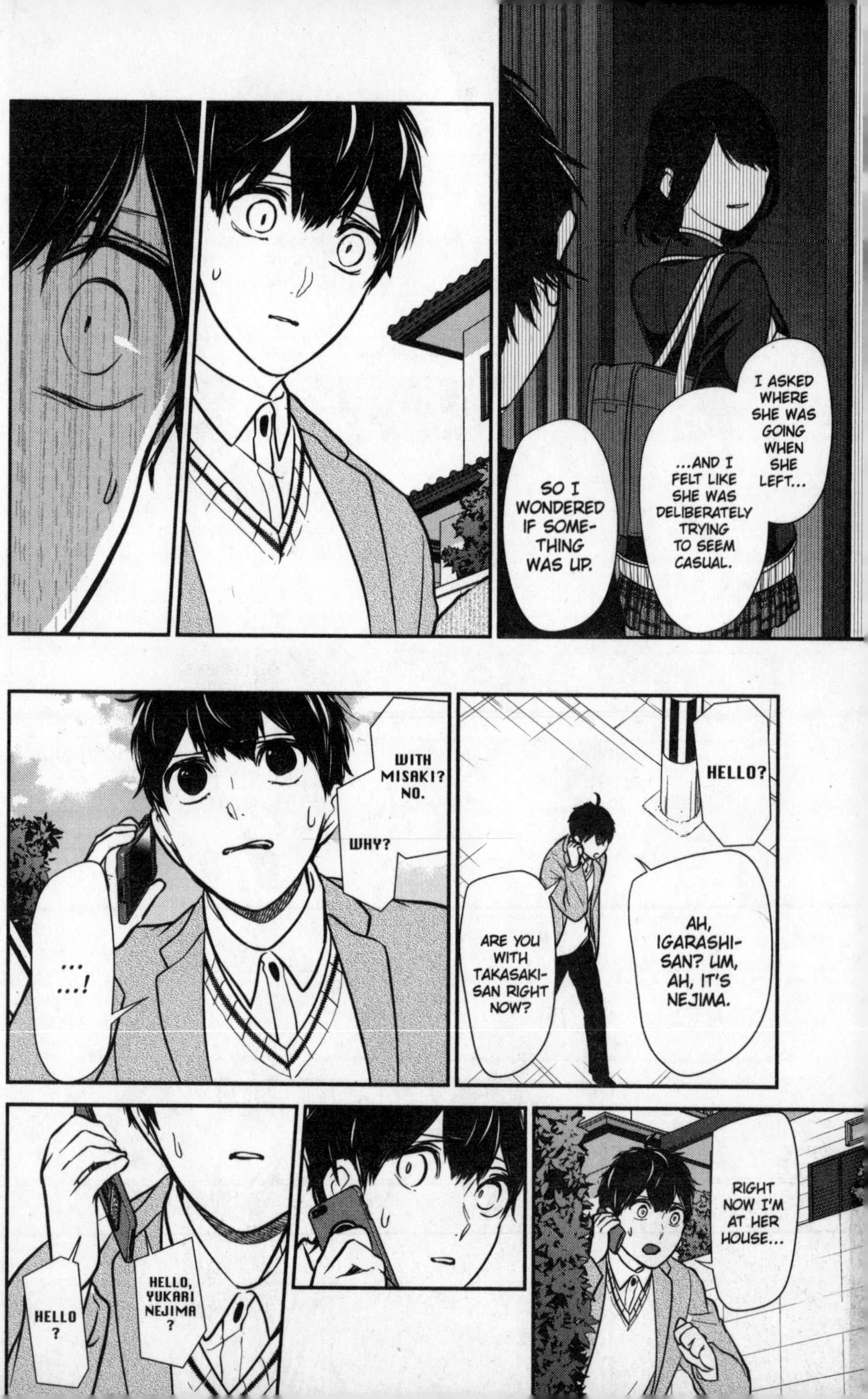
I ASKED WHERE SHE WAS GOING WHEN SHE LEFT...
...AND I FELT LIKE SHE WAS DELIBERATELY TRYING TO SEEM CASUAL.
SO I WONDERED IF SOME-THING WAS UP.
HELLO?
AH, IGARASHI-SAN? UM, AH, IT'S NEJIMA.
ARE YOU WITH TAKASAKI-SAN RIGHT NOW?
WITH MISAKI? NO.
WHY?
... ...!
RIGHT NOW I'M AT HER HOUSE...
HELLO, YUKARI NEJIMA?
HELLO?

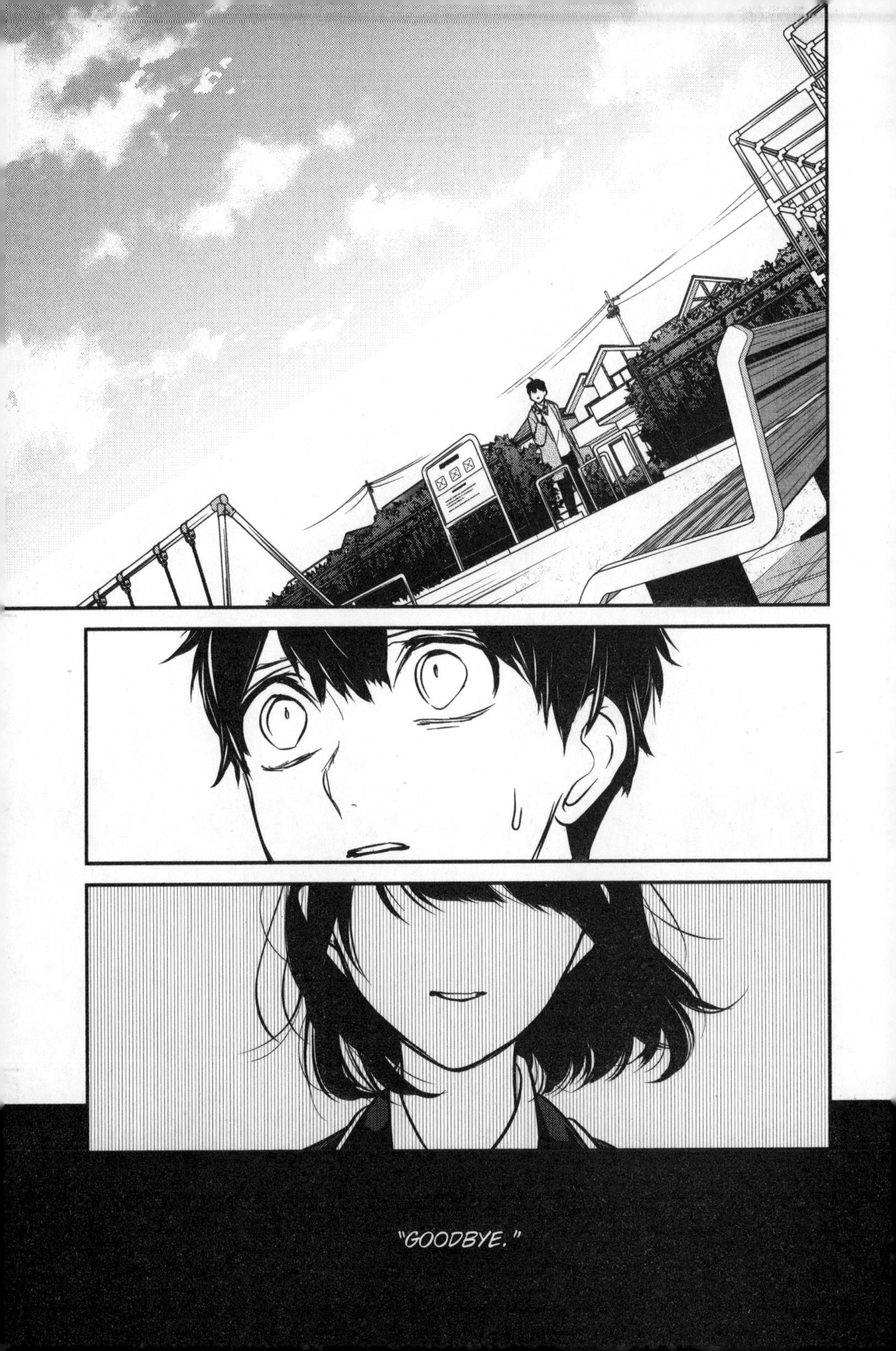
"GOODBYE."

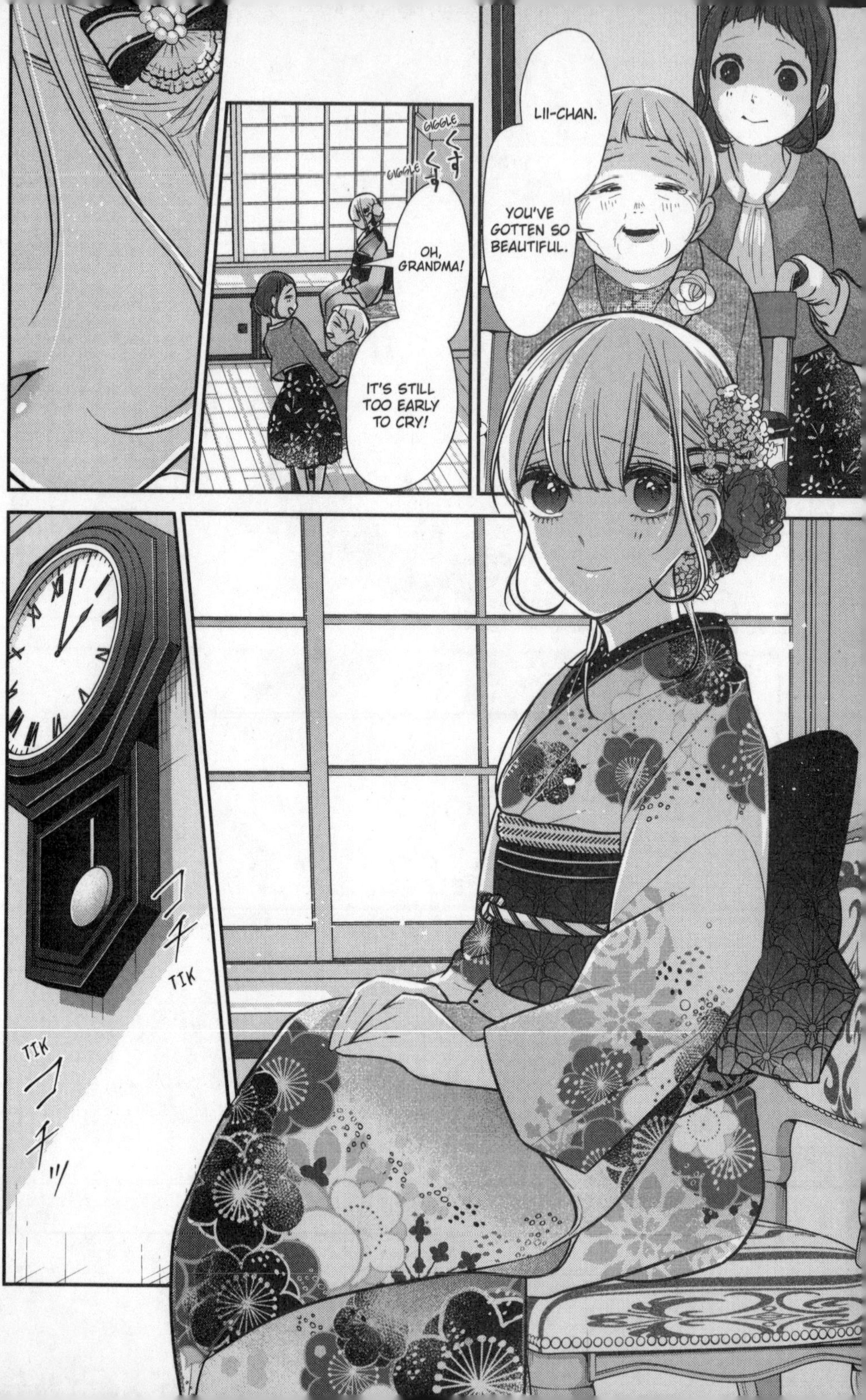
LII-CHAN.
YOU'VE GOTTEN SO BEAUTIFUL.
GIGGLE くす
GIGGLE くす
OH, GRANDMA!
IT'S STILL TOO EARLY TO CRY!
コチ TIK
TIK コチッ

Chapter 47: Accepting Love and Lies

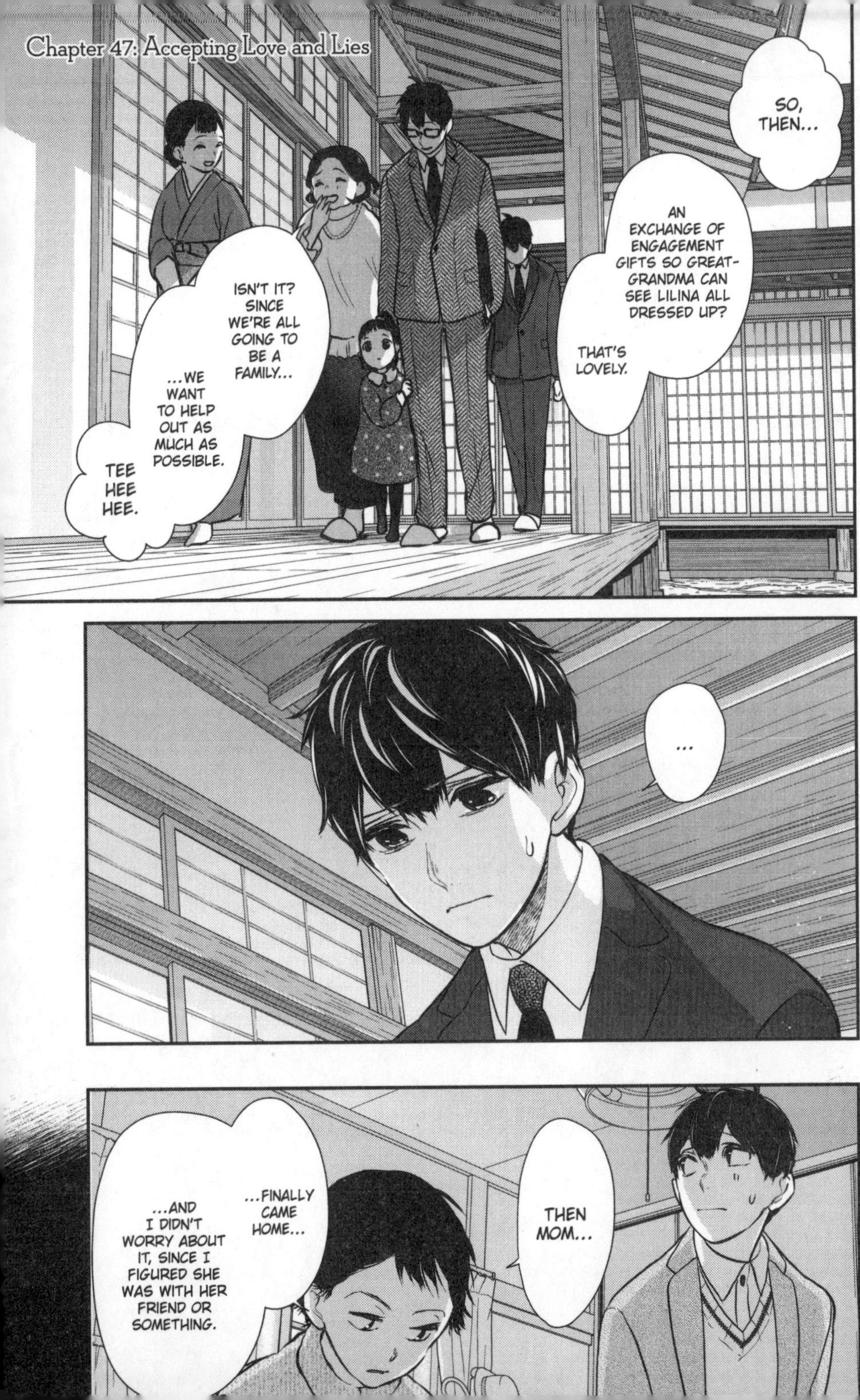
SO, THEN...
AN EXCHANGE OF ENGAGEMENT GIFTS SO GREAT-GRANDMA CAN SEE LILINA ALL DRESSED UP?
THAT'S LOVELY.
ISN'T IT? SINCE WE'RE ALL GOING TO BE A FAMILY...
...WE WANT TO HELP OUT AS MUCH AS POSSIBLE.
TEE HEE HEE.
...
THEN MOM...
...FINALLY CAME HOME...
...AND I DIDN'T WORRY ABOUT IT, SINCE I FIGURED SHE WAS WITH HER FRIEND OR SOMETHING.

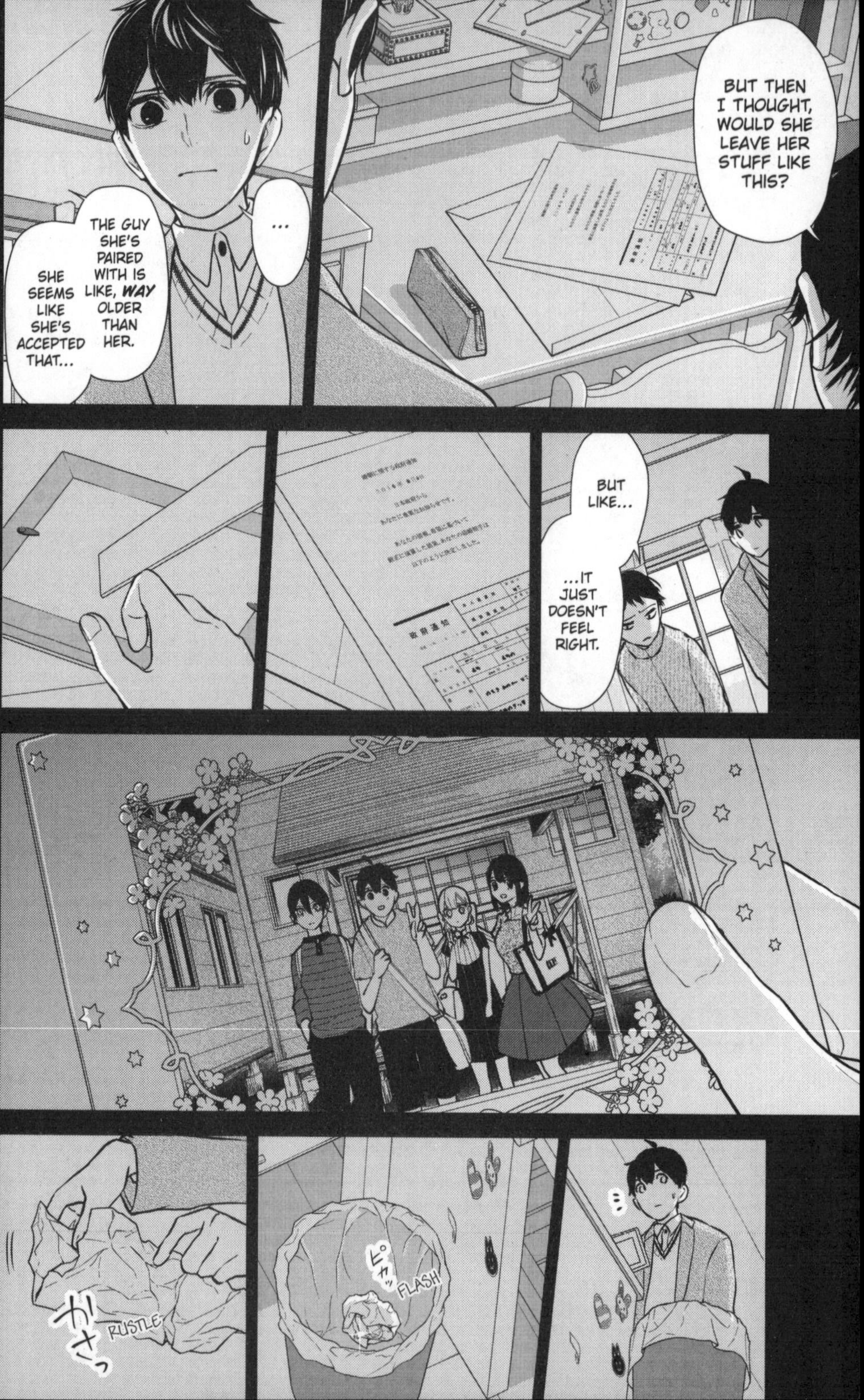
BUT THEN I THOUGHT, WOULD SHE LEAVE HER STUFF LIKE THIS?
...
THE GUY SHE'S PAIRED WITH IS LIKE, **WAY** OLDER THAN HER.
SHE SEEMS LIKE SHE'S ACCEPTED THAT...
BUT LIKE...
...IT JUST DOESN'T FEEL RIGHT.
...
ピカッ
FLASH
かさっ
RUSTLE

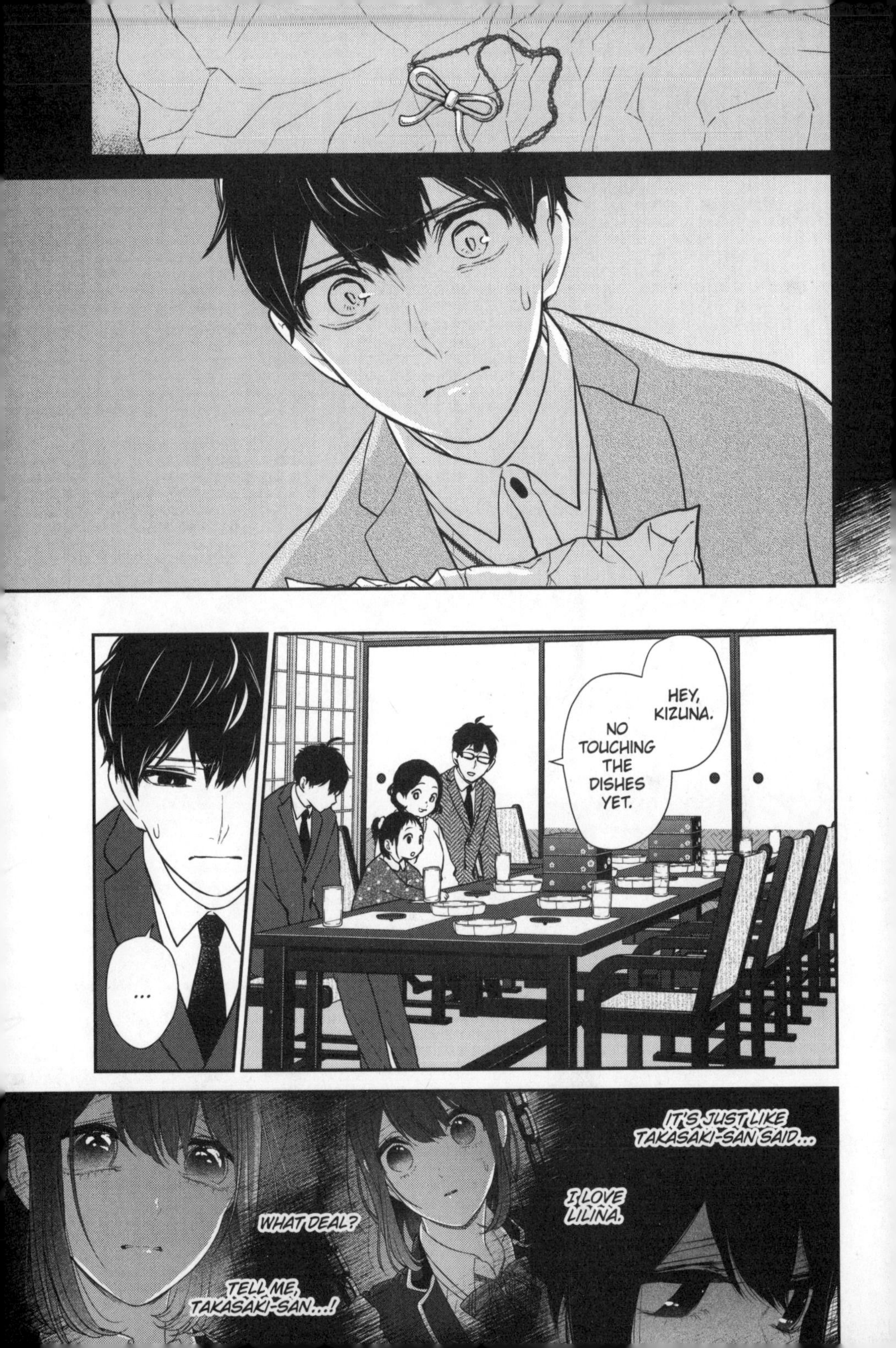
HEY, KIZUNA.
NO TOUCHING THE DISHES YET.
...
IT'S JUST LIKE TAKASAKI-SAN SAID...
I LOVE LILINA.
WHAT DEAL?
TELL ME, TAKASAKI-SAN...!

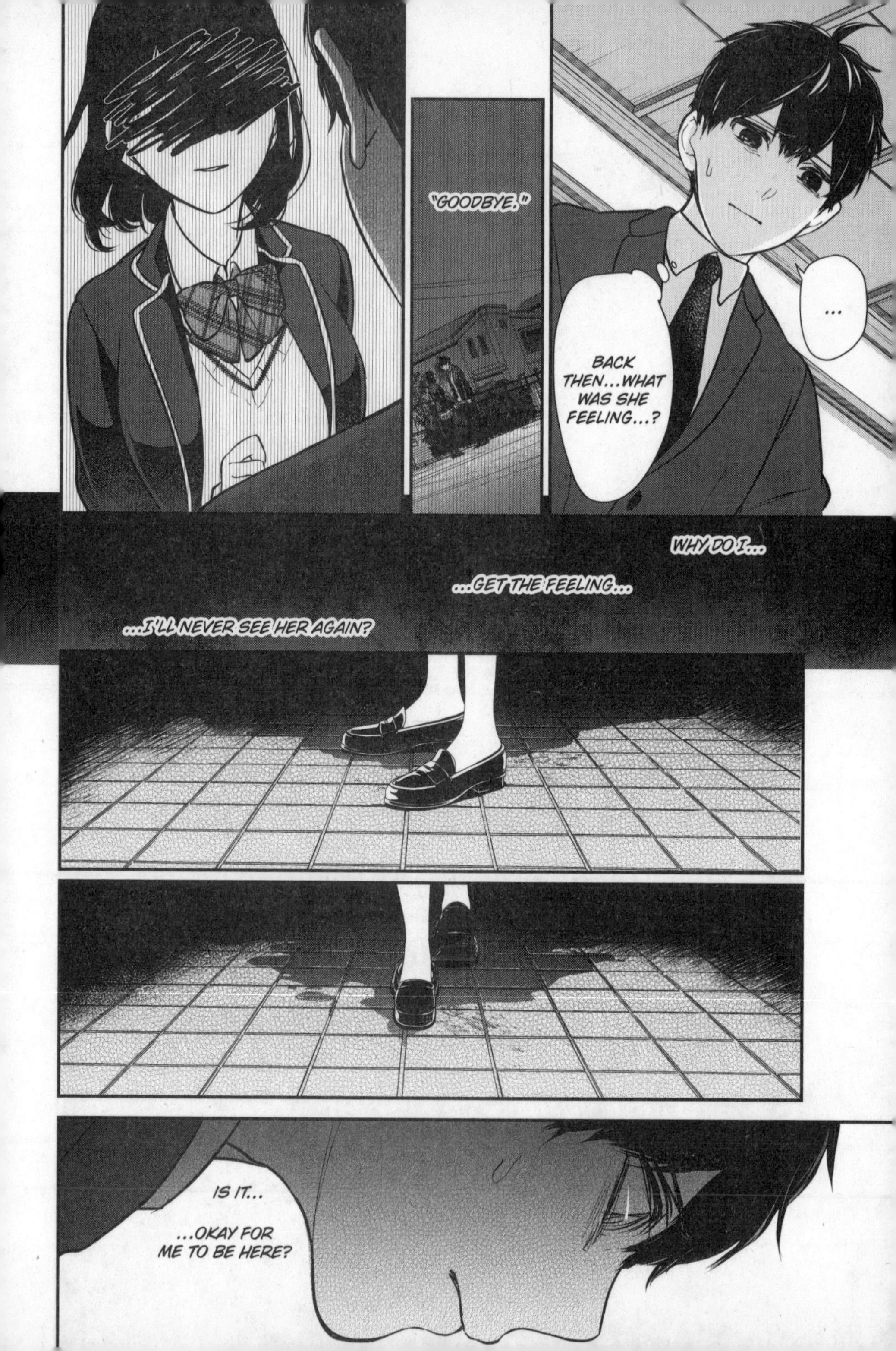
...
BACK THEN...WHAT WAS SHE FEELING...?
"GOODBYE."
WHY DO I...
...GET THE FEELING...
...I'LL NEVER SEE HER AGAIN?
IS IT...
...OKAY FOR ME TO BE HERE?

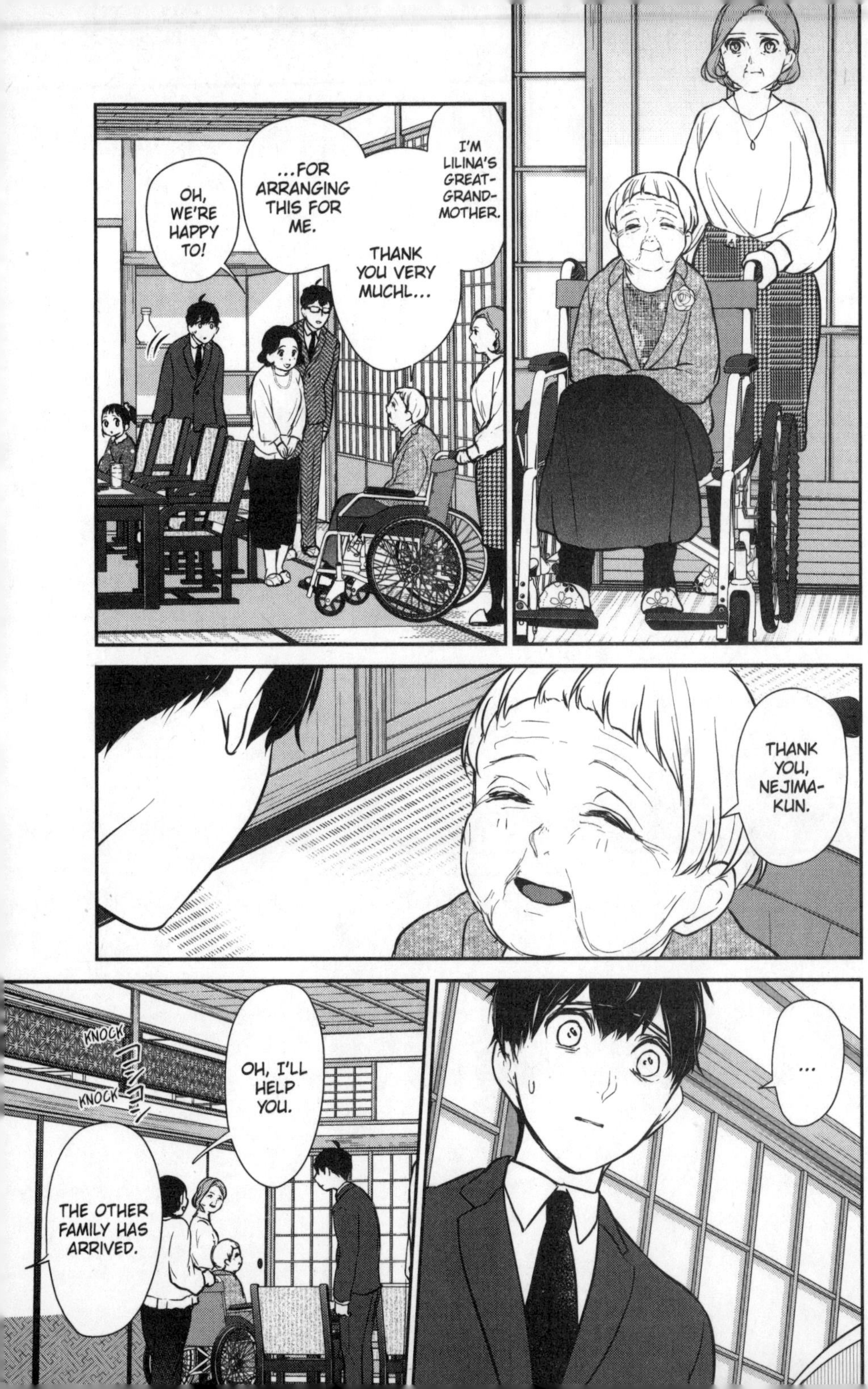
I'M LILINA'S GREAT-GRANDMOTHER.
THANK YOU VERY MUCHL...
...FOR ARRANGING THIS FOR ME.
OH, WE'RE HAPPY TO!
THANK YOU, NEJIMA-KUN.
...
OH, I'LL HELP YOU.
KNOCK
KNOCK
THE OTHER FAMILY HAS ARRIVED.

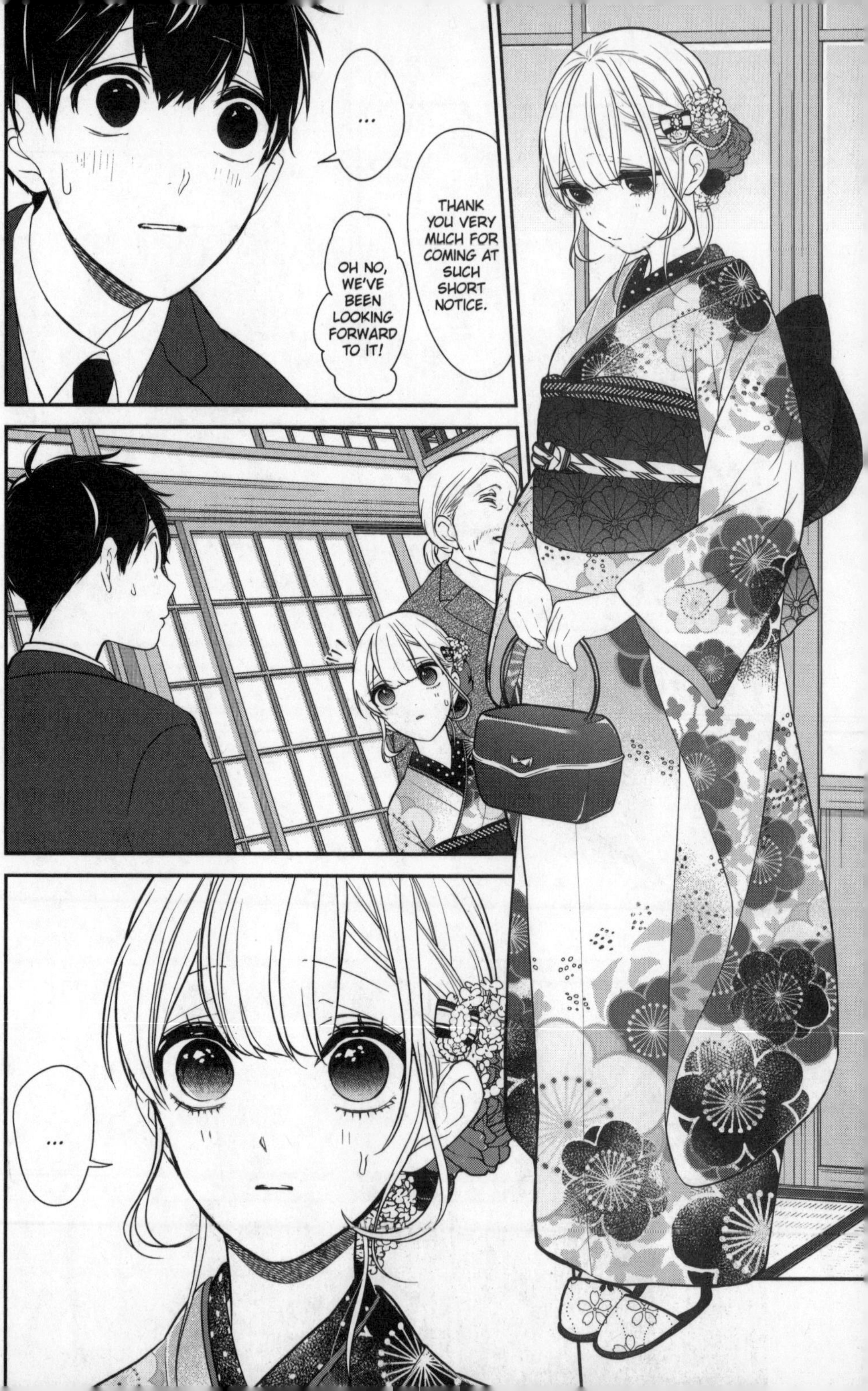
THANK YOU VERY MUCH FOR COMING AT SUCH SHORT NOTICE.
OH NO, WE'VE BEEN LOOKING FORWARD TO IT!
...
...

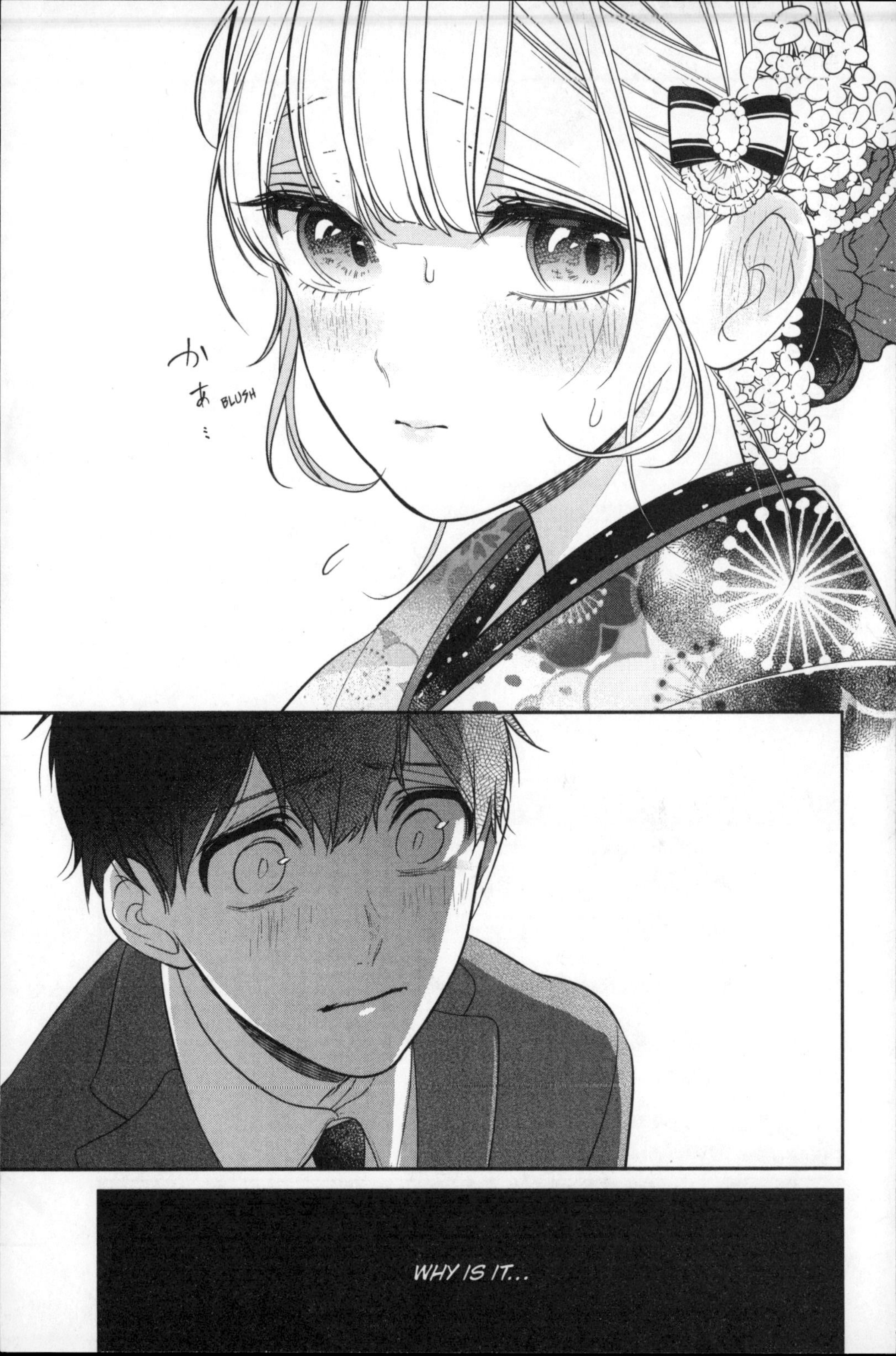
かあ
BLUSH
WHY IS IT...

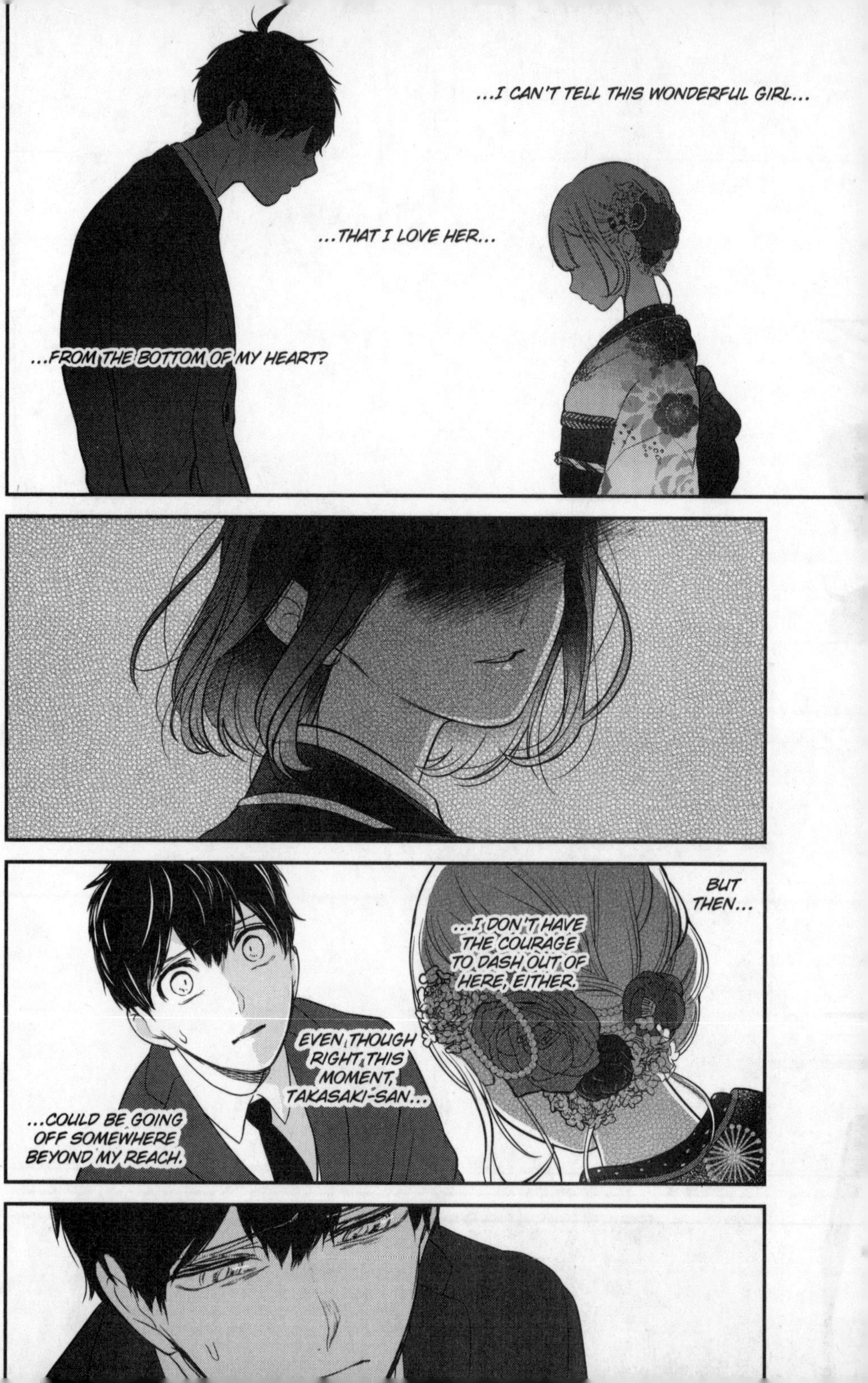
...I CAN'T TELL THIS WONDERFUL GIRL...
...THAT I LOVE HER...
...FROM THE BOTTOM OF MY HEART?
BUT THEN...
...I DON'T HAVE THE COURAGE TO DASH OUT OF HERE, EITHER.
EVEN THOUGH RIGHT THIS MOMENT, TAKASAKI-SAN...
...COULD BE GOING OFF SOMEWHERE BEYOND MY REACH.

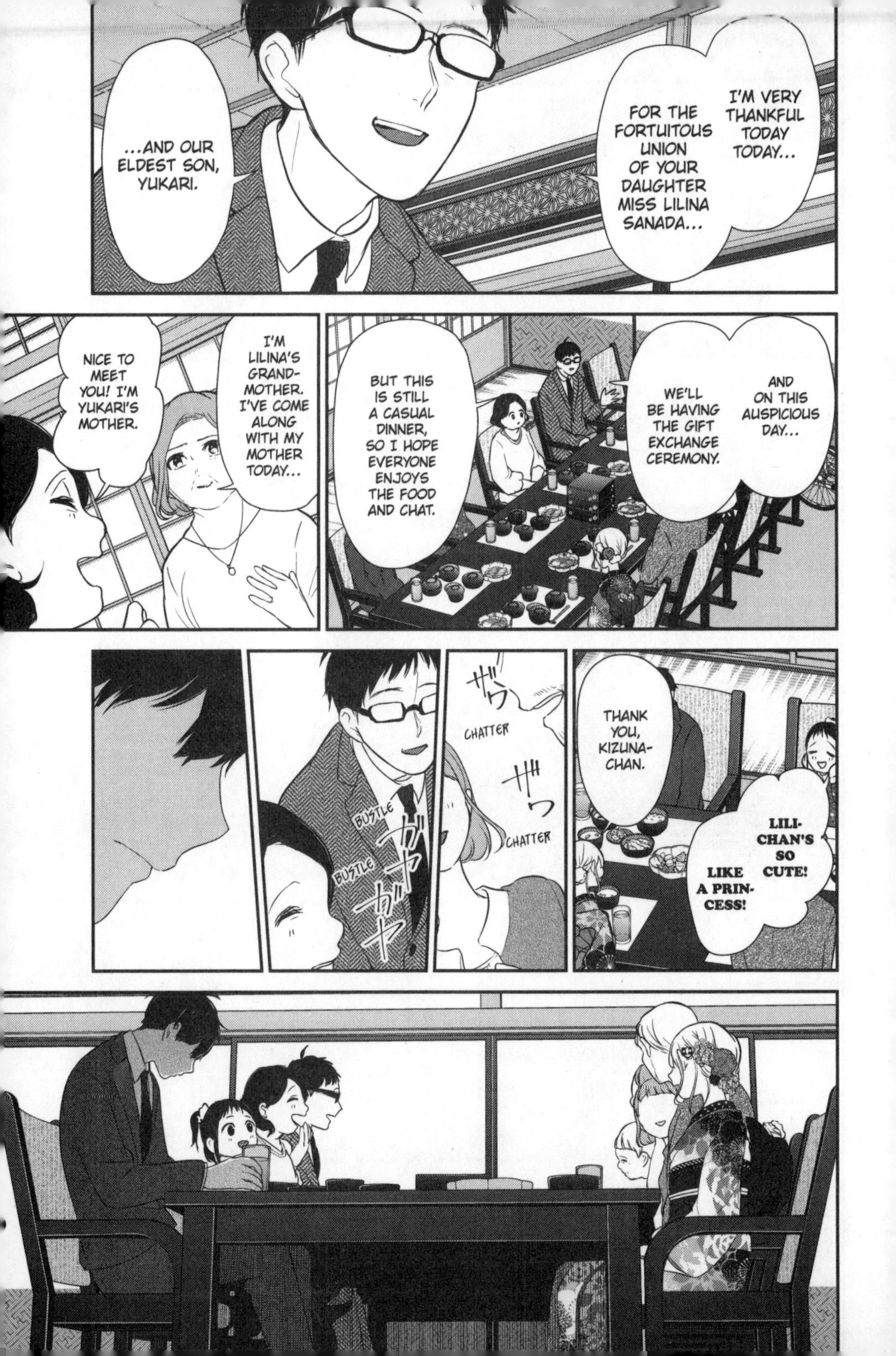
I'M VERY THANKFUL TODAY TODAY...
FOR THE FORTUITOUS UNION OF YOUR DAUGHTER MISS LILINA SANADA...
...AND OUR ELDEST SON, YUKARI.
AND ON THIS AUSPICIOUS DAY...
WE'LL BE HAVING THE GIFT EXCHANGE CEREMONY.
BUT THIS IS STILL A CASUAL DINNER, SO I HOPE EVERYONE ENJOYS THE FOOD AND CHAT.
I'M LILINA'S GRANDMOTHER. I'VE COME ALONG WITH MY MOTHER TODAY...
NICE TO MEET YOU! I'M YUKARI'S MOTHER.
LILI-CHAN'S SO CUTE!
LIKE A PRINCESS!
THANK YOU, KIZUNA-CHAN.
ザワ
CHATTER
ザワ
CHATTER
ガヤ
BUSTLE
ガヤ
BUSTLE

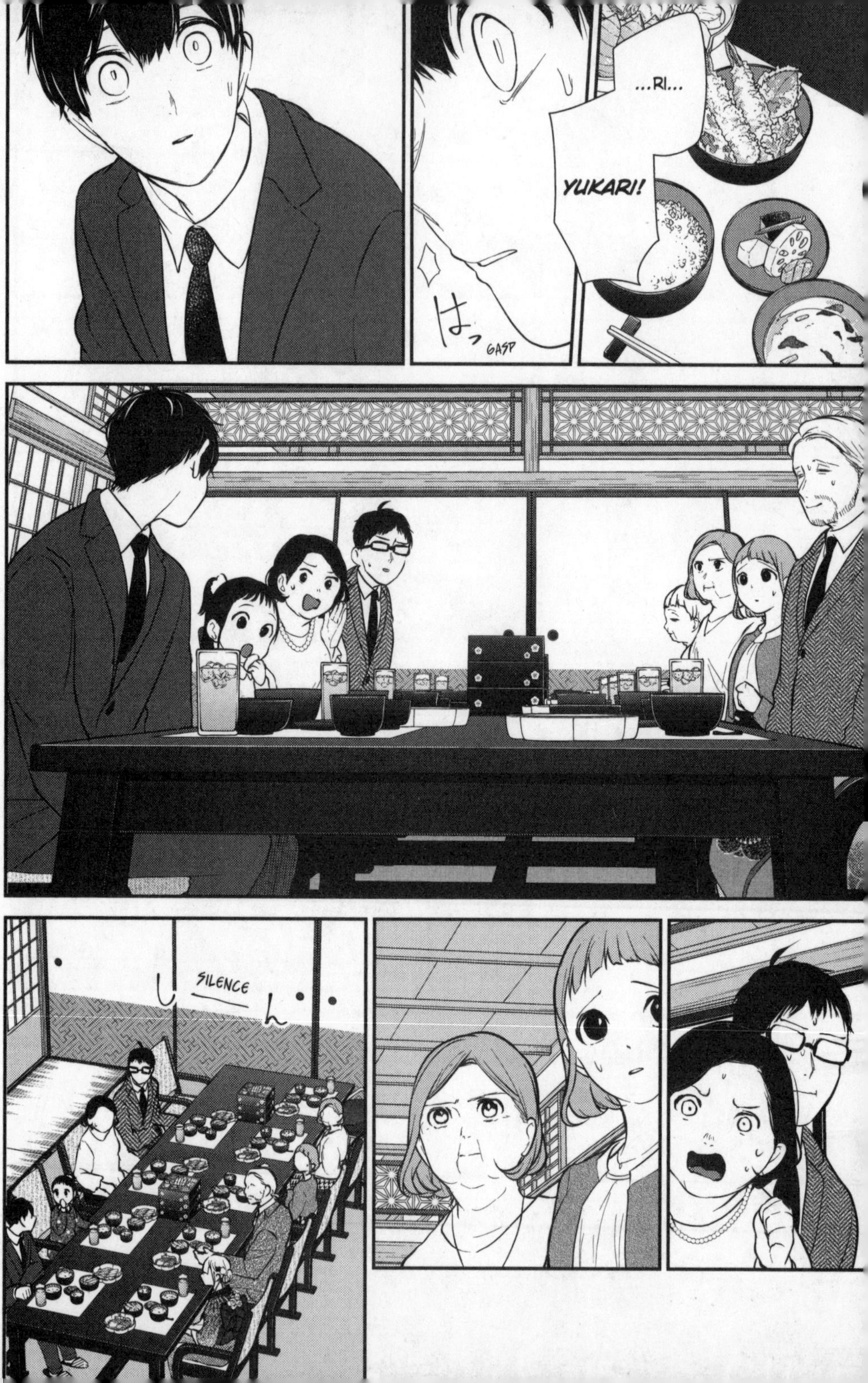
...RI...
YUKARI!
はっ
GASP
し ん
SILENCE

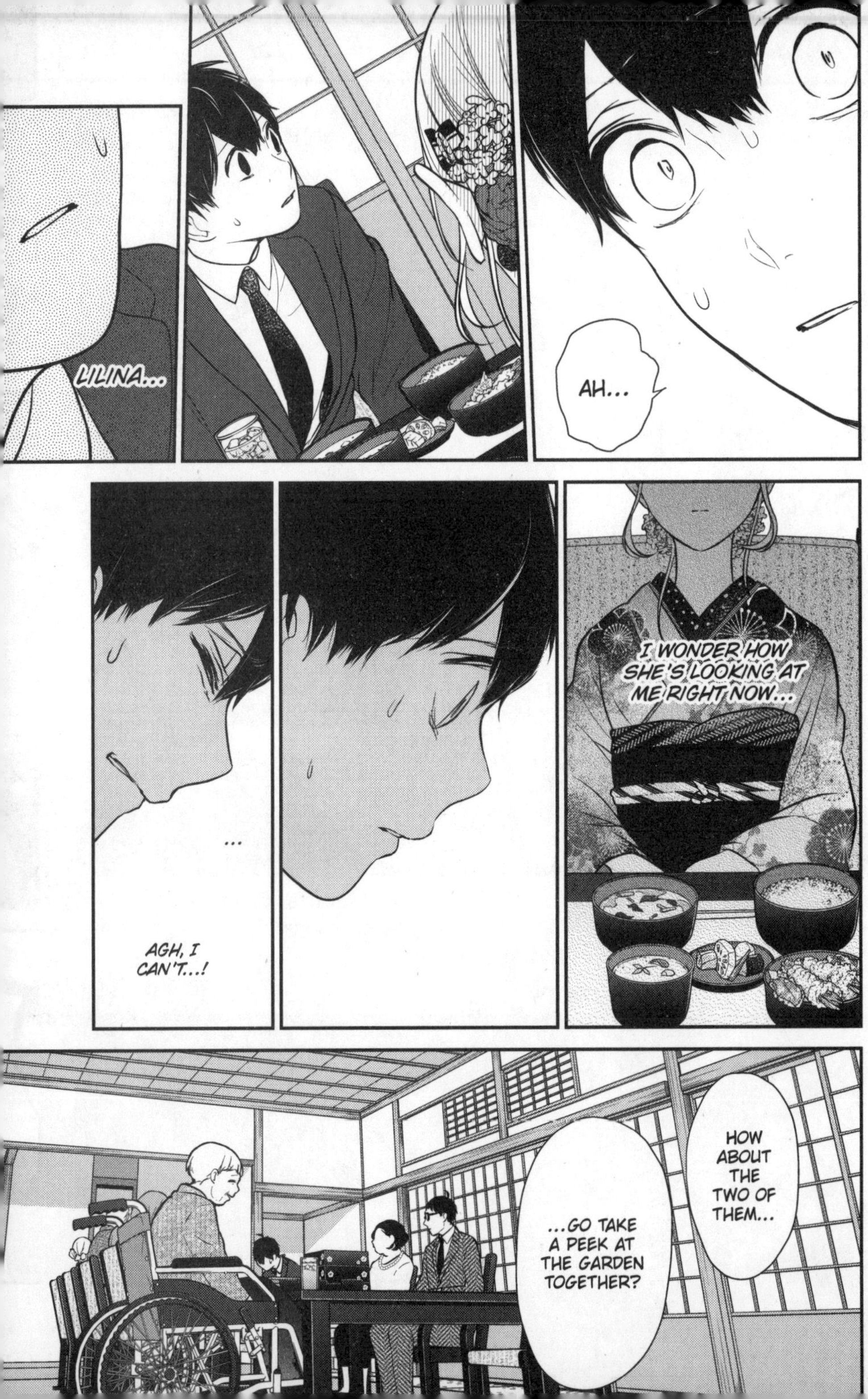
AH...
LILINA...
I WONDER HOW SHE'S LOOKING AT ME RIGHT NOW...
...
AGH, I CAN'T...!
HOW ABOUT THE TWO OF THEM...
...GO TAKE A PEEK AT THE GARDEN TOGETHER?

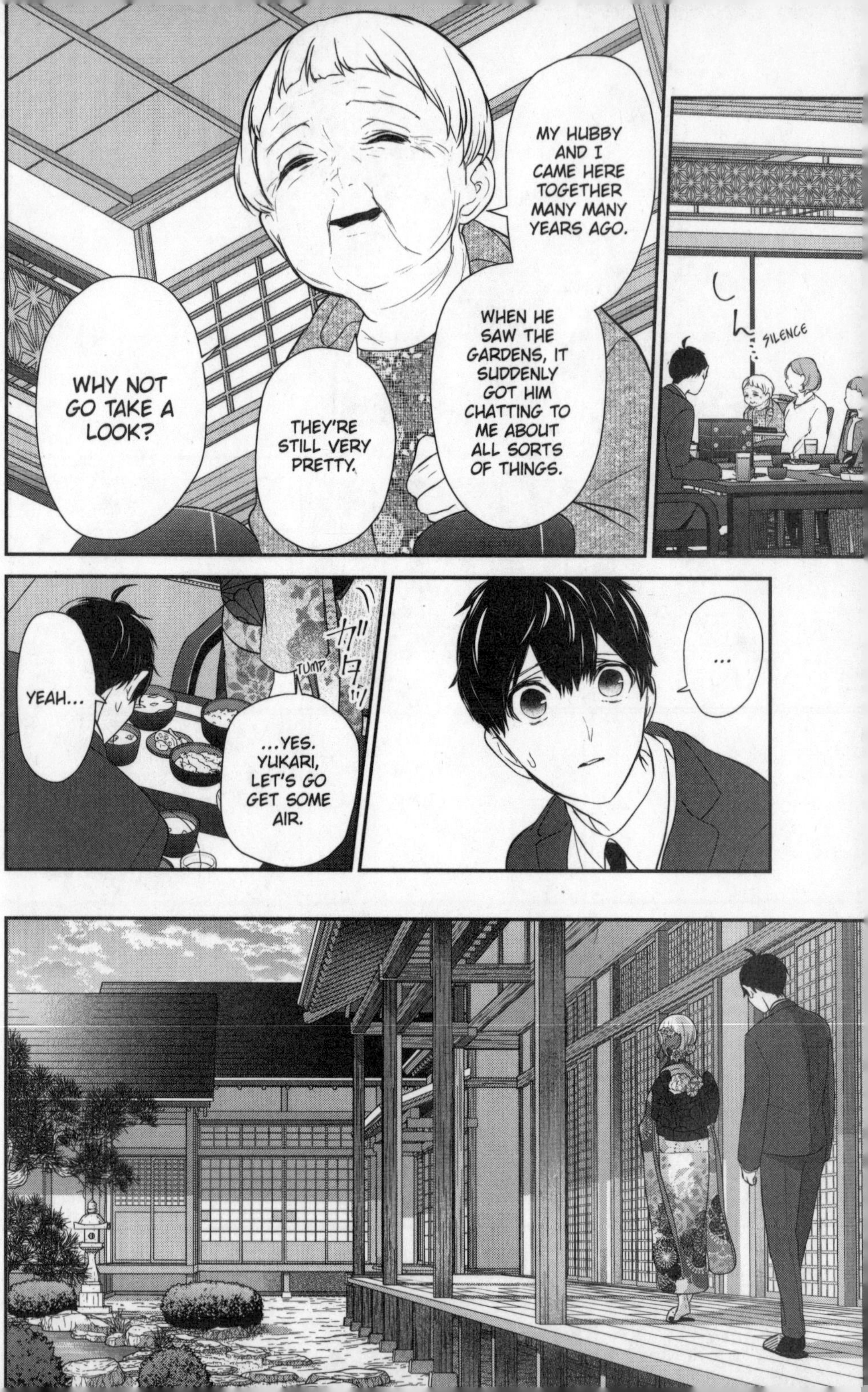
しん…
SILENCE
MY HUBBY AND I CAME HERE TOGETHER MANY MANY YEARS AGO.
WHEN HE SAW THE GARDENS, IT SUDDENLY GOT HIM CHATTING TO ME ABOUT ALL SORTS OF THINGS.
THEY'RE STILL VERY PRETTY.
WHY NOT GO TAKE A LOOK?
...
ガタッ
TUMP
...YES. YUKARI, LET'S GO GET SOME AIR.
YEAH...

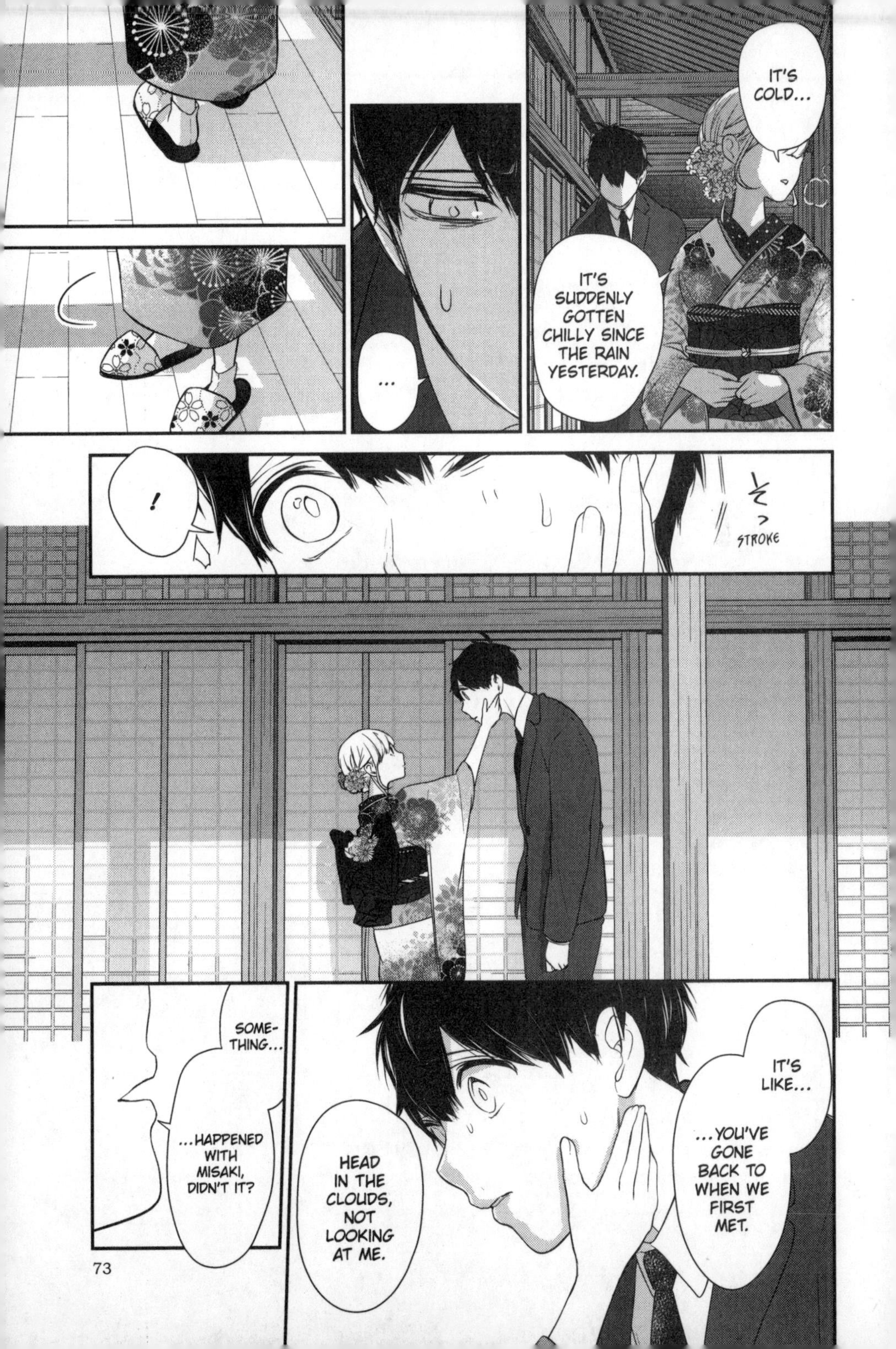
IT'S COLD...
IT'S SUDDENLY GOTTEN CHILLY SINCE THE RAIN YESTERDAY.
...
STROKE
!
IT'S LIKE...
...YOU'VE GONE BACK TO WHEN WE FIRST MET.
HEAD IN THE CLOUDS, NOT LOOKING AT ME.
SOME-THING...
...HAPPENED WITH MISAKI, DIDN'T IT?

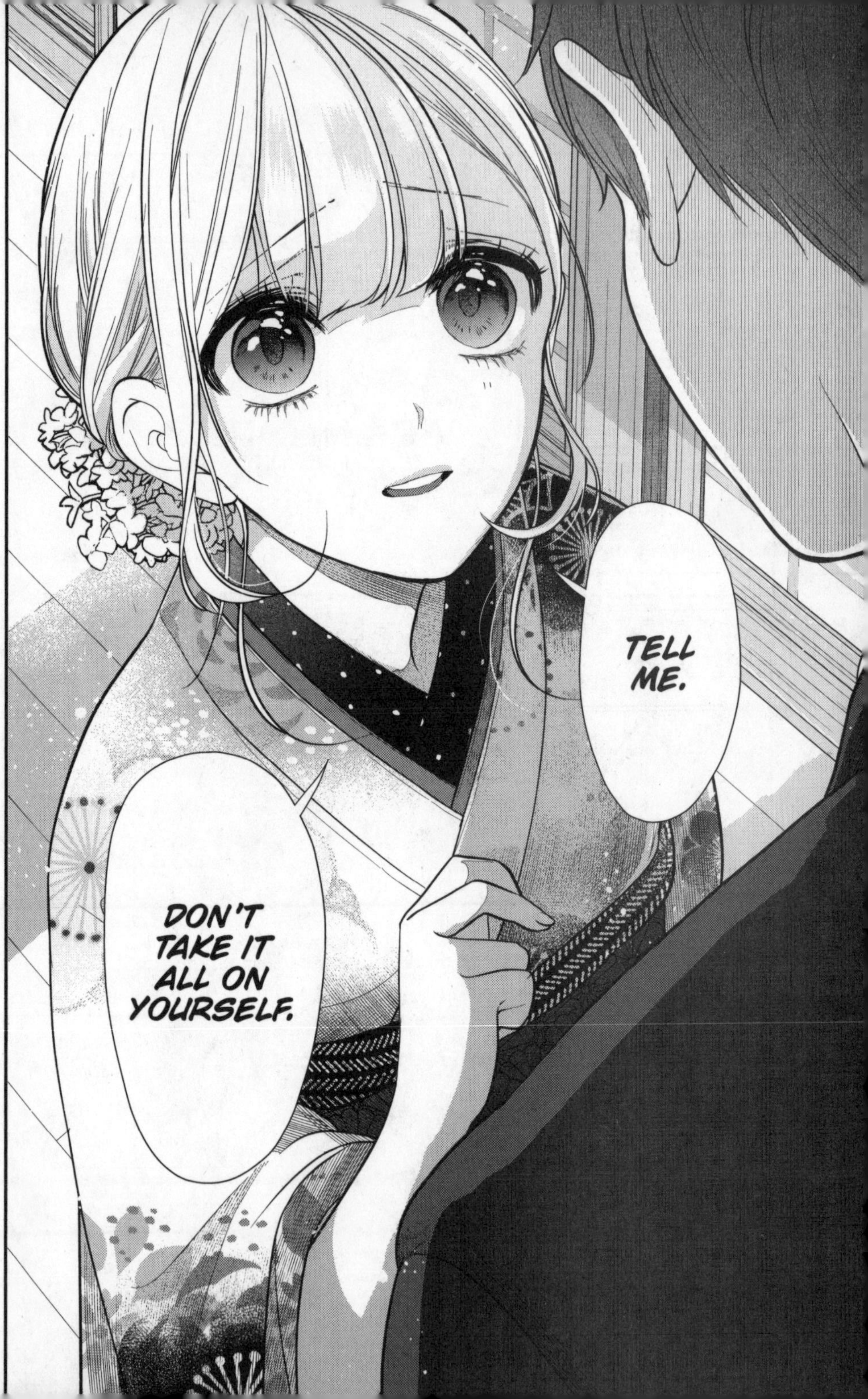
TELL ME.
DON'T TAKE IT ALL ON YOURSELF.

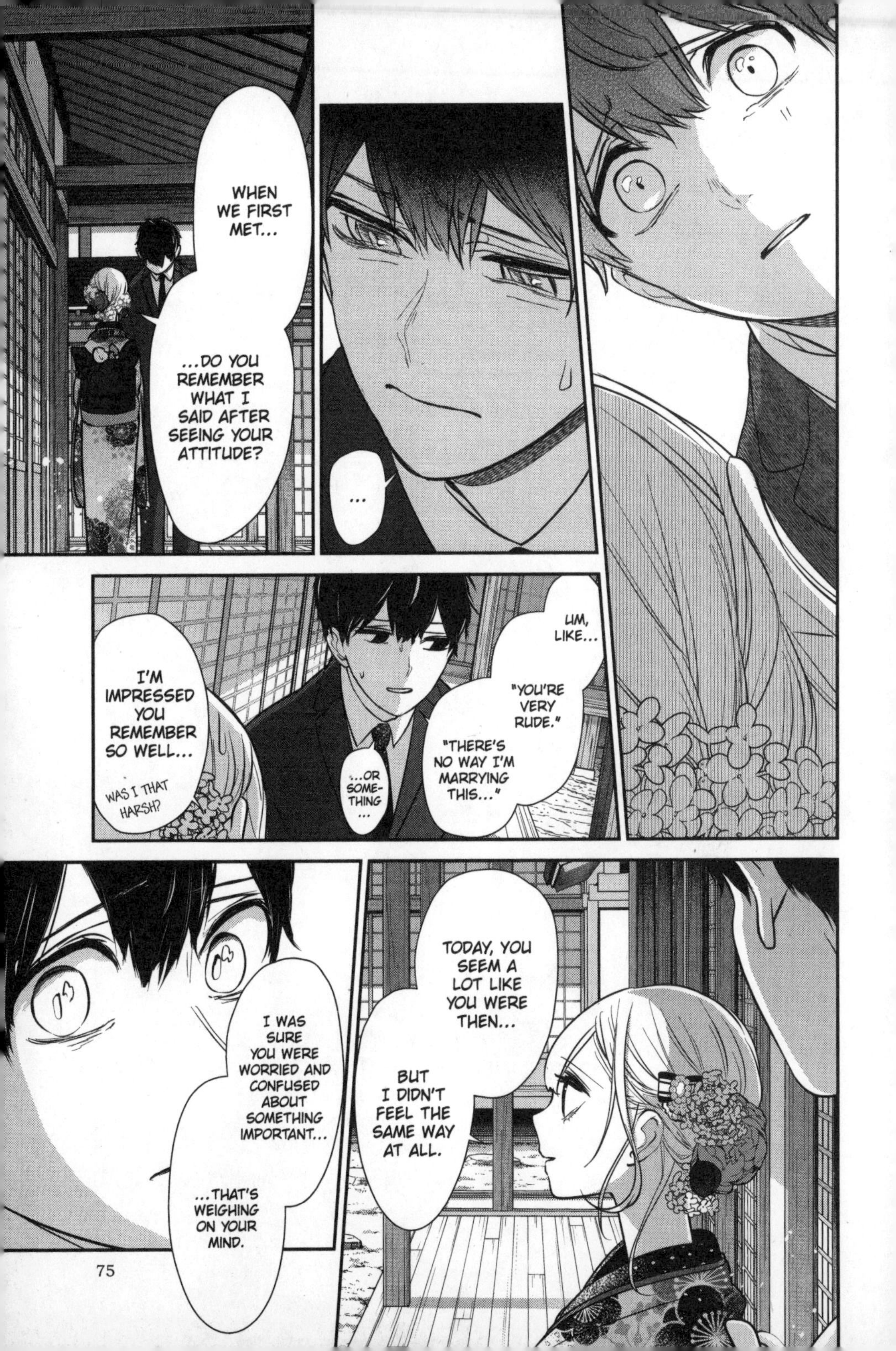
...
WHEN WE FIRST MET...
...DO YOU REMEMBER WHAT I SAID AFTER SEEING YOUR ATTITUDE?
UM, LIKE...
"YOU'RE VERY RUDE."
"THERE'S NO WAY I'M MARRYING THIS..."
...OR SOMETHING...
I'M IMPRESSED YOU REMEMBER SO WELL...
WAS I THAT HARSH?
TODAY, YOU SEEM A LOT LIKE YOU WERE THEN...
BUT I DIDN'T FEEL THE SAME WAY AT ALL.
I WAS SURE YOU WERE WORRIED AND CONFUSED ABOUT SOMETHING IMPORTANT...
...THAT'S WEIGHING ON YOUR MIND.

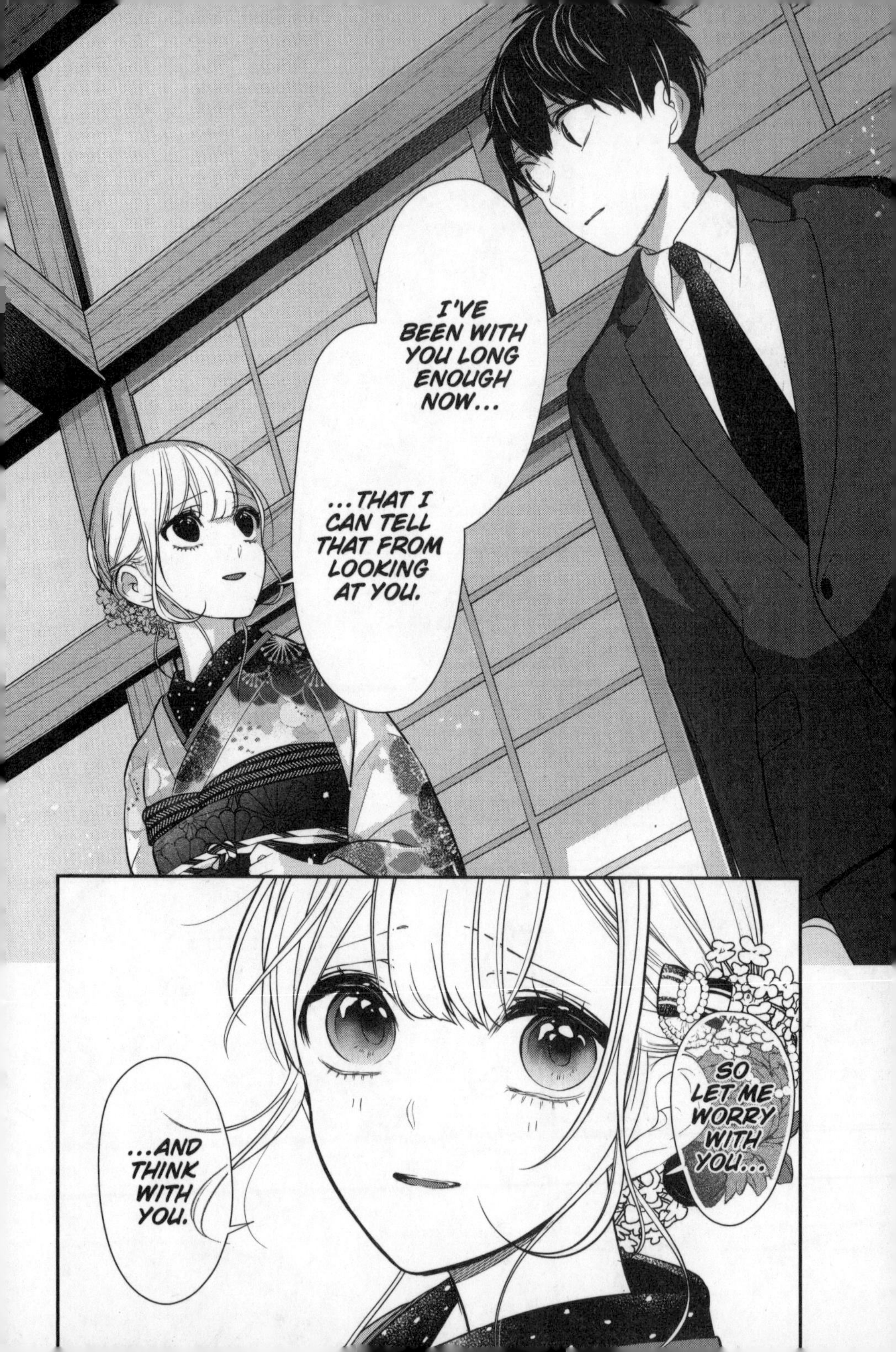
I'VE BEEN WITH YOU LONG ENOUGH NOW...
...THAT I CAN TELL THAT FROM LOOKING AT YOU.
SO LET ME WORRY WITH YOU...
...AND THINK WITH YOU.

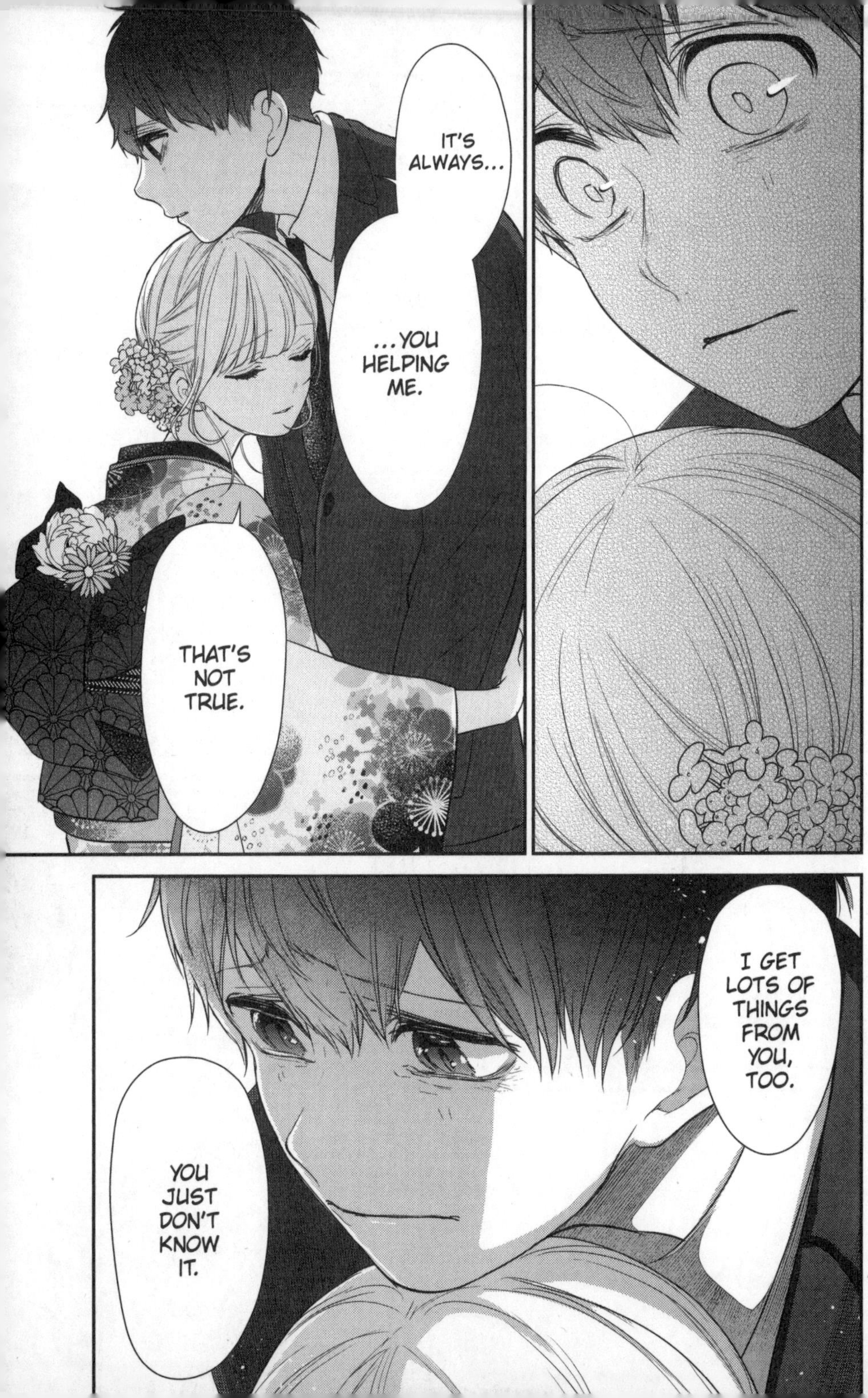
IT'S ALWAYS...
...YOU HELPING ME.
THAT'S NOT TRUE.
I GET LOTS OF THINGS FROM YOU, TOO.
YOU JUST DON'T KNOW IT.

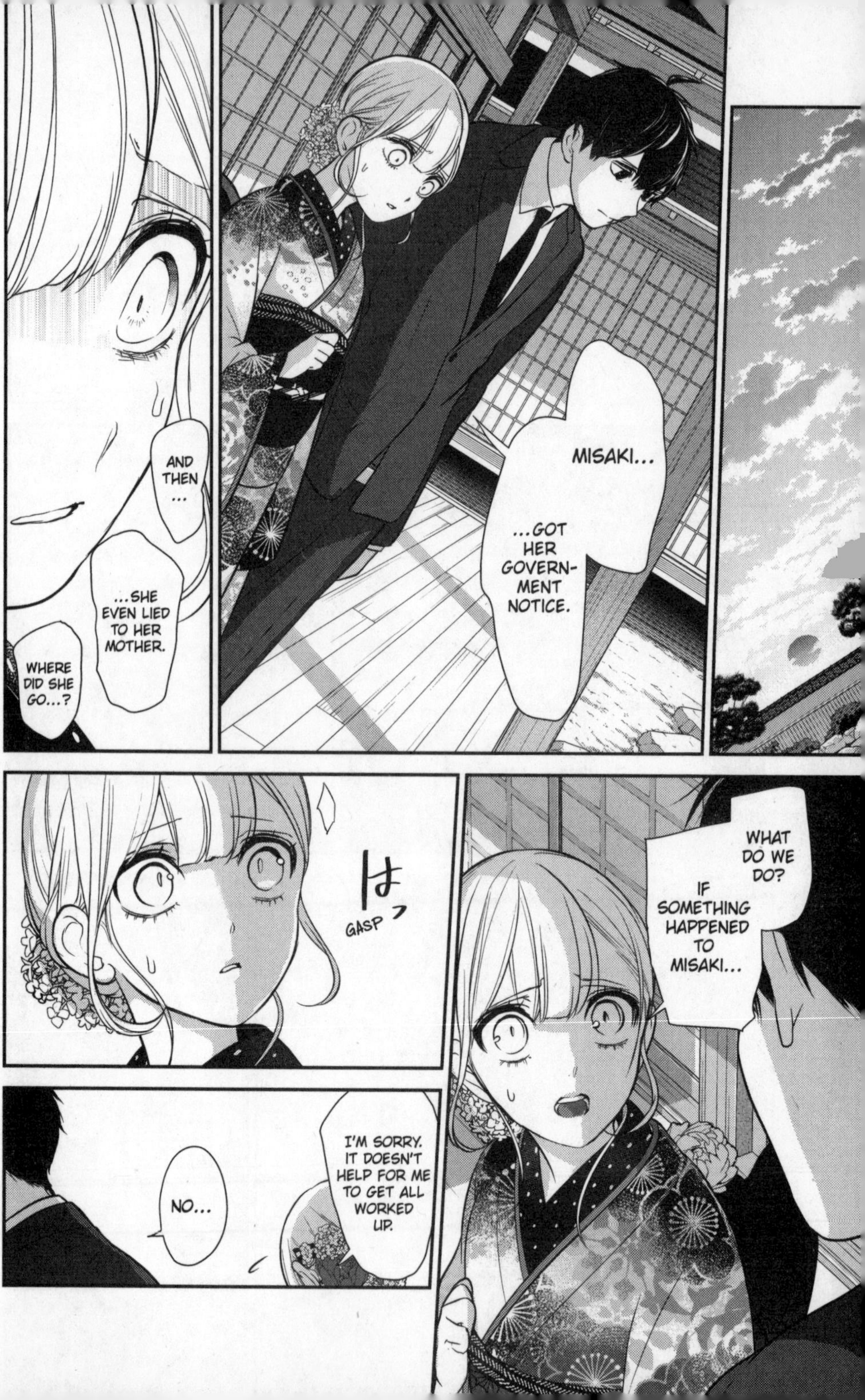
MISAKI...
...GOT HER GOVERNMENT NOTICE.
AND THEN ...
...SHE EVEN LIED TO HER MOTHER.
WHERE DID SHE GO...?
WHAT DO WE DO?
IF SOMETHING HAPPENED TO MISAKI...
は
GASP
I'M SORRY. IT DOESN'T HELP FOR ME TO GET ALL WORKED UP.
NO...

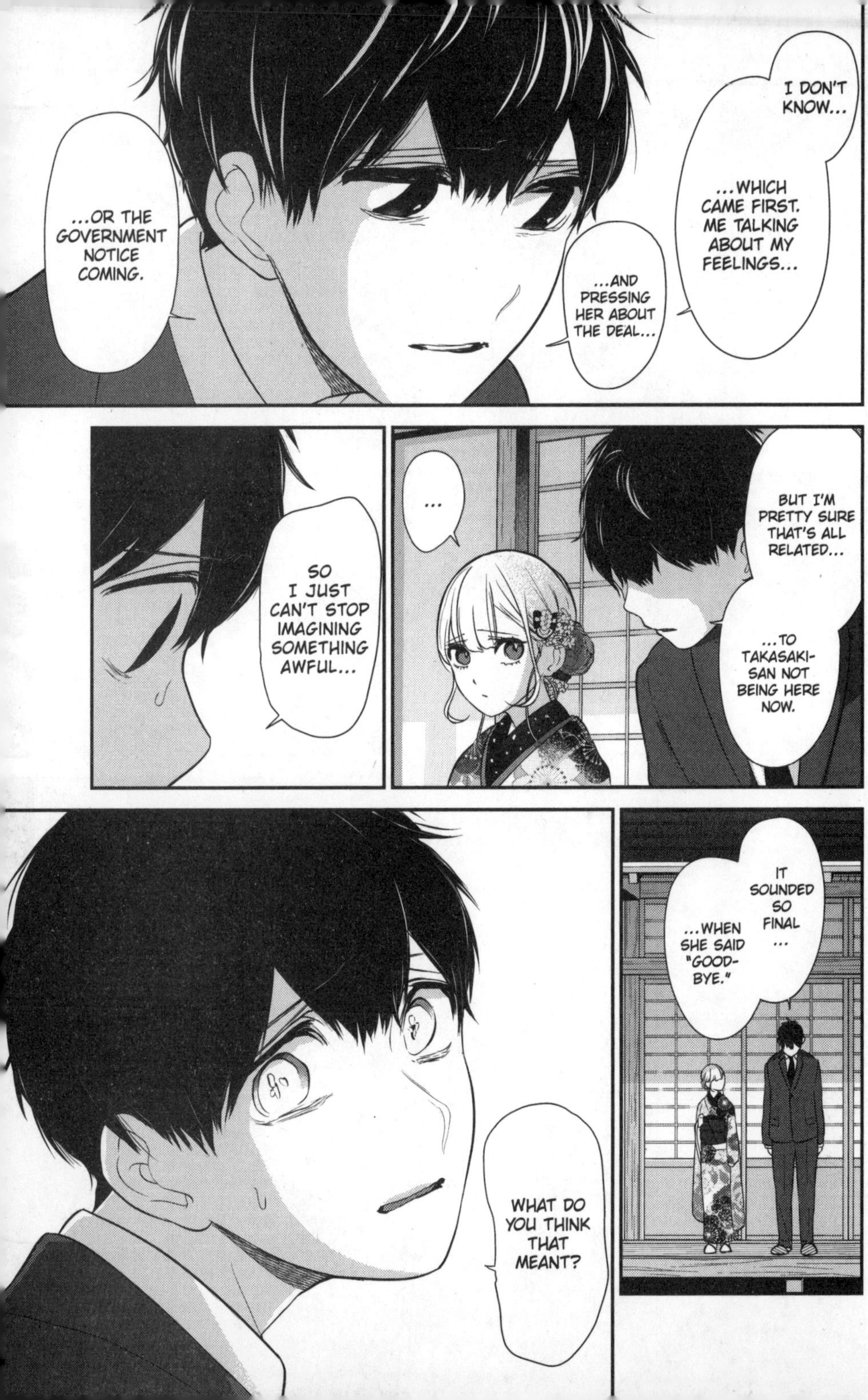
I DON'T KNOW...
...WHICH CAME FIRST. ME TALKING ABOUT MY FEELINGS...
...AND PRESSING HER ABOUT THE DEAL...
...OR THE GOVERNMENT NOTICE COMING.
BUT I'M PRETTY SURE THAT'S ALL RELATED...
...TO TAKASAKI-SAN NOT BEING HERE NOW.
...
SO I JUST CAN'T STOP IMAGINING SOMETHING AWFUL...
IT SOUNDED SO FINAL...
...WHEN SHE SAID "GOOD-BYE."
WHAT DO YOU THINK THAT MEANT?

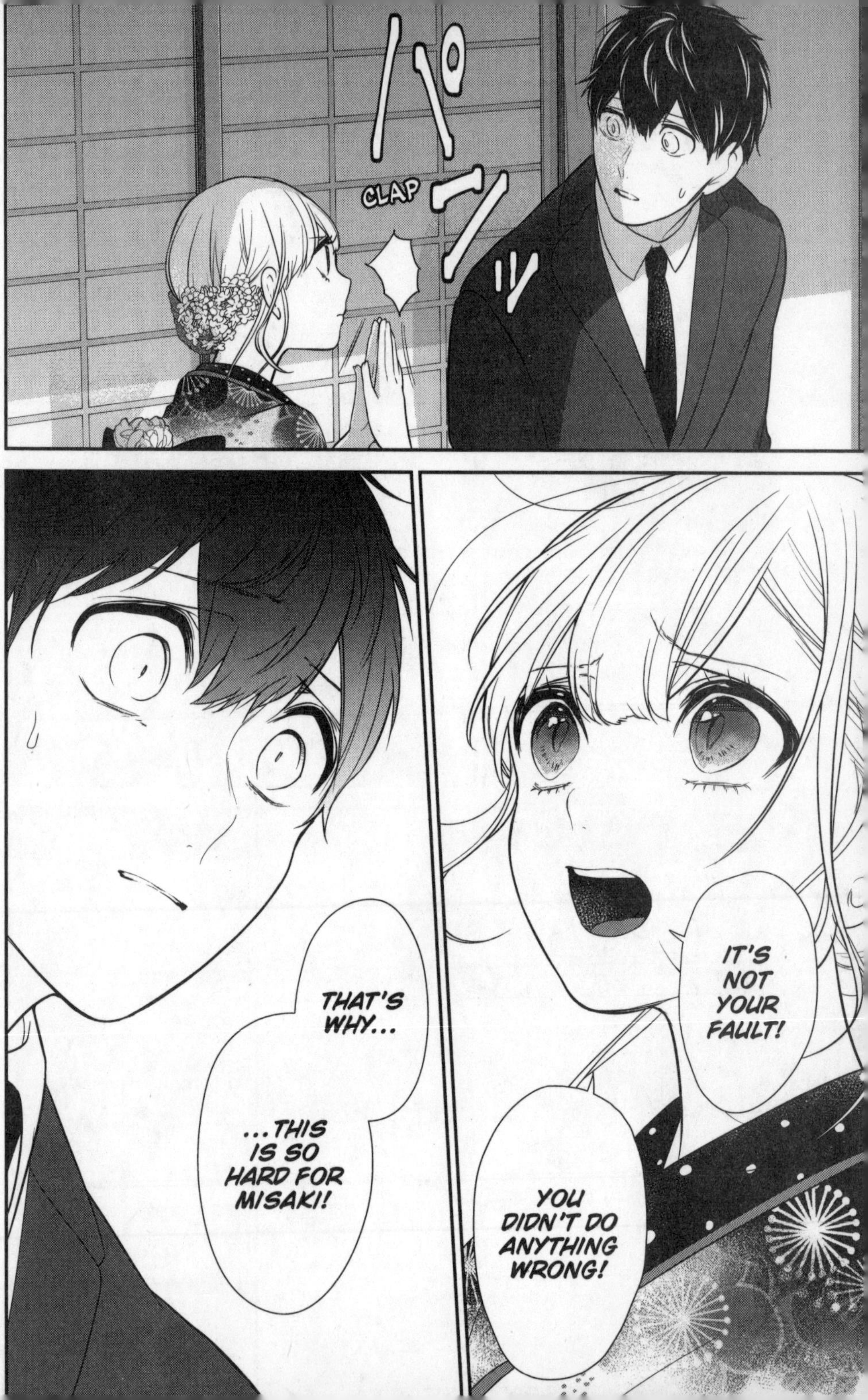
パン
CLAP
ッ
IT'S NOT YOUR FAULT!
YOU DIDN'T DO ANYTHING WRONG!
THAT'S WHY...
...THIS IS SO HARD FOR MISAKI!

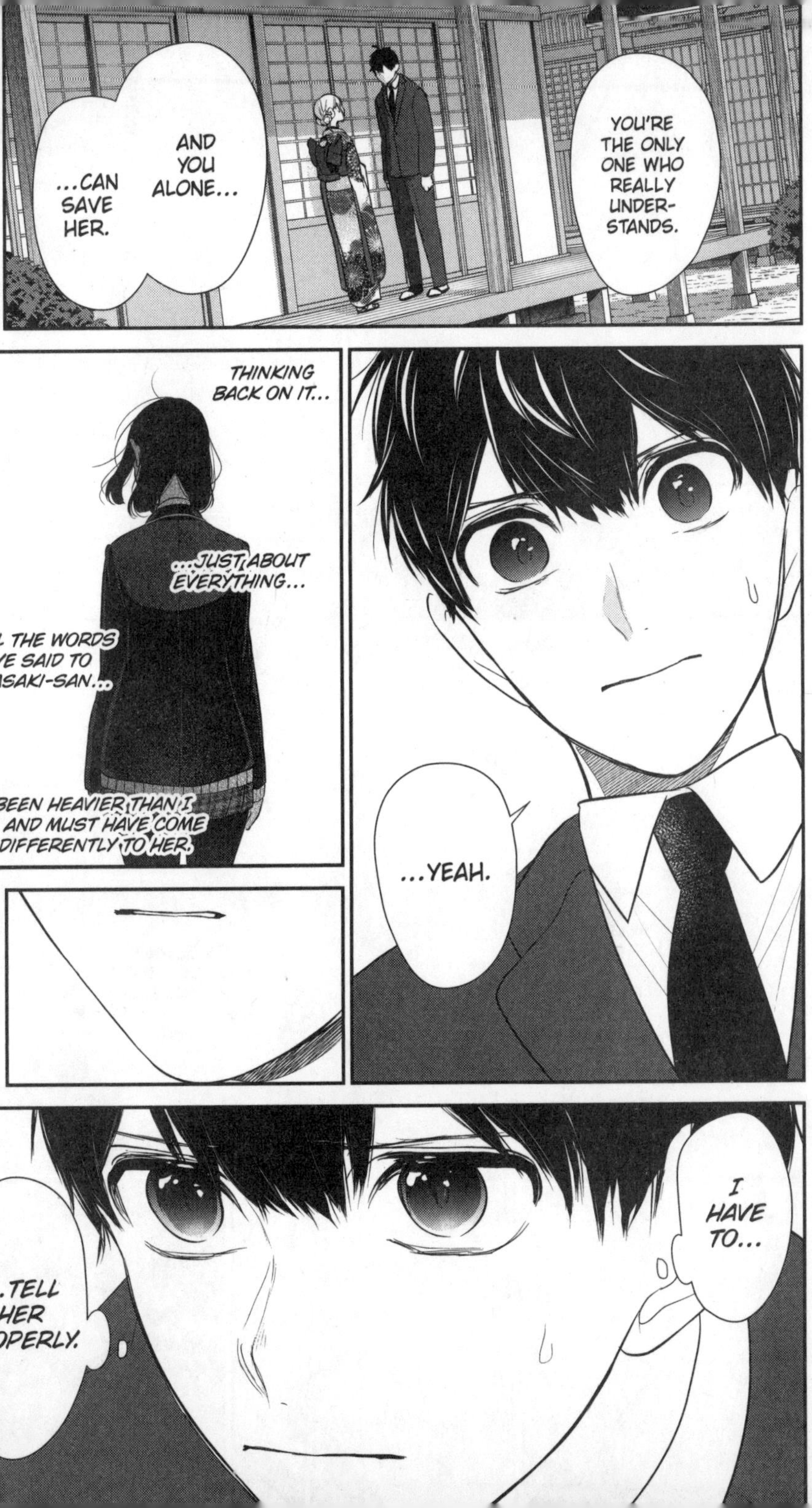
YOU'RE THE ONLY ONE WHO REALLY UNDERSTANDS.
AND YOU ALONE...
...CAN SAVE HER.
...YEAH.
THINKING BACK ON IT...
...JUST ABOUT EVERYTHING...
...ALL THE WORDS I'VE SAID TO TAKASAKI-SAN...
...HAVE BEEN HEAVIER THAN I REALIZED, AND MUST HAVE COME ACROSS DIFFERENTLY TO HER.
I HAVE TO...
...TELL HER PROPERLY.

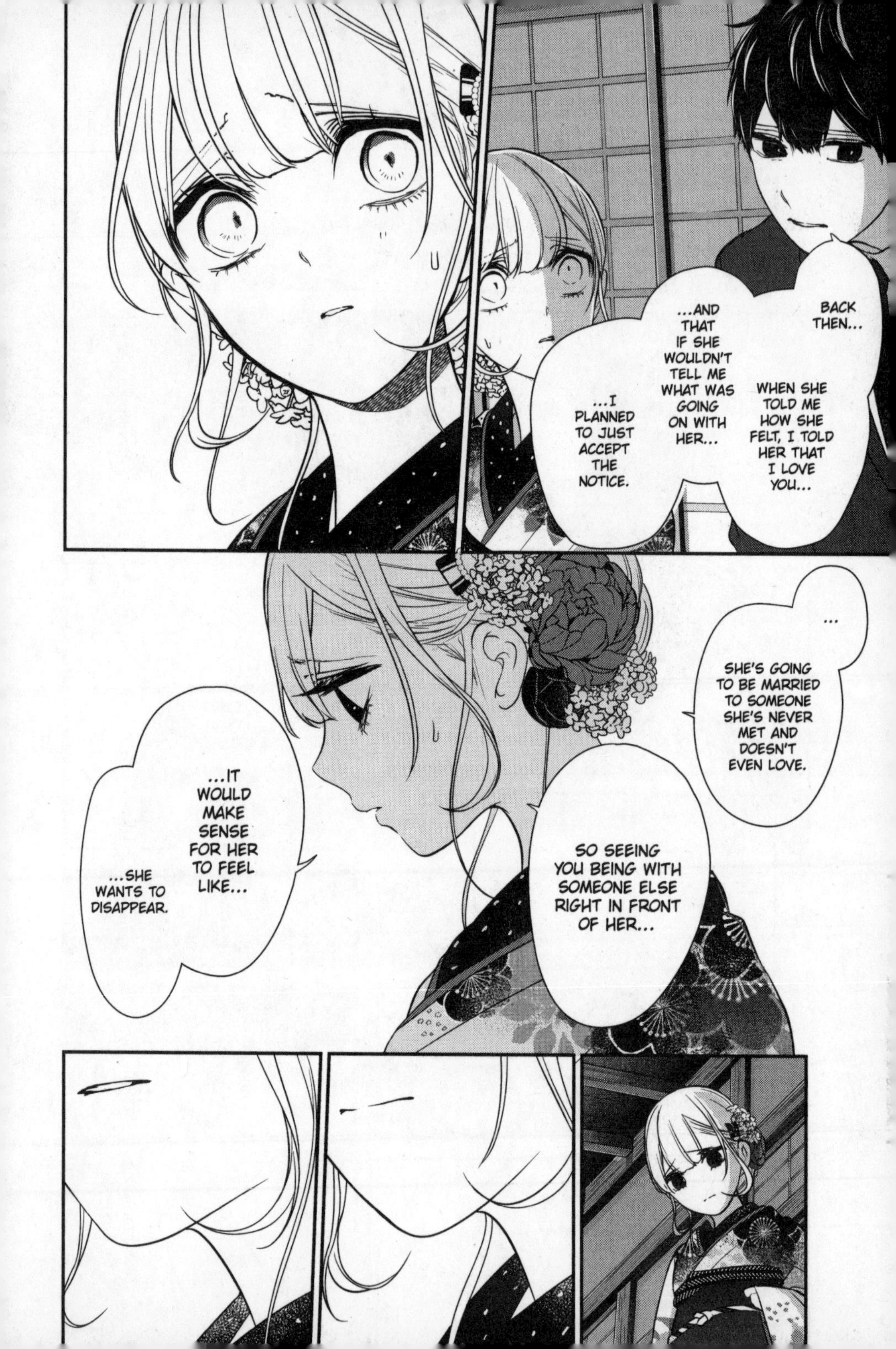
BACK THEN...
WHEN SHE TOLD ME HOW SHE FELT, I TOLD HER THAT I LOVE YOU...
...AND THAT IF SHE WOULDN'T TELL ME WHAT WAS GOING ON WITH HER...
...I PLANNED TO JUST ACCEPT THE NOTICE.
...
SHE'S GOING TO BE MARRIED TO SOMEONE SHE'S NEVER MET AND DOESN'T EVEN LOVE.
SO SEEING YOU BEING WITH SOMEONE ELSE RIGHT IN FRONT OF HER...
...IT WOULD MAKE SENSE FOR HER TO FEEL LIKE...
...SHE WANTS TO DISAPPEAR.

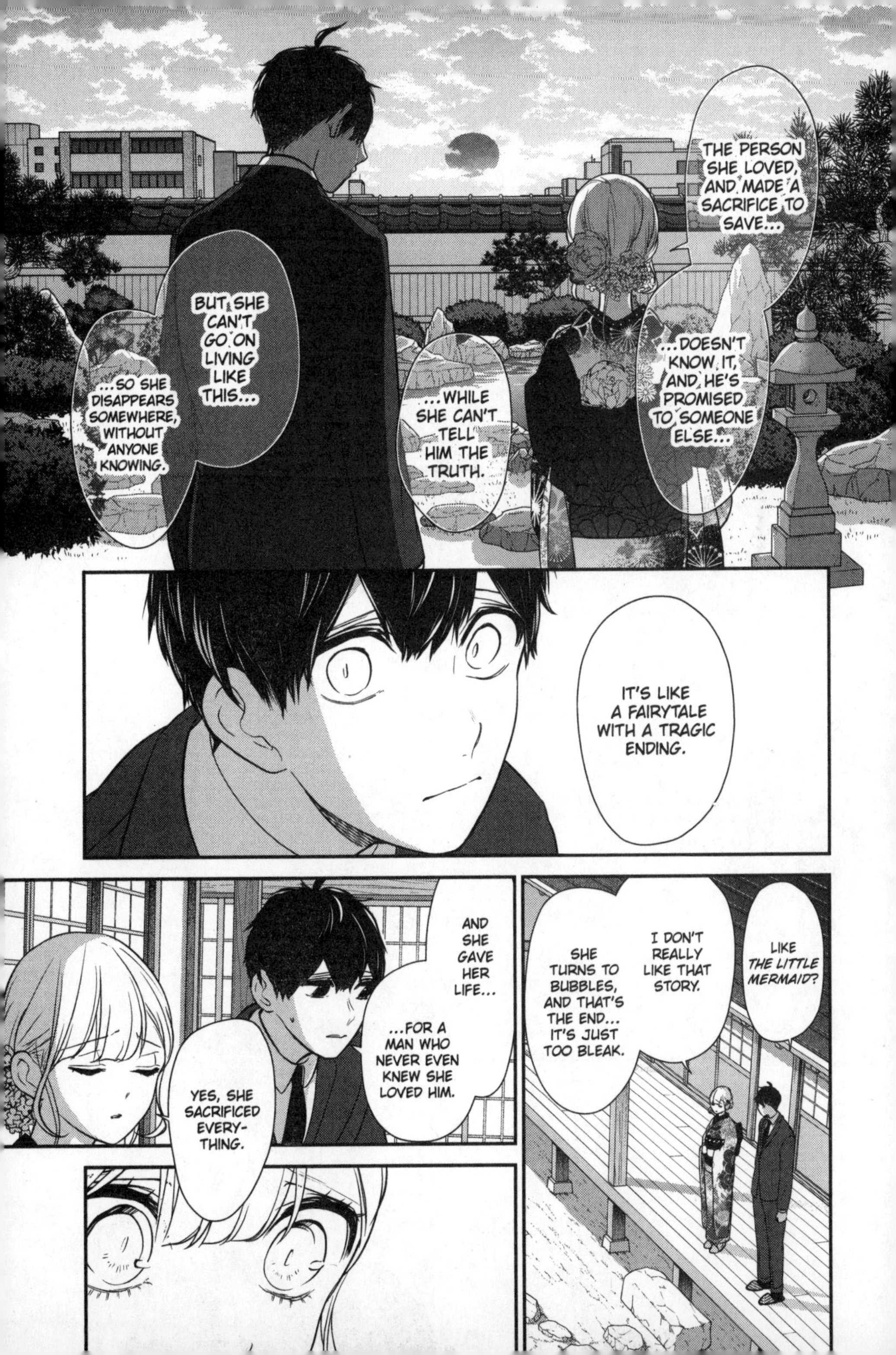
THE PERSON SHE LOVED, AND MADE A SACRIFICE TO SAVE...
...DOESN'T KNOW IT, AND HE'S PROMISED TO SOMEONE ELSE...
...WHILE SHE CAN'T TELL HIM THE TRUTH.
BUT SHE CAN'T GO ON LIVING LIKE THIS...
...SO SHE DISAPPEARS SOMEWHERE, WITHOUT ANYONE KNOWING.
IT'S LIKE A FAIRYTALE WITH A TRAGIC ENDING.
LIKE *THE LITTLE MERMAID*?
I DON'T REALLY LIKE THAT STORY.
SHE TURNS TO BUBBLES, AND THAT'S THE END... IT'S JUST TOO BLEAK.
AND SHE GAVE HER LIFE...
...FOR A MAN WHO NEVER EVEN KNEW SHE LOVED HIM.
YES, SHE SACRIFICED EVERY-THING.

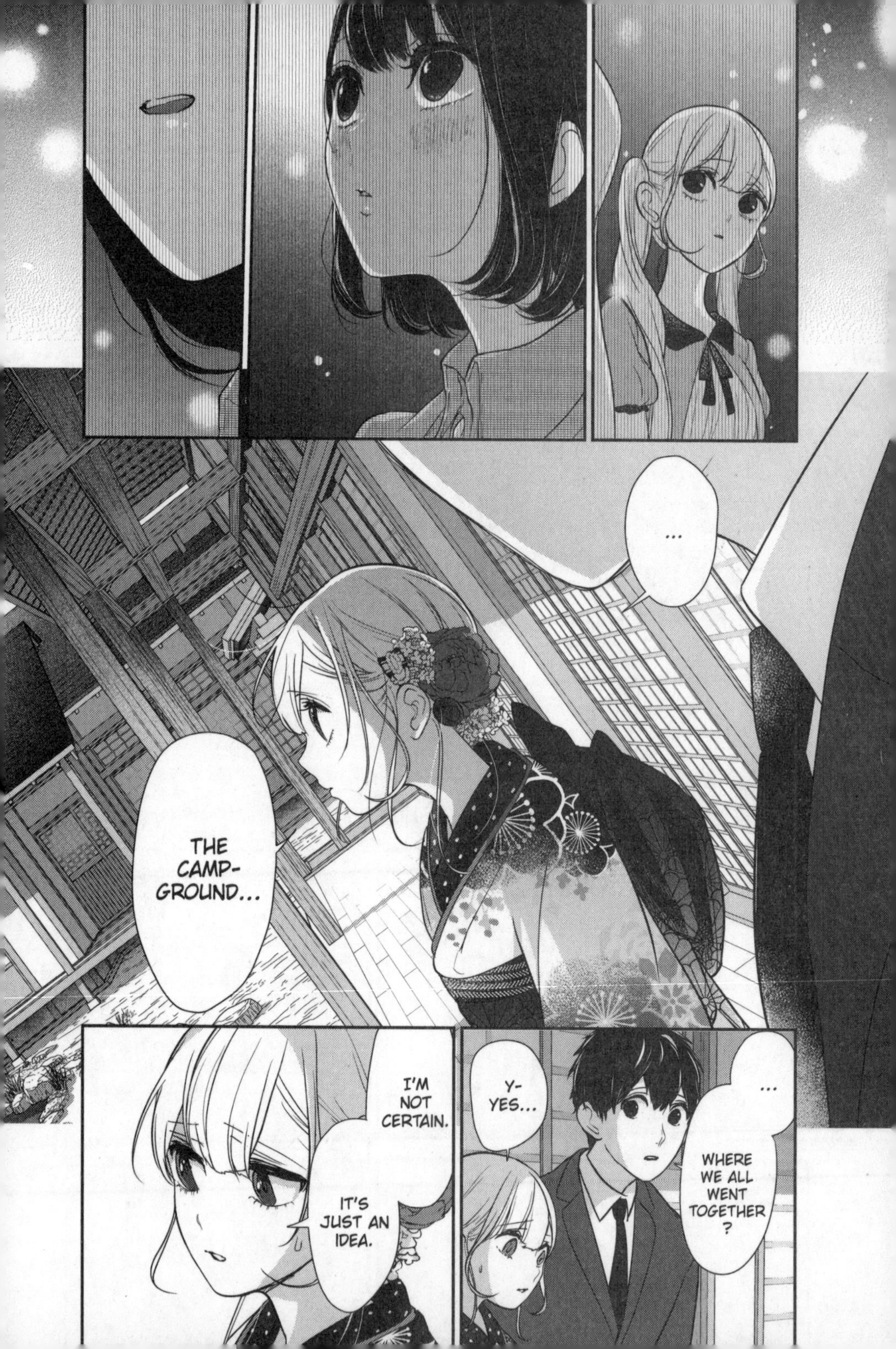
...
THE CAMP-GROUND...
...
WHERE WE ALL WENT TOGETHER?
Y-YES...
I'M NOT CERTAIN.
IT'S JUST AN IDEA.

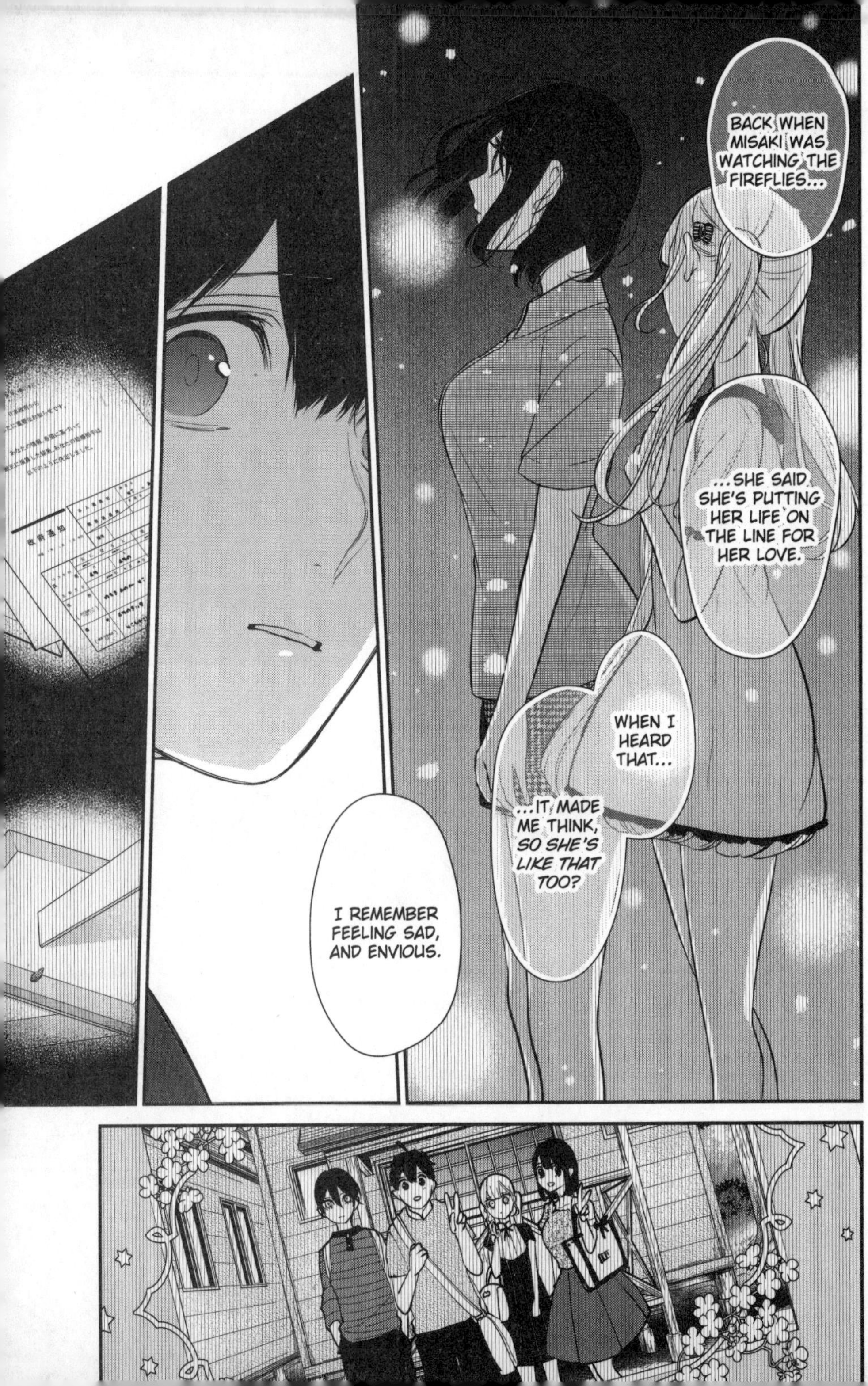
BACK WHEN MISAKI WAS WATCHING THE FIREFLIES...
...SHE SAID SHE'S PUTTING HER LIFE ON THE LINE FOR HER LOVE.
WHEN I HEARD THAT...
...IT MADE ME THINK, SO SHE'S LIKE THAT TOO?
I REMEMBER FEELING SAD, AND ENVIOUS.

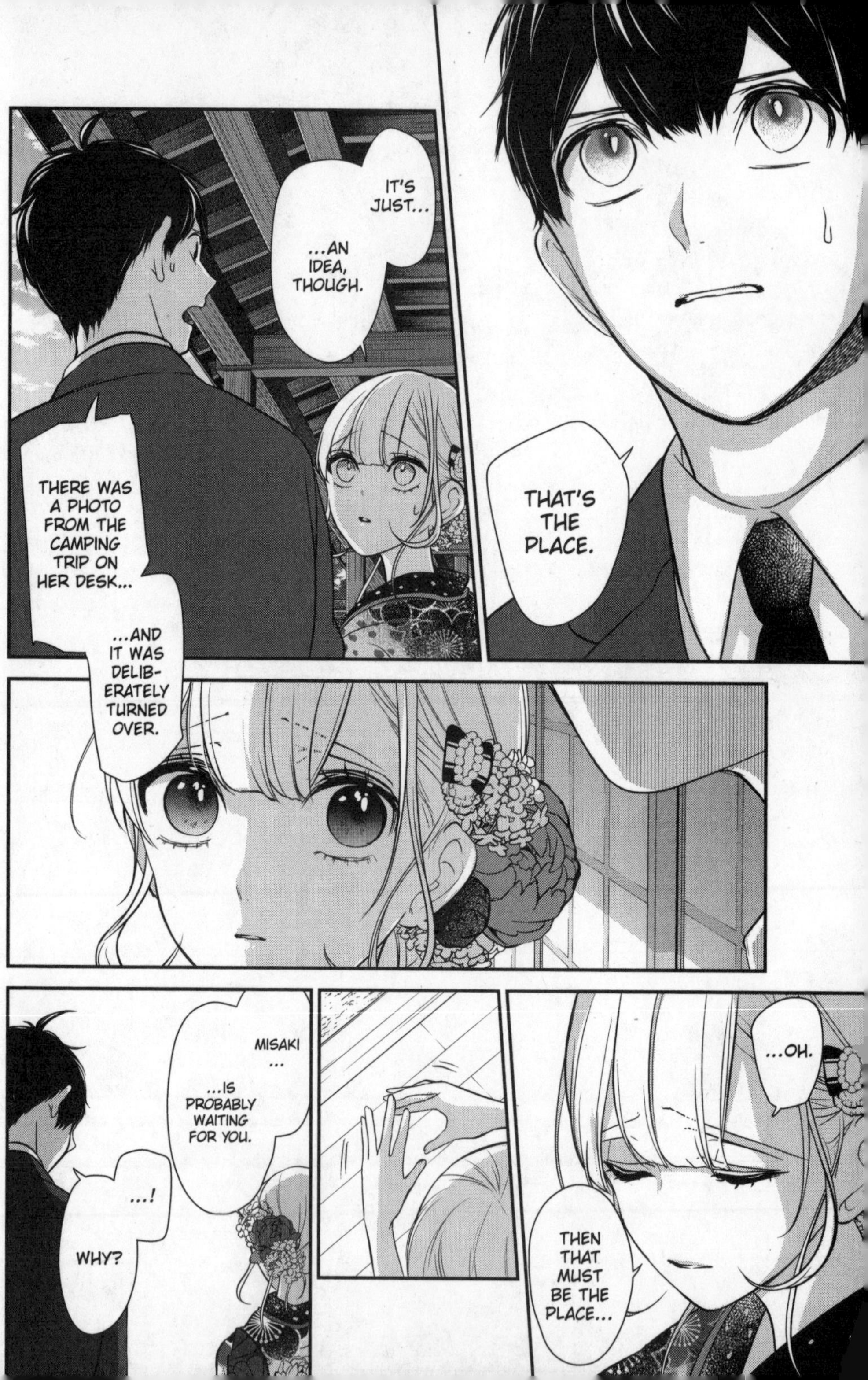
THAT'S THE PLACE.
IT'S JUST...
...AN IDEA, THOUGH.
THERE WAS A PHOTO FROM THE CAMPING TRIP ON HER DESK...
...AND IT WAS DELIB- ERATELY TURNED OVER.
...OH.
THEN THAT MUST BE THE PLACE...
MISAKI ...
...IS PROBABLY WAITING FOR YOU.
...!
WHY?

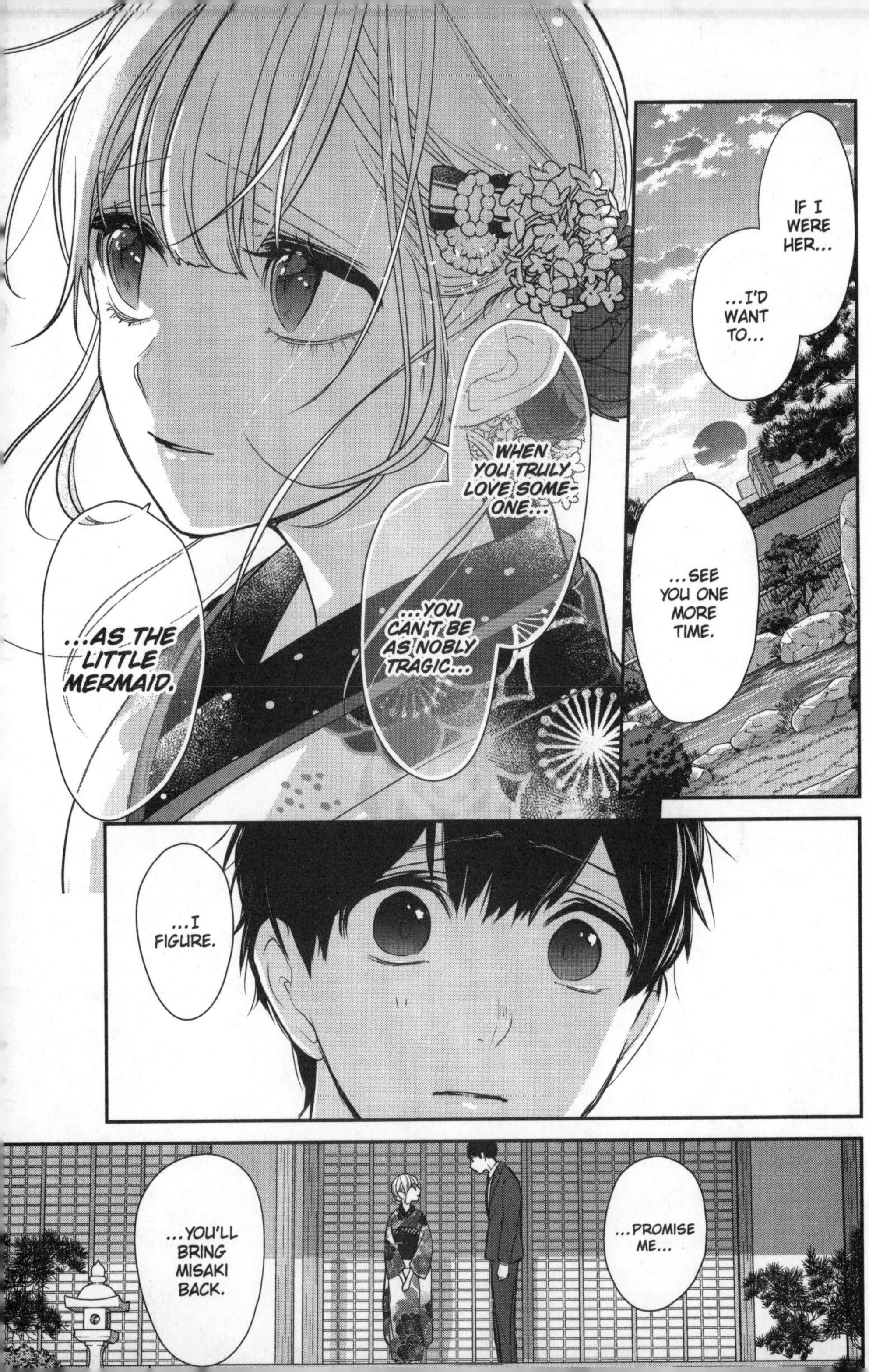
IF I WERE HER...
...I'D WANT TO...
...SEE YOU ONE MORE TIME.
WHEN YOU TRULY LOVE SOME-ONE...
...YOU CAN'T BE AS NOBLY TRAGIC...
...AS THE LITTLE MERMAID.
...I FIGURE.
...PROMISE ME...
...YOU'LL BRING MISAKI BACK.

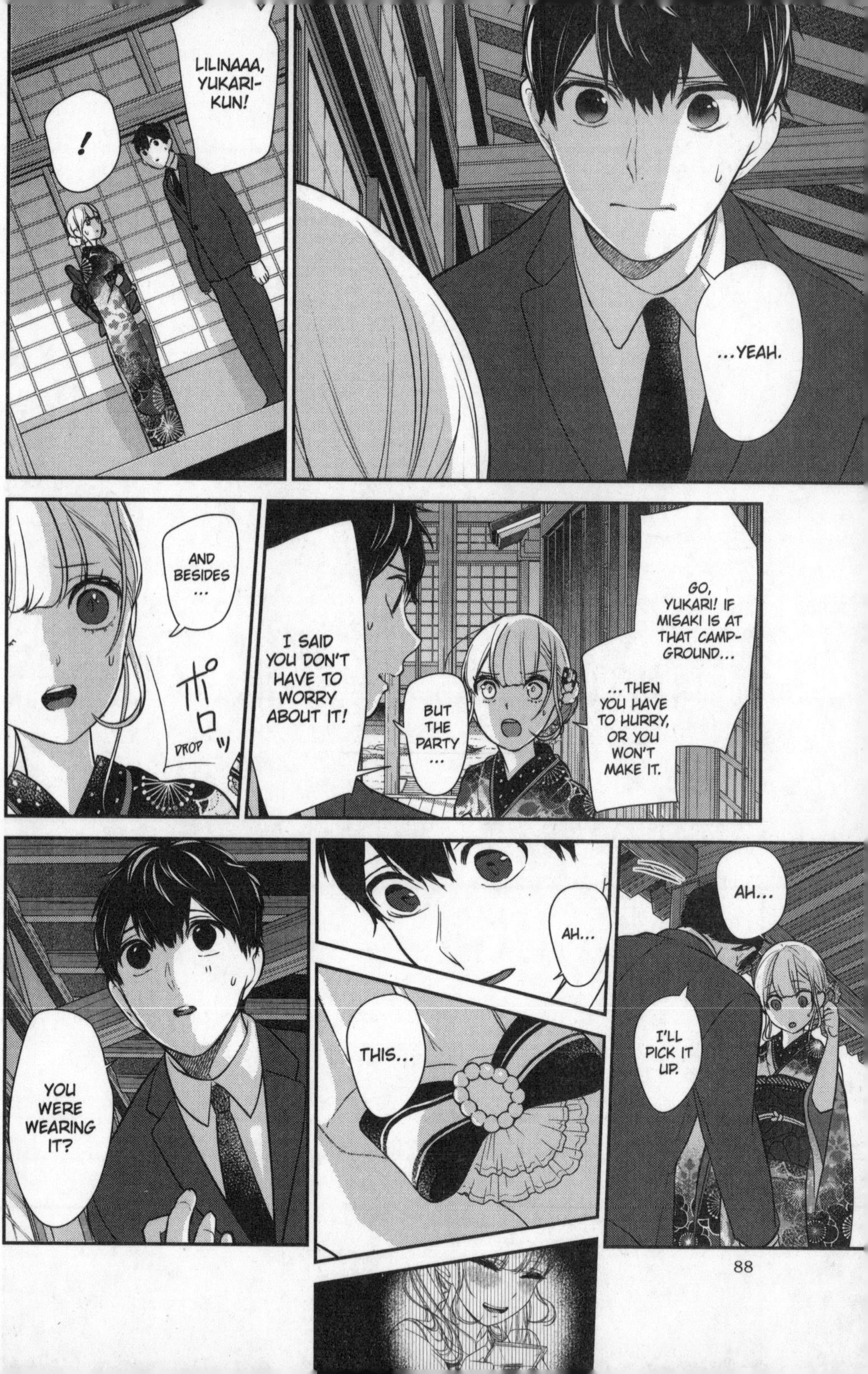
...YEAH.
LILINAAA, YUKARI-KUN!
!
GO, YUKARI! IF MISAKI IS AT THAT CAMP-GROUND...
...THEN YOU HAVE TO HURRY, OR YOU WON'T MAKE IT.
BUT THE PARTY...
I SAID YOU DON'T HAVE TO WORRY ABOUT IT!
AND BESIDES...
ポロッ
DROP
AH...
I'LL PICK IT UP.
AH...
THIS...
YOU WERE WEARING IT?

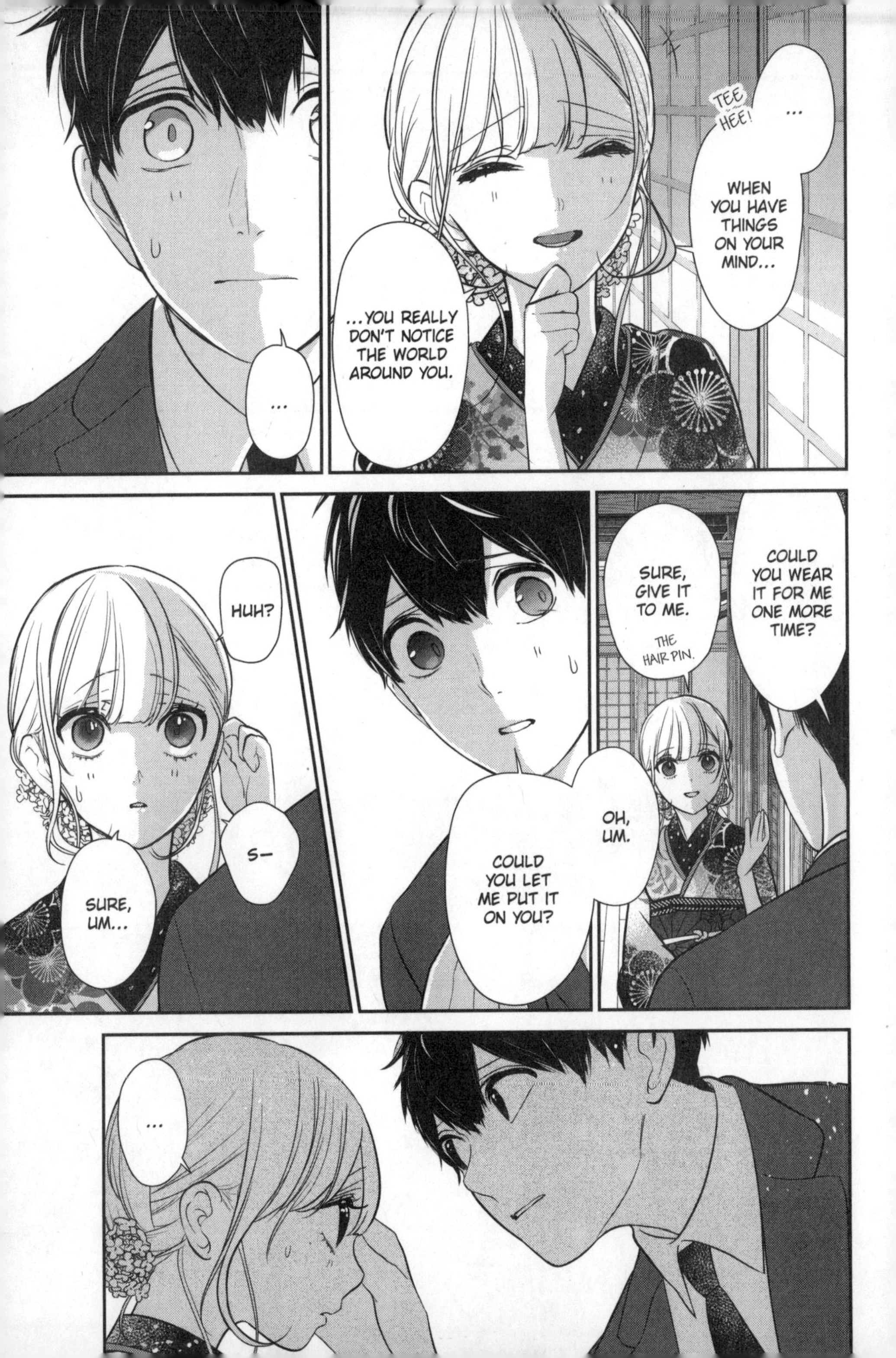
TEE HEE!
...
WHEN YOU HAVE THINGS ON YOUR MIND...
...YOU REALLY DON'T NOTICE THE WORLD AROUND YOU.
...
COULD YOU WEAR IT FOR ME ONE MORE TIME?
SURE, GIVE IT TO ME.
THE HAIR PIN.
OH, UM.
COULD YOU LET ME PUT IT ON YOU?
HUH?
S—
SURE, UM...
...

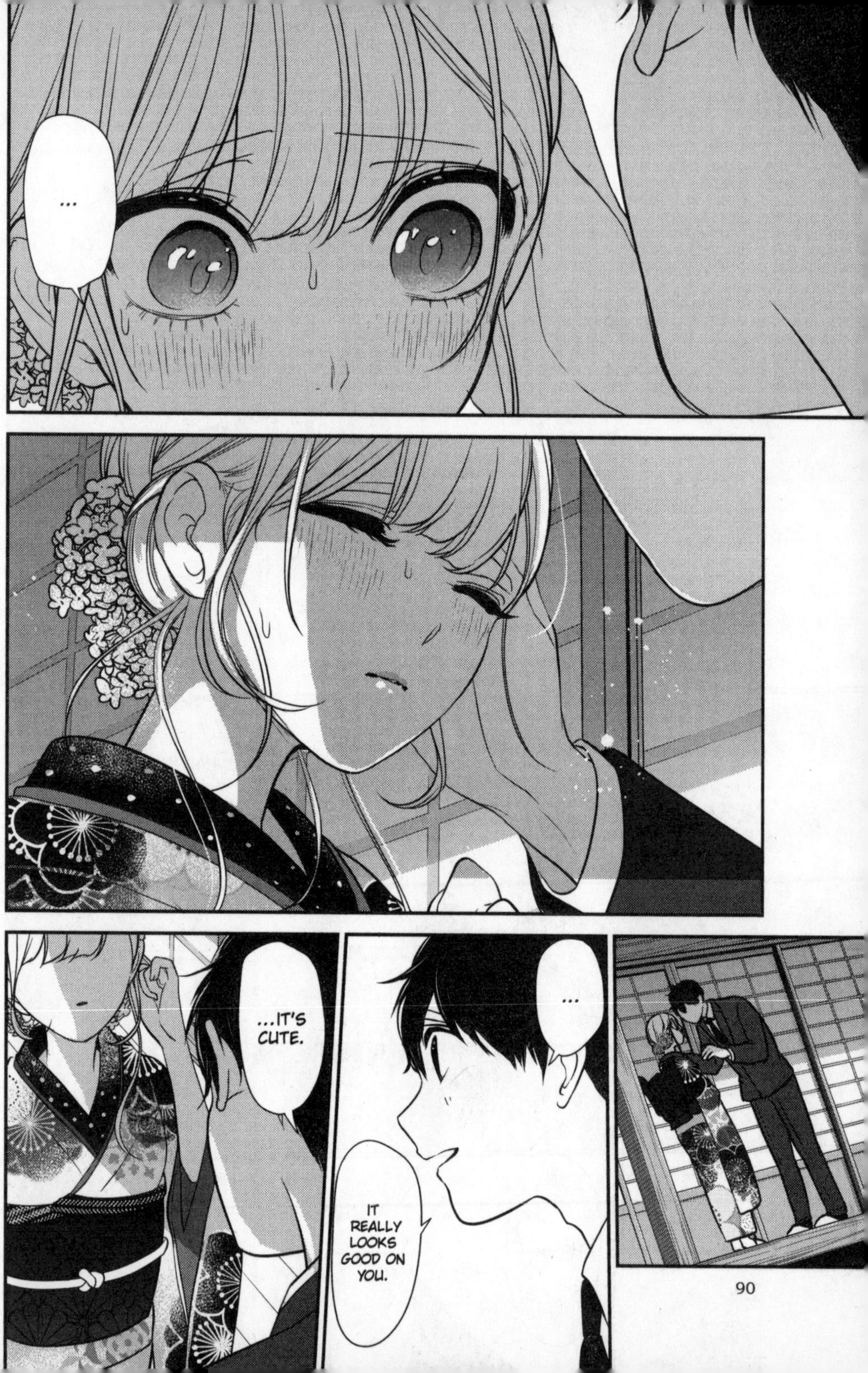
...
...
IT REALLY LOOKS GOOD ON YOU.
...IT'S CUTE.

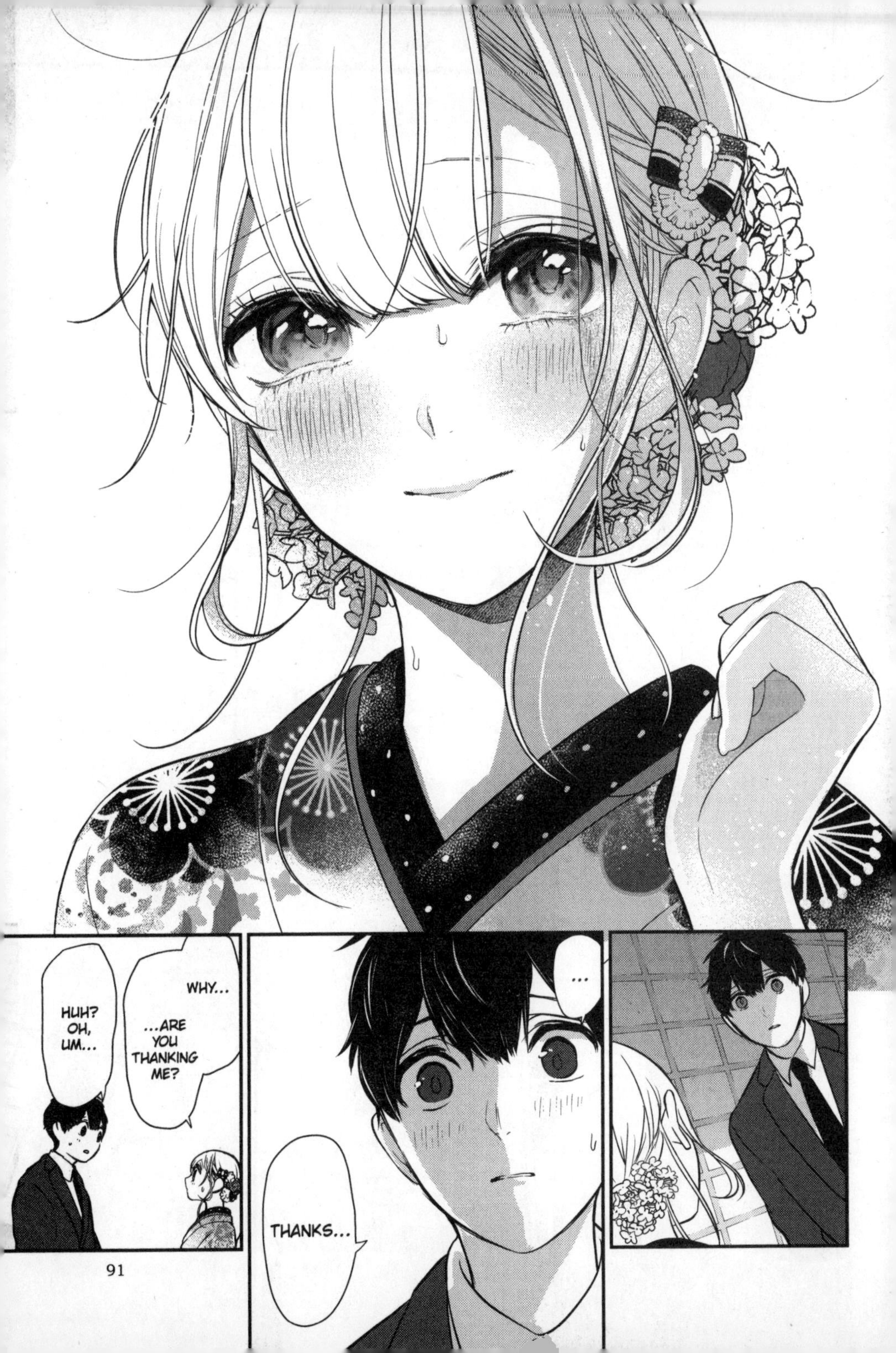
...
THANKS...
WHY... ...ARE YOU THANKING ME?
HUH? OH, UM...

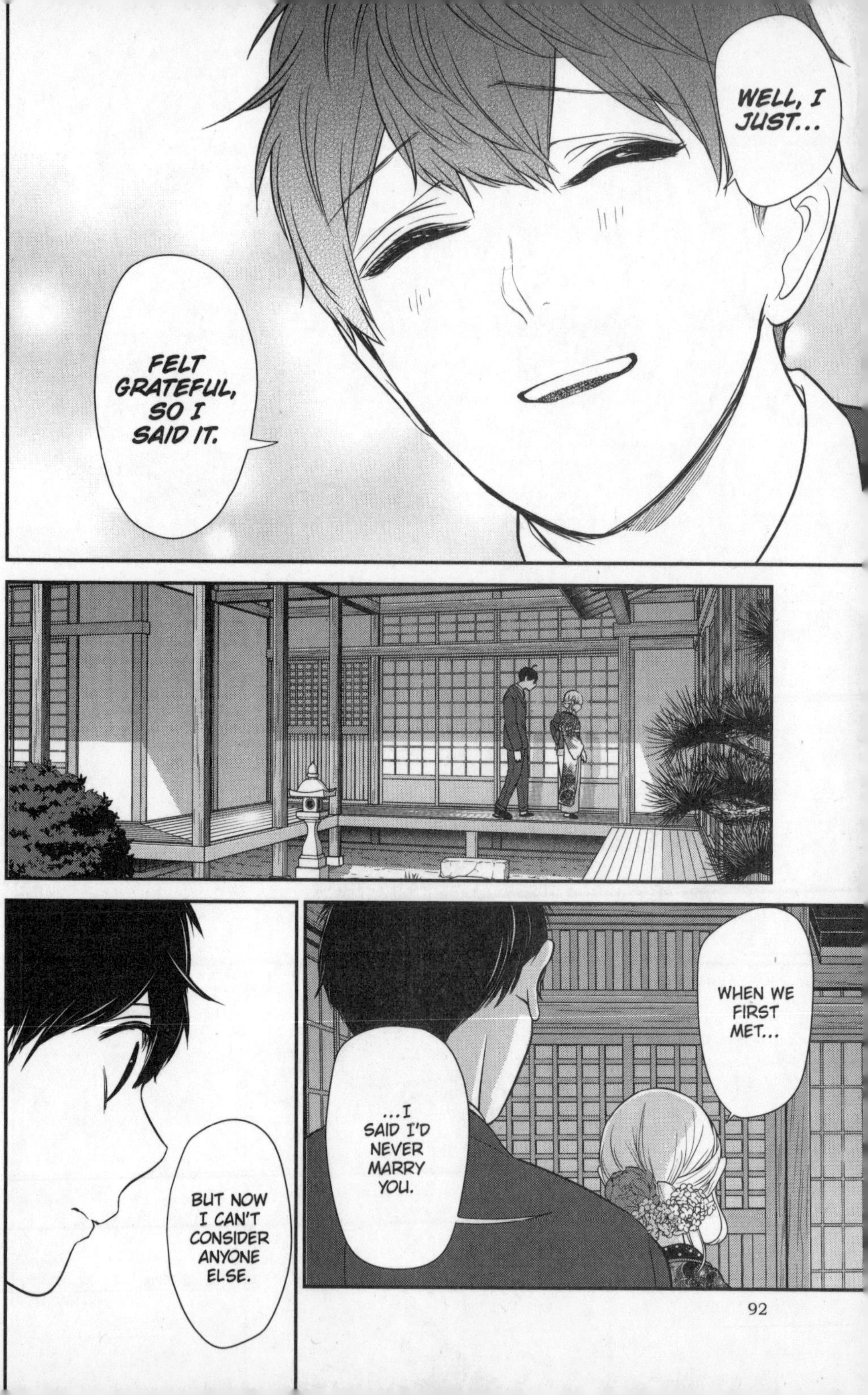
WELL, I JUST...
FELT GRATEFUL, SO I SAID IT.
WHEN WE FIRST MET...
...I SAID I'D NEVER MARRY YOU.
BUT NOW I CAN'T CONSIDER ANYONE ELSE.

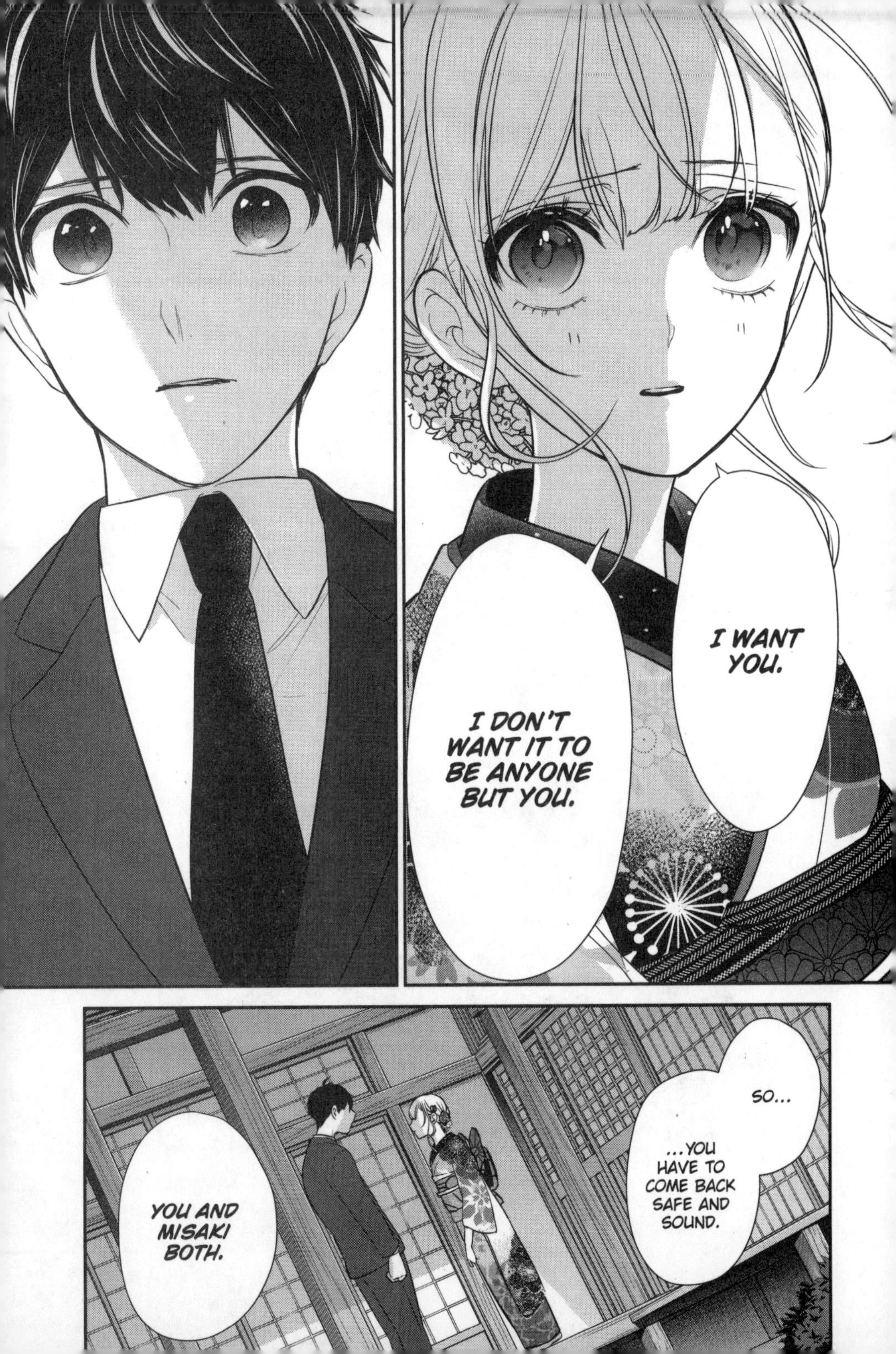
I WANT YOU.
I DON'T WANT IT TO BE ANYONE BUT YOU.
SO...
...YOU HAVE TO COME BACK SAFE AND SOUND.
YOU AND MISAKI BOTH.

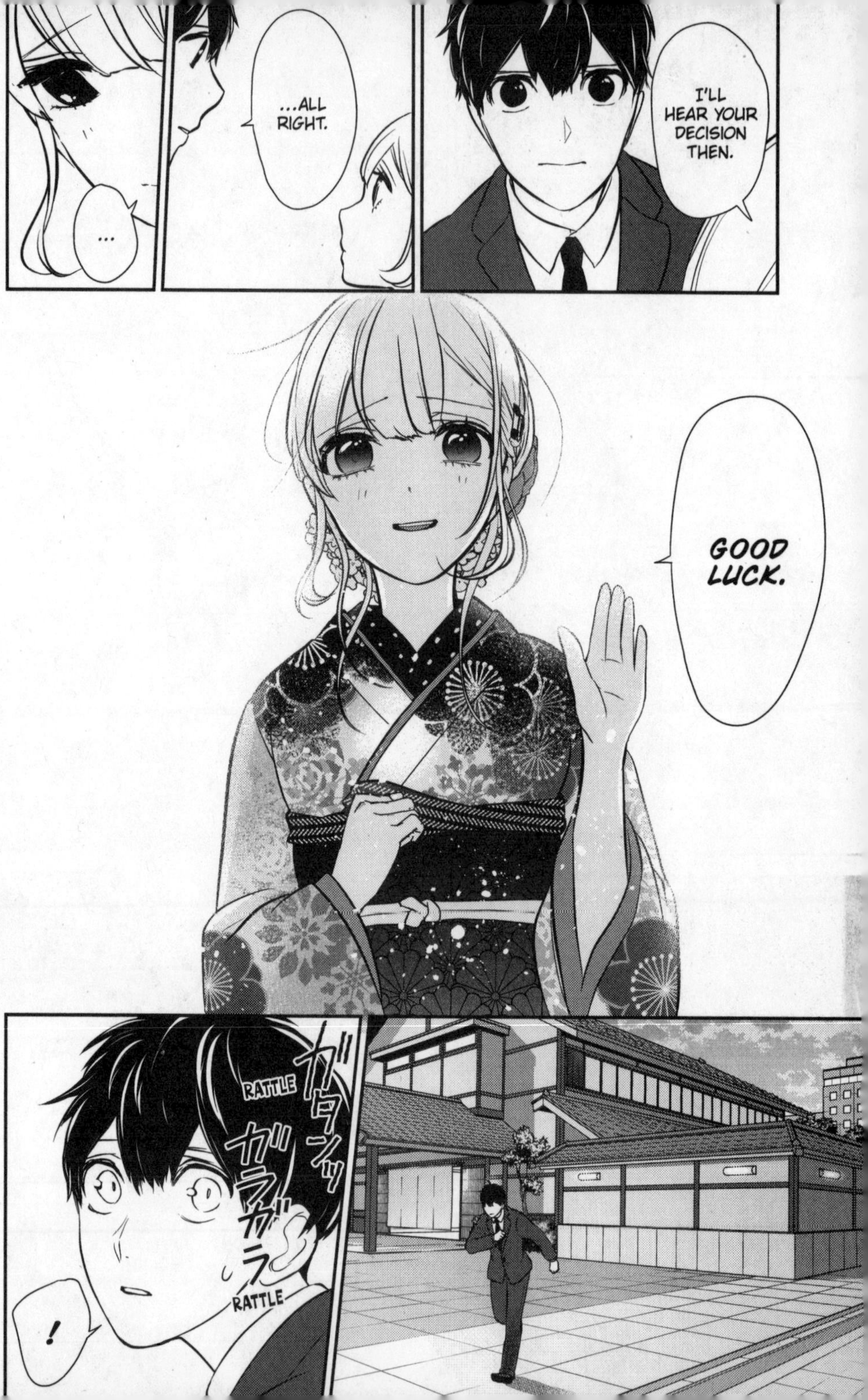
I'LL HEAR YOUR DECISION THEN.
...ALL RIGHT.
...
GOOD LUCK.
ガタンッ
RATTLE
ガラガラ
RATTLE
!

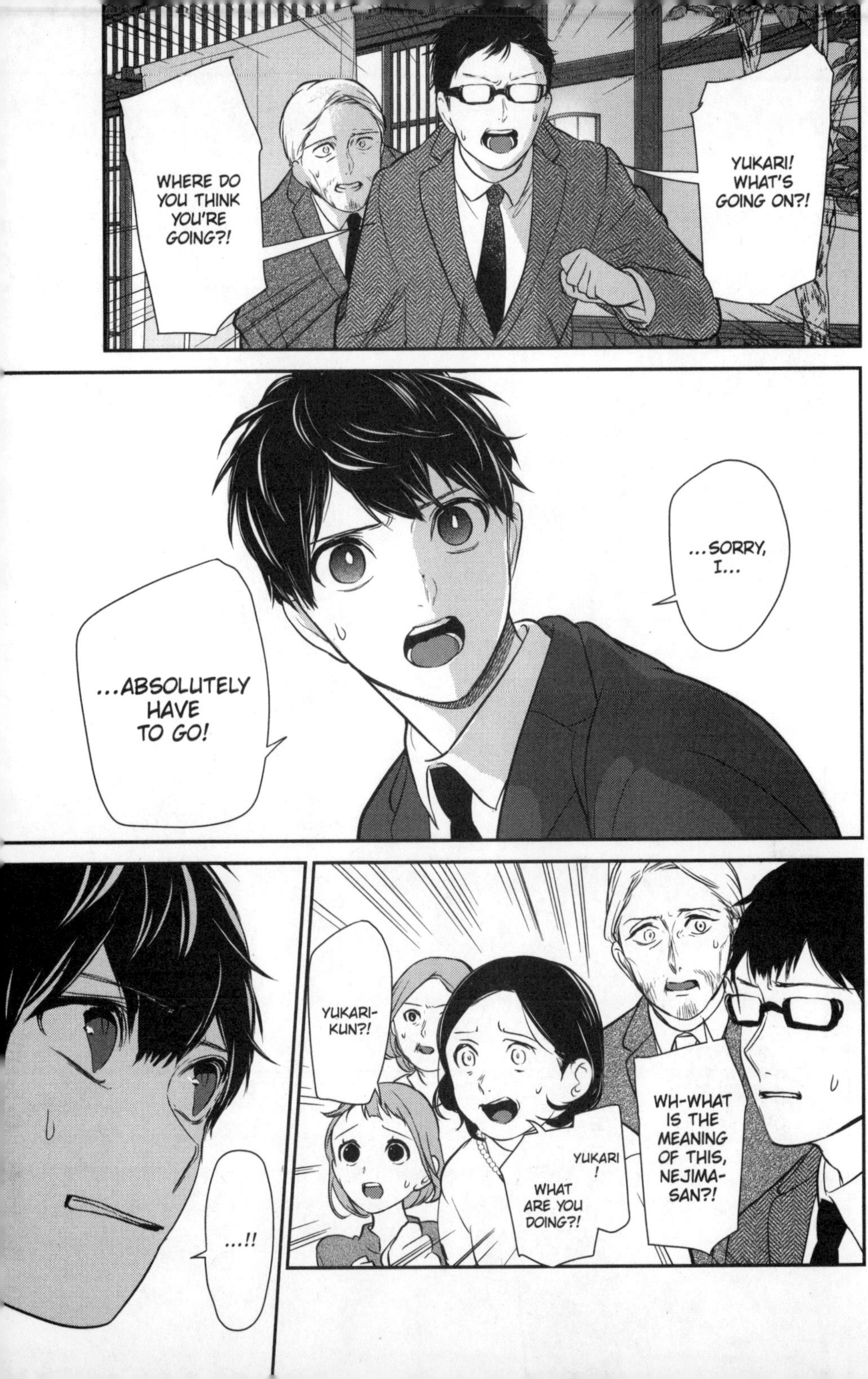
YUKARI! WHAT'S GOING ON?!
WHERE DO YOU THINK YOU'RE GOING?!
...SORRY, I...
...ABSOLUTELY HAVE TO GO!
WH-WHAT IS THE MEANING OF THIS, NEJIMA-SAN?!
YUKARI! WHAT ARE YOU DOING?!
YUKARI-KUN?!
...!!

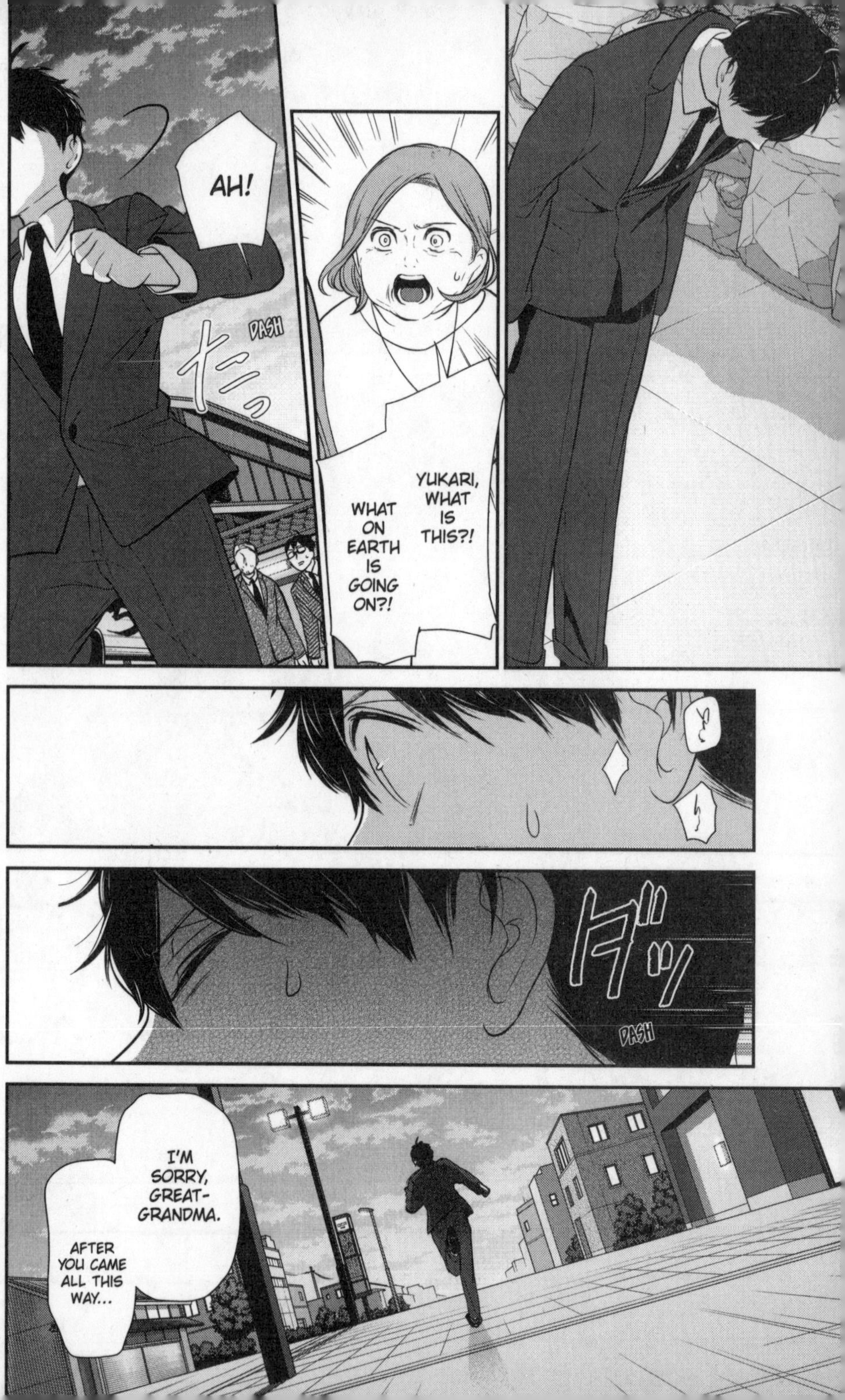
YUKARI, WHAT IS THIS?!
WHAT ON EARTH IS GOING ON?!
AH!
DASH
ダッ
DASH
I'M SORRY, GREAT-GRANDMA.
AFTER YOU CAME ALL THIS WAY...

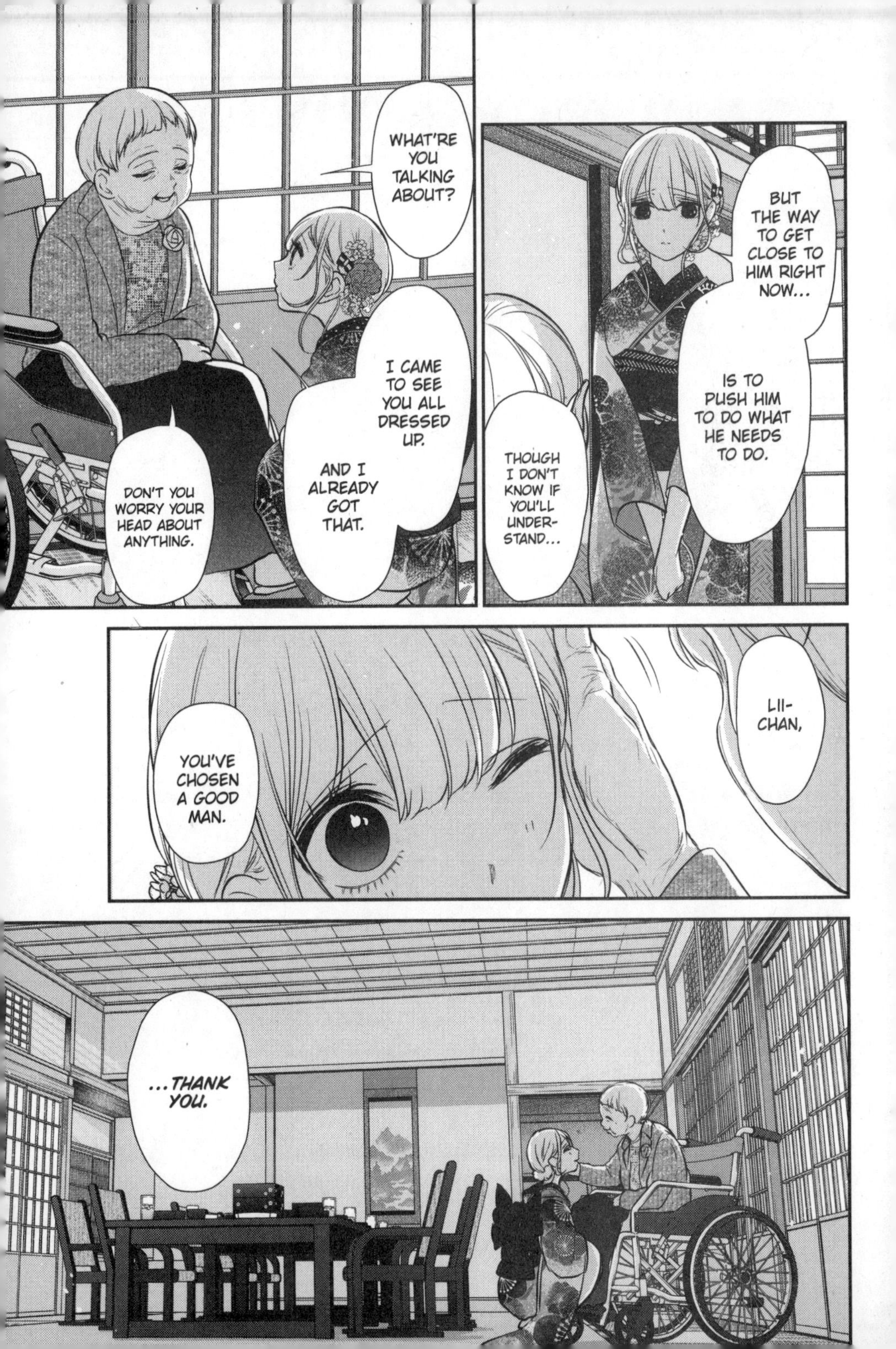
BUT THE WAY TO GET CLOSE TO HIM RIGHT NOW...
IS TO PUSH HIM TO DO WHAT HE NEEDS TO DO.
THOUGH I DON'T KNOW IF YOU'LL UNDER-STAND...
WHAT'RE YOU TALKING ABOUT?
I CAME TO SEE YOU ALL DRESSED UP.
AND I ALREADY GOT THAT.
DON'T YOU WORRY YOUR HEAD ABOUT ANYTHING.
LII-CHAN,
YOU'VE CHOSEN A GOOD MAN.
...THANK YOU.

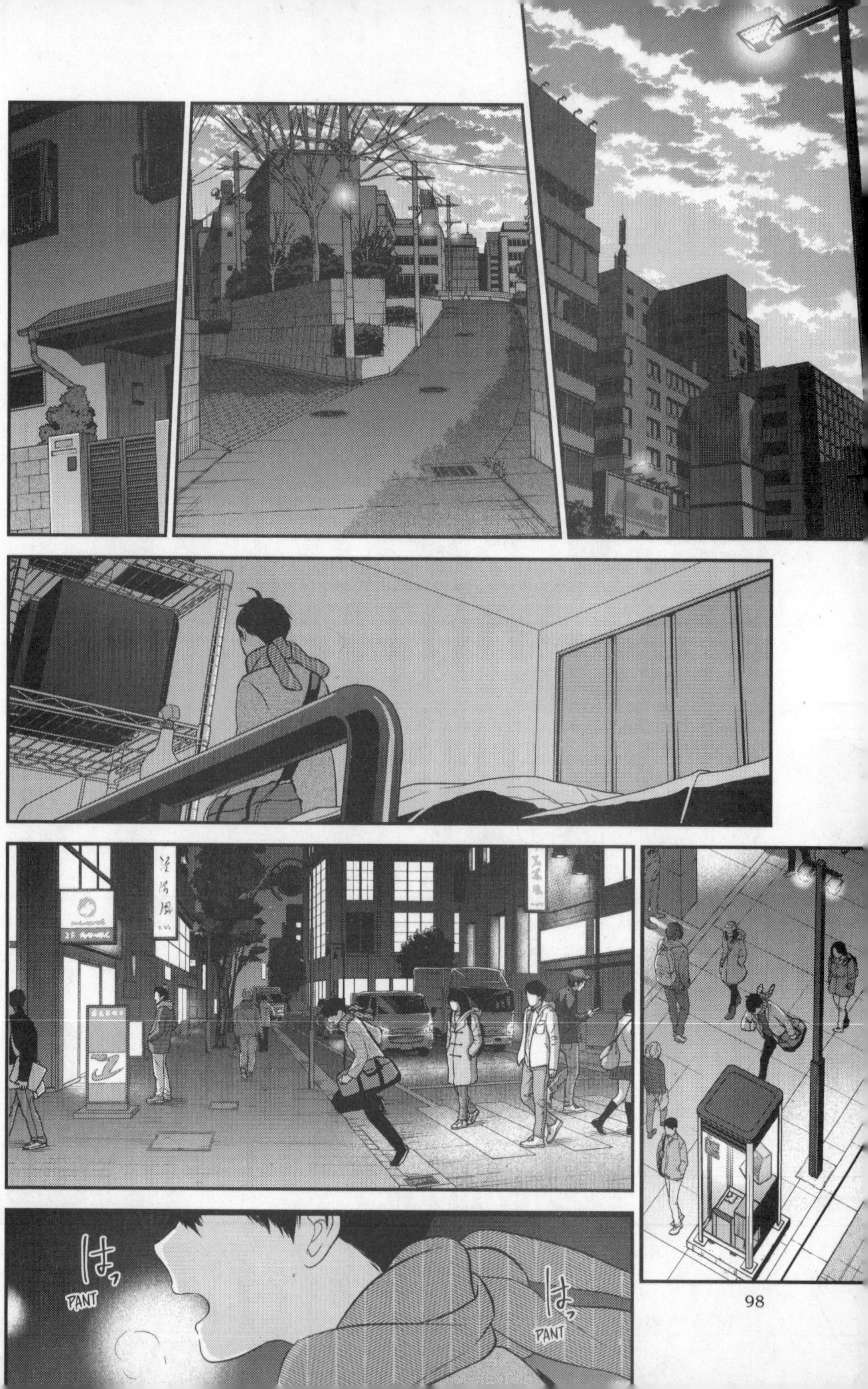
はっ
PANT
はっ
PANT

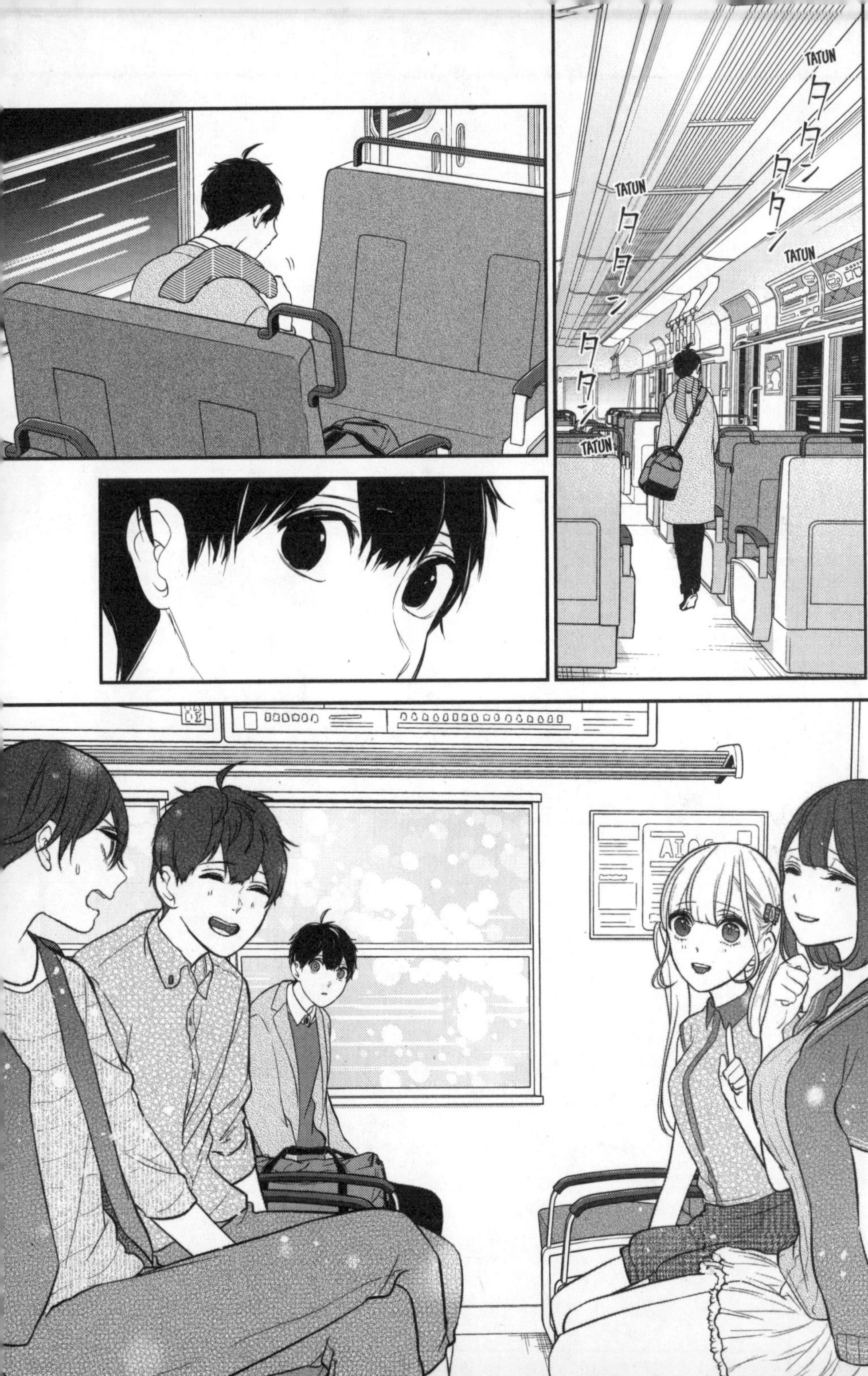
TATUN
タタン
タタン
TATUN
TATUN
タタン
タタン
TATUN

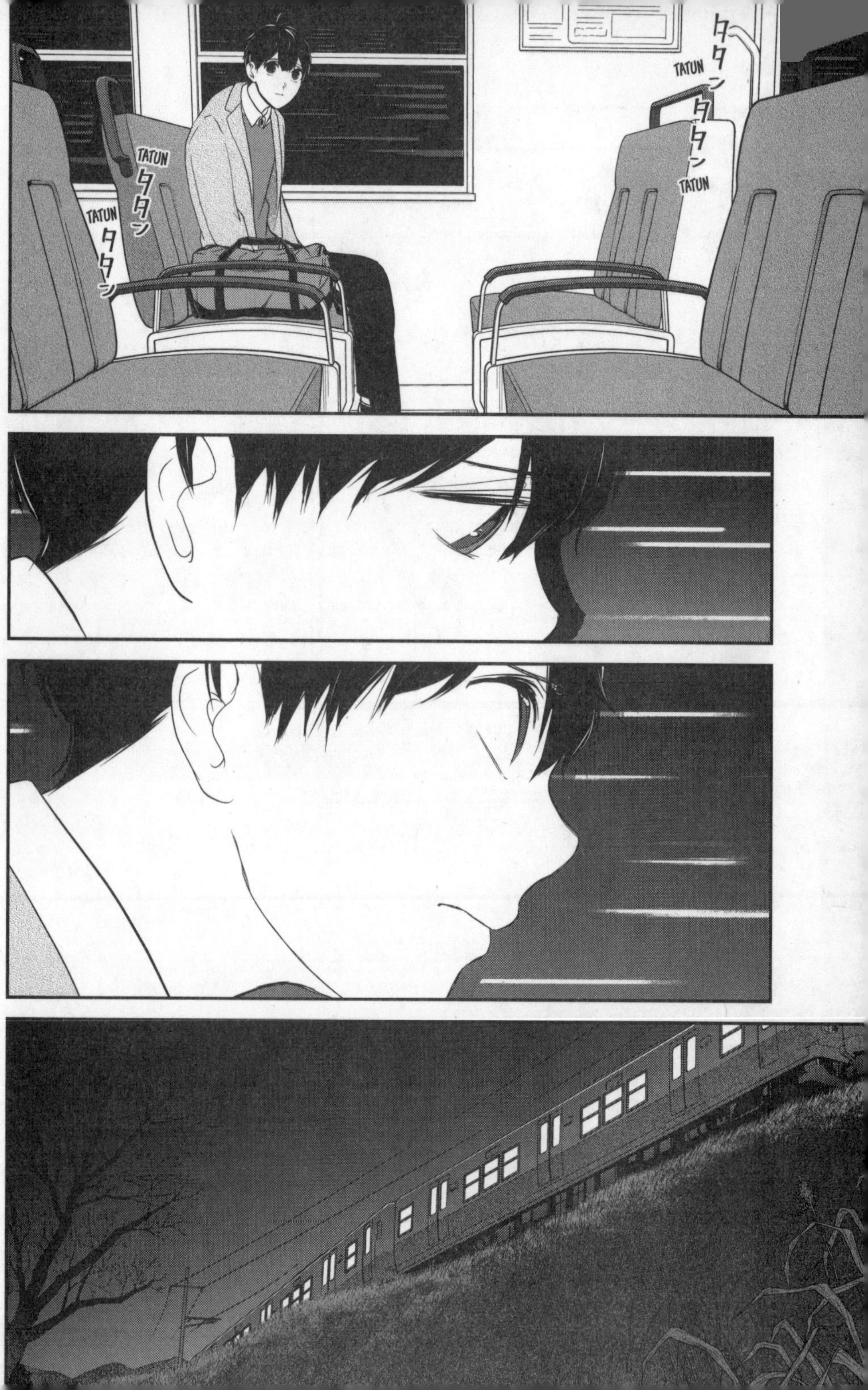

タタン
TATUN
タタン
TATUN
TATUN
タタン
TATUN
タタン

Chapter 48: Thank You

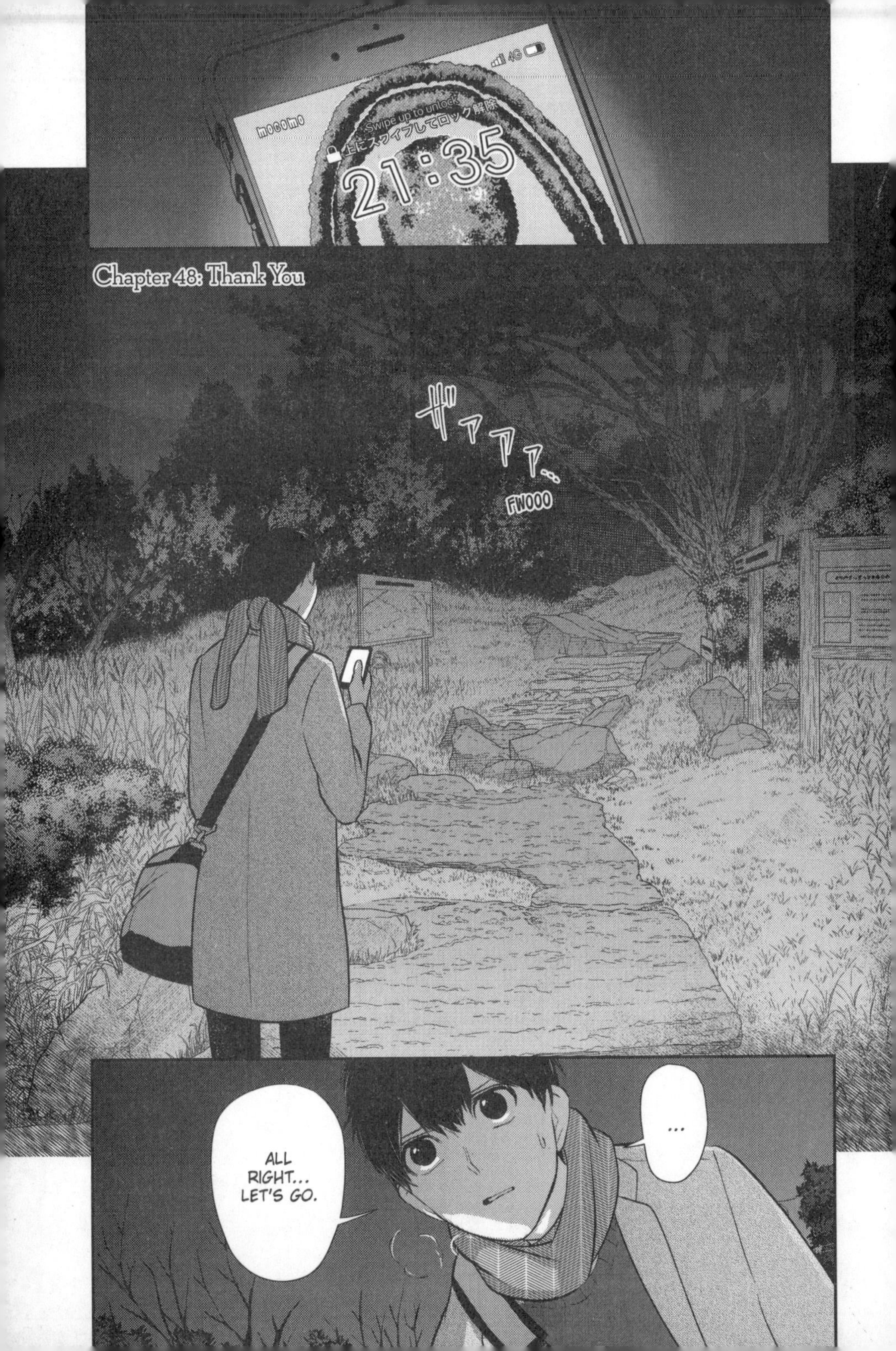
4G
mocomo
Swipe up to unlock
上にスワイプしてロック解除
21:35
ザァァァ…
FWOOO
...
ALL RIGHT... LET'S GO.

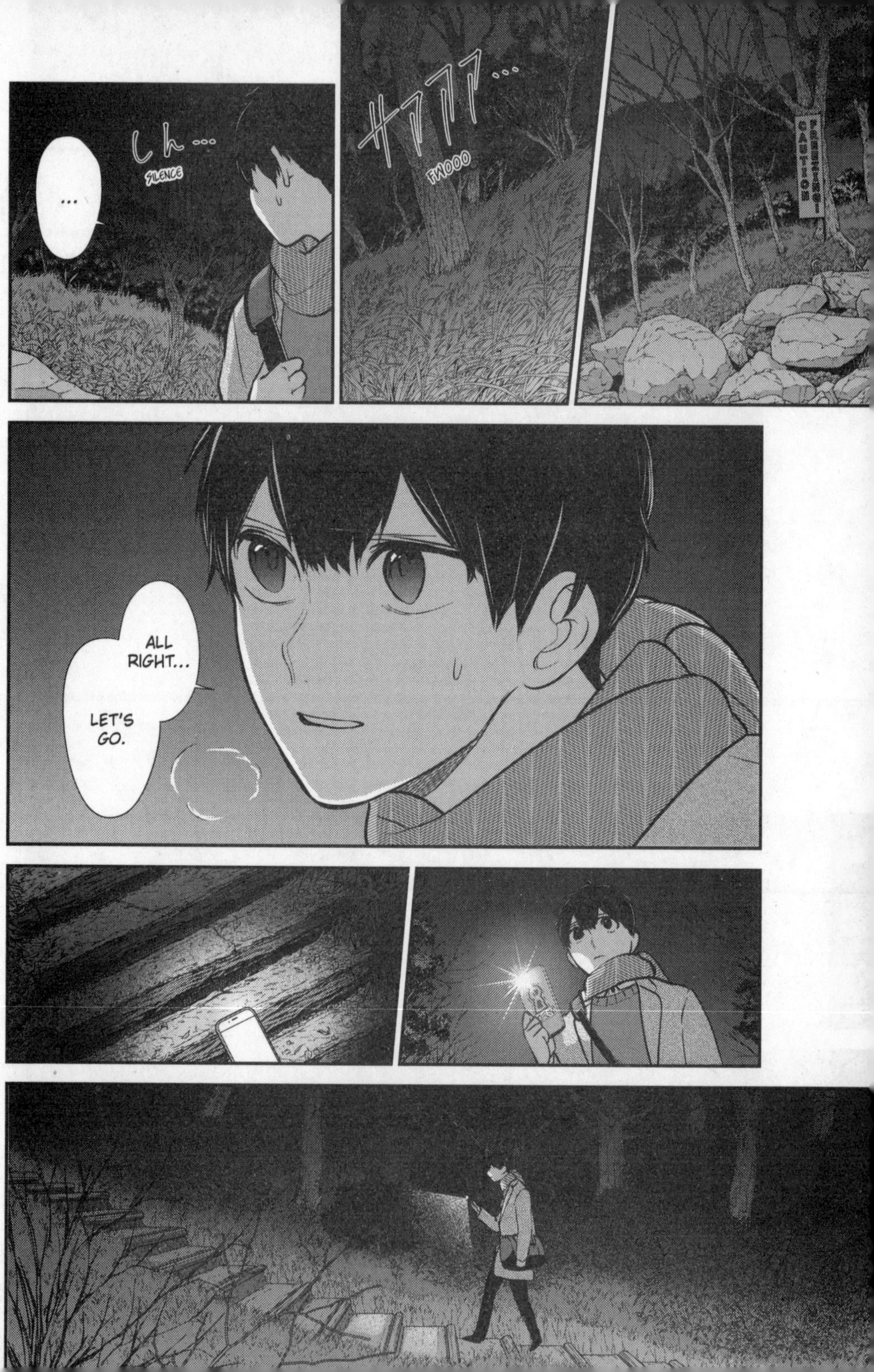
FREEZING!
CAUTION
サァァァ…
FWOOO
しん…
SILENCE
…
ALL RIGHT…
LET'S GO.

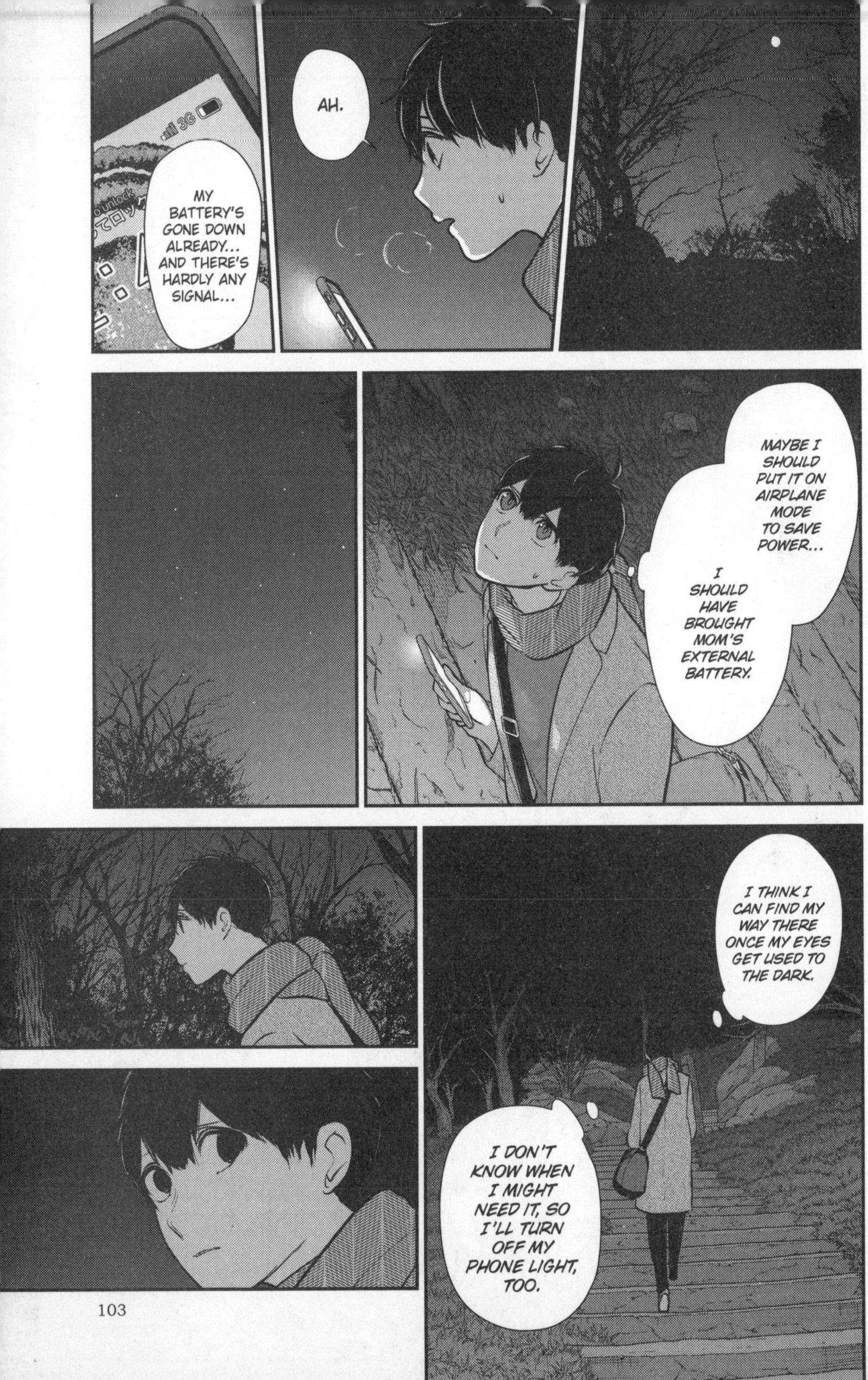
AH.
MY BATTERY'S GONE DOWN ALREADY... AND THERE'S HARDLY ANY SIGNAL...
MAYBE I SHOULD PUT IT ON AIRPLANE MODE TO SAVE POWER...
I SHOULD HAVE BROUGHT MOM'S EXTERNAL BATTERY.
I THINK I CAN FIND MY WAY THERE ONCE MY EYES GET USED TO THE DARK.
I DON'T KNOW WHEN I MIGHT NEED IT, SO I'LL TURN OFF MY PHONE LIGHT, TOO.

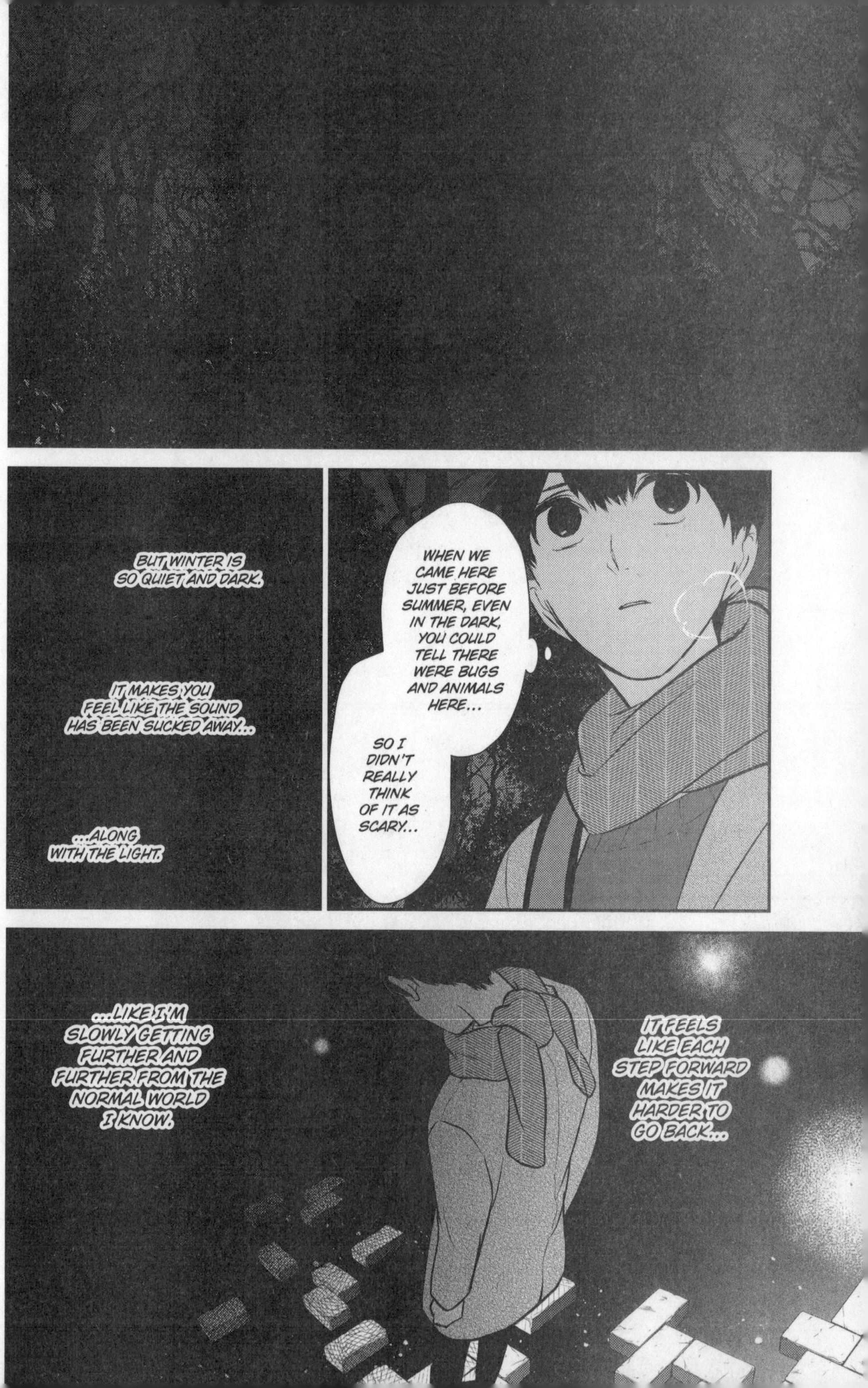
WHEN WE CAME HERE JUST BEFORE SUMMER, EVEN IN THE DARK, YOU COULD TELL THERE WERE BUGS AND ANIMALS HERE...
SO I DIDN'T REALLY THINK OF IT AS SCARY...
BUT WINTER IS SO QUIET AND DARK.
IT MAKES YOU FEEL LIKE THE SOUND HAS BEEN SUCKED AWAY...
...ALONG WITH THE LIGHT.
IT FEELS LIKE EACH STEP FORWARD MAKES IT HARDER TO GO BACK...
...LIKE I'M SLOWLY GETTING FURTHER AND FURTHER FROM THE NORMAL WORLD I KNOW.

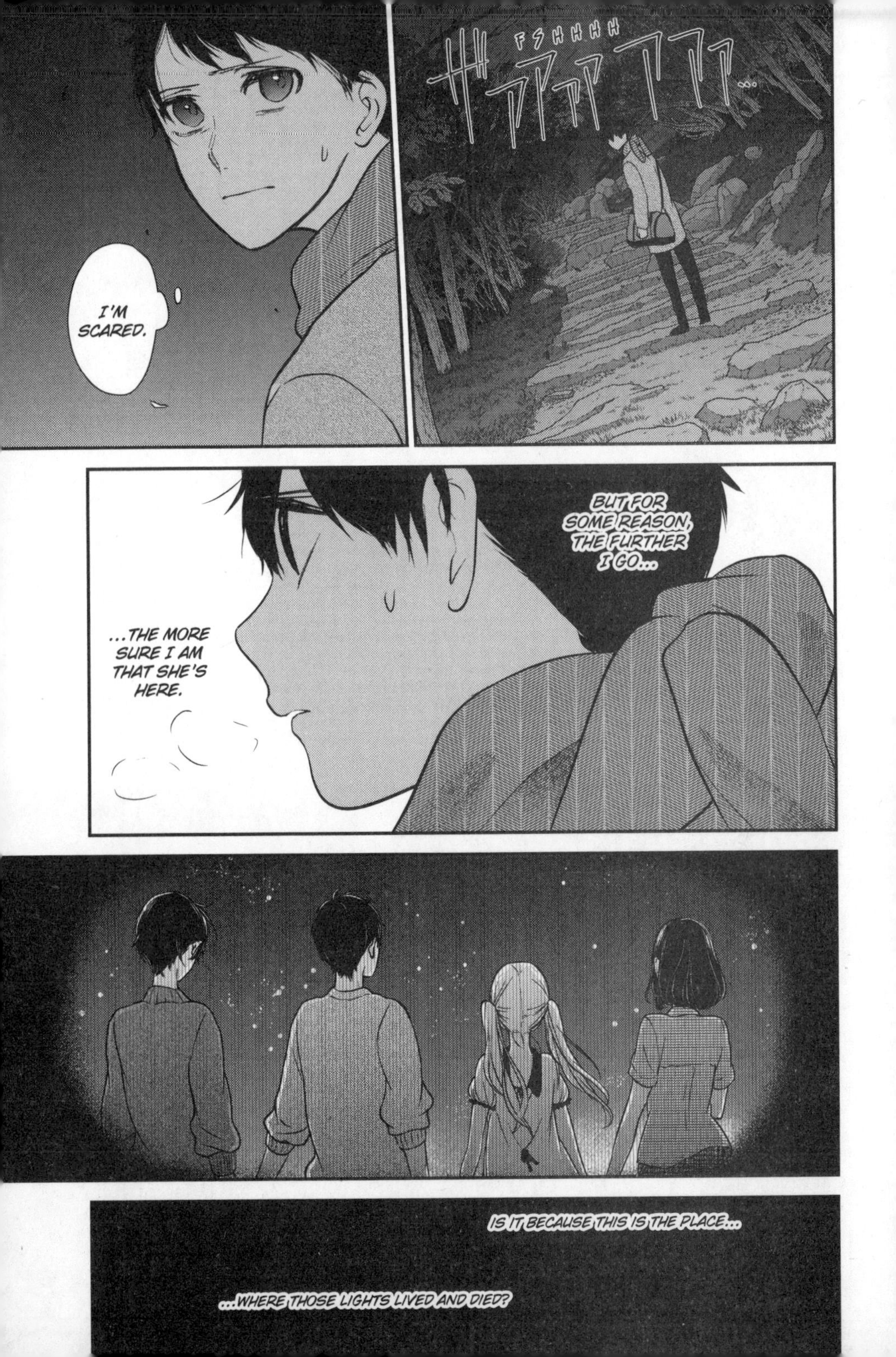
ザアァァアアア…
FSHHHH
I'M SCARED.
BUT FOR SOME REASON, THE FURTHER I GO...
...THE MORE SURE I AM THAT SHE'S HERE.
IS IT BECAUSE THIS IS THE PLACE...
...WHERE THOSE LIGHTS LIVED AND DIED?

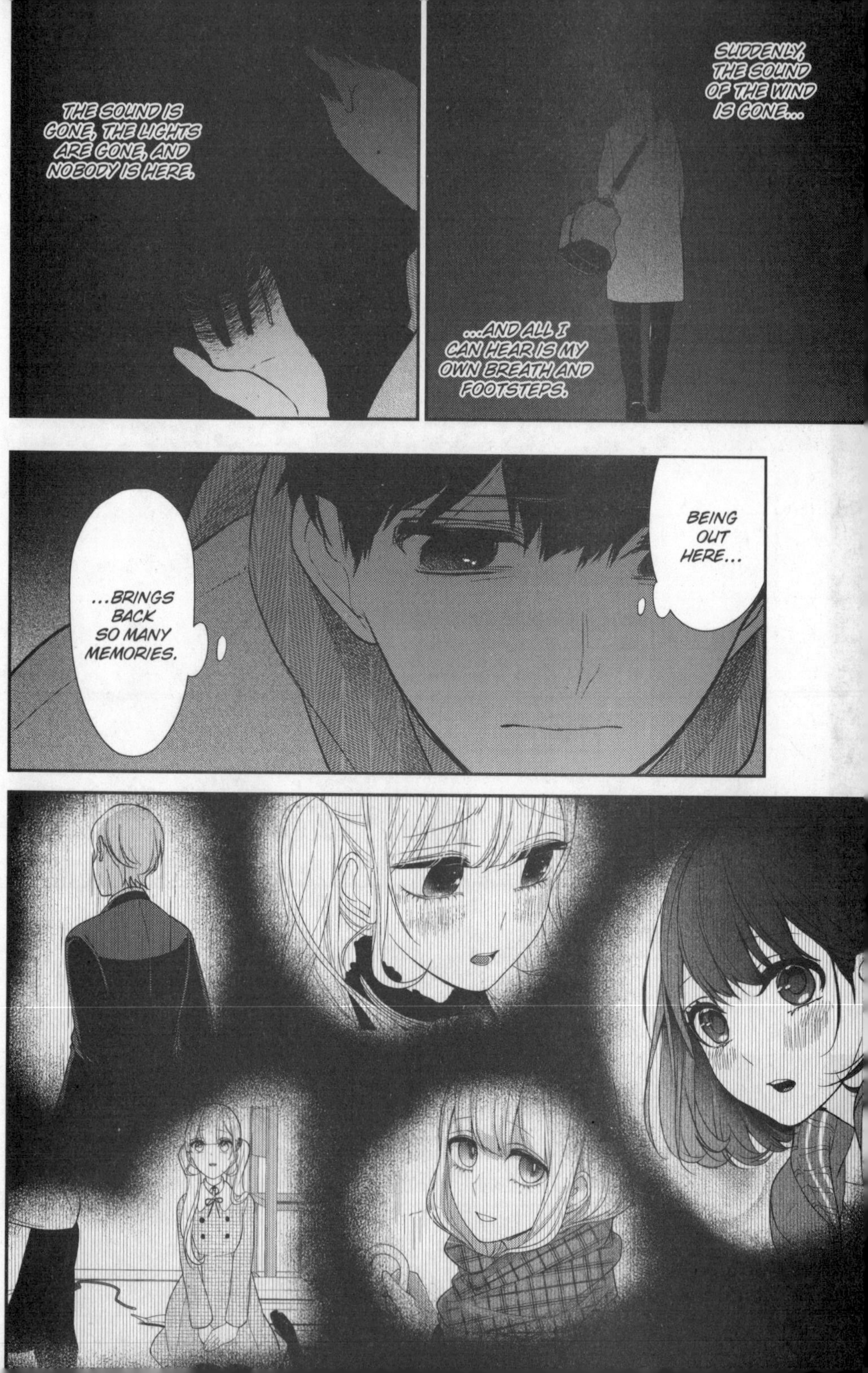
SUDDENLY, THE SOUND OF THE WIND IS GONE...
...AND ALL I CAN HEAR IS MY OWN BREATH AND FOOTSTEPS.
THE SOUND IS GONE, THE LIGHTS ARE GONE, AND NOBODY IS HERE.
BEING OUT HERE...
...BRINGS BACK SO MANY MEMORIES.

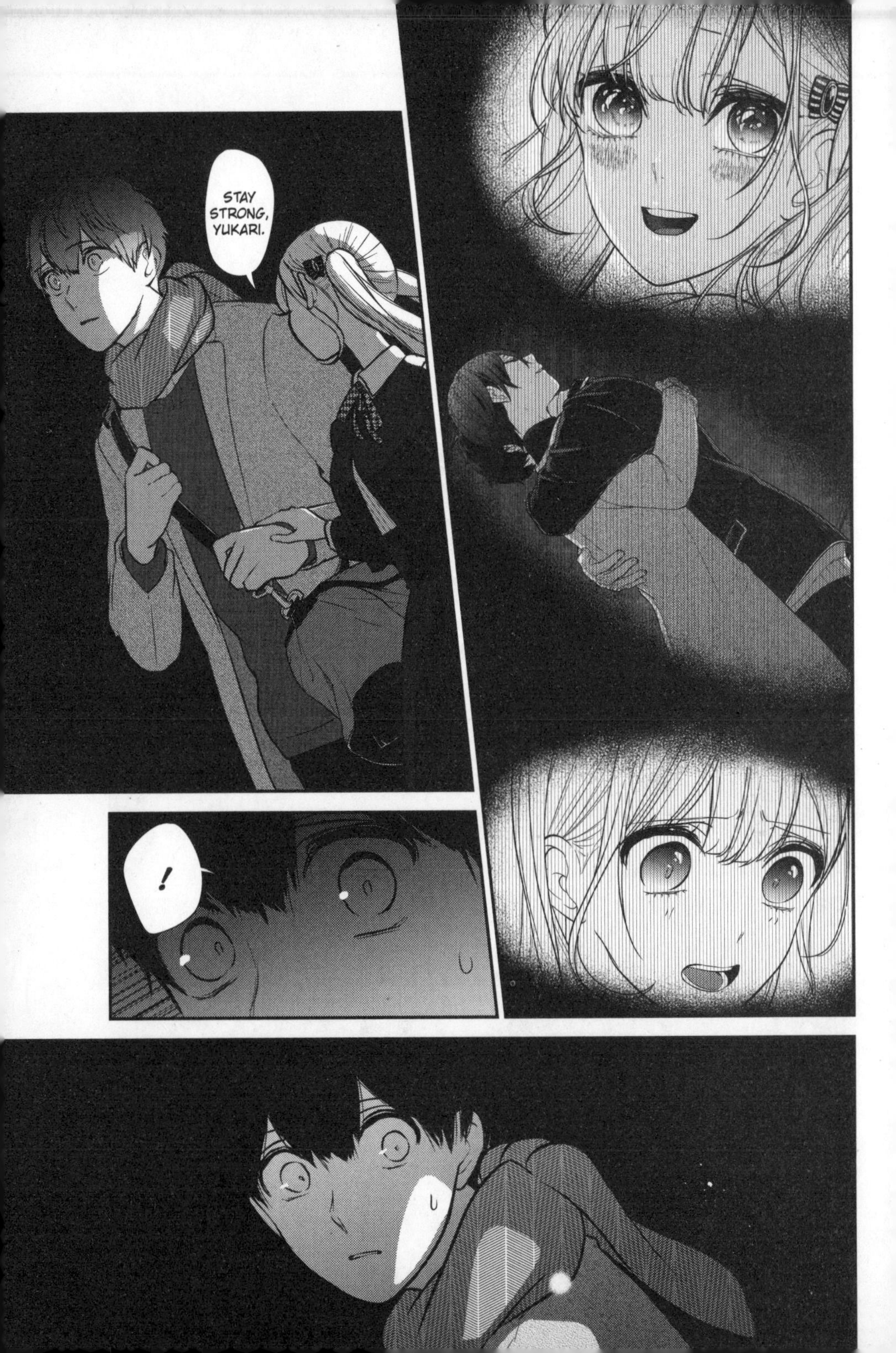
STAY STRONG, YUKARI.
!

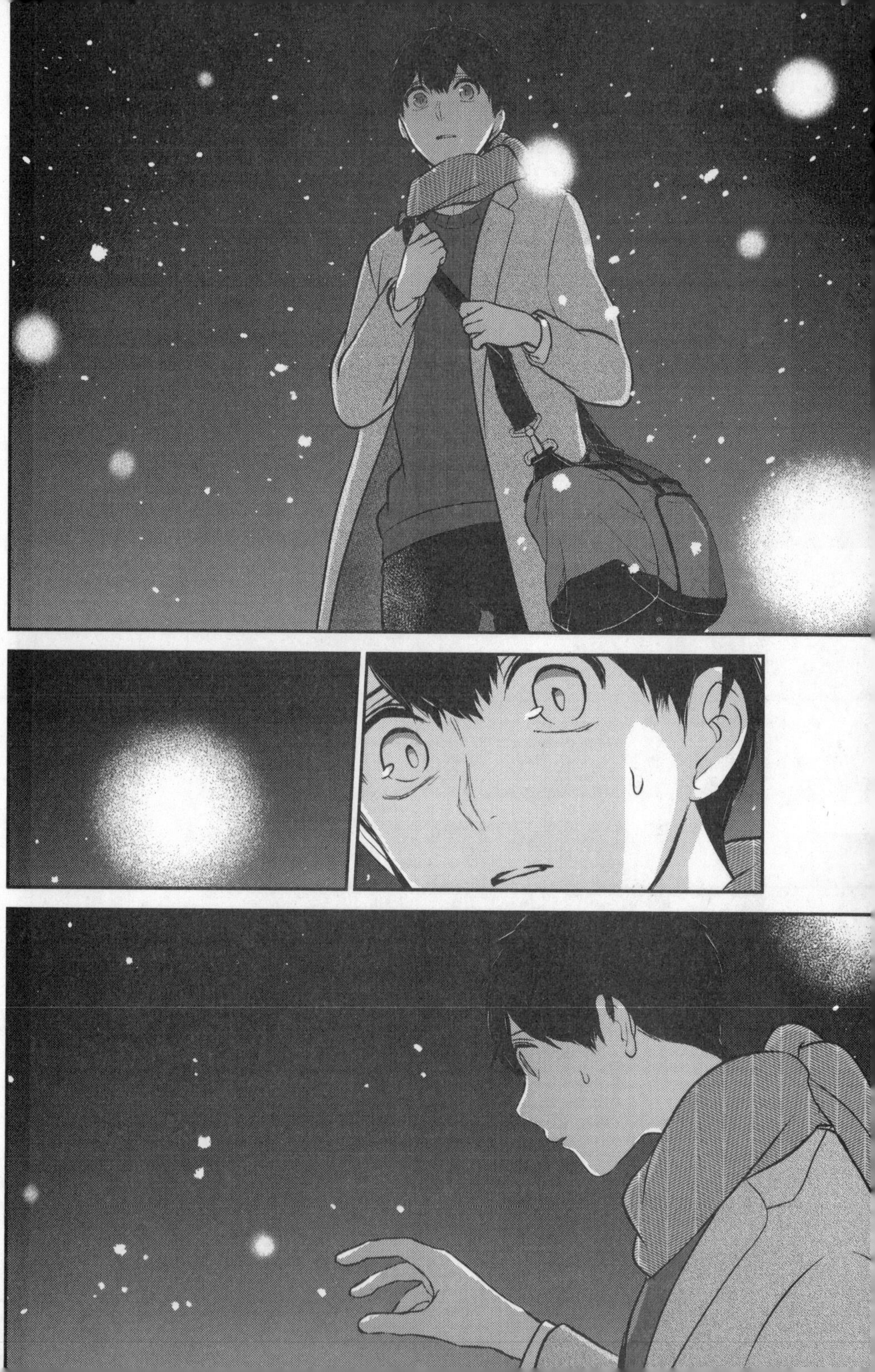

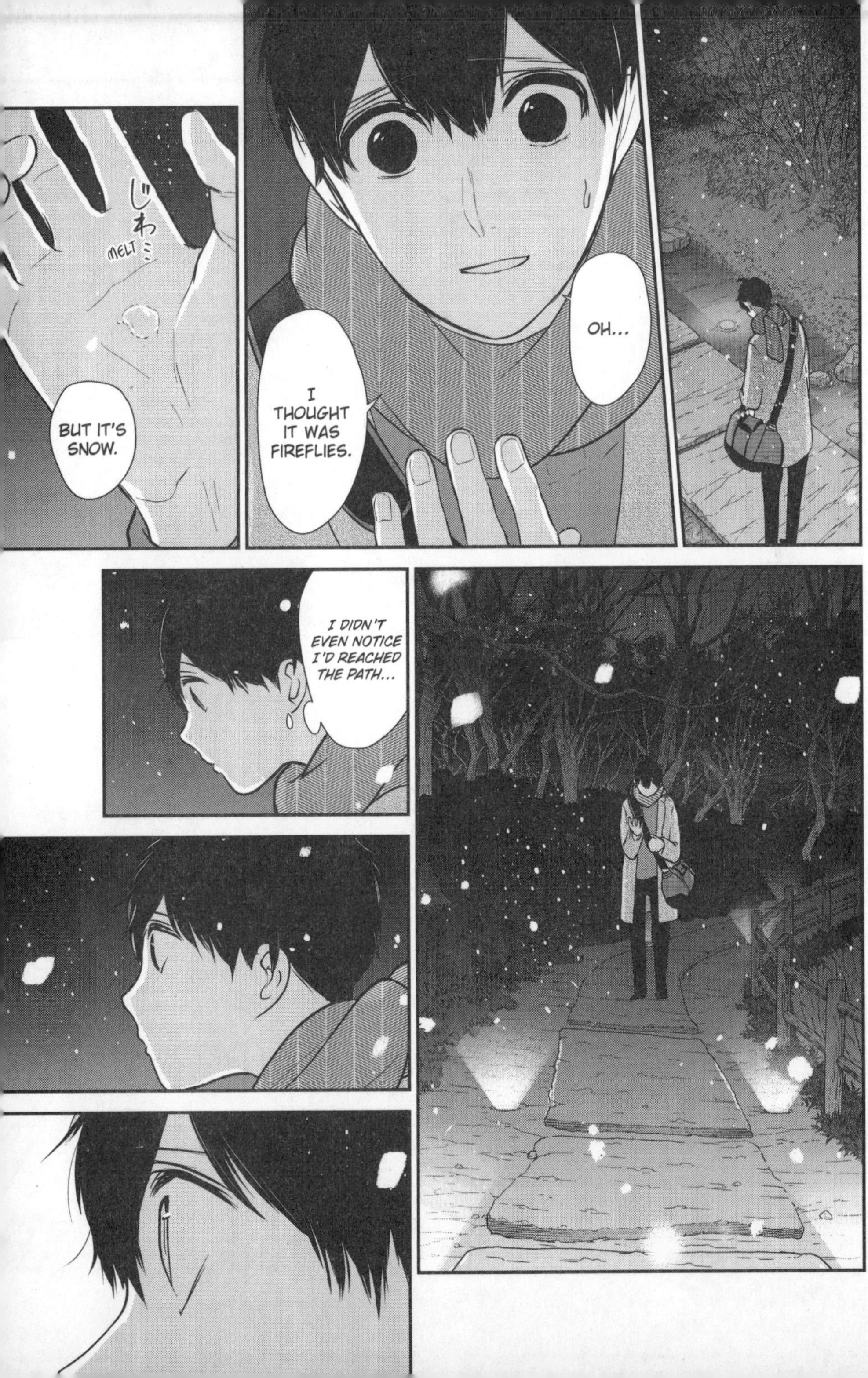
OH...
I THOUGHT IT WAS FIREFLIES.
じわ
MELT
BUT IT'S SNOW.
I DIDN'T EVEN NOTICE I'D REACHED THE PATH...

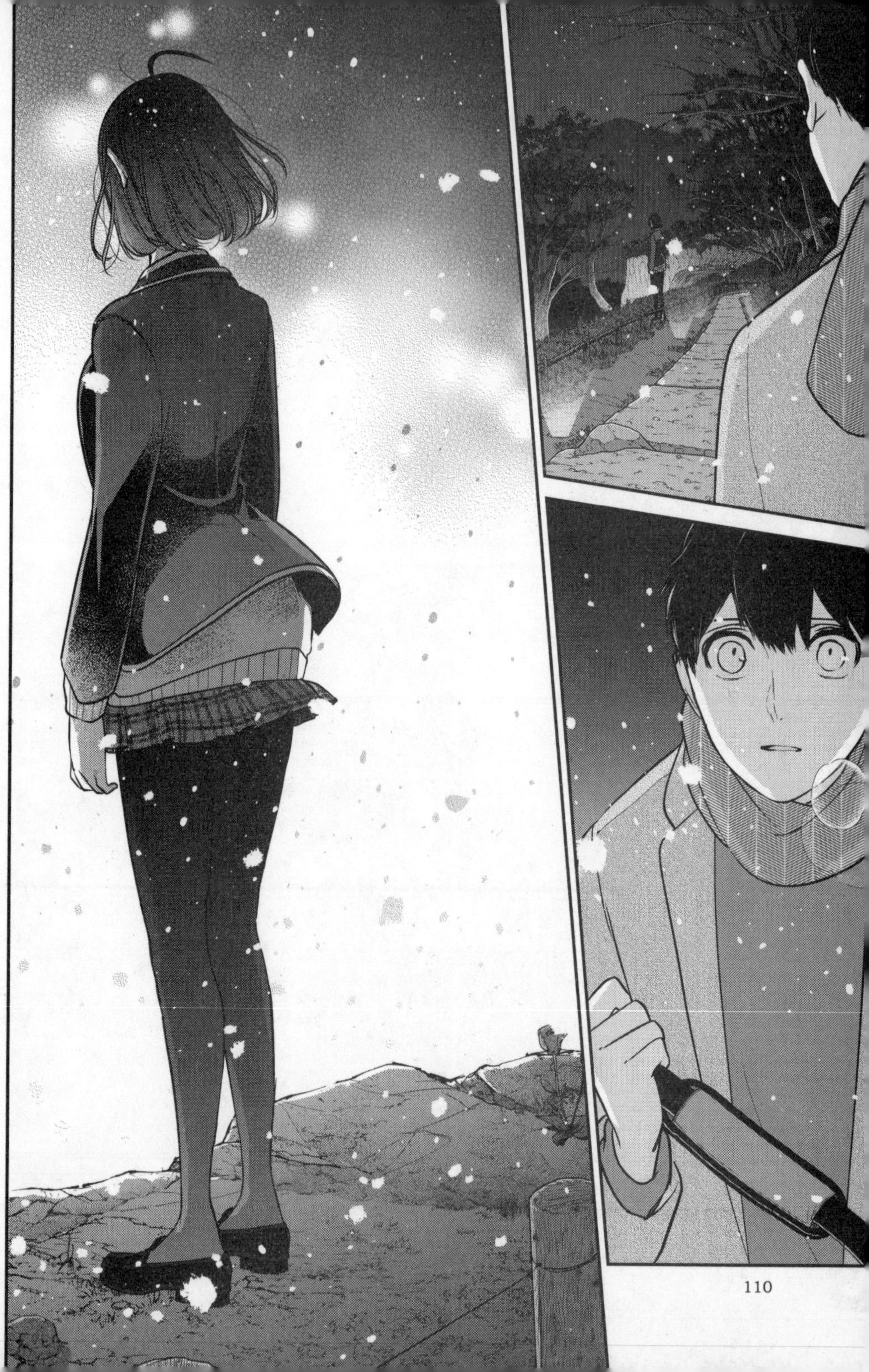

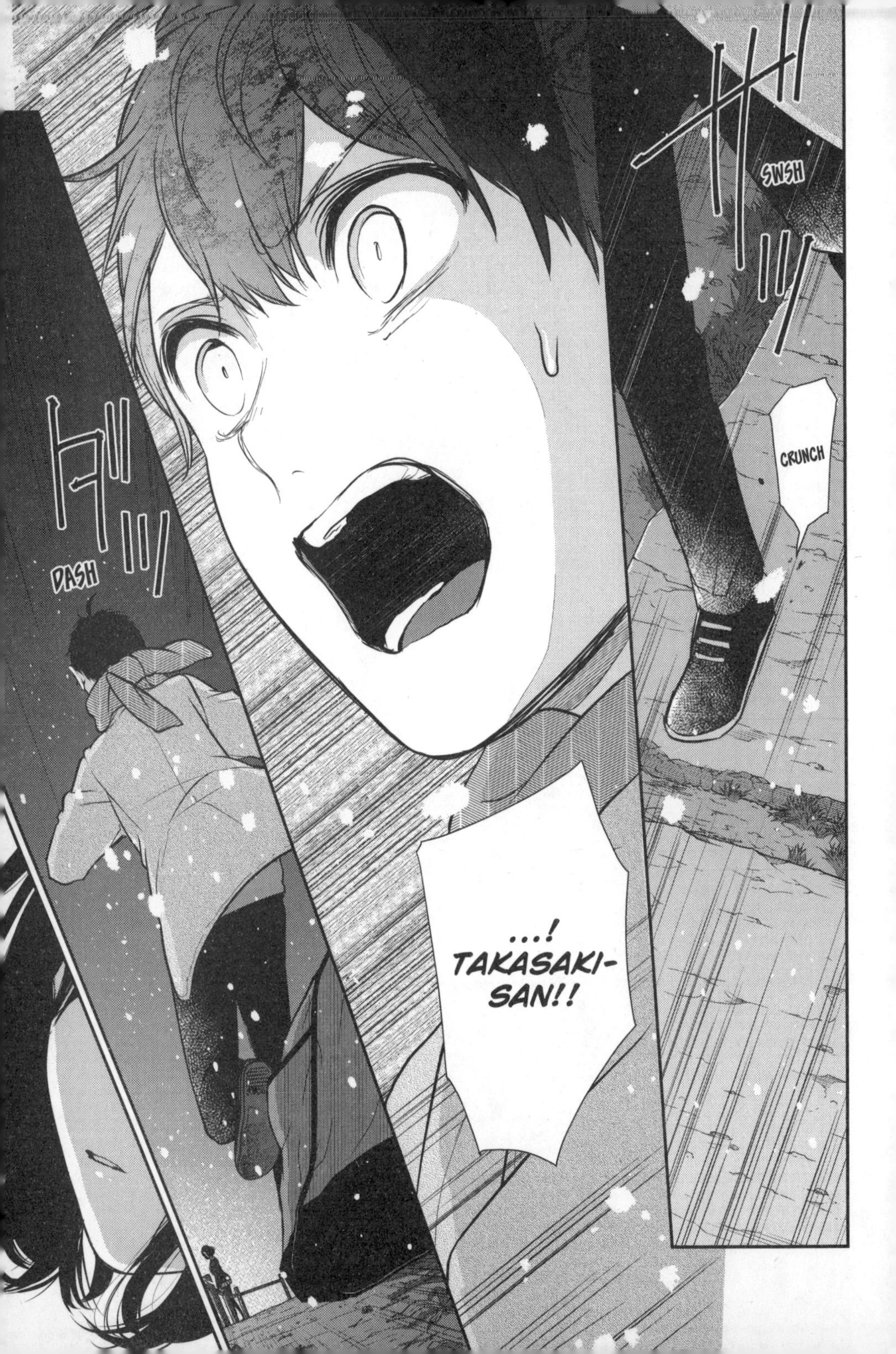
SWSH
CRUNCH
...! TAKASAKI-SAN!!
DASH

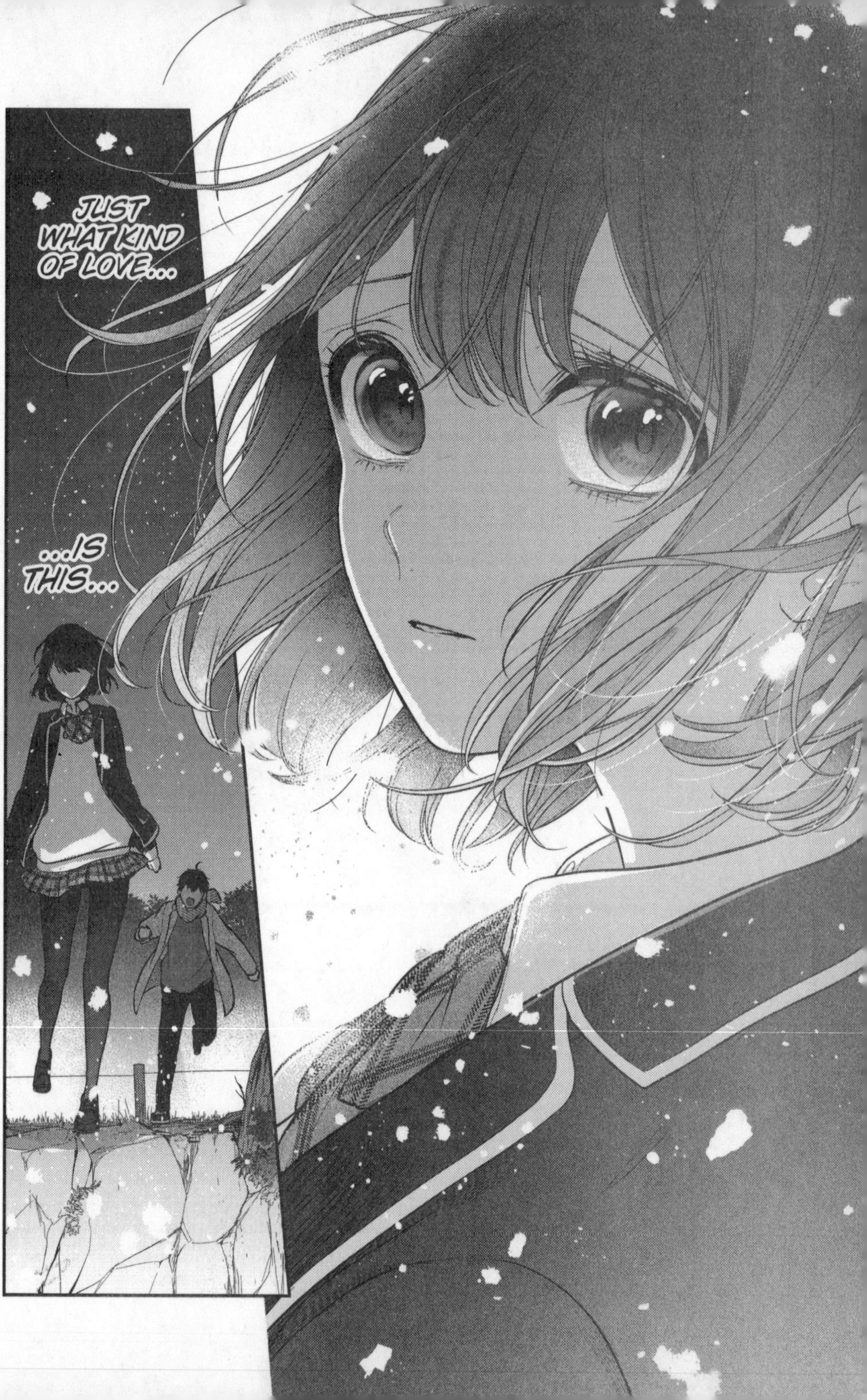
JUST WHAT KIND OF LOVE...
...IS THIS...

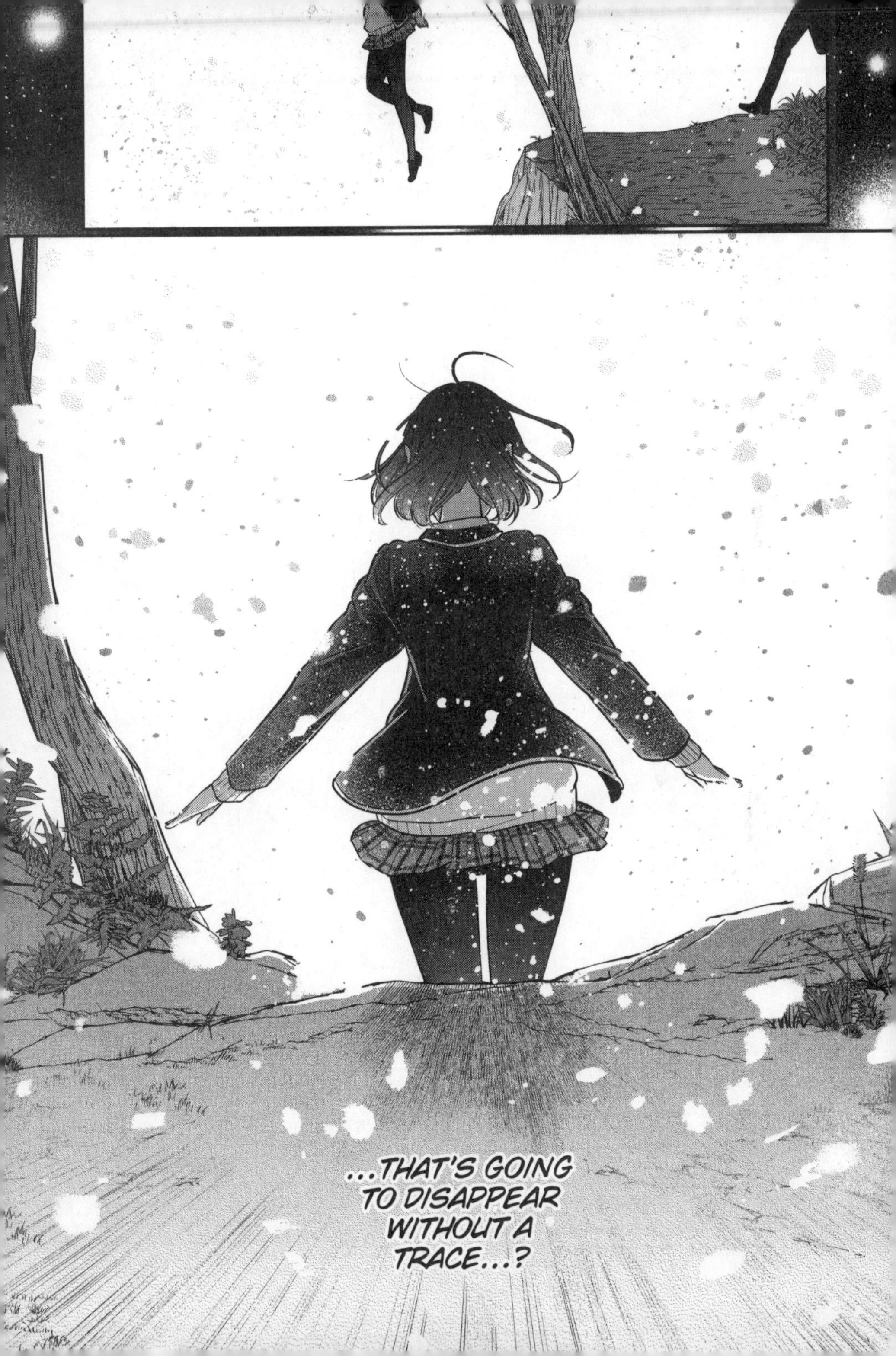
...THAT'S GOING TO DISAPPEAR WITHOUT A TRACE...?

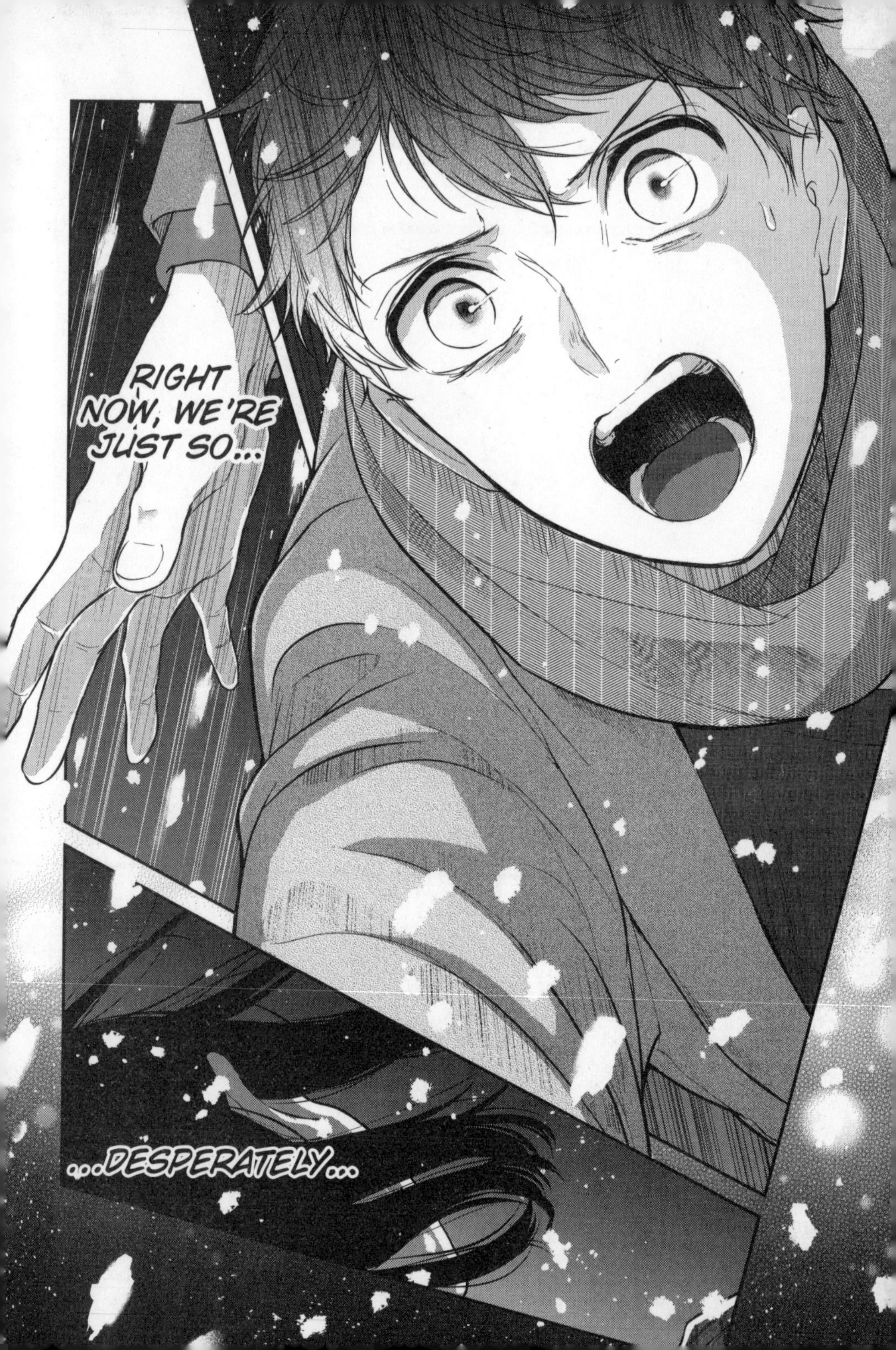
RIGHT NOW, WE'RE JUST SO...
...DESPERATELY...

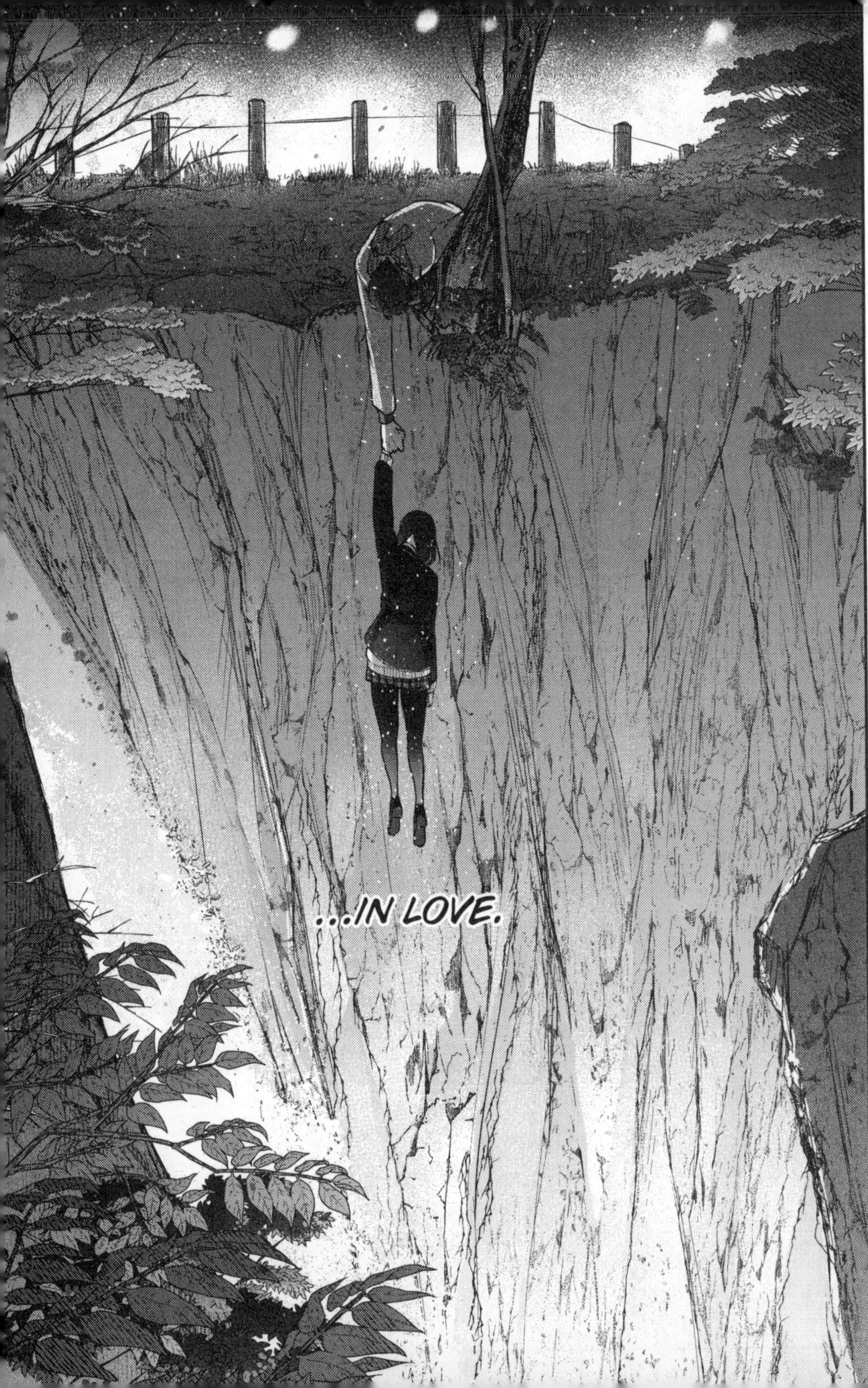
...IN LOVE.

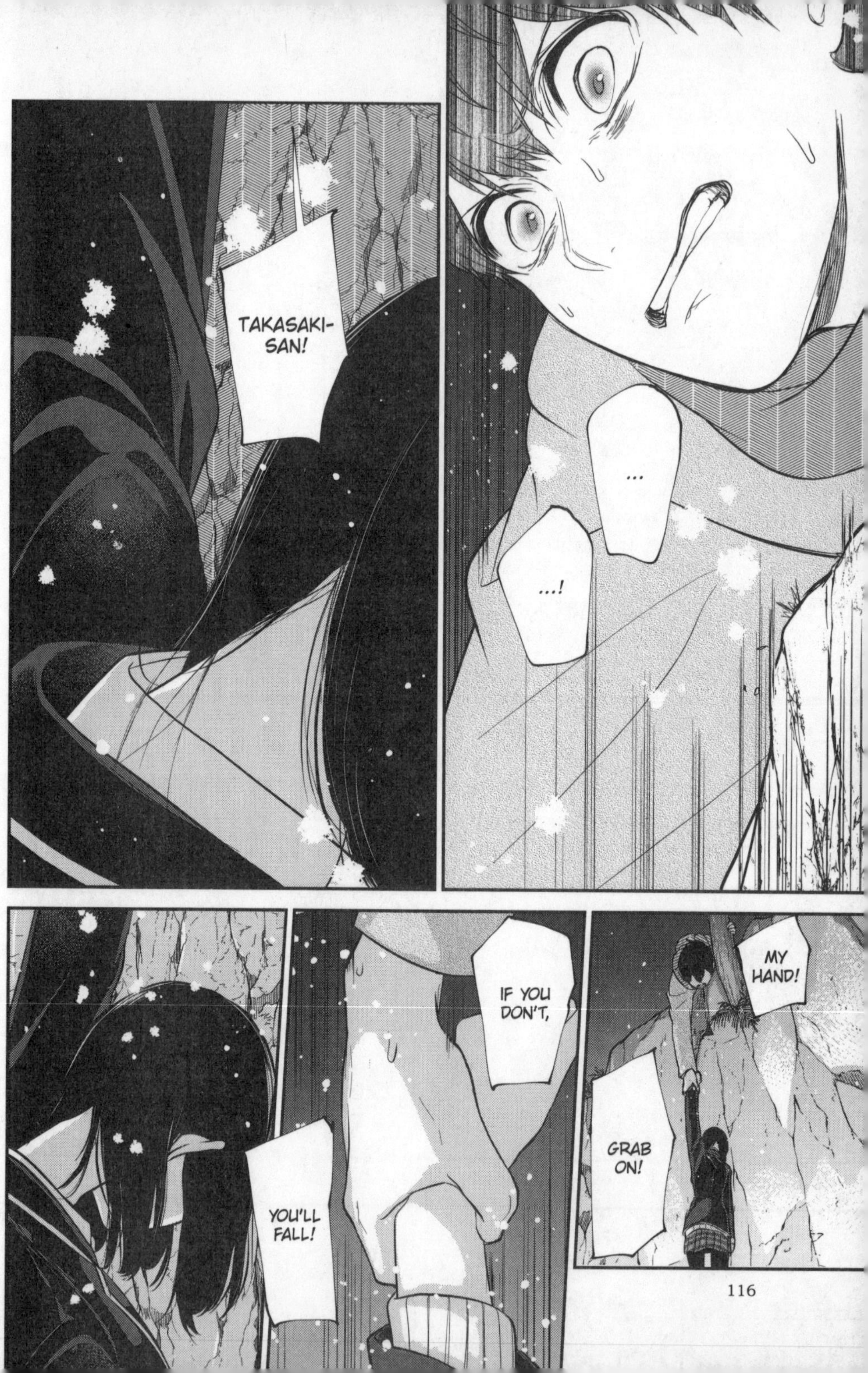
...
...!
TAKASAKI-SAN!
MY HAND!
GRAB ON!
IF YOU DON'T,
YOU'LL FALL!

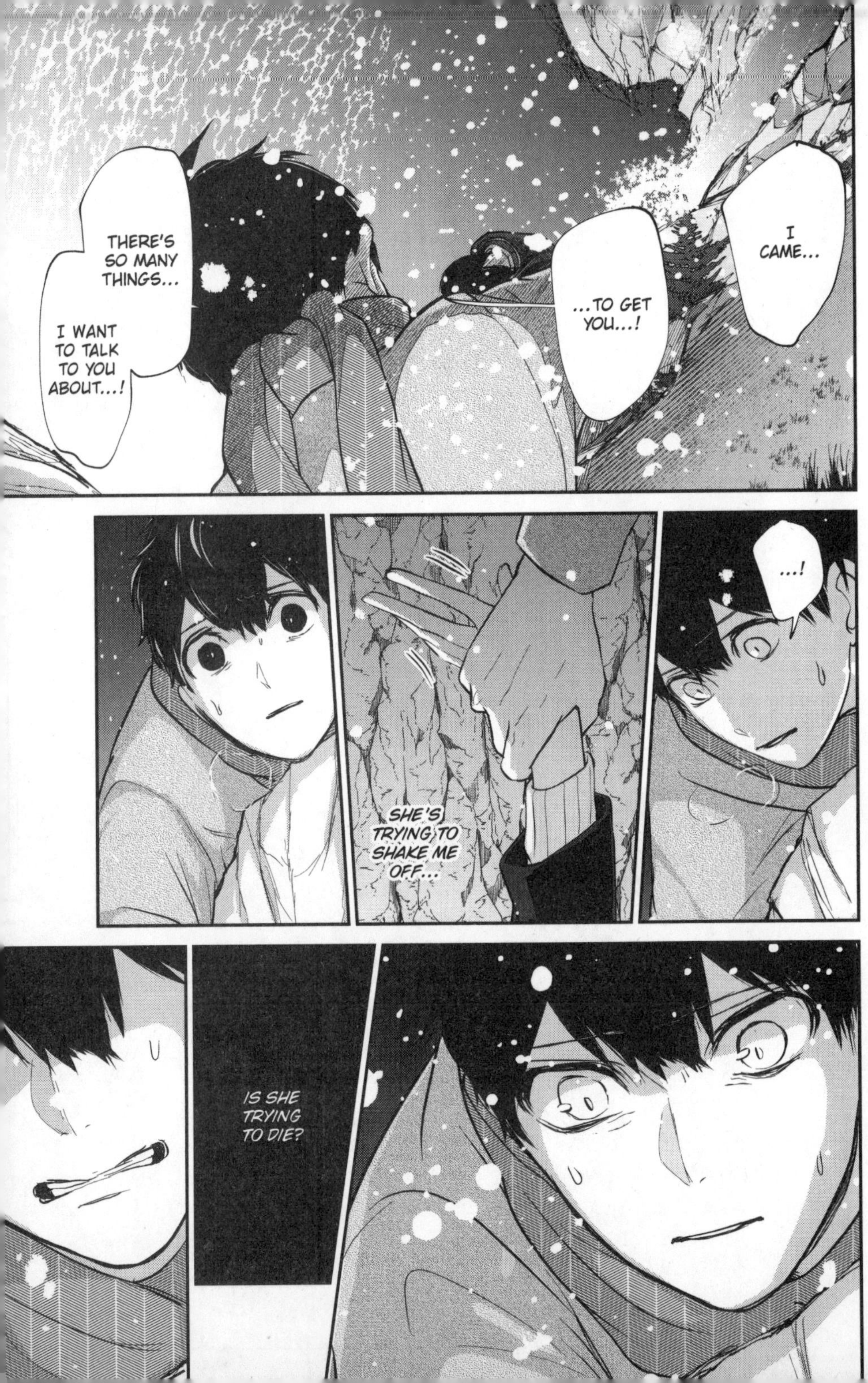
I CAME...
...TO GET YOU...!
THERE'S SO MANY THINGS...
I WANT TO TALK TO YOU ABOUT...!
...!
SHE'S TRYING TO SHAKE ME OFF...
IS SHE TRYING TO DIE?

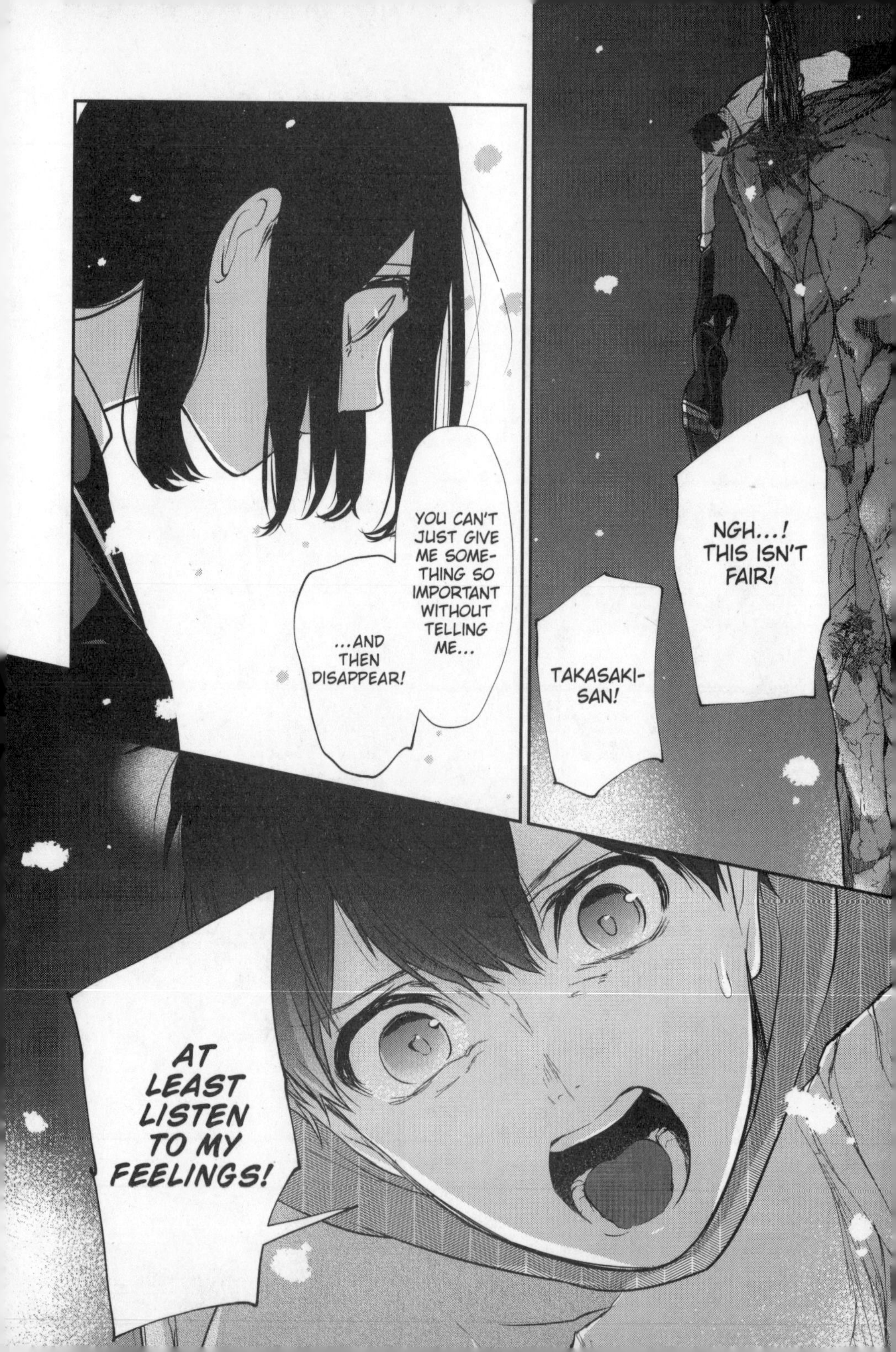
NGH...! THIS ISN'T FAIR!
TAKASAKI-SAN!
YOU CAN'T JUST GIVE ME SOMETHING SO IMPORTANT WITHOUT TELLING ME...
...AND THEN DISAPPEAR!
AT LEAST LISTEN TO MY FEELINGS!

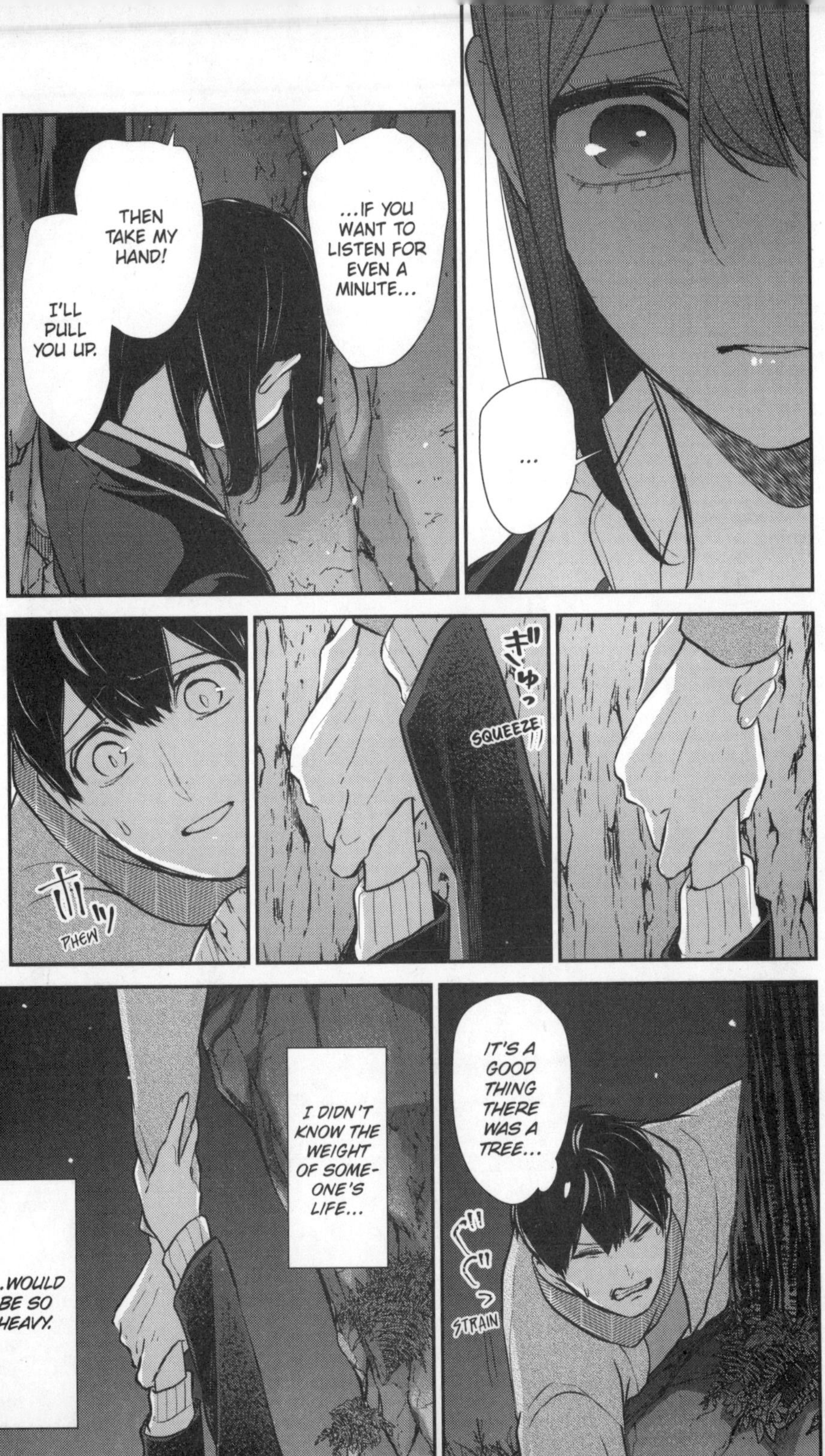
...
...IF YOU WANT TO LISTEN FOR EVEN A MINUTE...
THEN TAKE MY HAND!
I'LL PULL YOU UP.
SQUEEZE
PHEW
IT'S A GOOD THING THERE WAS A TREE...
STRAIN
I DIDN'T KNOW THE WEIGHT OF SOME-ONE'S LIFE...
...WOULD BE SO HEAVY.

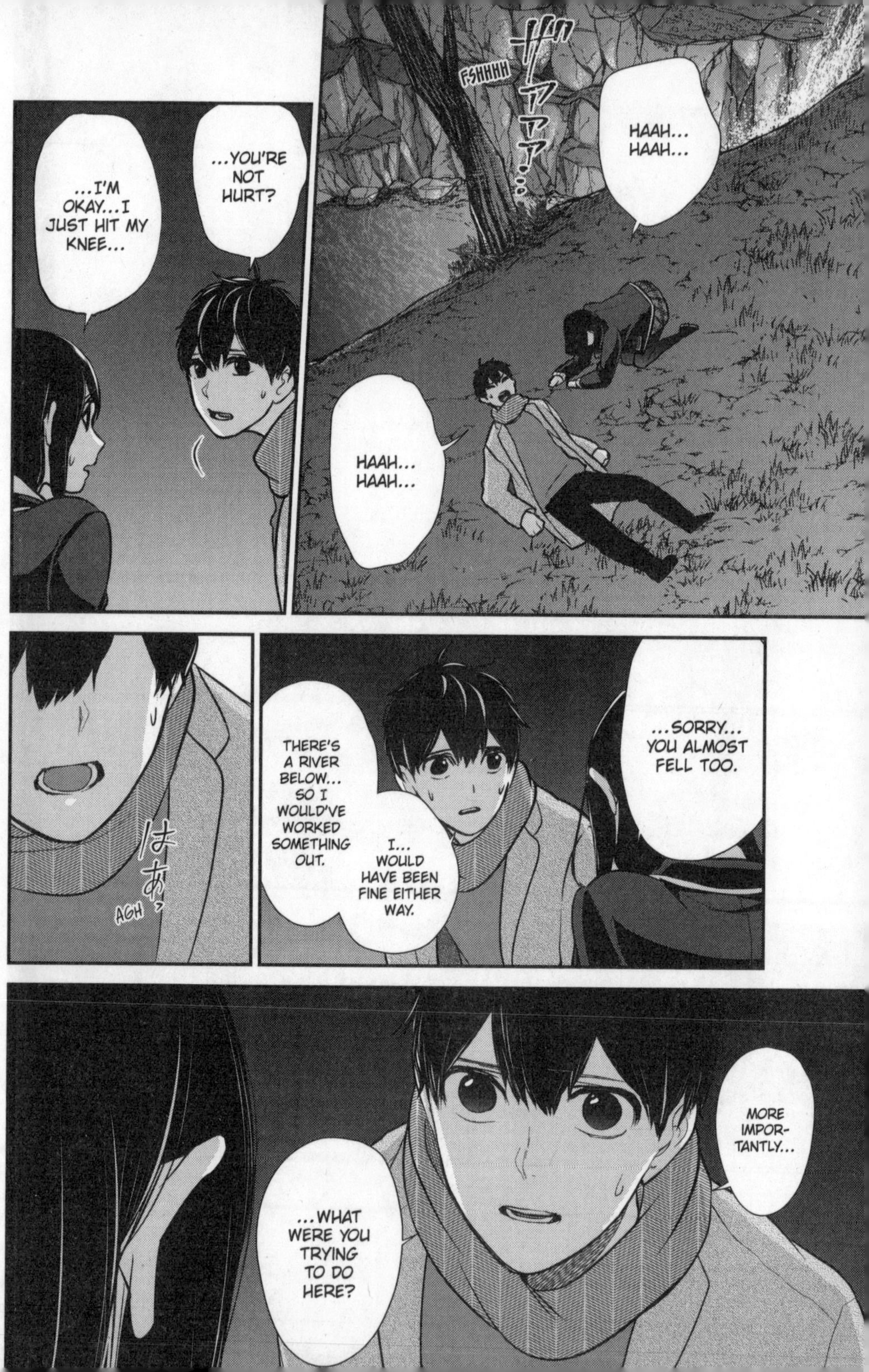
FSHHHH
HAAH... HAAH...
HAAH... HAAH...
...YOU'RE NOT HURT?
...I'M OKAY...I JUST HIT MY KNEE...
...SORRY... YOU ALMOST FELL TOO.
I... WOULD HAVE BEEN FINE EITHER WAY.
THERE'S A RIVER BELOW... SO I WOULD'VE WORKED SOMETHING OUT.
AGH
MORE IMPOR-TANTLY...
...WHAT WERE YOU TRYING TO DO HERE?

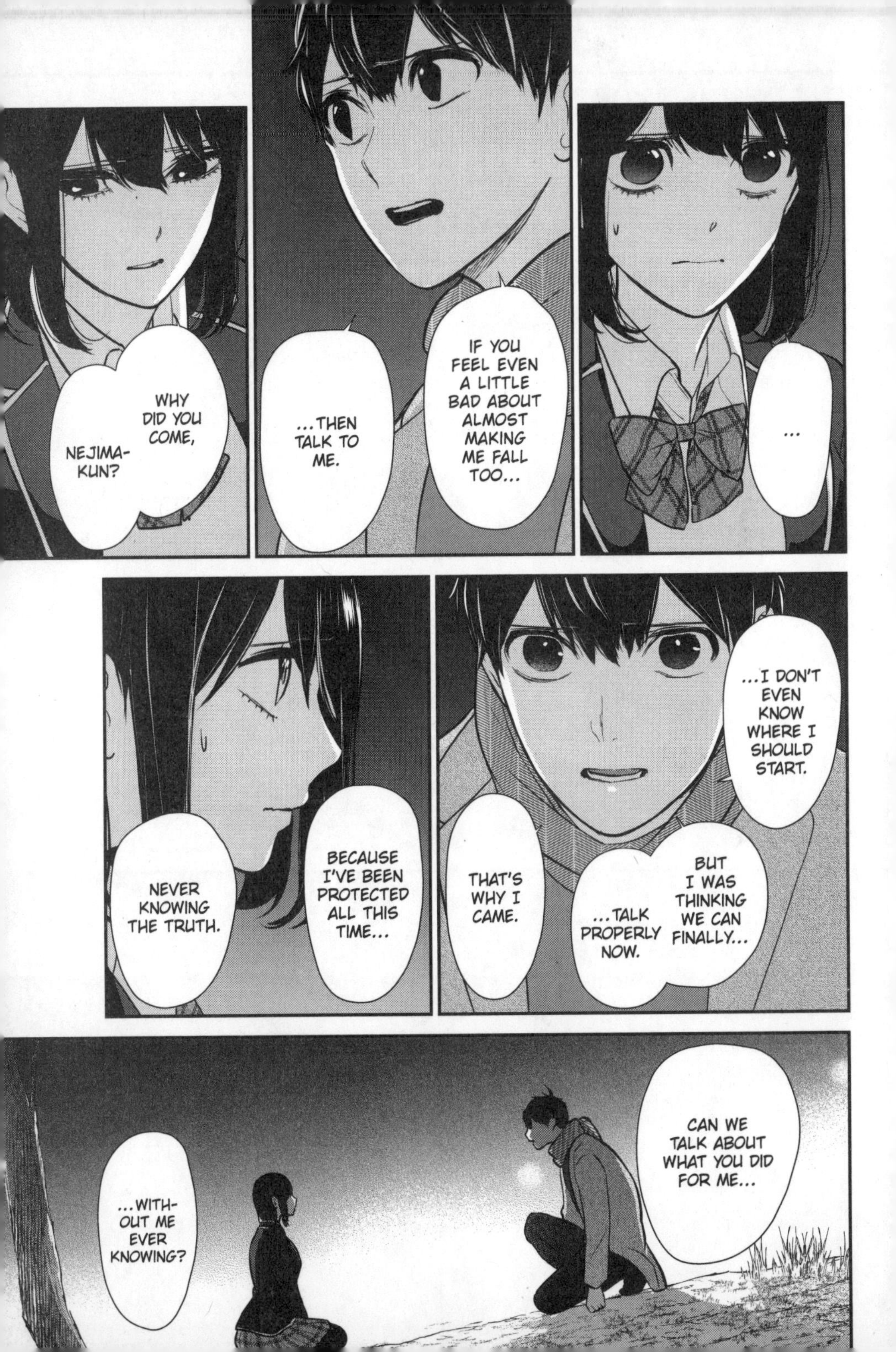
...
IF YOU FEEL EVEN A LITTLE BAD ABOUT ALMOST MAKING ME FALL TOO...
...THEN TALK TO ME.
WHY DID YOU COME, NEJIMA-KUN?
...I DON'T EVEN KNOW WHERE I SHOULD START.
BUT I WAS THINKING WE CAN FINALLY...
...TALK PROPERLY NOW.
THAT'S WHY I CAME.
BECAUSE I'VE BEEN PROTECTED ALL THIS TIME...
NEVER KNOWING THE TRUTH.
CAN WE TALK ABOUT WHAT YOU DID FOR ME...
...WITHOUT ME EVER KNOWING?

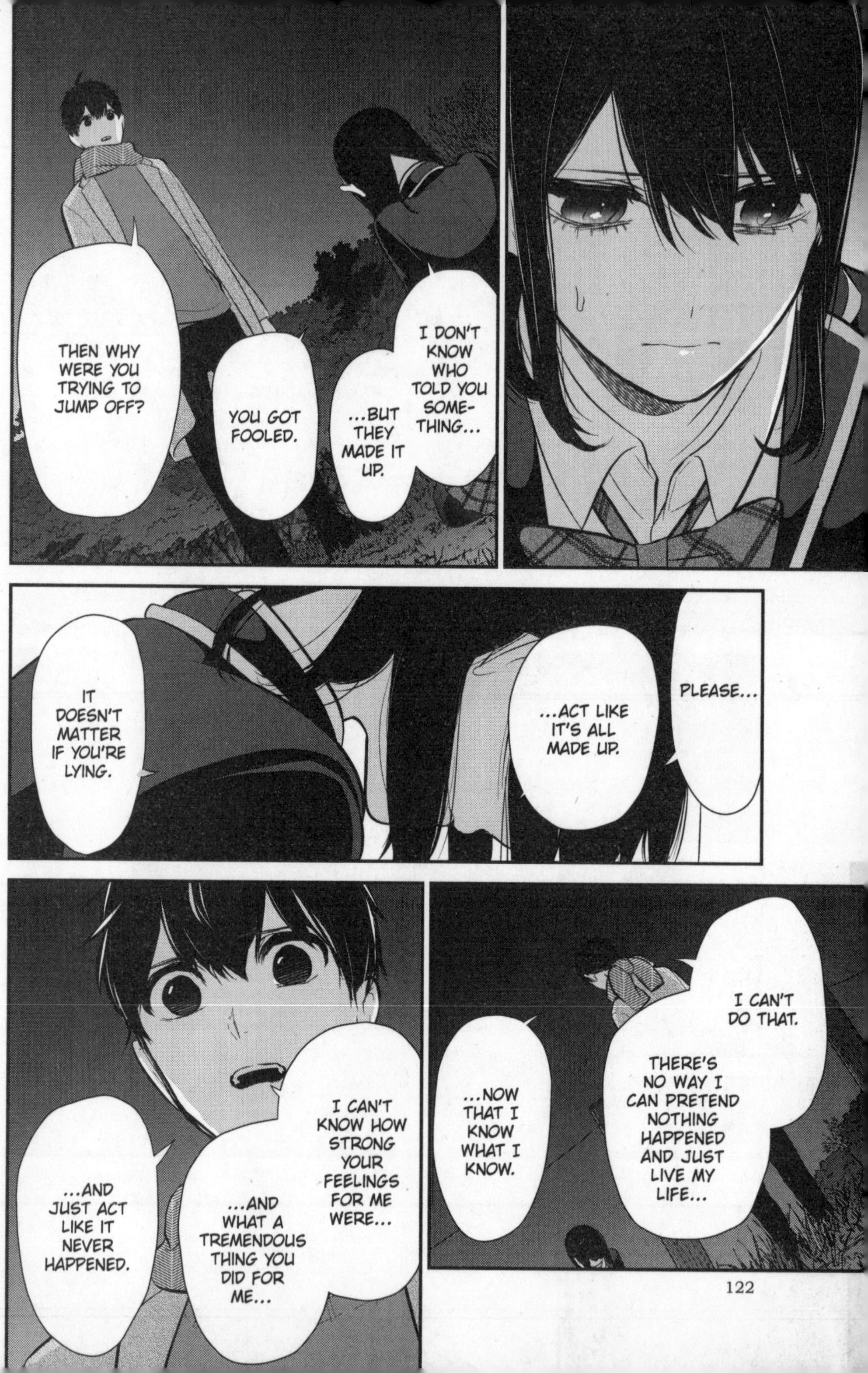
I DON'T KNOW WHO TOLD YOU SOME-THING...
...BUT THEY MADE IT UP.
YOU GOT FOOLED.
THEN WHY WERE YOU TRYING TO JUMP OFF?
PLEASE...
...ACT LIKE IT'S ALL MADE UP.
IT DOESN'T MATTER IF YOU'RE LYING.
I CAN'T DO THAT.
THERE'S NO WAY I CAN PRETEND NOTHING HAPPENED AND JUST LIVE MY LIFE...
...NOW THAT I KNOW WHAT I KNOW.
I CAN'T KNOW HOW STRONG YOUR FEELINGS FOR ME WERE...
...AND WHAT A TREMENDOUS THING YOU DID FOR ME...
...AND JUST ACT LIKE IT NEVER HAPPENED.

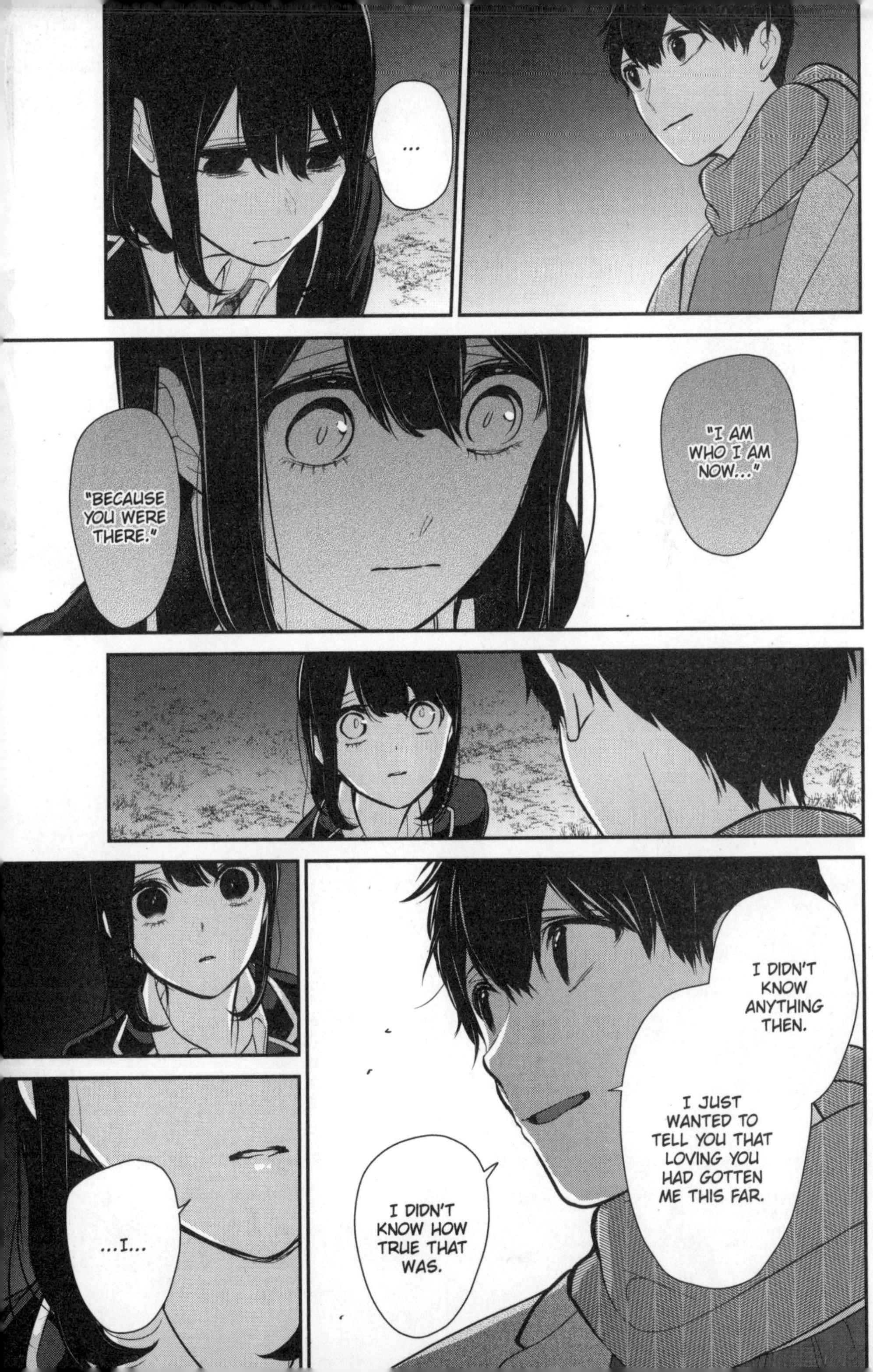
...
"I AM WHO I AM NOW..."
"BECAUSE YOU WERE THERE."
I DIDN'T KNOW ANYTHING THEN.
I JUST WANTED TO TELL YOU THAT LOVING YOU HAD GOTTEN ME THIS FAR.
I DIDN'T KNOW HOW TRUE THAT WAS.
...I...

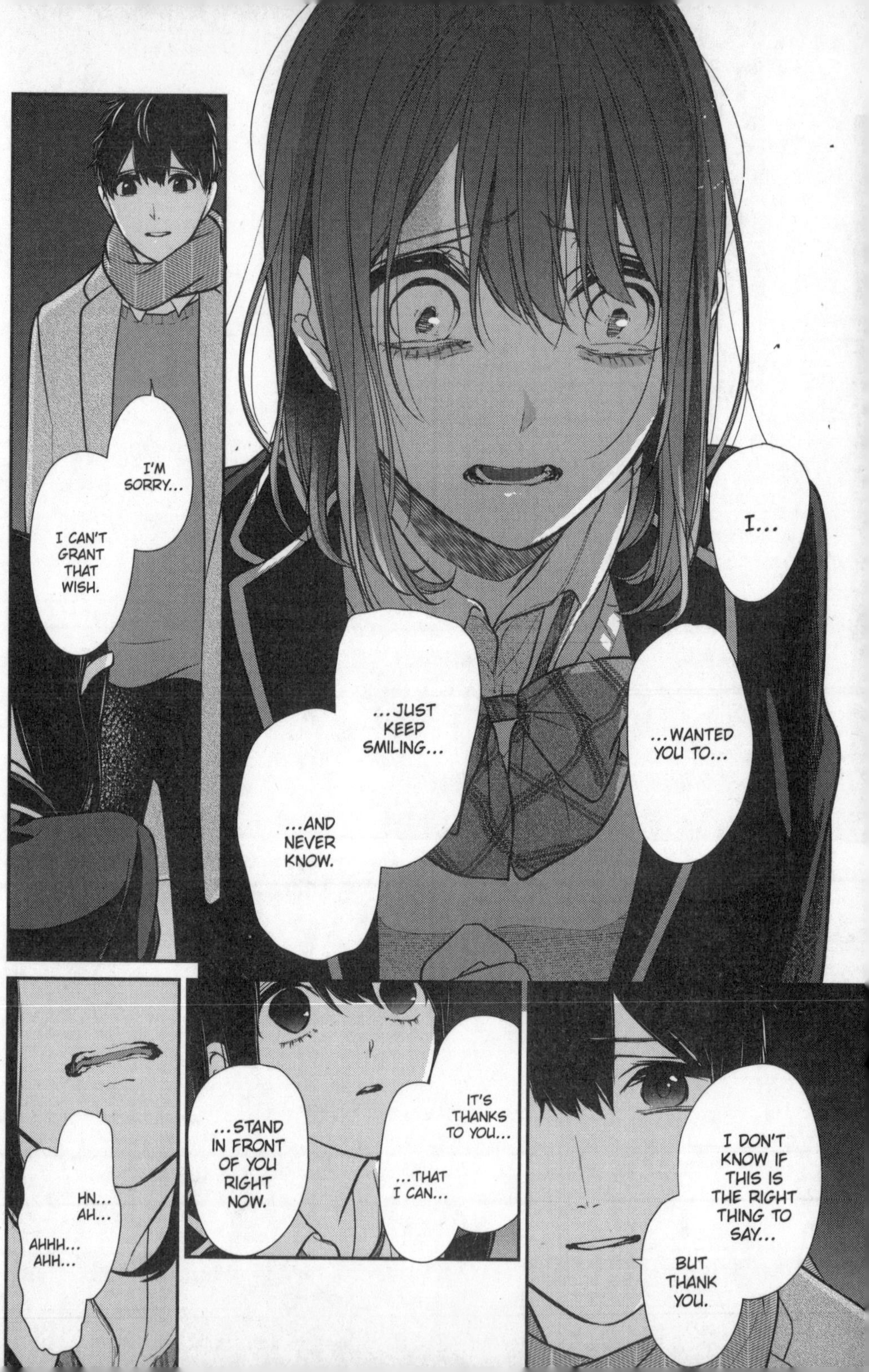
I...
...WANTED YOU TO...
...JUST KEEP SMILING...
...AND NEVER KNOW.
I'M SORRY...
I CAN'T GRANT THAT WISH.
I DON'T KNOW IF THIS IS THE RIGHT THING TO SAY...
BUT THANK YOU.
IT'S THANKS TO YOU...
...THAT I CAN...
...STAND IN FRONT OF YOU RIGHT NOW.
HN... AH...
AHHH... AHH...

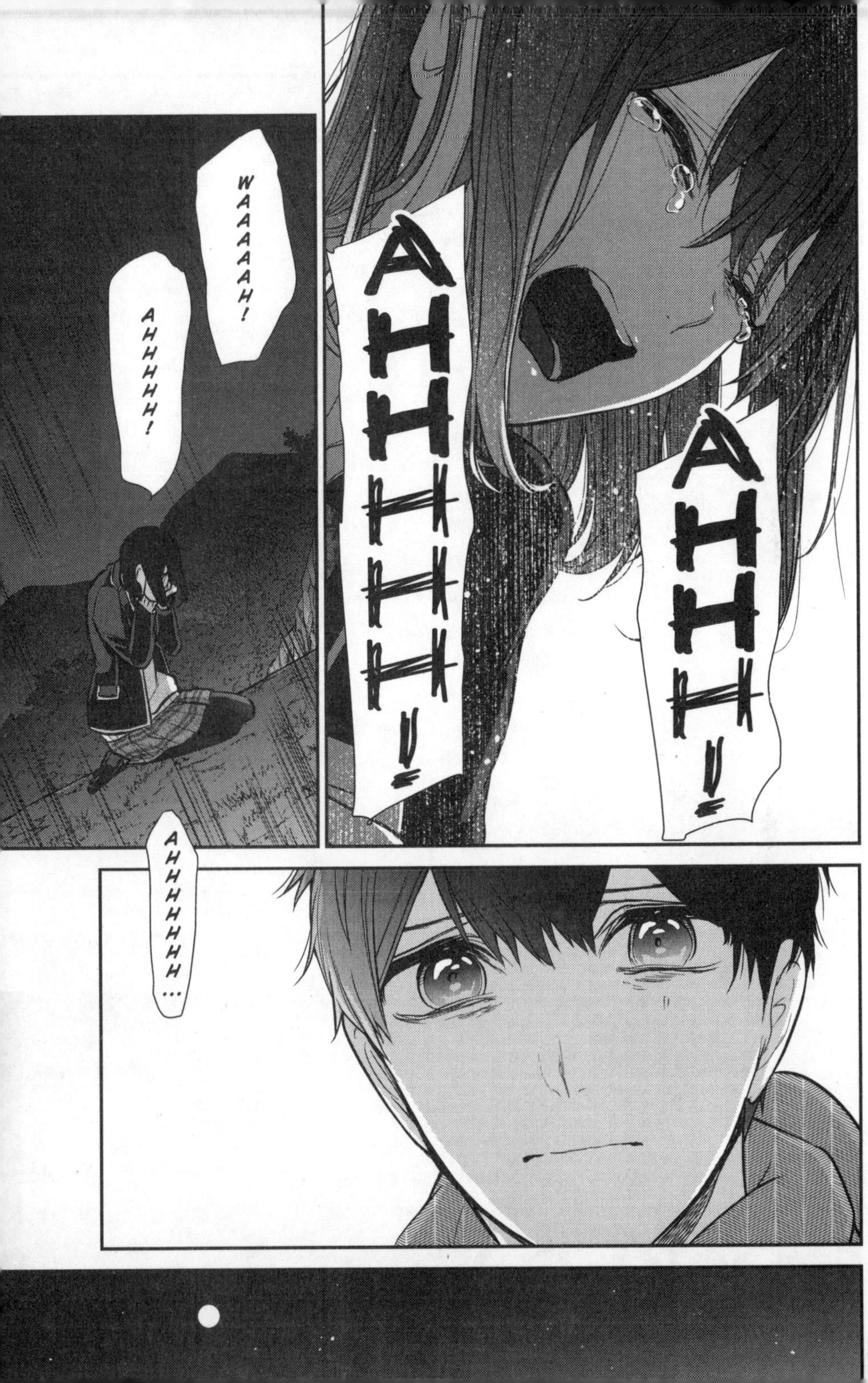
AHHH!!
AHHHHH!!
WAAAAAAH!
AHHHHHH!
AHHHHHHHH...

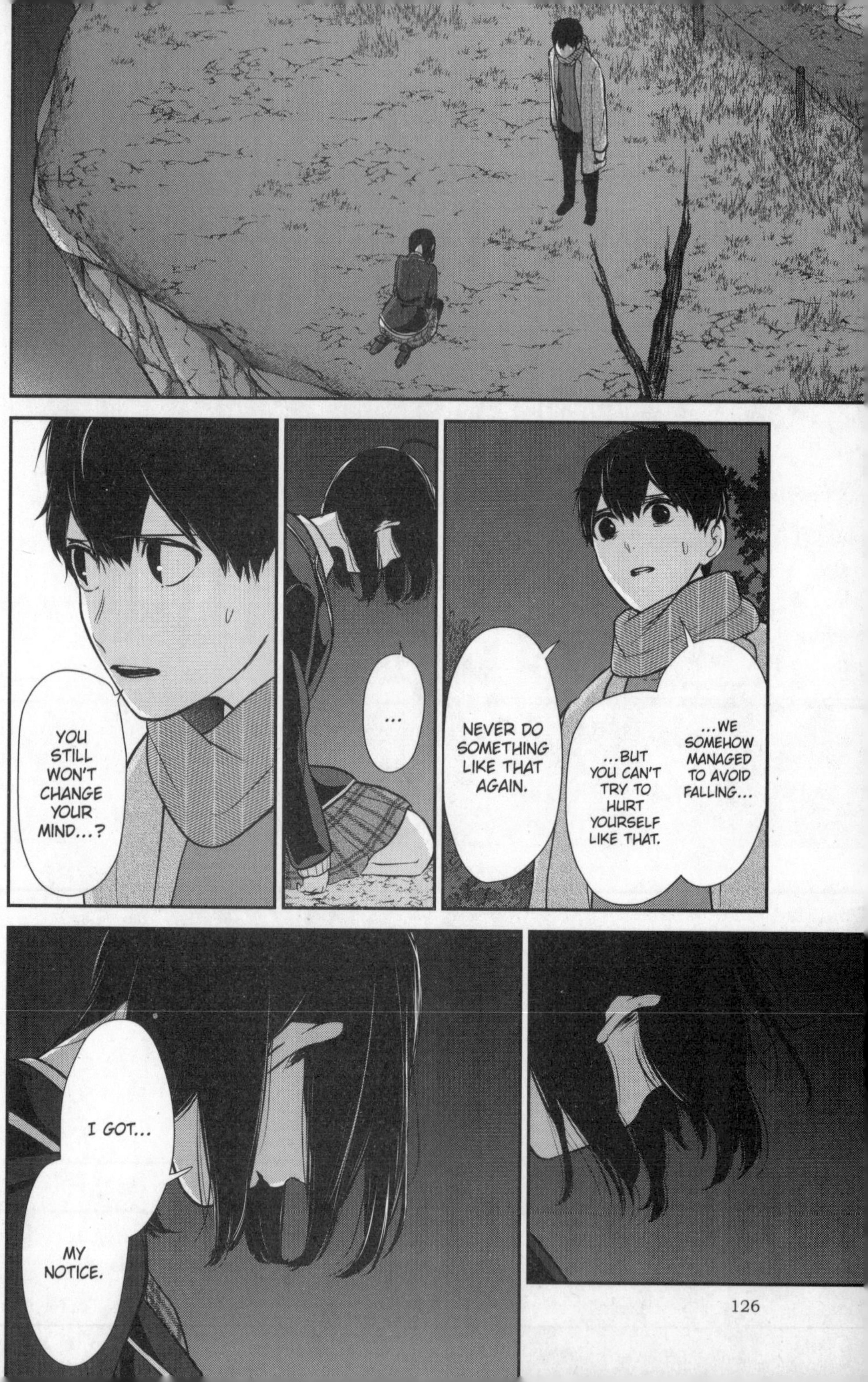
...WE SOMEHOW MANAGED TO AVOID FALLING...
...BUT YOU CAN'T TRY TO HURT YOURSELF LIKE THAT.
NEVER DO SOMETHING LIKE THAT AGAIN.
...
YOU STILL WON'T CHANGE YOUR MIND...?
I GOT...
MY NOTICE.

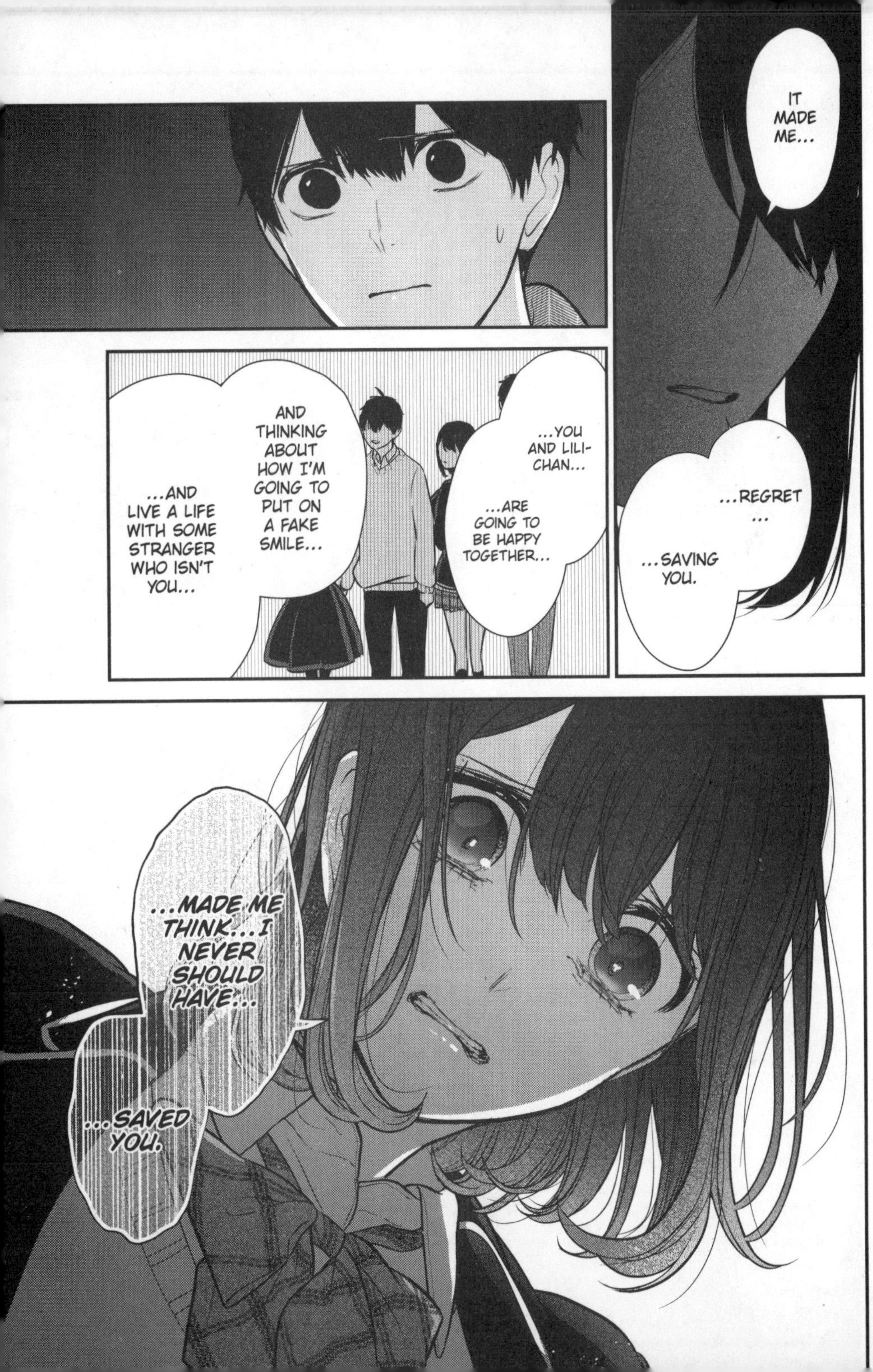
IT MADE ME...
...REGRET ...
...SAVING YOU.
...YOU AND LILI-CHAN...
...ARE GOING TO BE HAPPY TOGETHER...
AND THINKING ABOUT HOW I'M GOING TO PUT ON A FAKE SMILE...
...AND LIVE A LIFE WITH SOME STRANGER WHO ISN'T YOU...
...MADE ME THINK...I NEVER SHOULD HAVE...
...SAVED YOU.

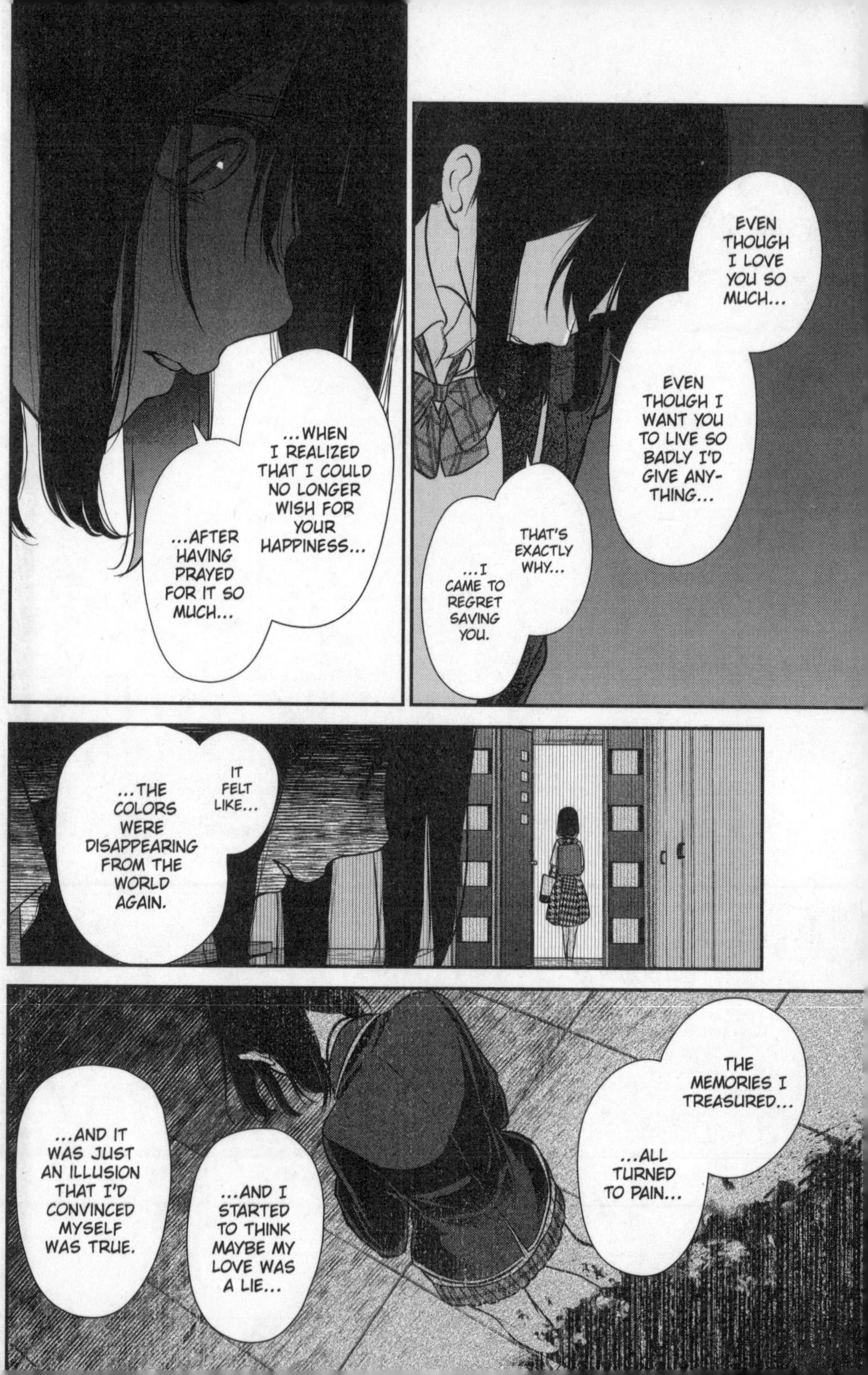
EVEN THOUGH I LOVE YOU SO MUCH...
EVEN THOUGH I WANT YOU TO LIVE SO BADLY I'D GIVE ANY-THING...
THAT'S EXACTLY WHY...
...I CAME TO REGRET SAVING YOU.
...WHEN I REALIZED THAT I COULD NO LONGER WISH FOR YOUR HAPPINESS...
...AFTER HAVING PRAYED FOR IT SO MUCH...
IT FELT LIKE...
...THE COLORS WERE DISAPPEARING FROM THE WORLD AGAIN.
THE MEMORIES I TREASURED...
...ALL TURNED TO PAIN...
...AND I STARTED TO THINK MAYBE MY LOVE WAS A LIE...
...AND IT WAS JUST AN ILLUSION THAT I'D CONVINCED MYSELF WAS TRUE.

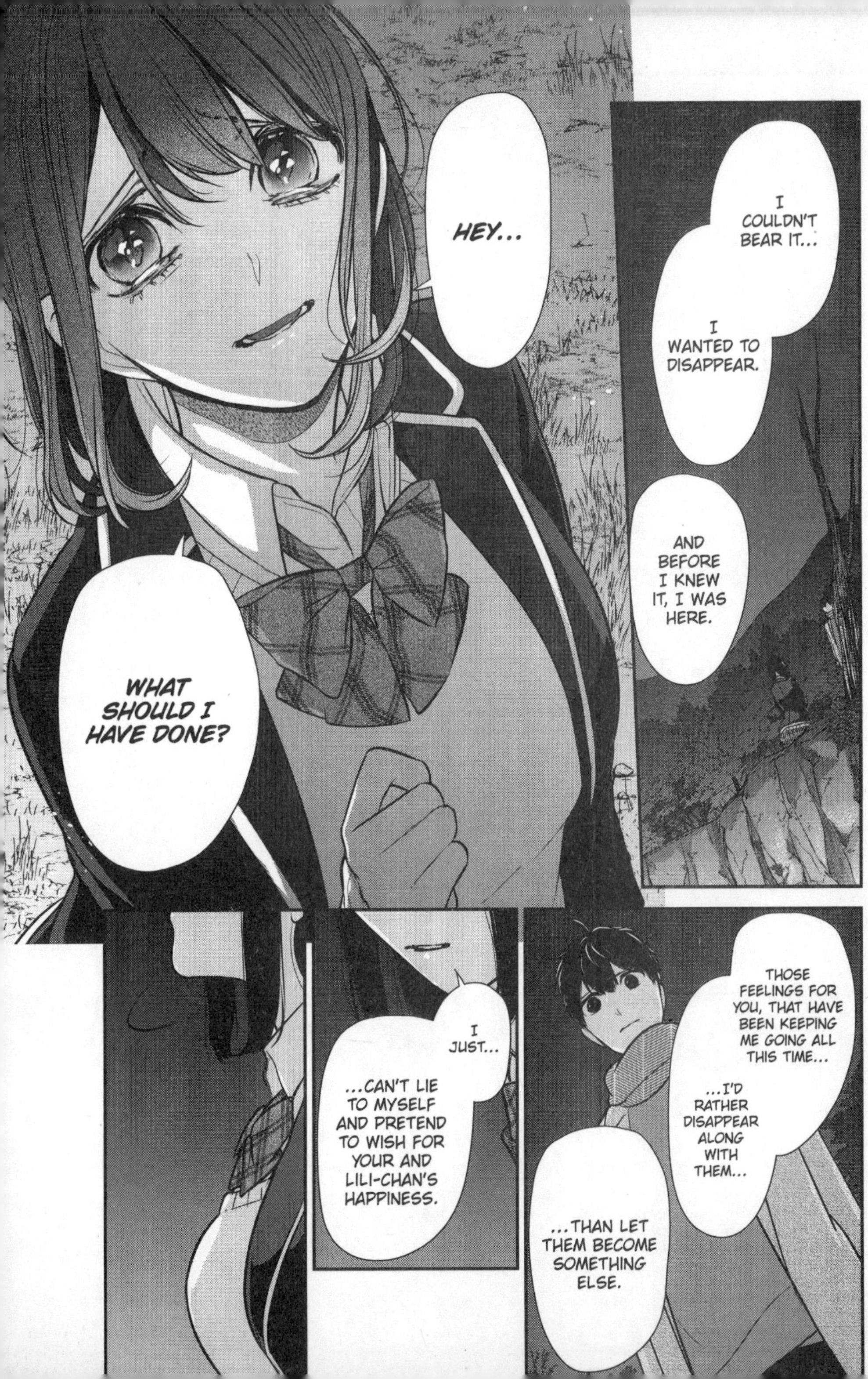
I COULDN'T BEAR IT...
I WANTED TO DISAPPEAR.
AND BEFORE I KNEW IT, I WAS HERE.
HEY...
WHAT SHOULD I HAVE DONE?
THOSE FEELINGS FOR YOU, THAT HAVE BEEN KEEPING ME GOING ALL THIS TIME...
...I'D RATHER DISAPPEAR ALONG WITH THEM...
...THAN LET THEM BECOME SOMETHING ELSE.
I JUST...
...CAN'T LIE TO MYSELF AND PRETEND TO WISH FOR YOUR AND LILI-CHAN'S HAPPINESS.

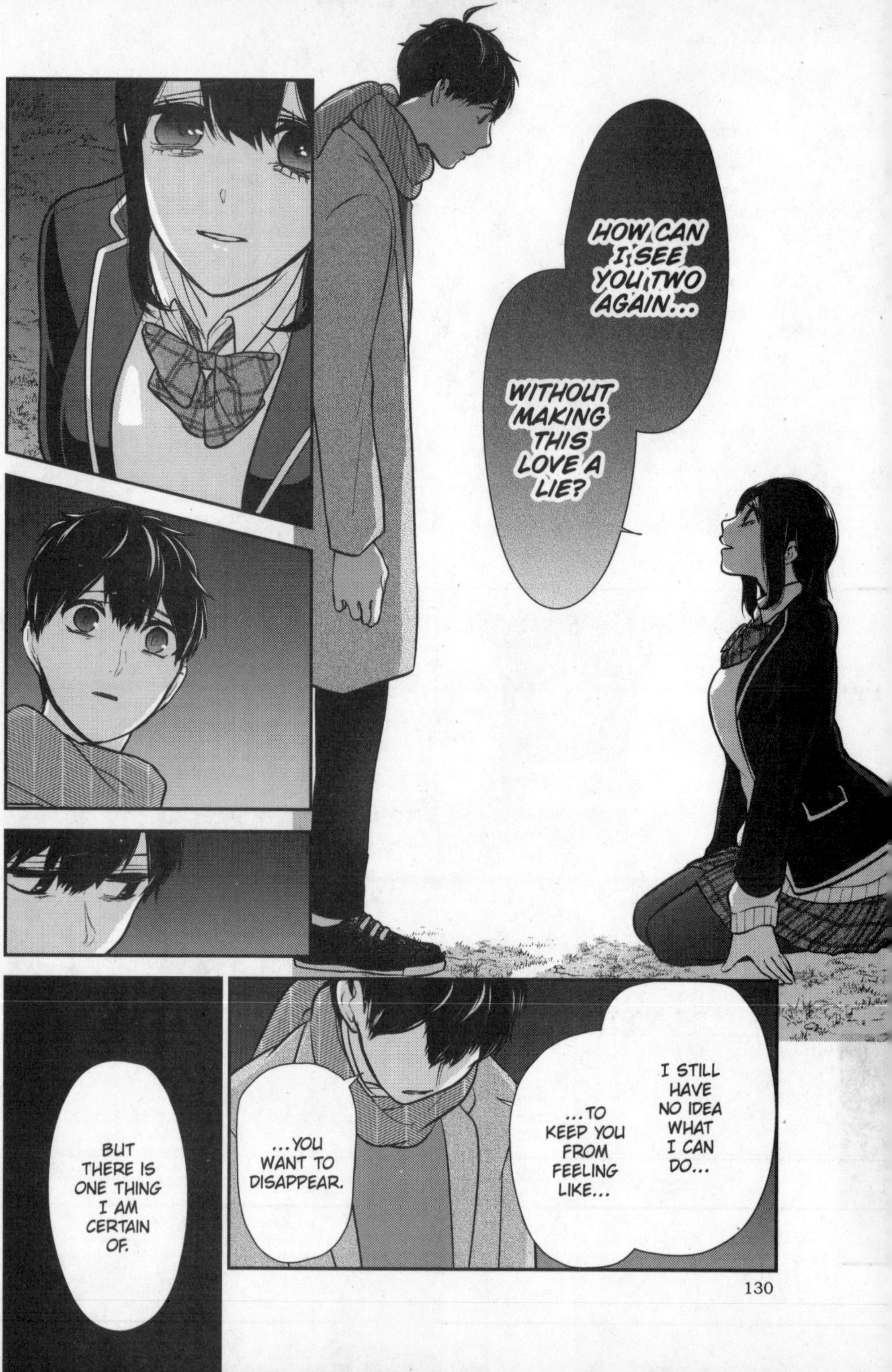
HOW CAN I SEE YOU TWO AGAIN...
WITHOUT MAKING THIS LOVE A LIE?
I STILL HAVE NO IDEA WHAT I CAN DO...
...TO KEEP YOU FROM FEELING LIKE...
...YOU WANT TO DISAPPEAR.
BUT THERE IS ONE THING I AM CERTAIN OF.

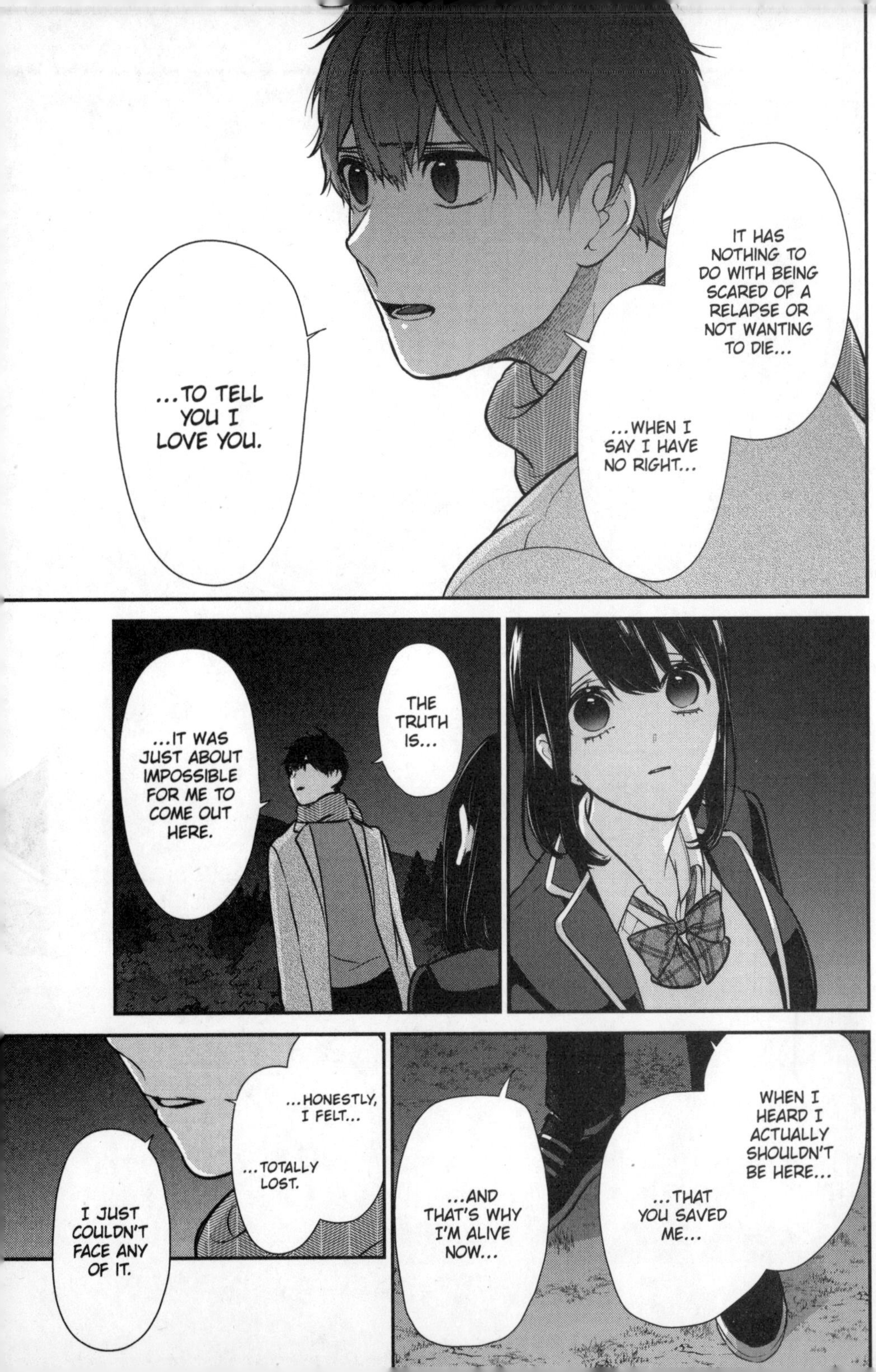
IT HAS NOTHING TO DO WITH BEING SCARED OF A RELAPSE OR NOT WANTING TO DIE...
...WHEN I SAY I HAVE NO RIGHT...
...TO TELL YOU I LOVE YOU.
THE TRUTH IS...
...IT WAS JUST ABOUT IMPOSSIBLE FOR ME TO COME OUT HERE.
WHEN I HEARD I ACTUALLY SHOULDN'T BE HERE...
...THAT YOU SAVED ME...
...AND THAT'S WHY I'M ALIVE NOW...
...HONESTLY, I FELT...
...TOTALLY LOST.
I JUST COULDN'T FACE ANY OF IT.

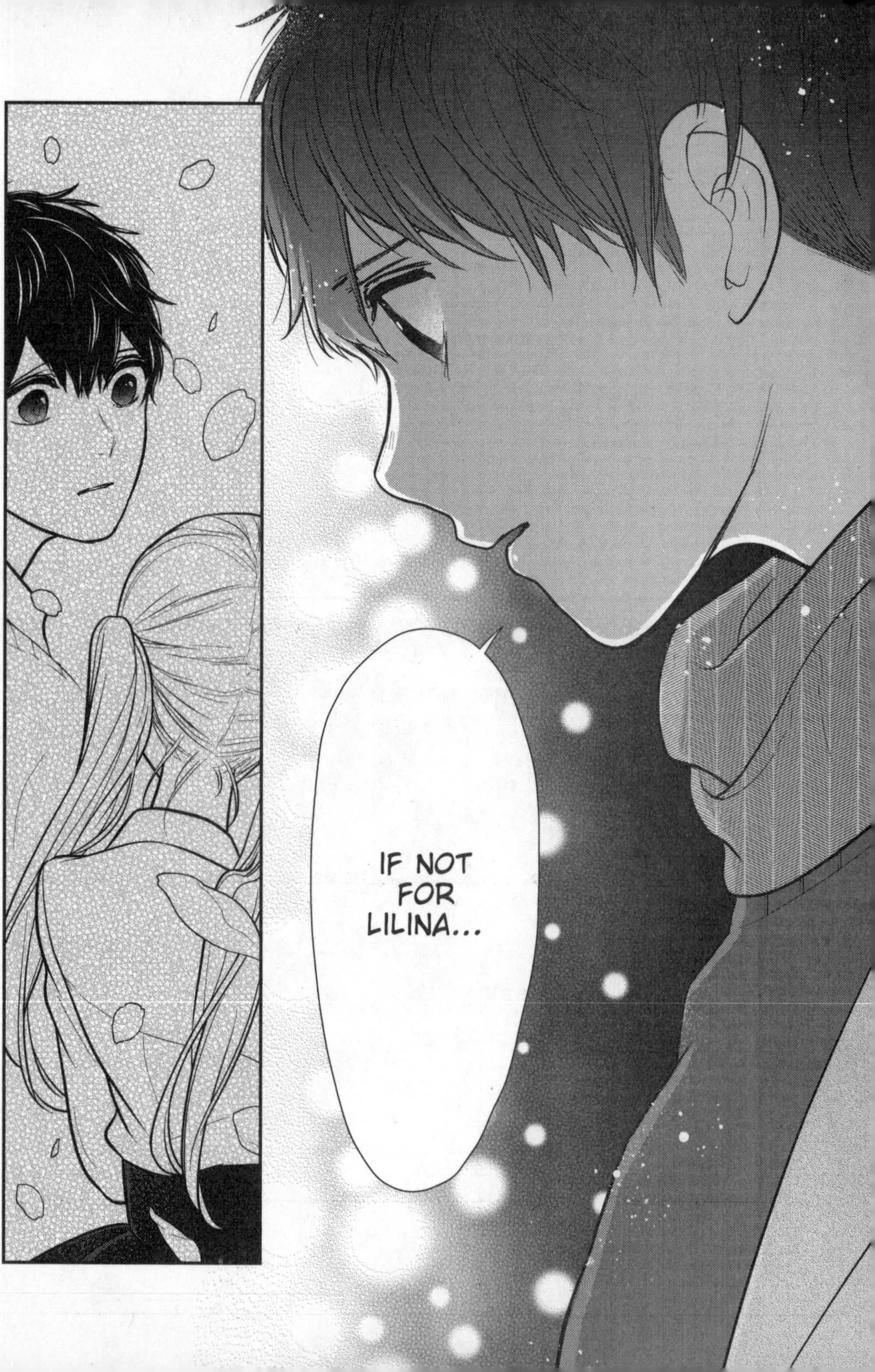
IF NOT FOR LILINA...

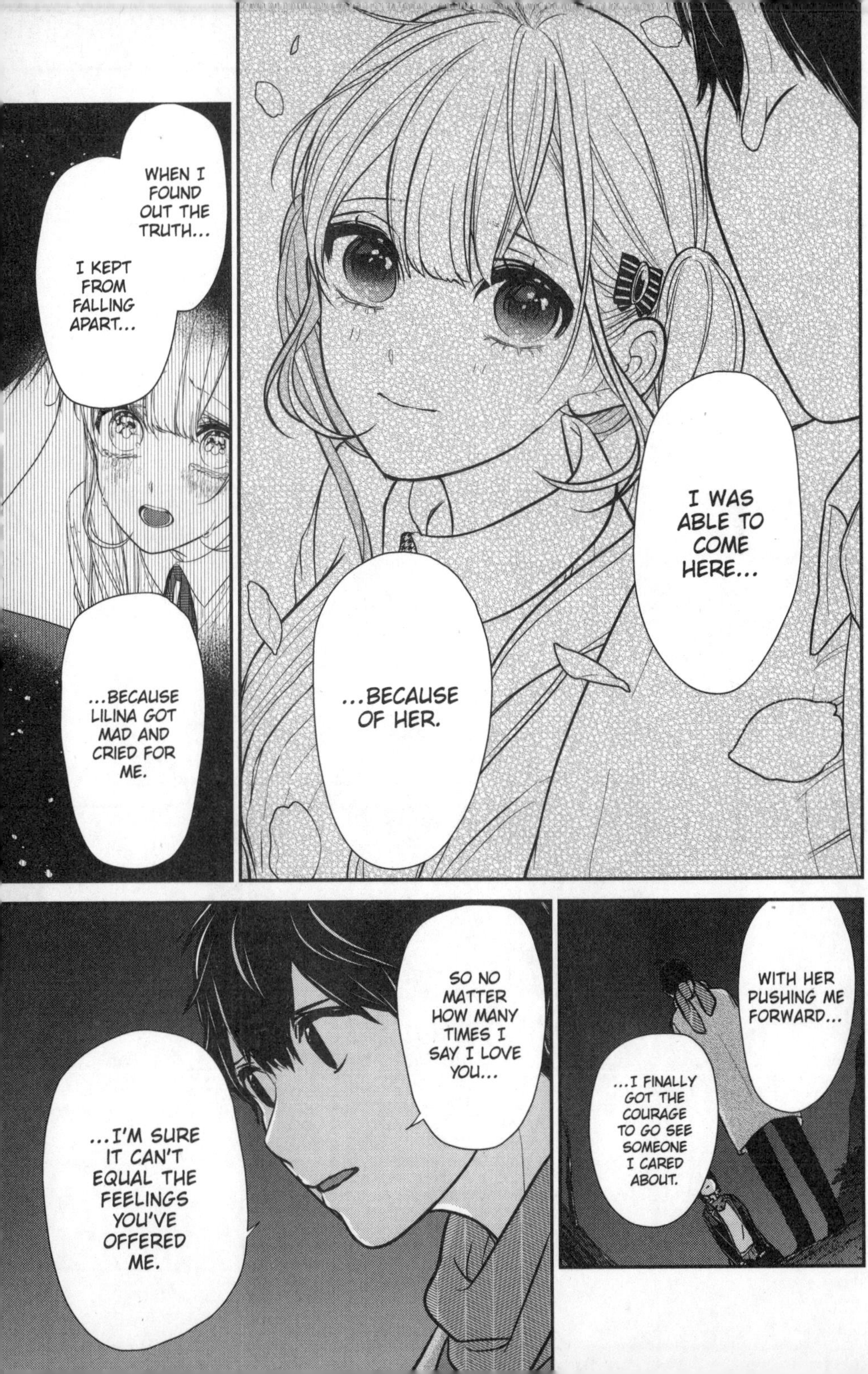
I WAS ABLE TO COME HERE...
...BECAUSE OF HER.
WHEN I FOUND OUT THE TRUTH...
I KEPT FROM FALLING APART...
...BECAUSE LILINA GOT MAD AND CRIED FOR ME.
WITH HER PUSHING ME FORWARD...
...I FINALLY GOT THE COURAGE TO GO SEE SOMEONE I CARED ABOUT.
SO NO MATTER HOW MANY TIMES I SAY I LOVE YOU...
...I'M SURE IT CAN'T EQUAL THE FEELINGS YOU'VE OFFERED ME.

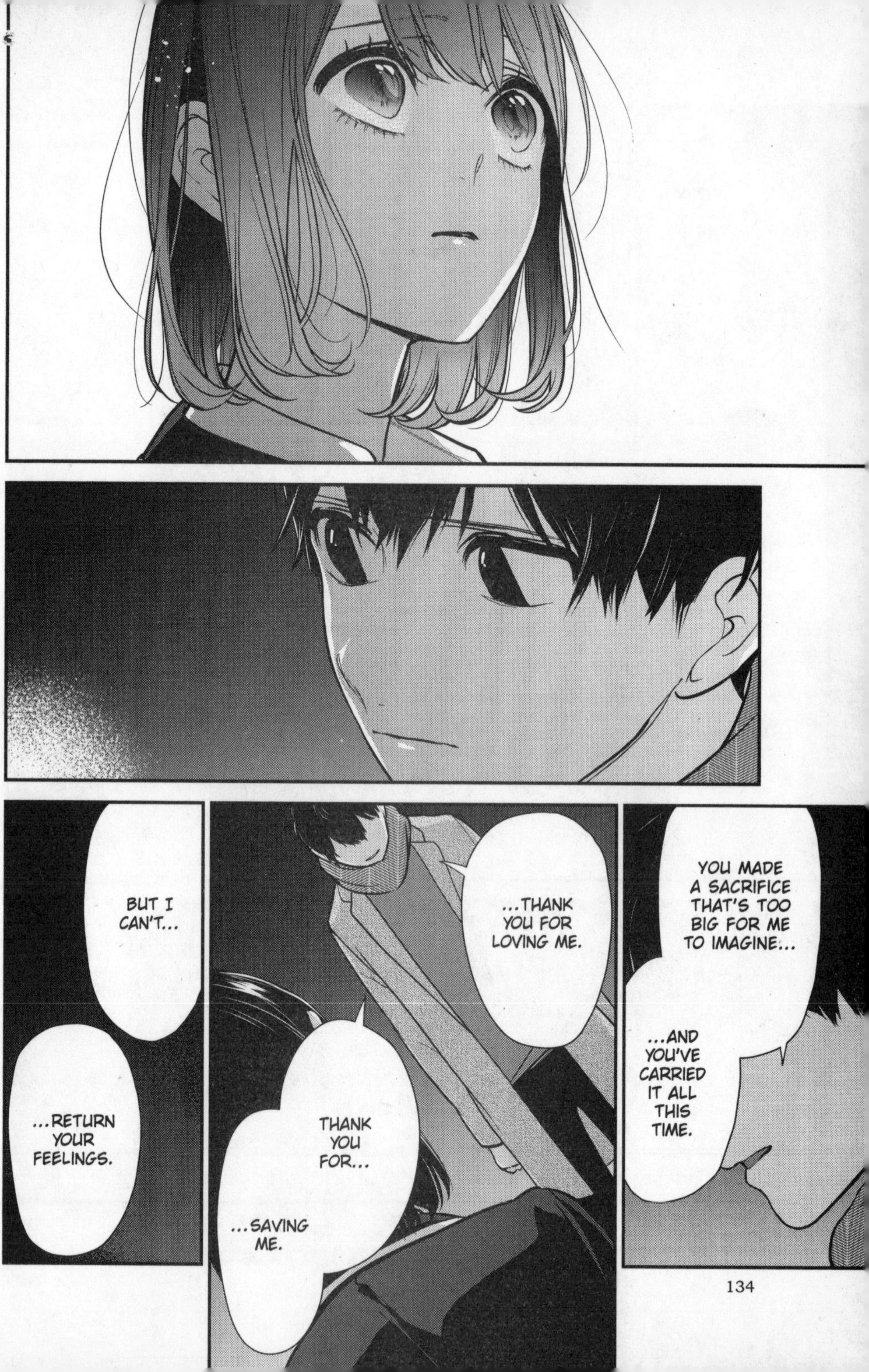
YOU MADE A SACRIFICE THAT'S TOO BIG FOR ME TO IMAGINE...
...AND YOU'VE CARRIED IT ALL THIS TIME.
...THANK YOU FOR LOVING ME.
THANK YOU FOR...
...SAVING ME.
BUT I CAN'T...
...RETURN YOUR FEELINGS.

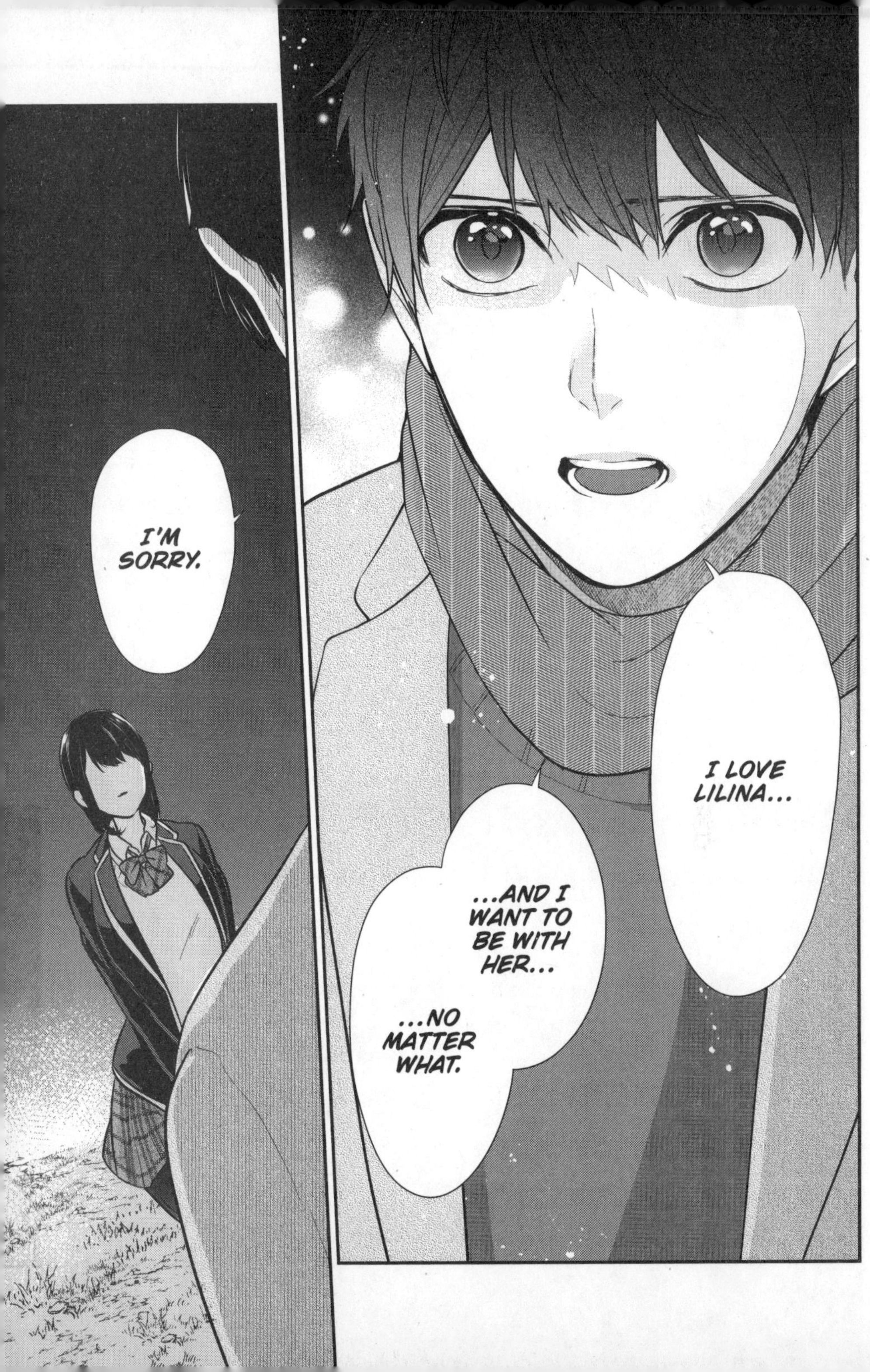
I LOVE LILINA...
...AND I WANT TO BE WITH HER...
...NO MATTER WHAT.
I'M SORRY.

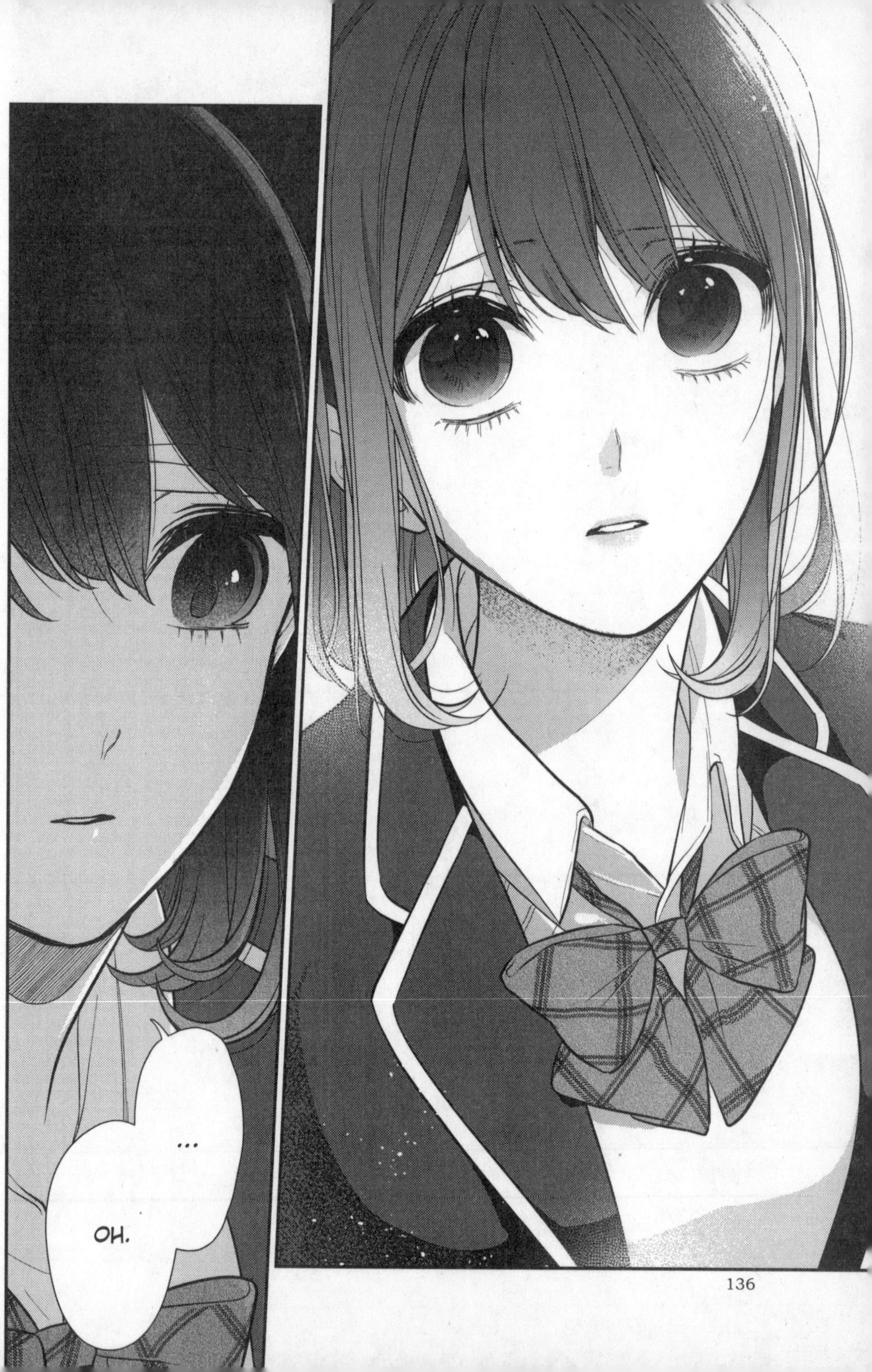
...
OH.

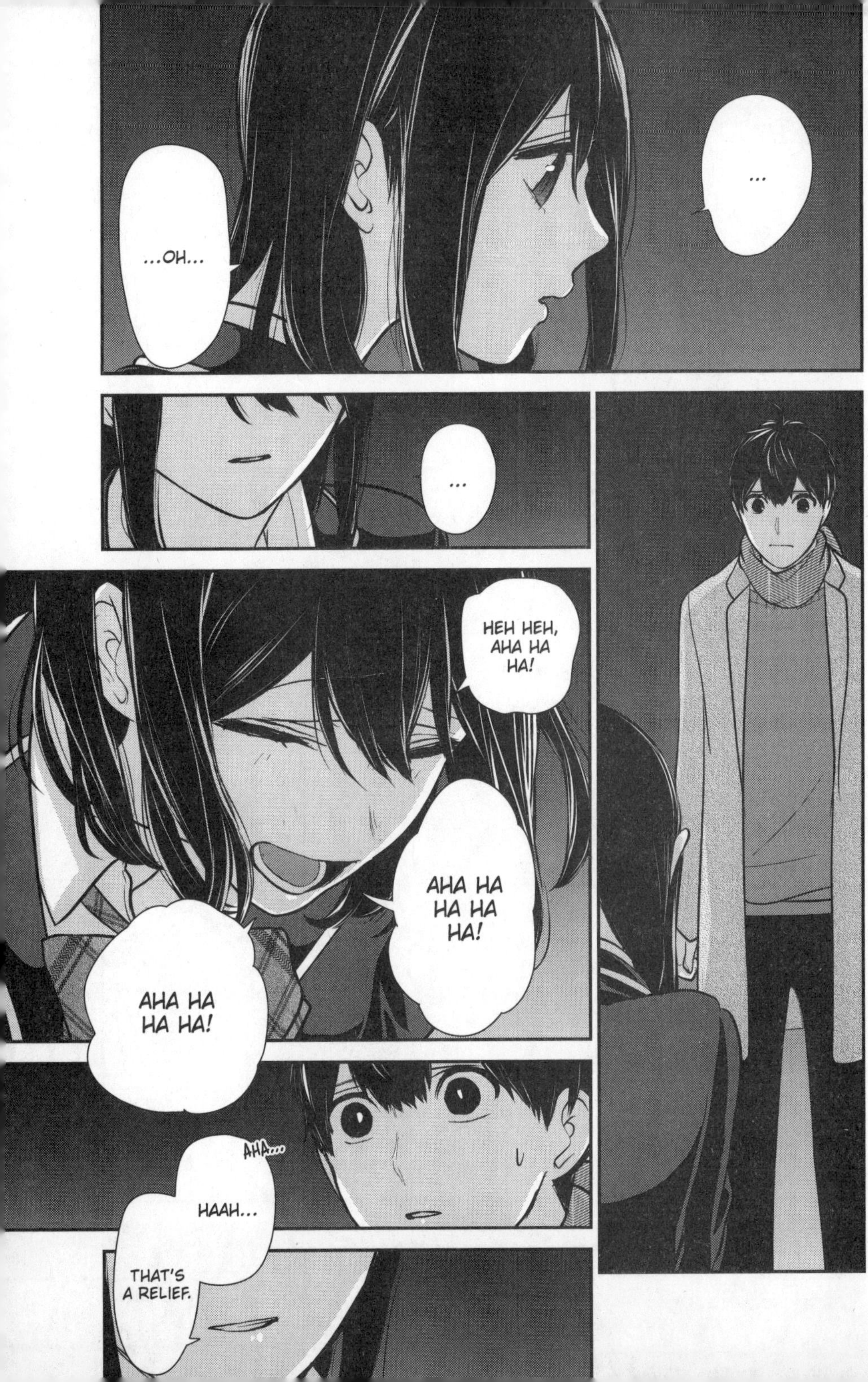
...
...OH...
...
HEH HEH, AHA HA HA!
AHA HA HA HA HA!
AHA HA HA HA!
AHA...
HAAH...
THAT'S A RELIEF.

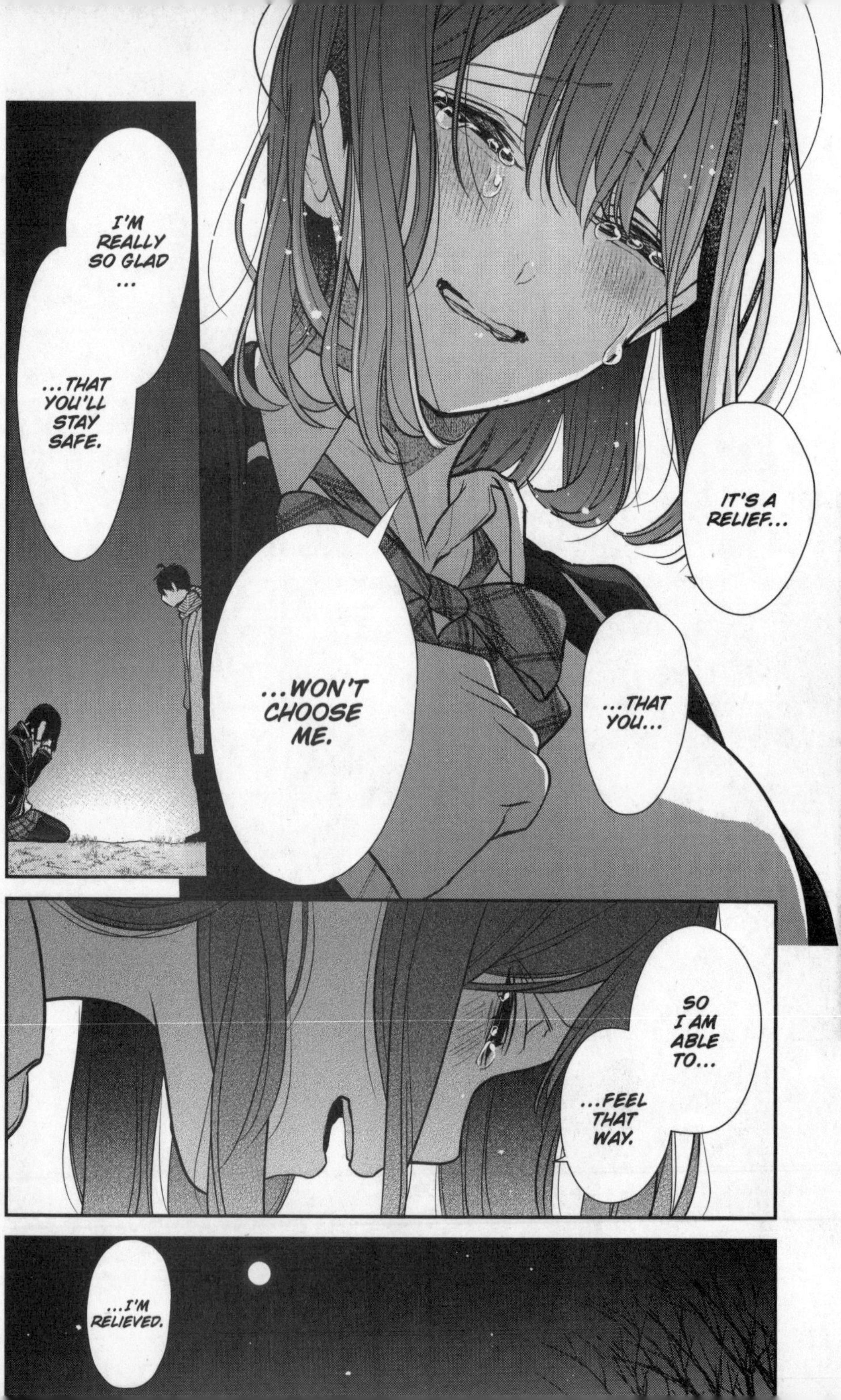
IT'S A RELIEF...
...THAT YOU...
...WON'T CHOOSE ME.
I'M REALLY SO GLAD ...
...THAT YOU'LL STAY SAFE.
SO I AM ABLE TO...
...FEEL THAT WAY.
...I'M RELIEVED.

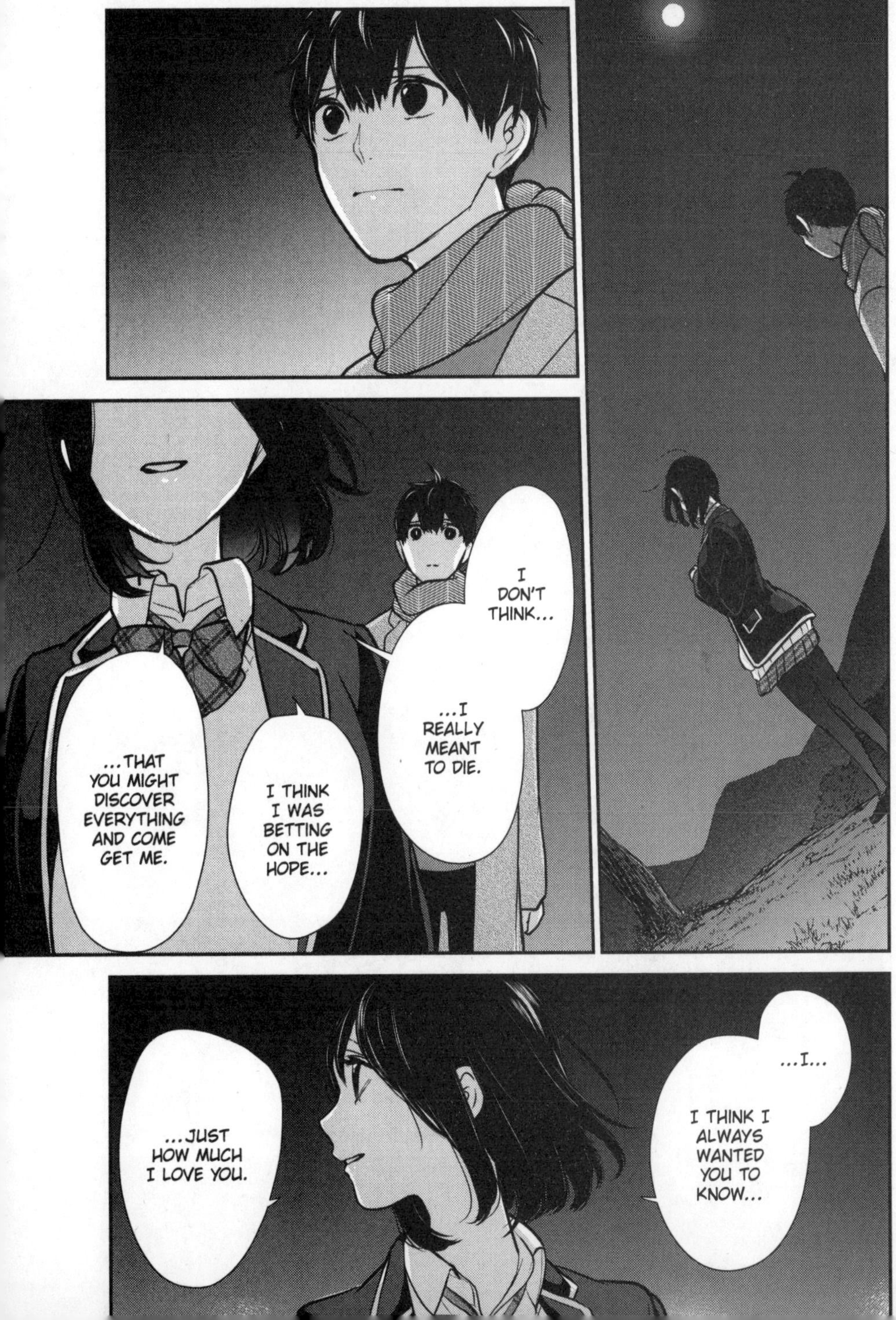
I DON'T THINK...
...I REALLY MEANT TO DIE.
I THINK I WAS BETTING ON THE HOPE...
...THAT YOU MIGHT DISCOVER EVERYTHING AND COME GET ME.
...I...
I THINK I ALWAYS WANTED YOU TO KNOW...
...JUST HOW MUCH I LOVE YOU.

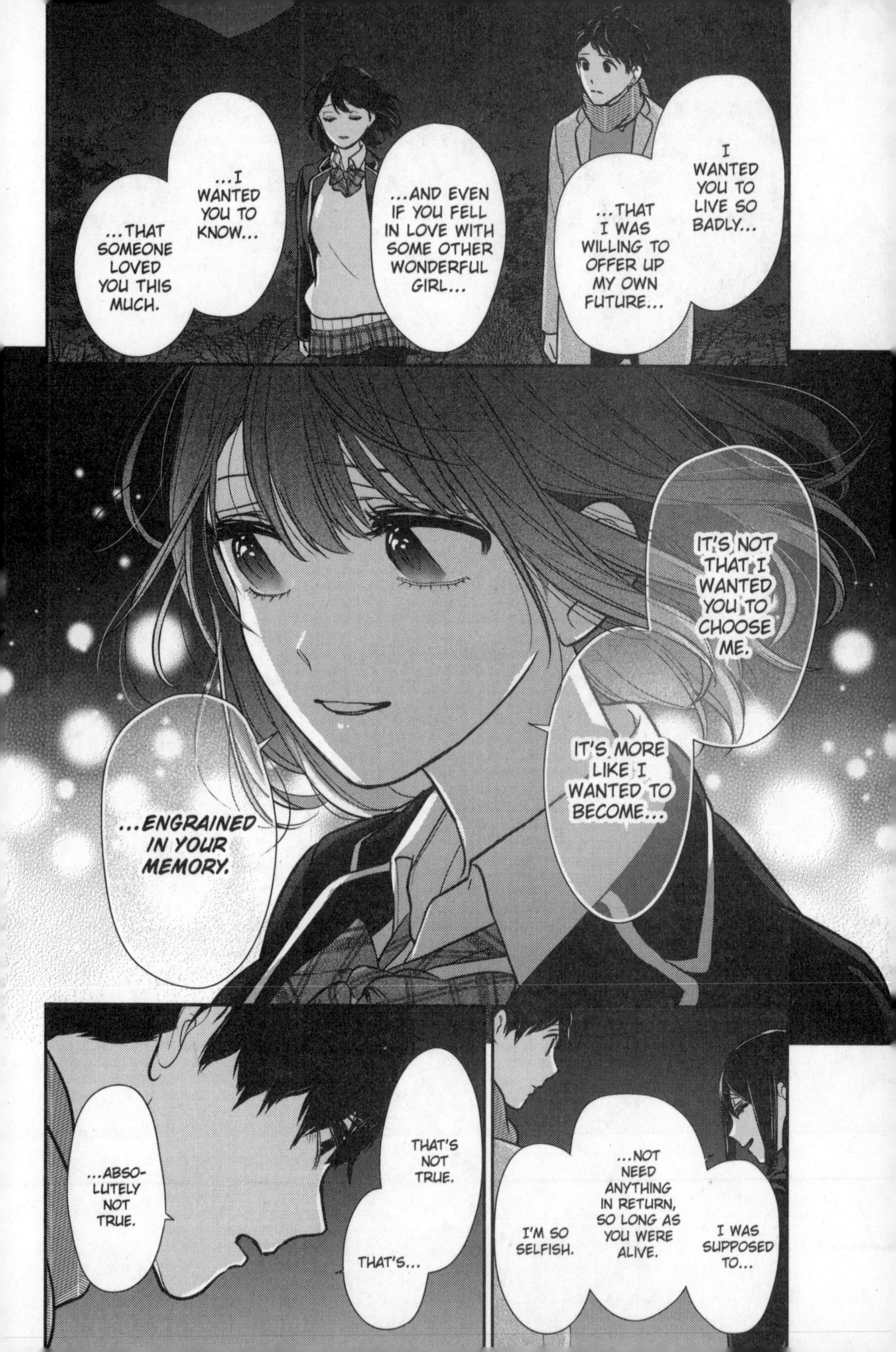
I WANTED YOU TO LIVE SO BADLY...
...THAT I WAS WILLING TO OFFER UP MY OWN FUTURE...
...AND EVEN IF YOU FELL IN LOVE WITH SOME OTHER WONDERFUL GIRL...
...I WANTED YOU TO KNOW...
...THAT SOMEONE LOVED YOU THIS MUCH.
IT'S NOT THAT I WANTED YOU TO CHOOSE ME.
IT'S MORE LIKE I WANTED TO BECOME...
...ENGRAINED IN YOUR MEMORY.
I WAS SUPPOSED TO...
...NOT NEED ANYTHING IN RETURN, SO LONG AS YOU WERE ALIVE.
I'M SO SELFISH.
THAT'S NOT TRUE.
THAT'S...
...ABSO-LUTELY NOT TRUE.

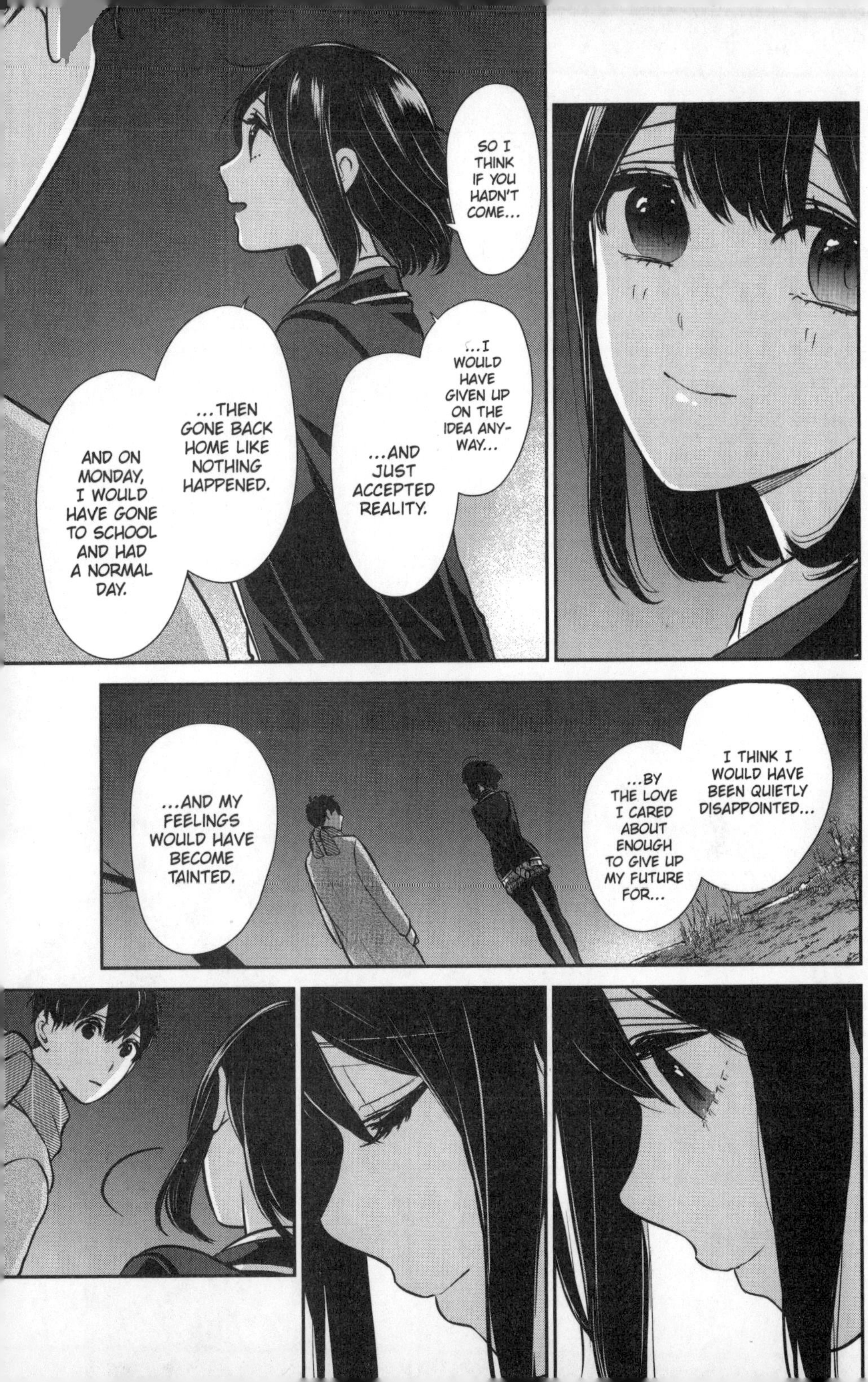
SO I THINK IF YOU HADN'T COME...
...I WOULD HAVE GIVEN UP ON THE IDEA ANYWAY...
...AND JUST ACCEPTED REALITY.
...THEN GONE BACK HOME LIKE NOTHING HAPPENED.
AND ON MONDAY, I WOULD HAVE GONE TO SCHOOL AND HAD A NORMAL DAY.
I THINK I WOULD HAVE BEEN QUIETLY DISAPPOINTED...
...BY THE LOVE I CARED ABOUT ENOUGH TO GIVE UP MY FUTURE FOR...
...AND MY FEELINGS WOULD HAVE BECOME TAINTED.

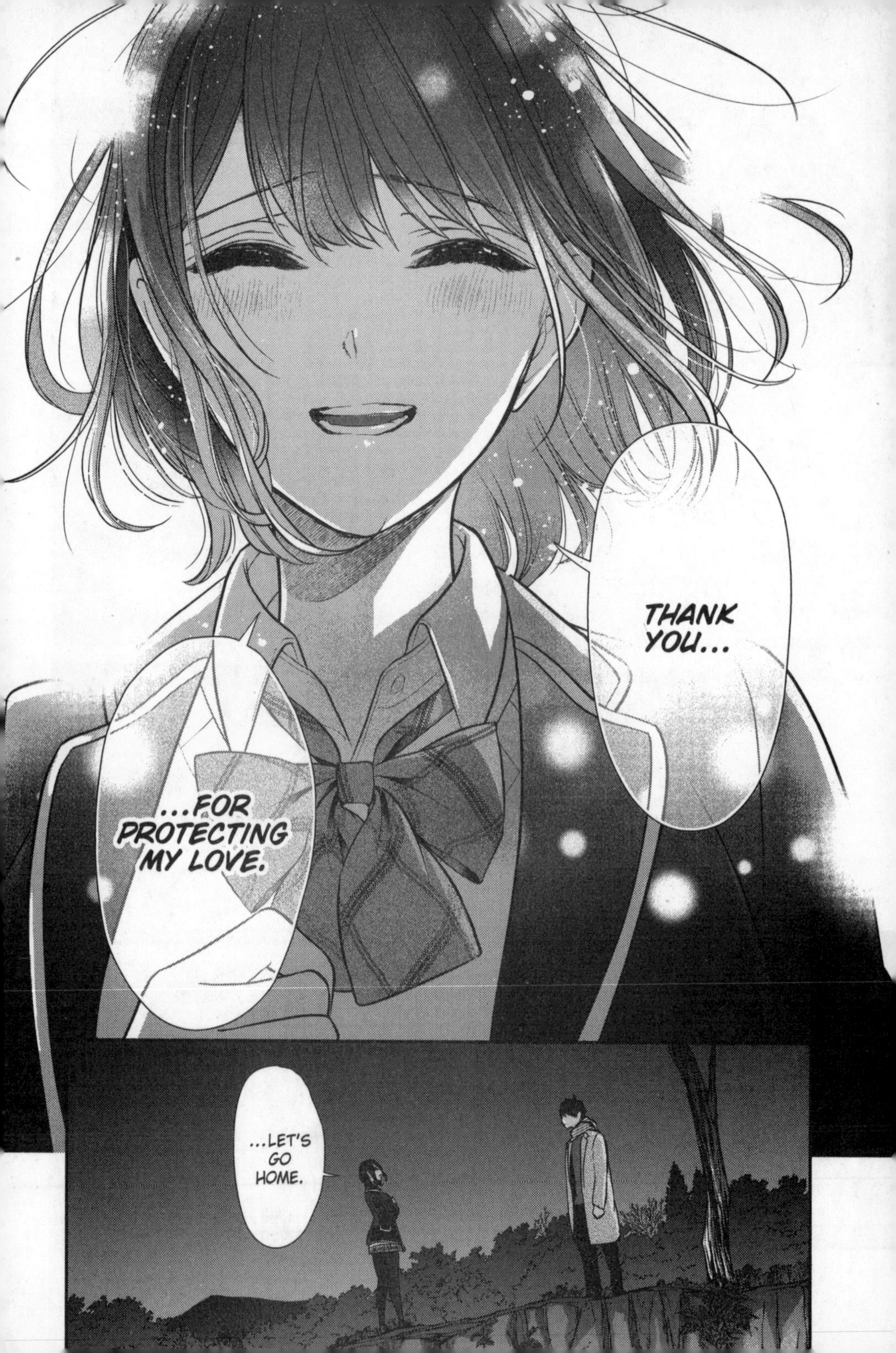
THANK YOU...
...FOR PROTECTING MY LOVE.
...LET'S GO HOME.

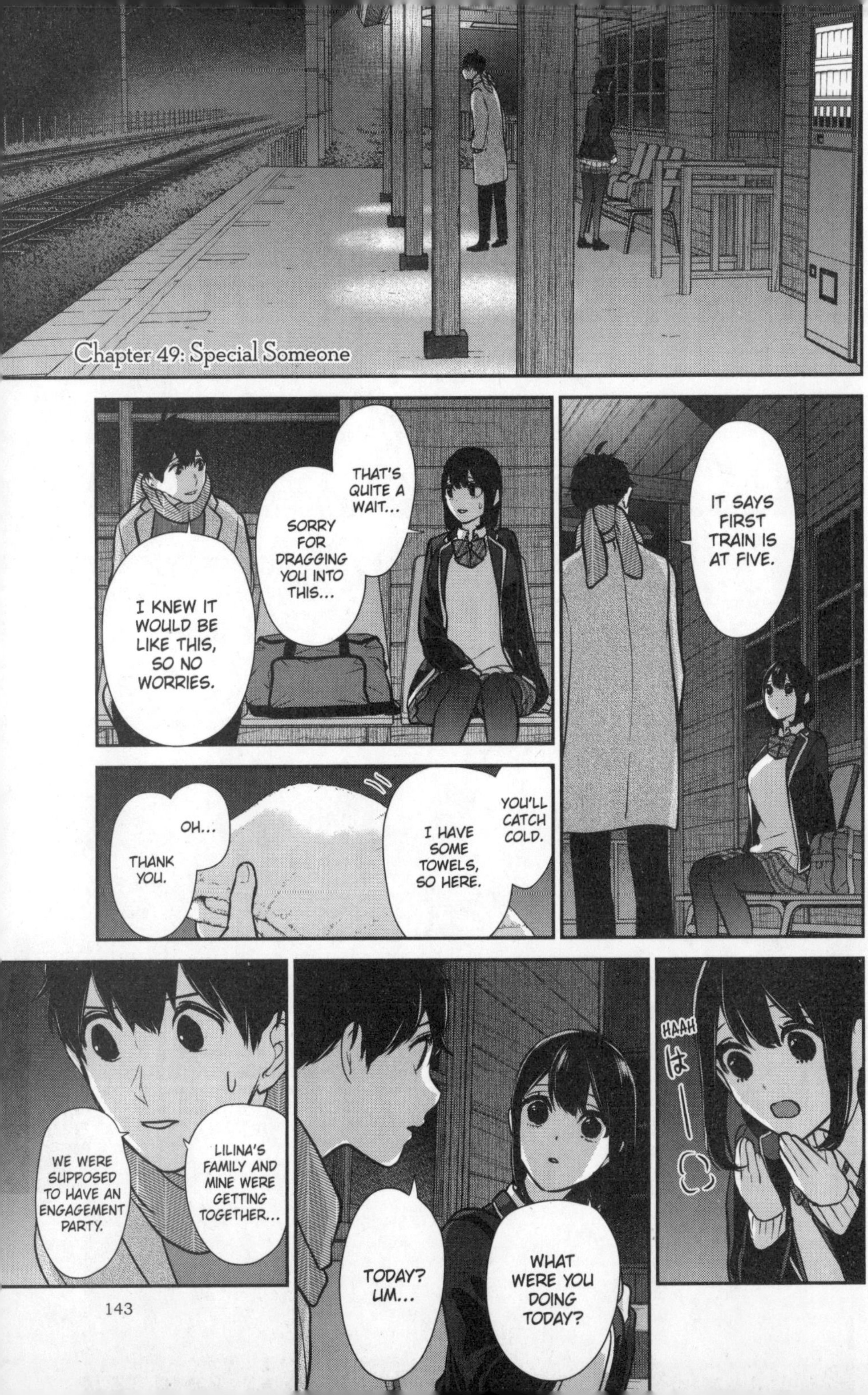
Chapter 49: Special Someone
IT SAYS FIRST TRAIN IS AT FIVE.
THAT'S QUITE A WAIT...
SORRY FOR DRAGGING YOU INTO THIS...
I KNEW IT WOULD BE LIKE THIS, SO NO WORRIES.
YOU'LL CATCH COLD.
I HAVE SOME TOWELS, SO HERE.
OH...
THANK YOU.
HAAH
はー
WHAT WERE YOU DOING TODAY?
TODAY? UM...
LILINA'S FAMILY AND MINE WERE GETTING TOGETHER...
WE WERE SUPPOSED TO HAVE AN ENGAGEMENT PARTY.

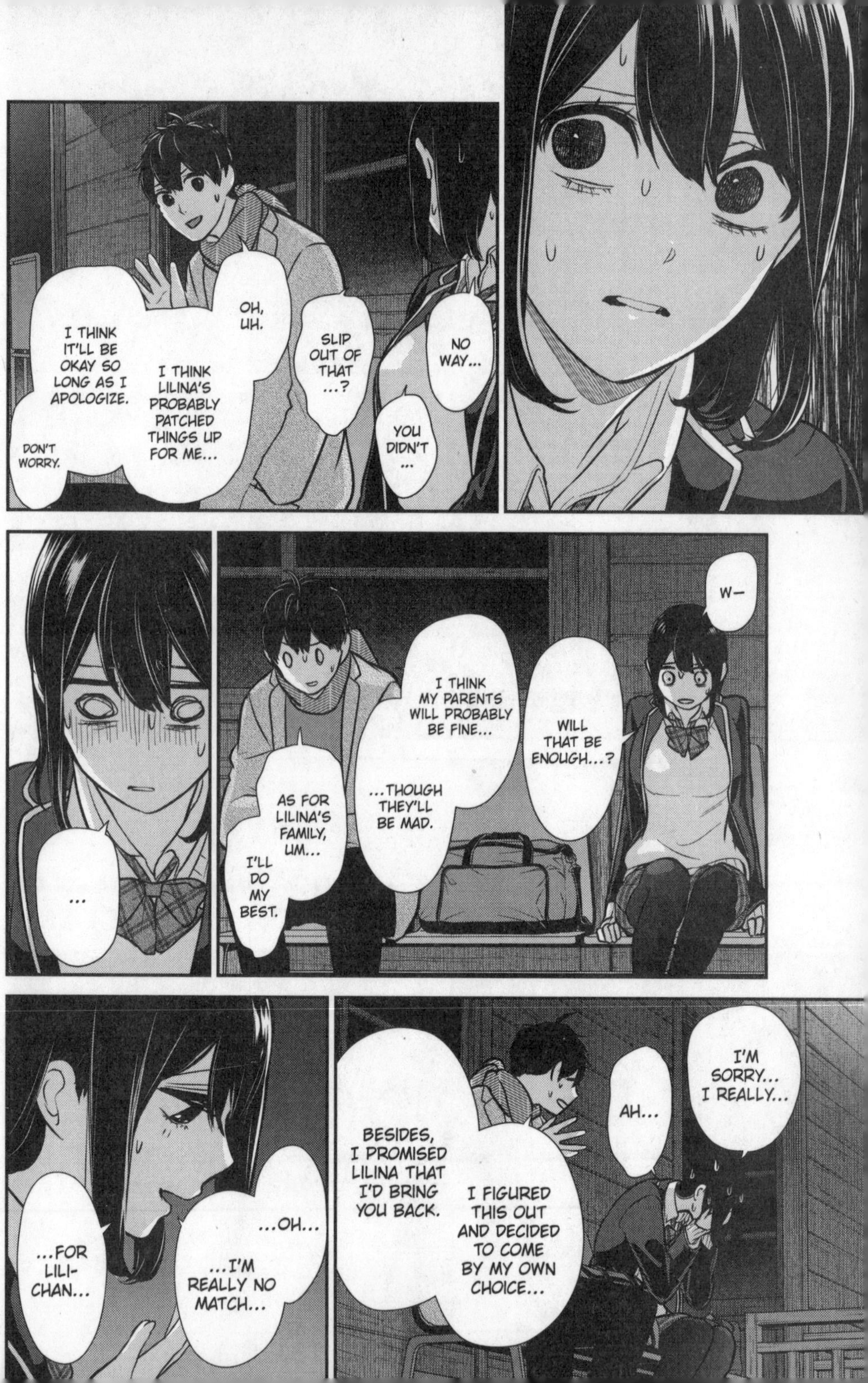
NO WAY...
YOU DIDN'T ...
SLIP OUT OF THAT ...?
OH, UH.
I THINK LILINA'S PROBABLY PATCHED THINGS UP FOR ME...
I THINK IT'LL BE OKAY SO LONG AS I APOLOGIZE.
DON'T WORRY.
W—
WILL THAT BE ENOUGH...?
I THINK MY PARENTS WILL PROBABLY BE FINE...
...THOUGH THEY'LL BE MAD.
AS FOR LILINA'S FAMILY, UM...
I'LL DO MY BEST.
...
I'M SORRY... I REALLY...
AH...
I FIGURED THIS OUT AND DECIDED TO COME BY MY OWN CHOICE...
BESIDES, I PROMISED LILINA THAT I'D BRING YOU BACK.
...OH...
...I'M REALLY NO MATCH...
...FOR LILI-CHAN...

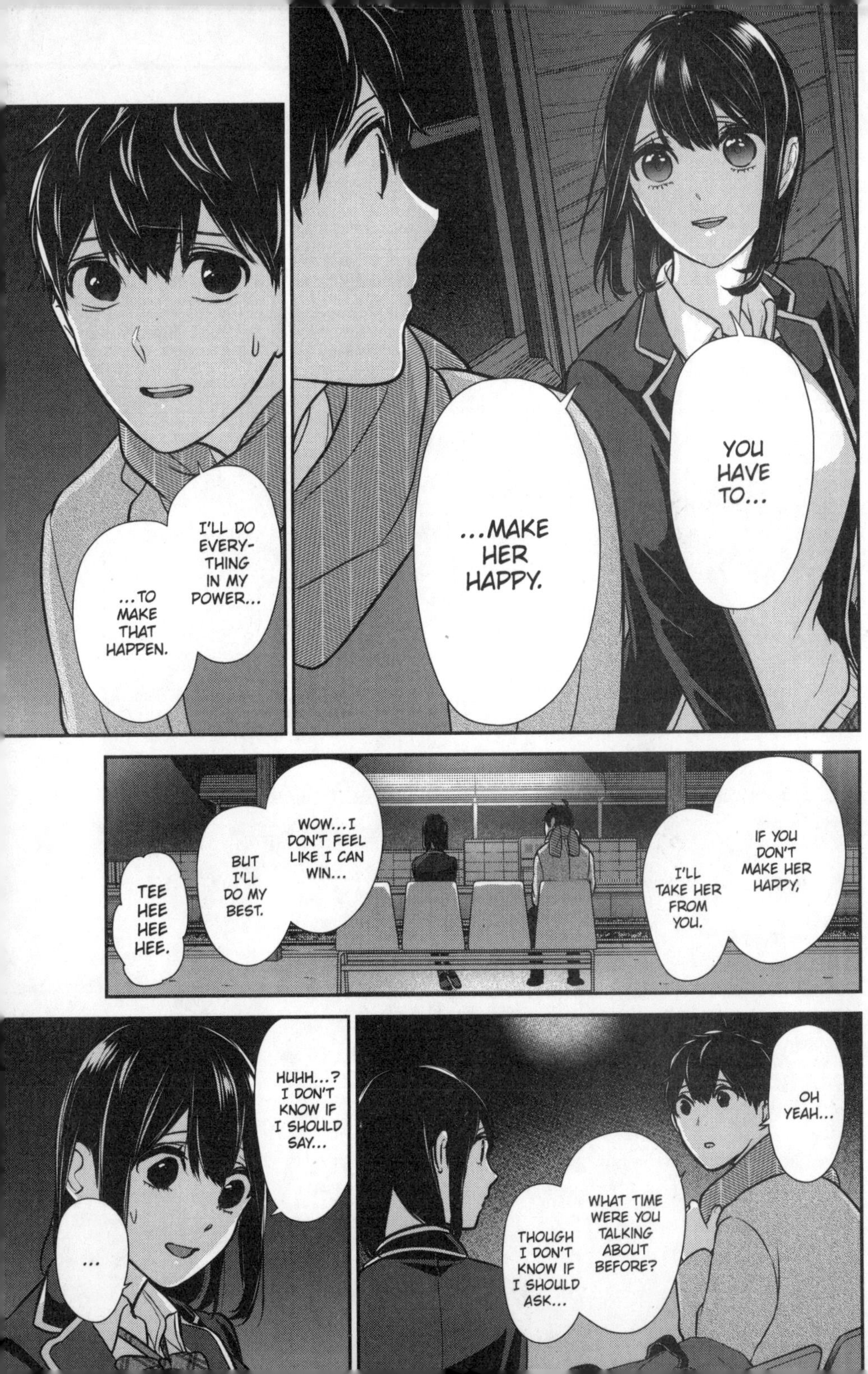
YOU HAVE TO...
...MAKE HER HAPPY.
I'LL DO EVERY-THING IN MY POWER...
...TO MAKE THAT HAPPEN.
IF YOU DON'T MAKE HER HAPPY,
I'LL TAKE HER FROM YOU.
WOW...I DON'T FEEL LIKE I CAN WIN...
BUT I'LL DO MY BEST.
TEE HEE HEE HEE.
OH YEAH...
WHAT TIME WERE YOU TALKING ABOUT BEFORE?
THOUGH I DON'T KNOW IF I SHOULD ASK...
HUHH...? I DON'T KNOW IF I SHOULD SAY...
...

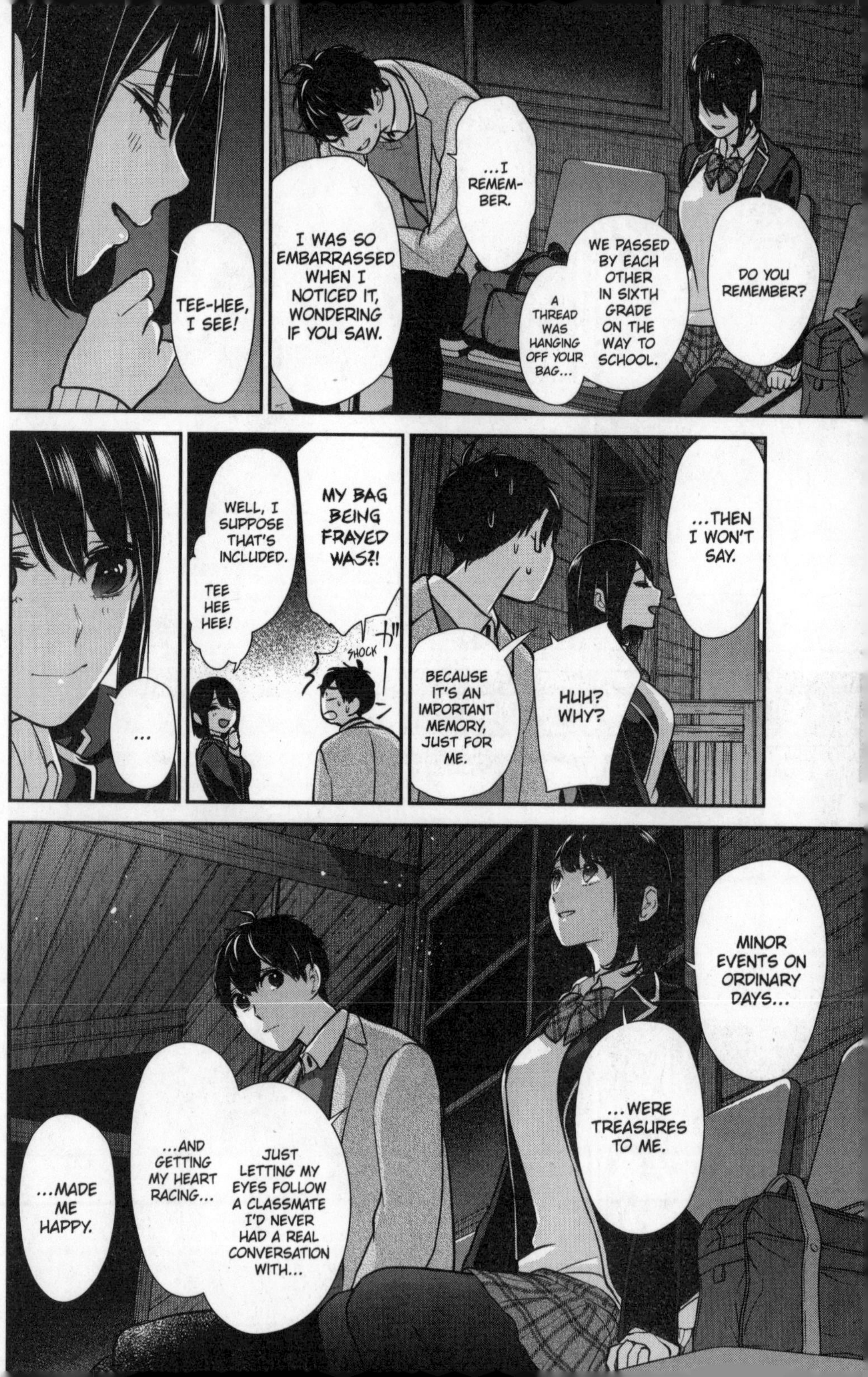
DO YOU REMEMBER?
WE PASSED BY EACH OTHER IN SIXTH GRADE ON THE WAY TO SCHOOL.
A THREAD WAS HANGING OFF YOUR BAG...
...I REMEM-BER.
I WAS SO EMBARRASSED WHEN I NOTICED IT, WONDERING IF YOU SAW.
TEE-HEE, I SEE!
...THEN I WON'T SAY.
HUH? WHY?
BECAUSE IT'S AN IMPORTANT MEMORY, JUST FOR ME.
MY BAG BEING FRAYED WAS?!
SHOCK
WELL, I SUPPOSE THAT'S INCLUDED.
TEE HEE HEE!
...
MINOR EVENTS ON ORDINARY DAYS...
...WERE TREASURES TO ME.
JUST LETTING MY EYES FOLLOW A CLASSMATE I'D NEVER HAD A REAL CONVERSATION WITH...
...AND GETTING MY HEART RACING...
...MADE ME HAPPY.

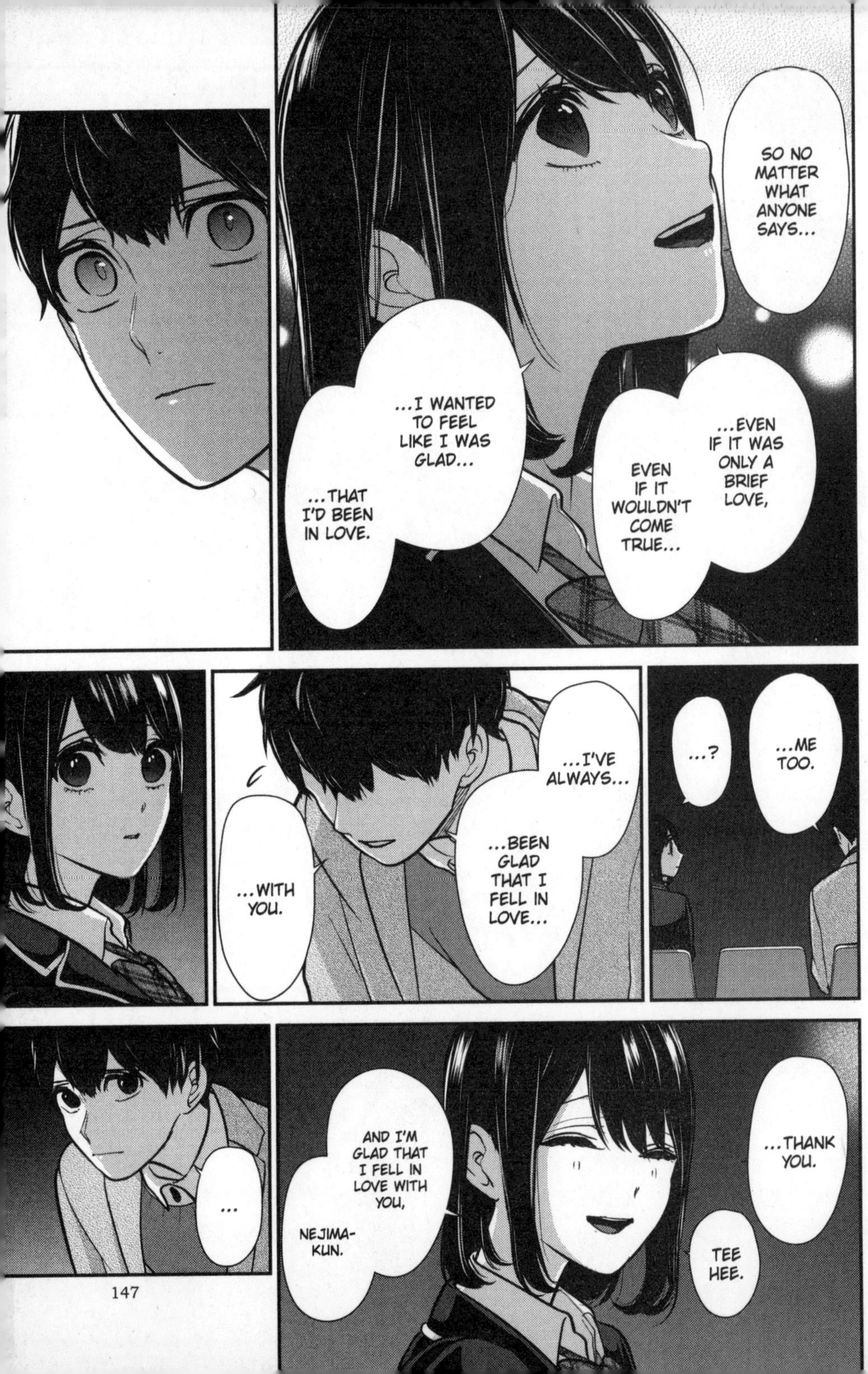
SO NO MATTER WHAT ANYONE SAYS...
...EVEN IF IT WAS ONLY A BRIEF LOVE,
EVEN IF IT WOULDN'T COME TRUE...
...I WANTED TO FEEL LIKE I WAS GLAD...
...THAT I'D BEEN IN LOVE.
...ME TOO.
...?
...I'VE ALWAYS...
...BEEN GLAD THAT I FELL IN LOVE...
...WITH YOU.
...THANK YOU.
TEE HEE.
AND I'M GLAD THAT I FELL IN LOVE WITH YOU,
NEJIMA-KUN.
...

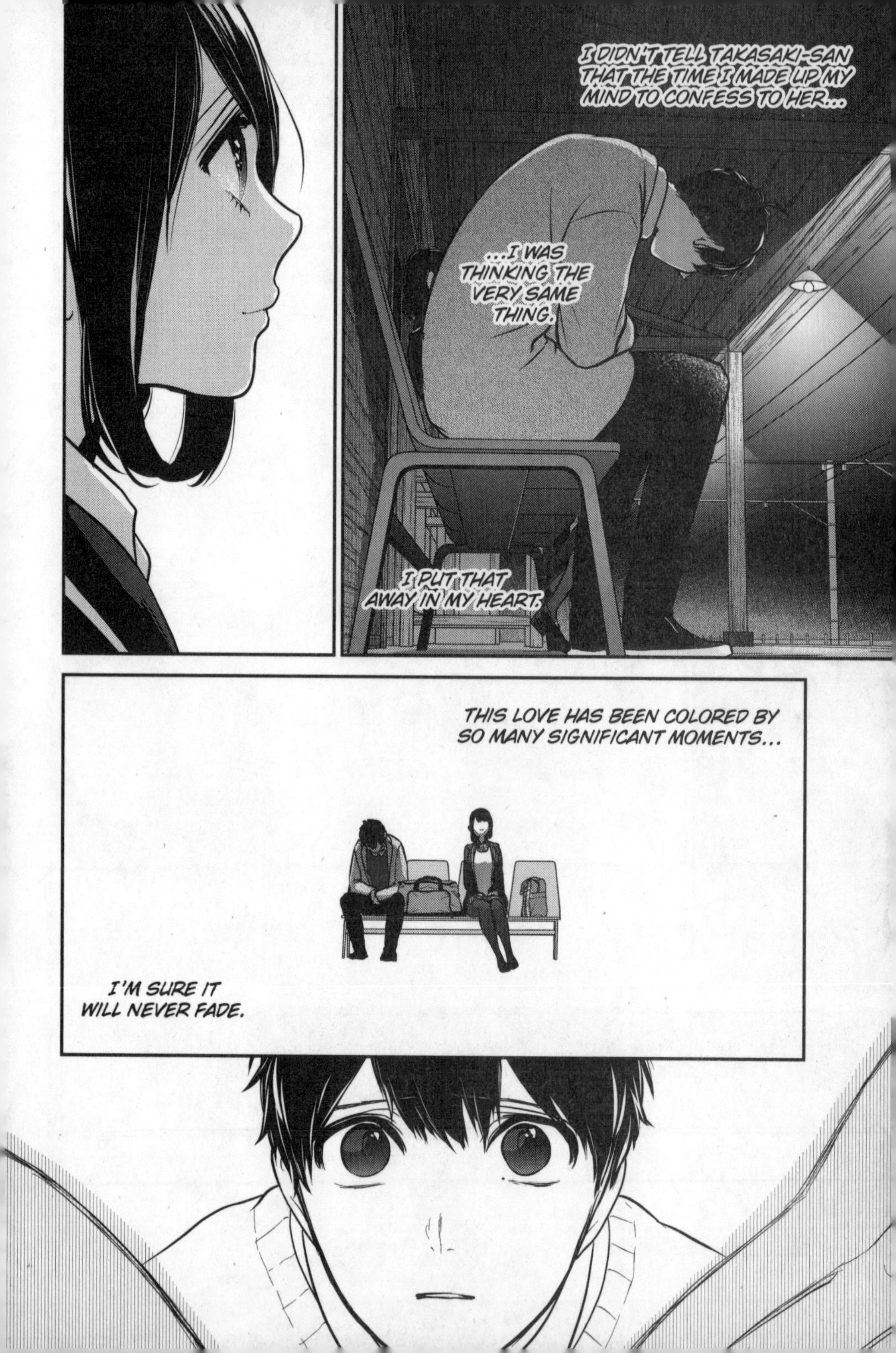
I DIDN'T TELL TAKASAKI-SAN THAT THE TIME I MADE UP MY MIND TO CONFESS TO HER...
...I WAS THINKING THE VERY SAME THING.
I PUT THAT AWAY IN MY HEART.
THIS LOVE HAS BEEN COLORED BY SO MANY SIGNIFICANT MOMENTS...
I'M SURE IT WILL NEVER FADE.

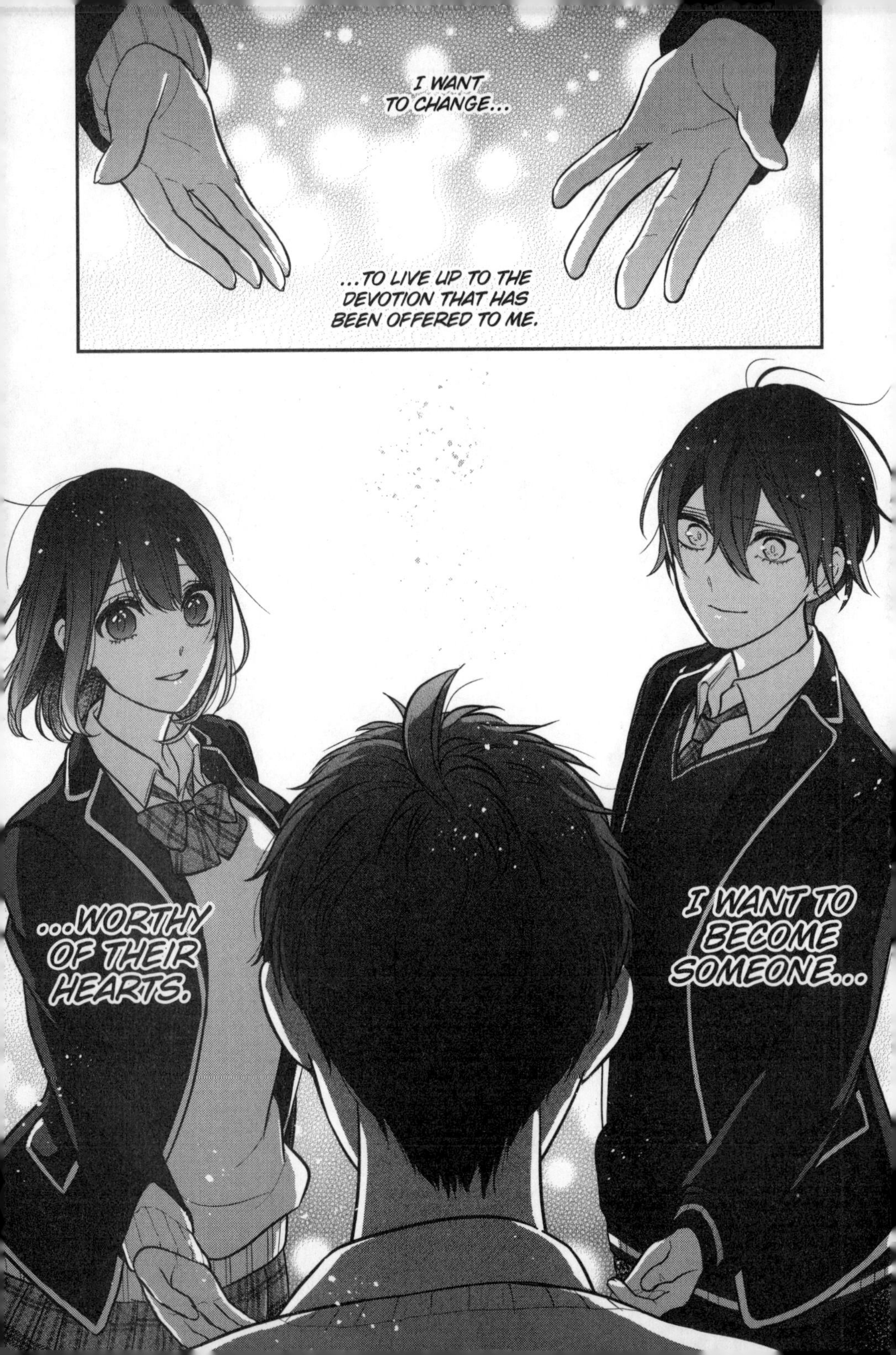
I WANT TO CHANGE...
...TO LIVE UP TO THE DEVOTION THAT HAS BEEN OFFERED TO ME.
I WANT TO BECOME SOMEONE...
...WORTHY OF THEIR HEARTS.

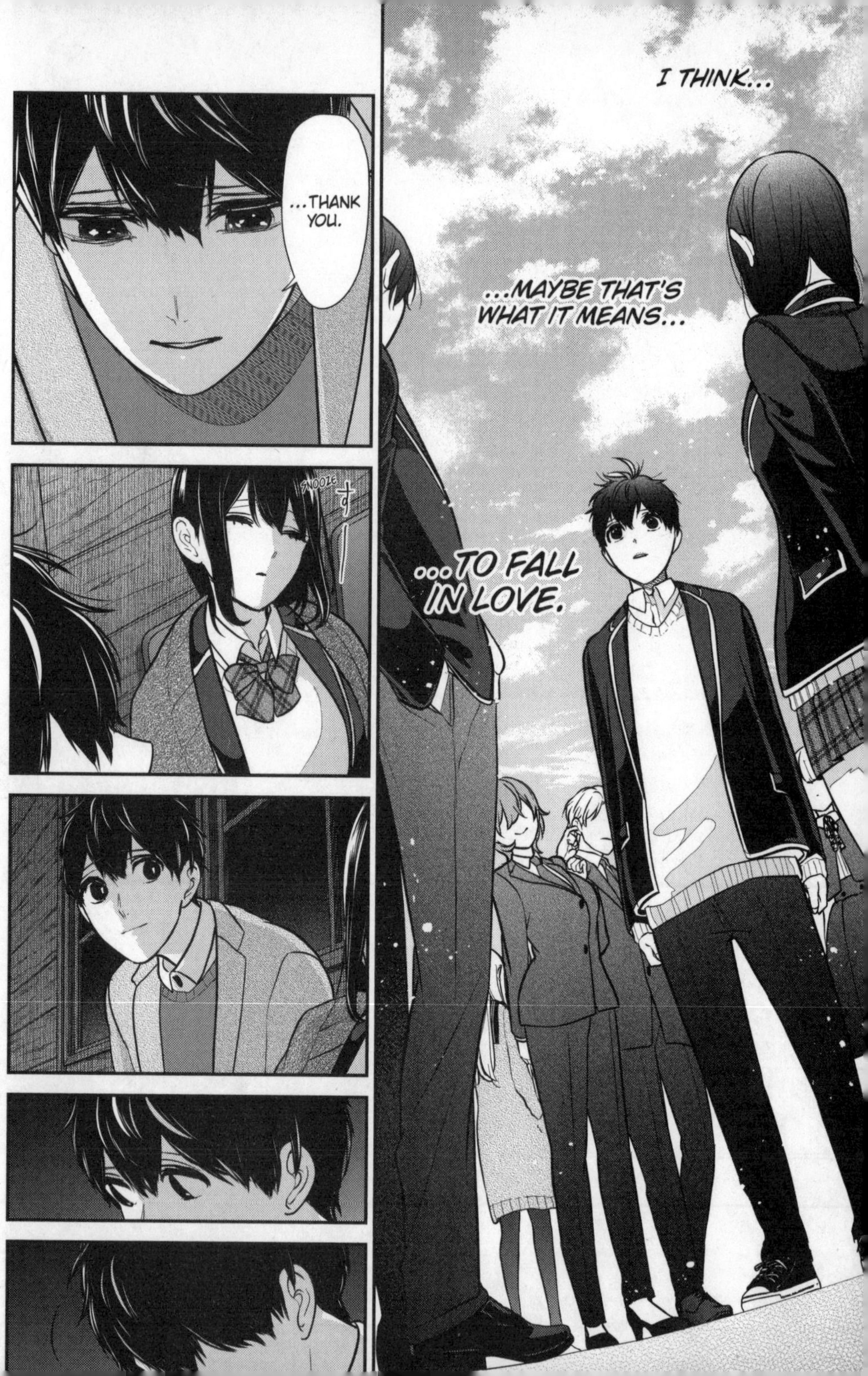
I THINK...
...MAYBE THAT'S WHAT IT MEANS...
...TO FALL IN LOVE.
...THANK YOU.
SNOOZE

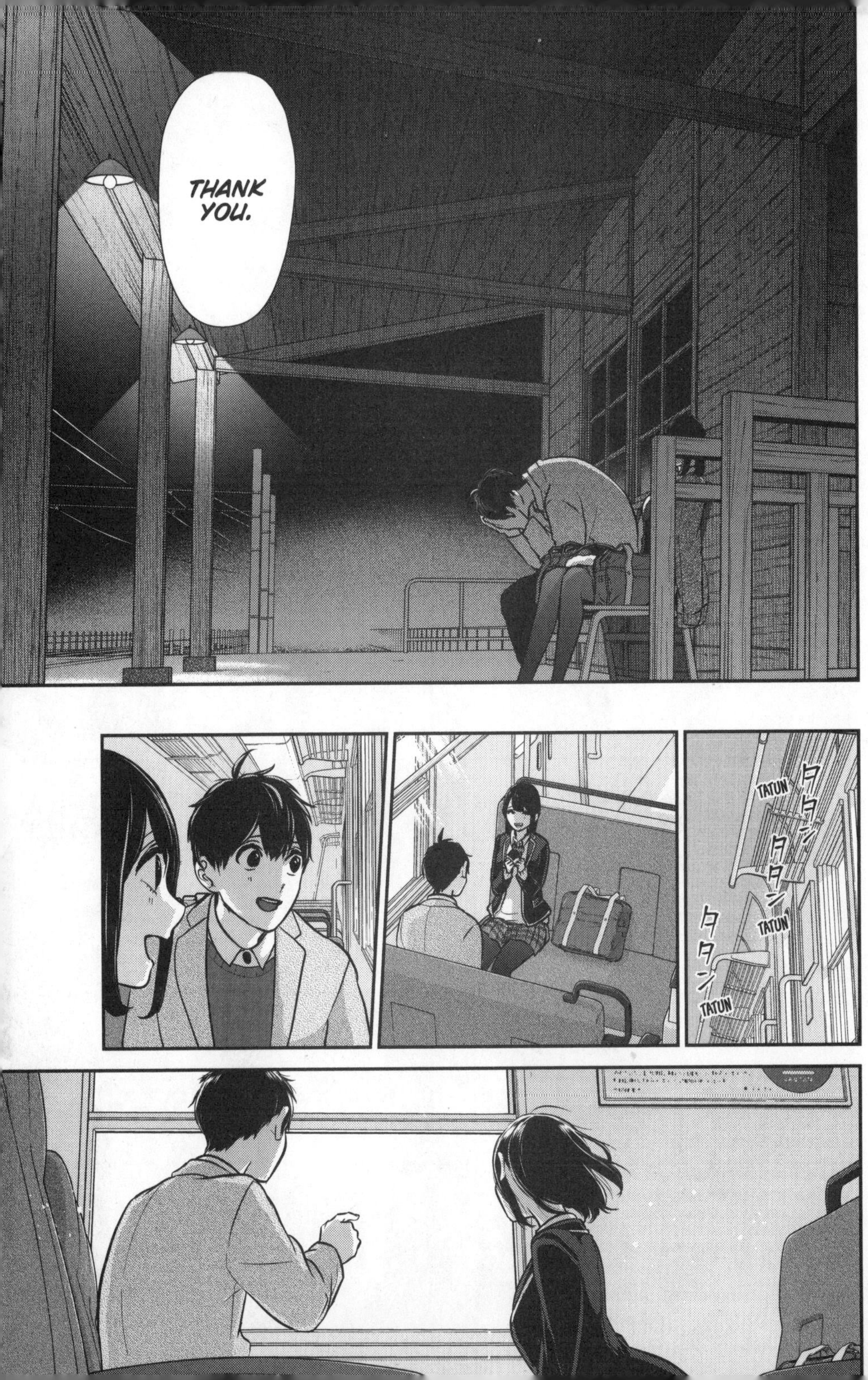
THANK YOU.
タタン
TATUN
タタン
TATUN
タタン
TATUN

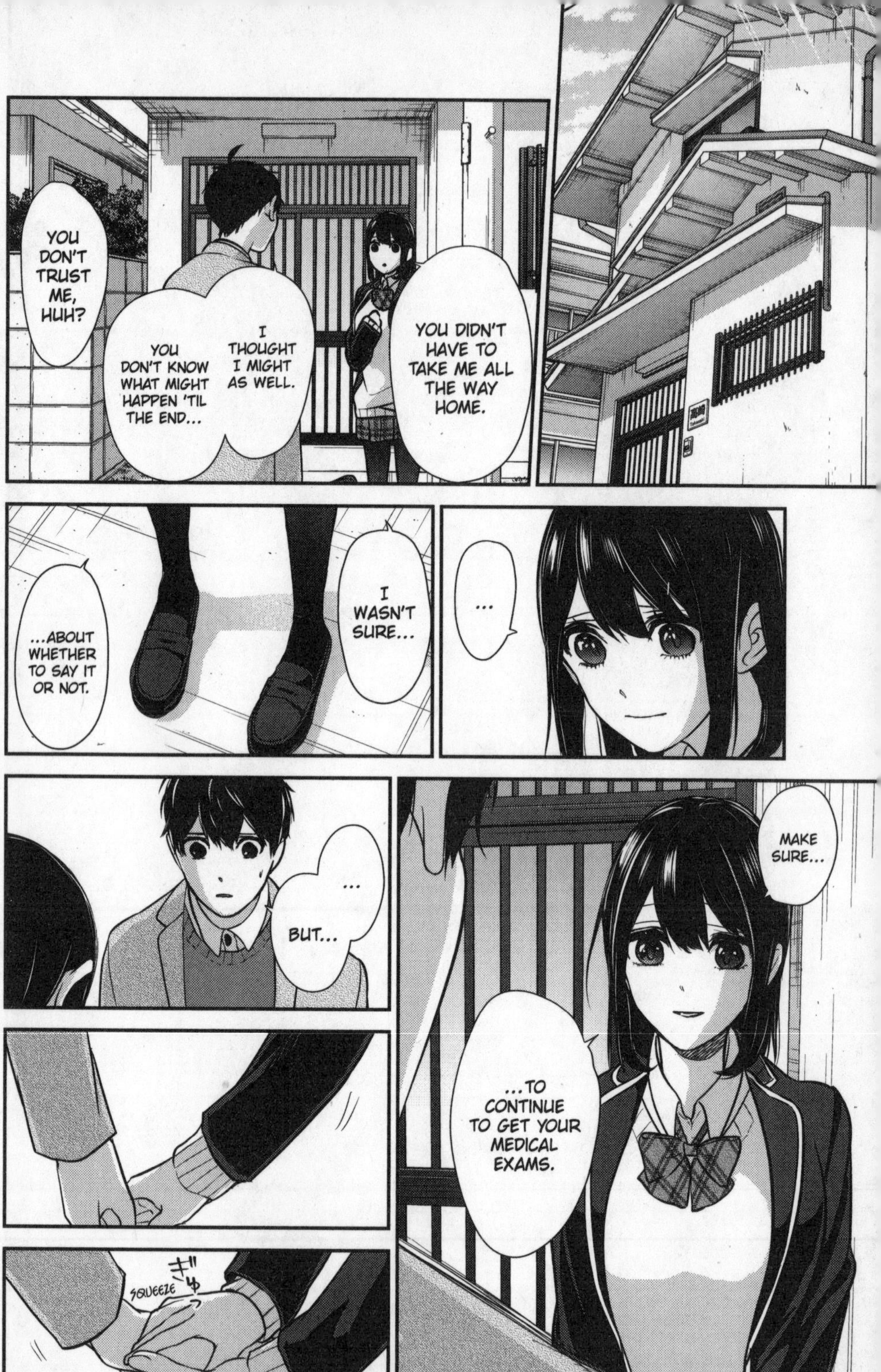
YOU DIDN'T HAVE TO TAKE ME ALL THE WAY HOME.
I THOUGHT I MIGHT AS WELL.
YOU DON'T KNOW WHAT MIGHT HAPPEN 'TIL THE END...
YOU DON'T TRUST ME, HUH?
...
I WASN'T SURE...
...ABOUT WHETHER TO SAY IT OR NOT.
MAKE SURE...
...TO CONTINUE TO GET YOUR MEDICAL EXAMS.
...
BUT...
ギュッ
SQUEEZE

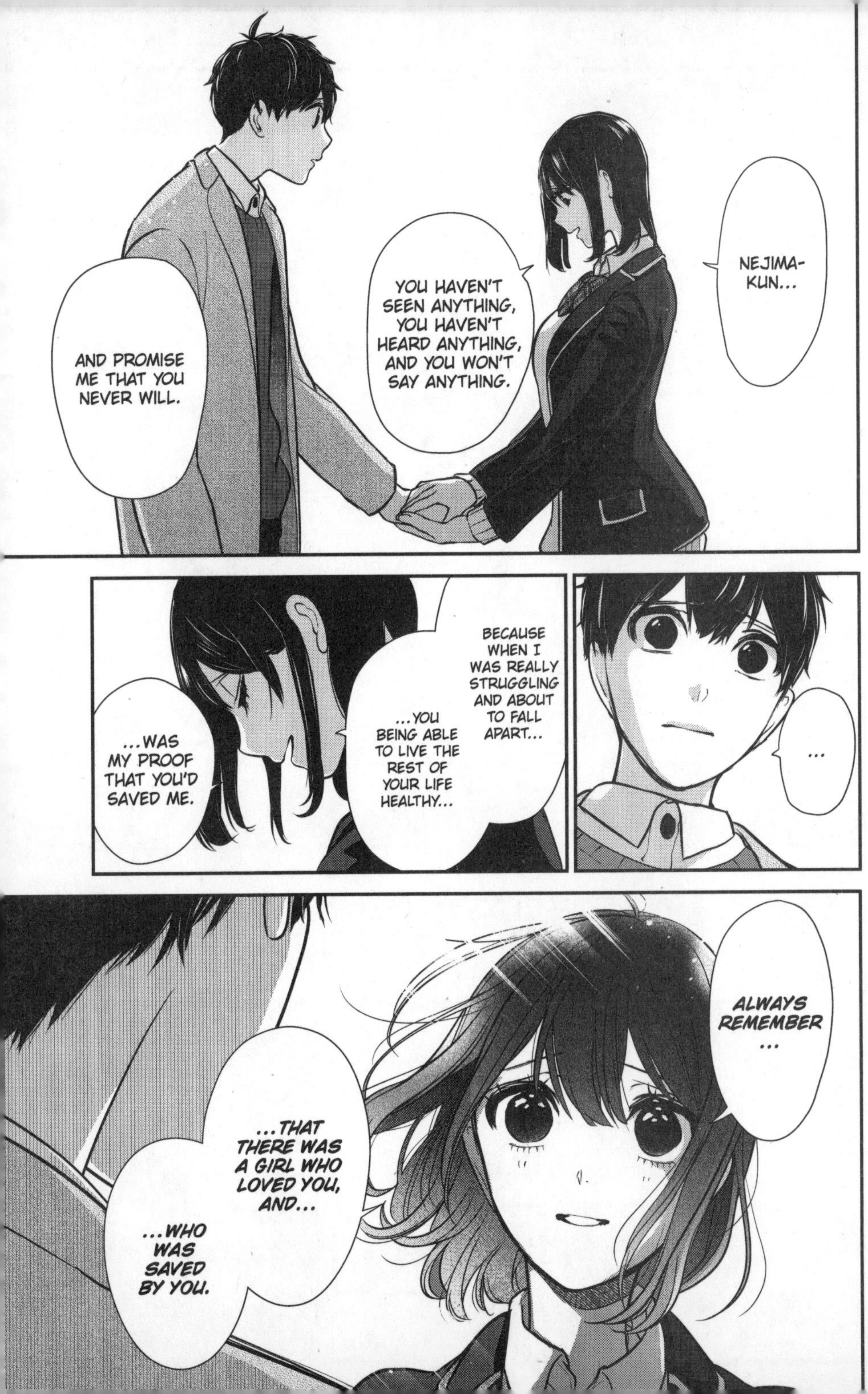
NEJIMA-KUN...
YOU HAVEN'T SEEN ANYTHING, YOU HAVEN'T HEARD ANYTHING, AND YOU WON'T SAY ANYTHING.
AND PROMISE ME THAT YOU NEVER WILL.
...
BECAUSE WHEN I WAS REALLY STRUGGLING AND ABOUT TO FALL APART...
...YOU BEING ABLE TO LIVE THE REST OF YOUR LIFE HEALTHY...
...WAS MY PROOF THAT YOU'D SAVED ME.
ALWAYS REMEMBER ...
...THAT THERE WAS A GIRL WHO LOVED YOU, AND...
...WHO WAS SAVED BY YOU.

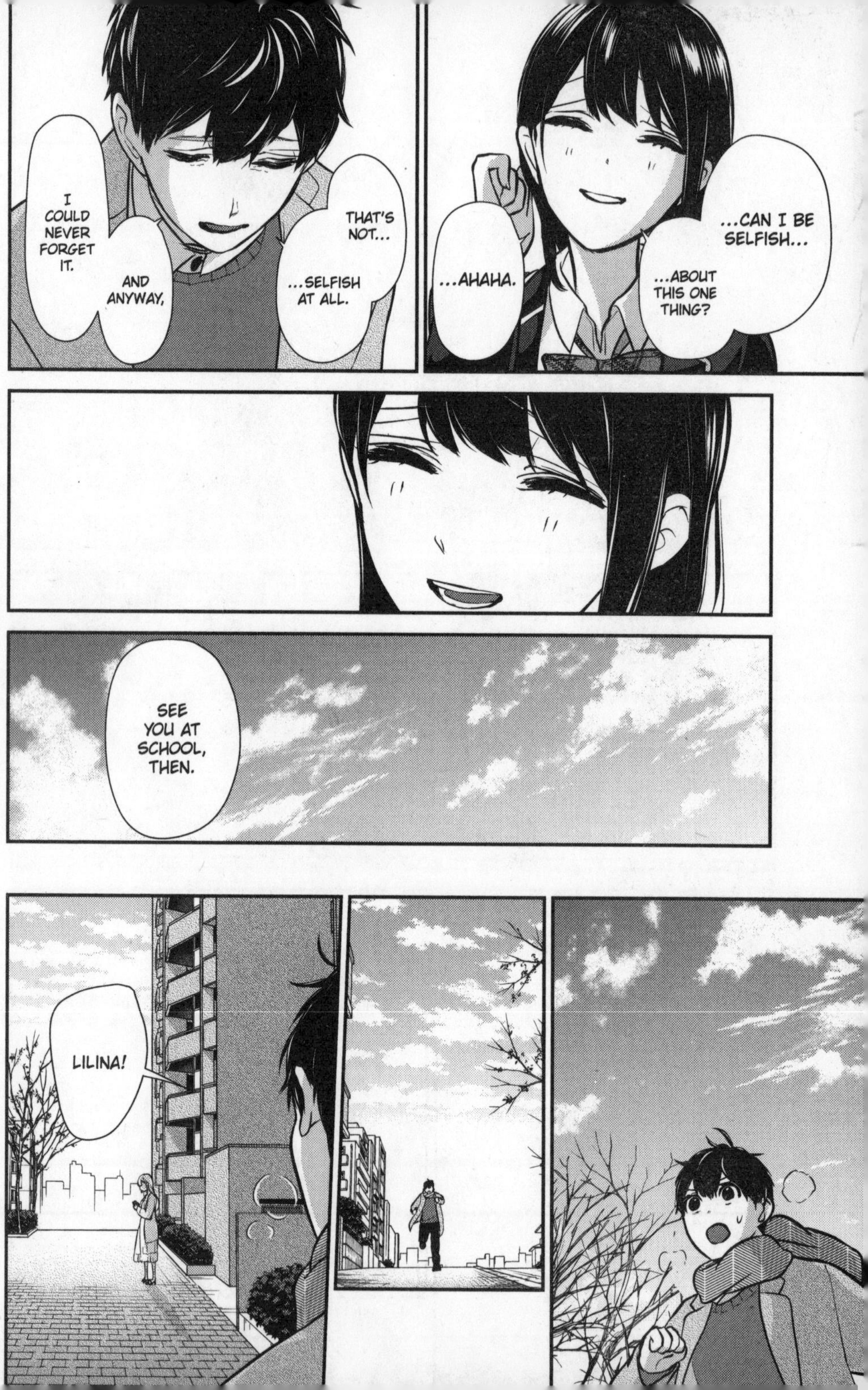
...CAN I BE SELFISH...
...ABOUT THIS ONE THING?
...AHAHA.
THAT'S NOT...
...SELFISH AT ALL.
AND ANYWAY,
I COULD NEVER FORGET IT.
SEE YOU AT SCHOOL, THEN.
LILINA!

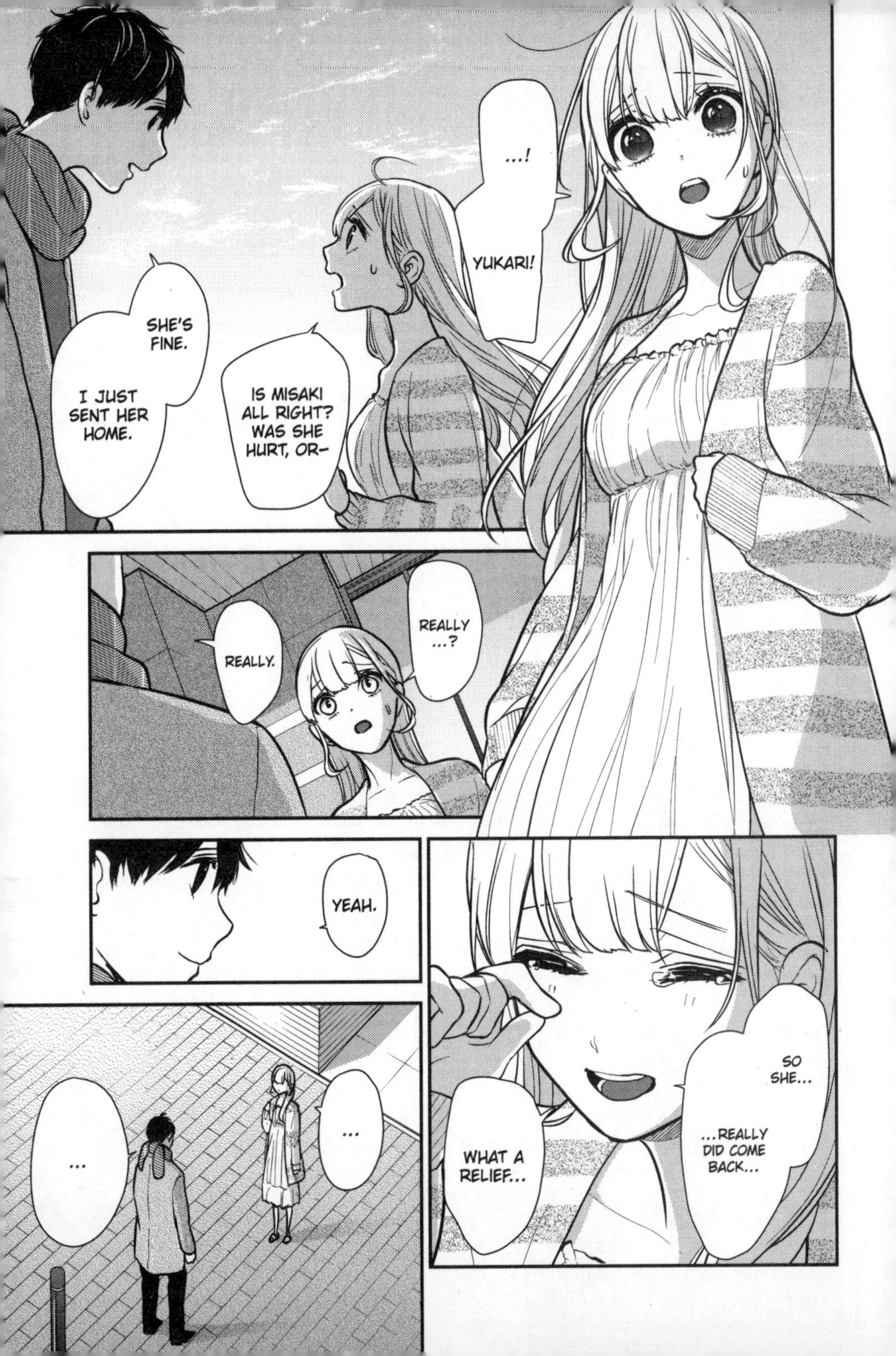
...!
YUKARI!
IS MISAKI ALL RIGHT? WAS SHE HURT, OR–
SHE'S FINE.
I JUST SENT HER HOME.
REALLY ...?
REALLY.
SO SHE...
...REALLY DID COME BACK...
WHAT A RELIEF...
YEAH.
...
...

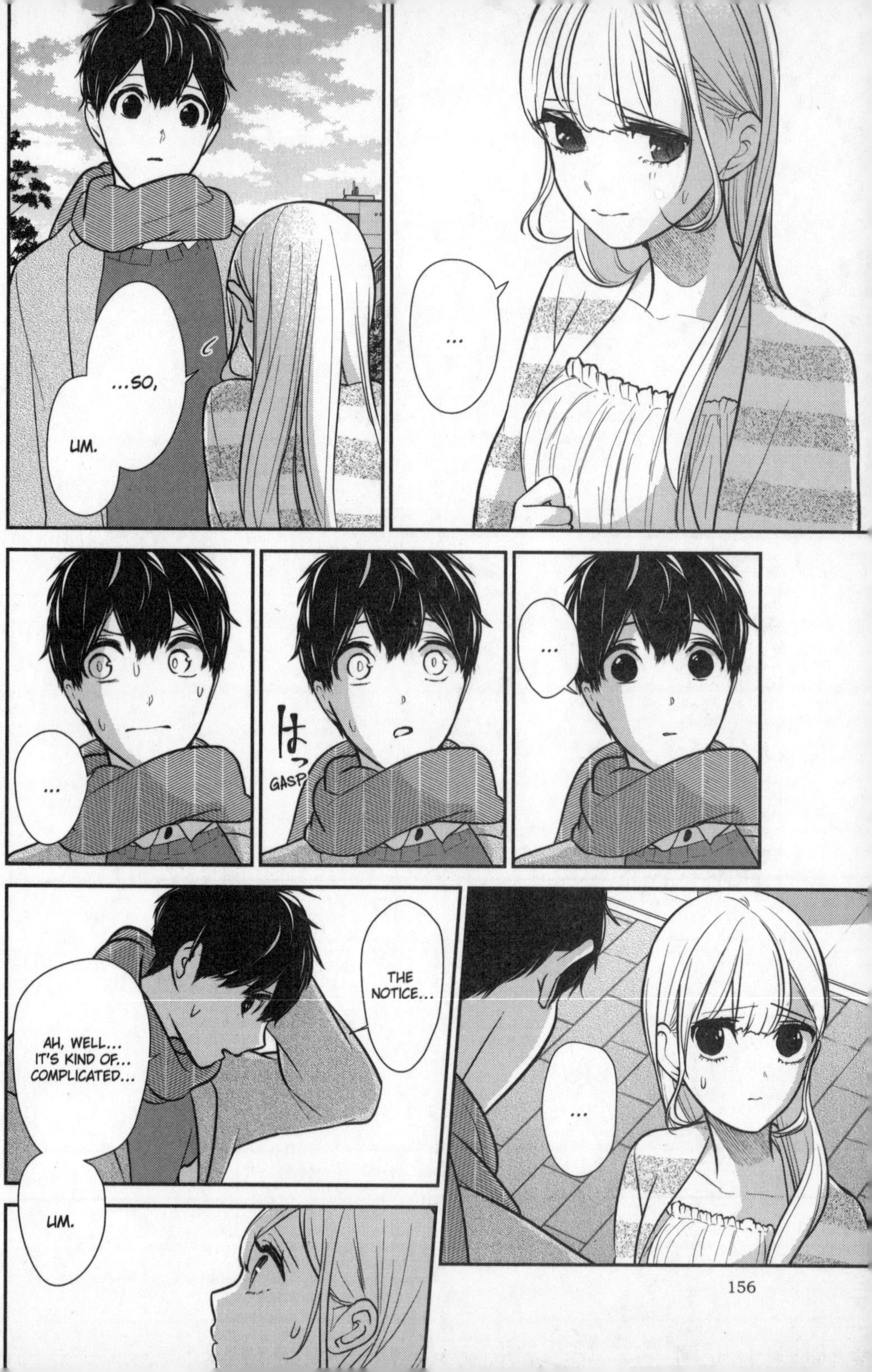
...
...SO,
UM.
...
はっ
GASP
...
...
THE NOTICE...
AH, WELL... IT'S KIND OF... COMPLICATED...
UM.

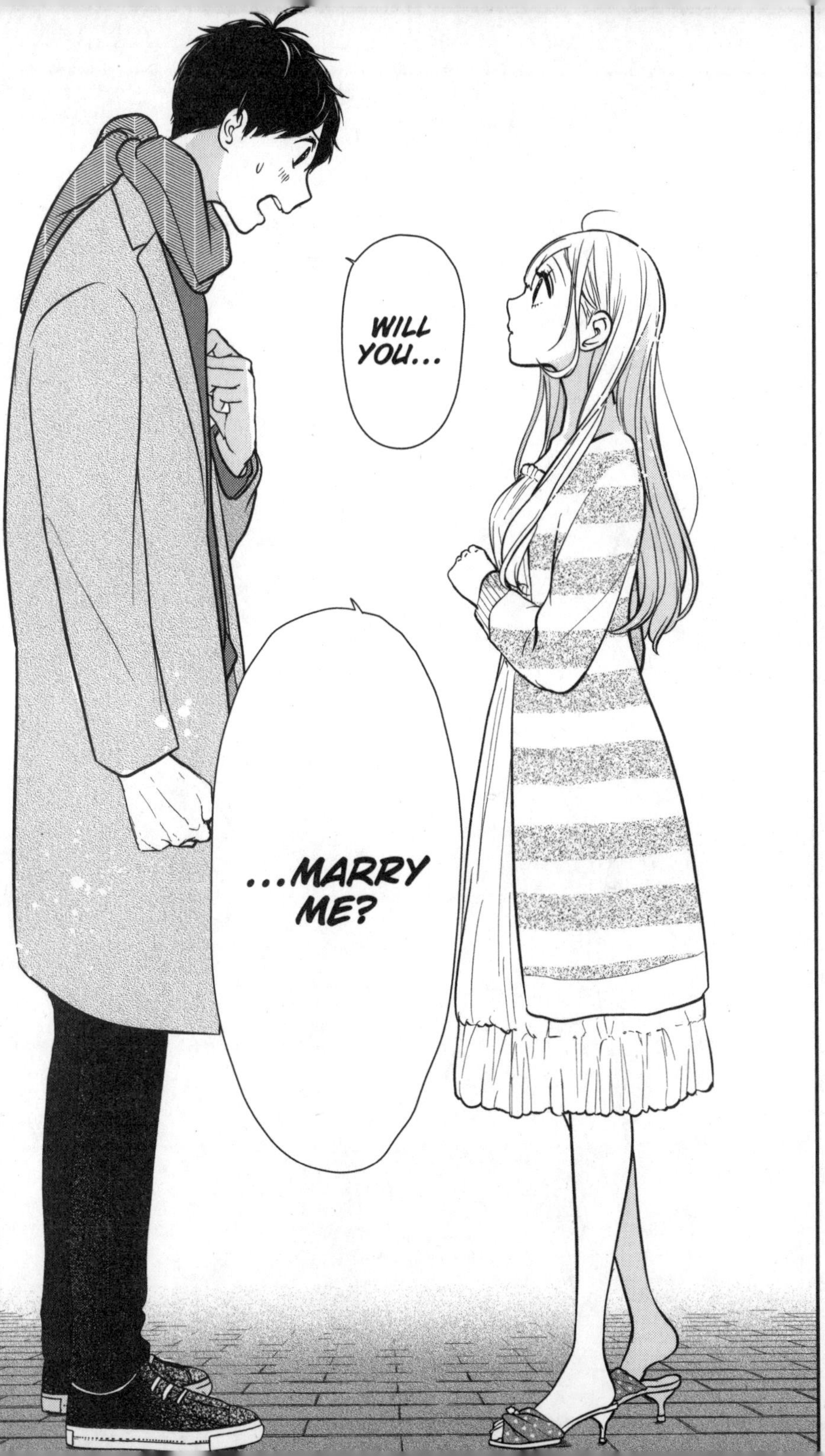
WILL YOU...
...MARRY ME?

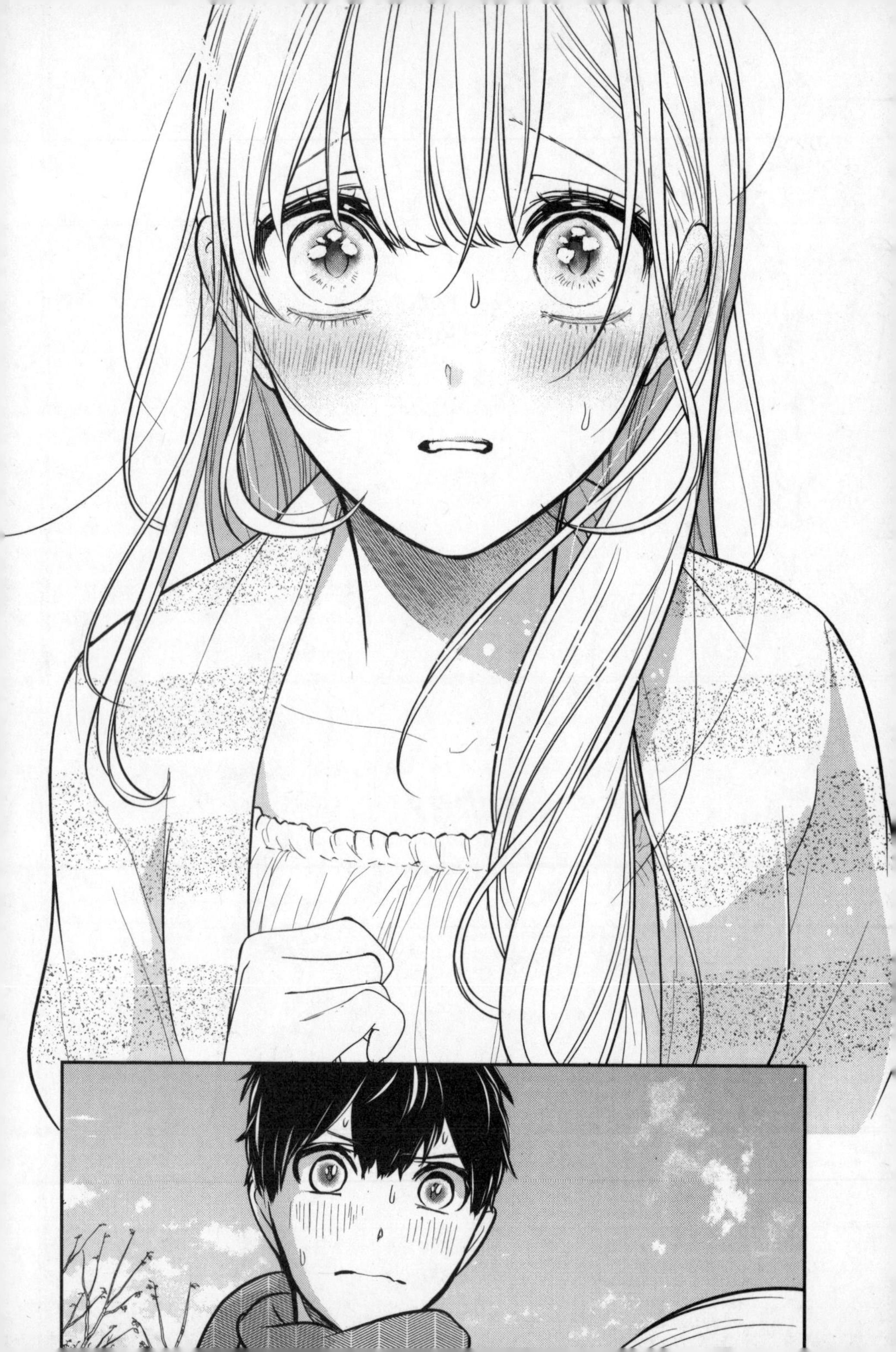

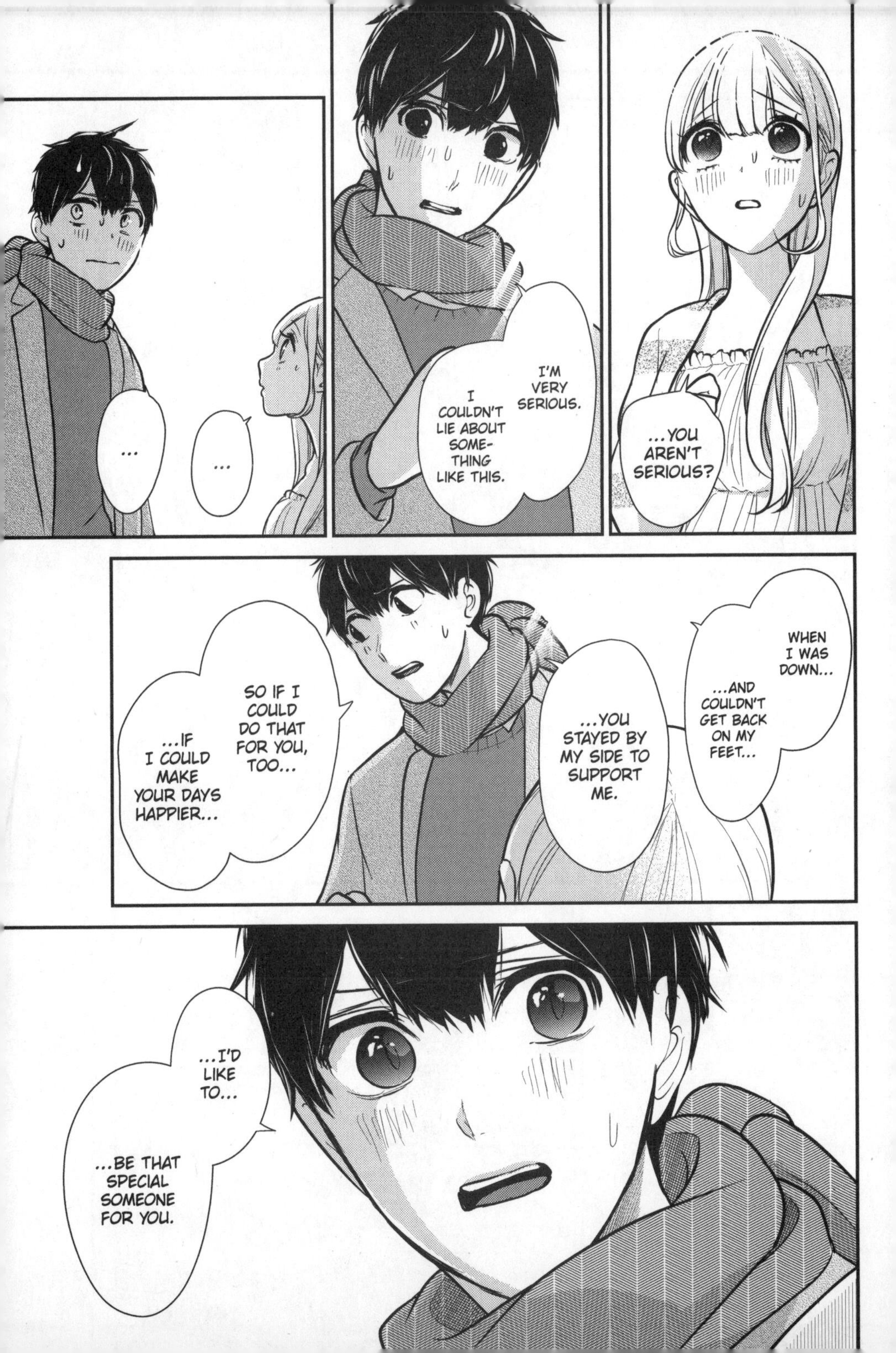
...YOU AREN'T SERIOUS?
I'M VERY SERIOUS.
I COULDN'T LIE ABOUT SOME-THING LIKE THIS.
...
...
WHEN I WAS DOWN...
...AND COULDN'T GET BACK ON MY FEET...
...YOU STAYED BY MY SIDE TO SUPPORT ME.
SO IF I COULD DO THAT FOR YOU, TOO...
...IF I COULD MAKE YOUR DAYS HAPPIER...
...I'D LIKE TO...
...BE THAT SPECIAL SOMEONE FOR YOU.

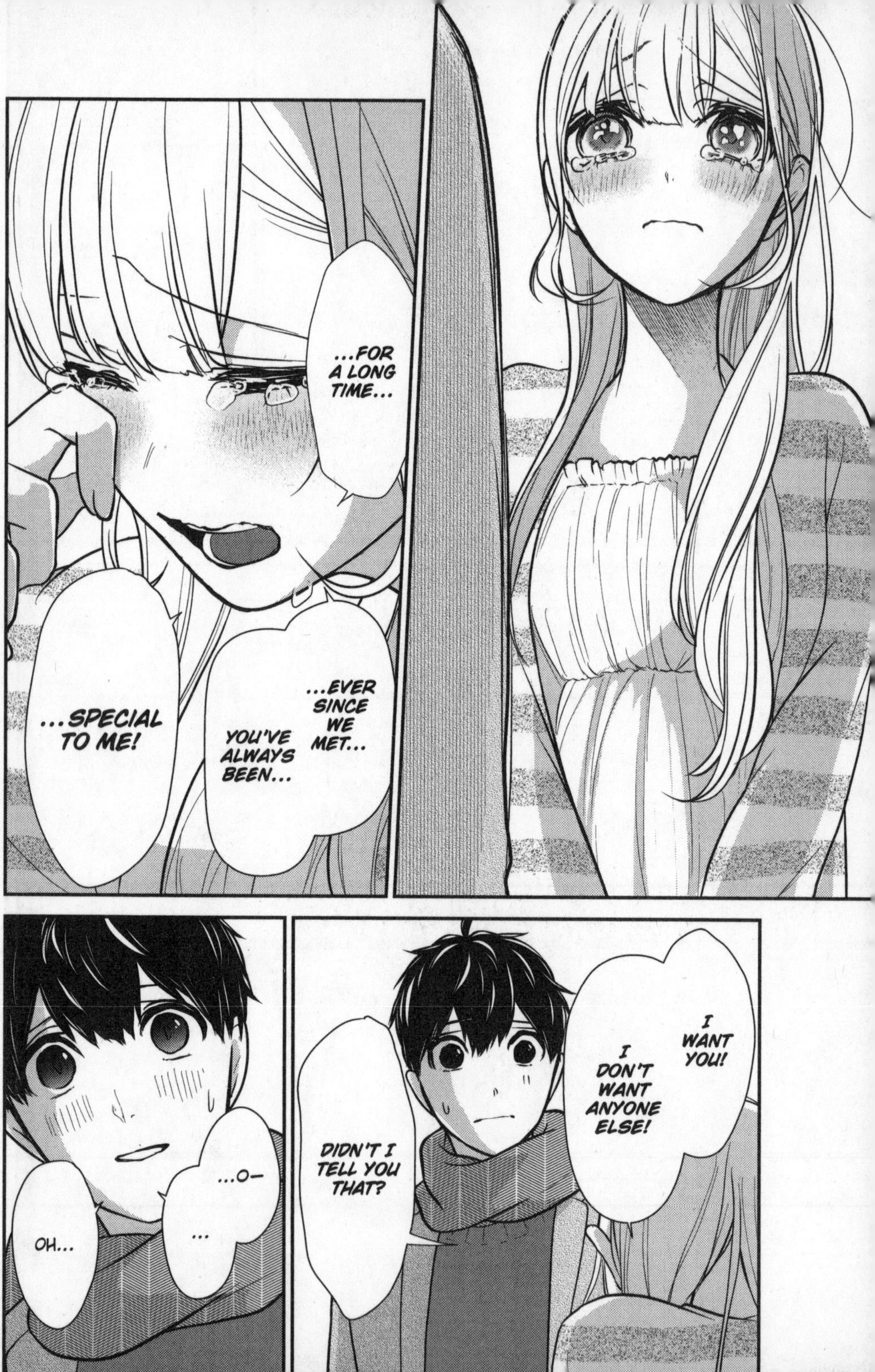
...FOR A LONG TIME...
...EVER SINCE WE MET...
YOU'VE ALWAYS BEEN...
...SPECIAL TO ME!
I WANT YOU!
I DON'T WANT ANYONE ELSE!
DIDN'T I TELL YOU THAT?
...O—
...
OH...

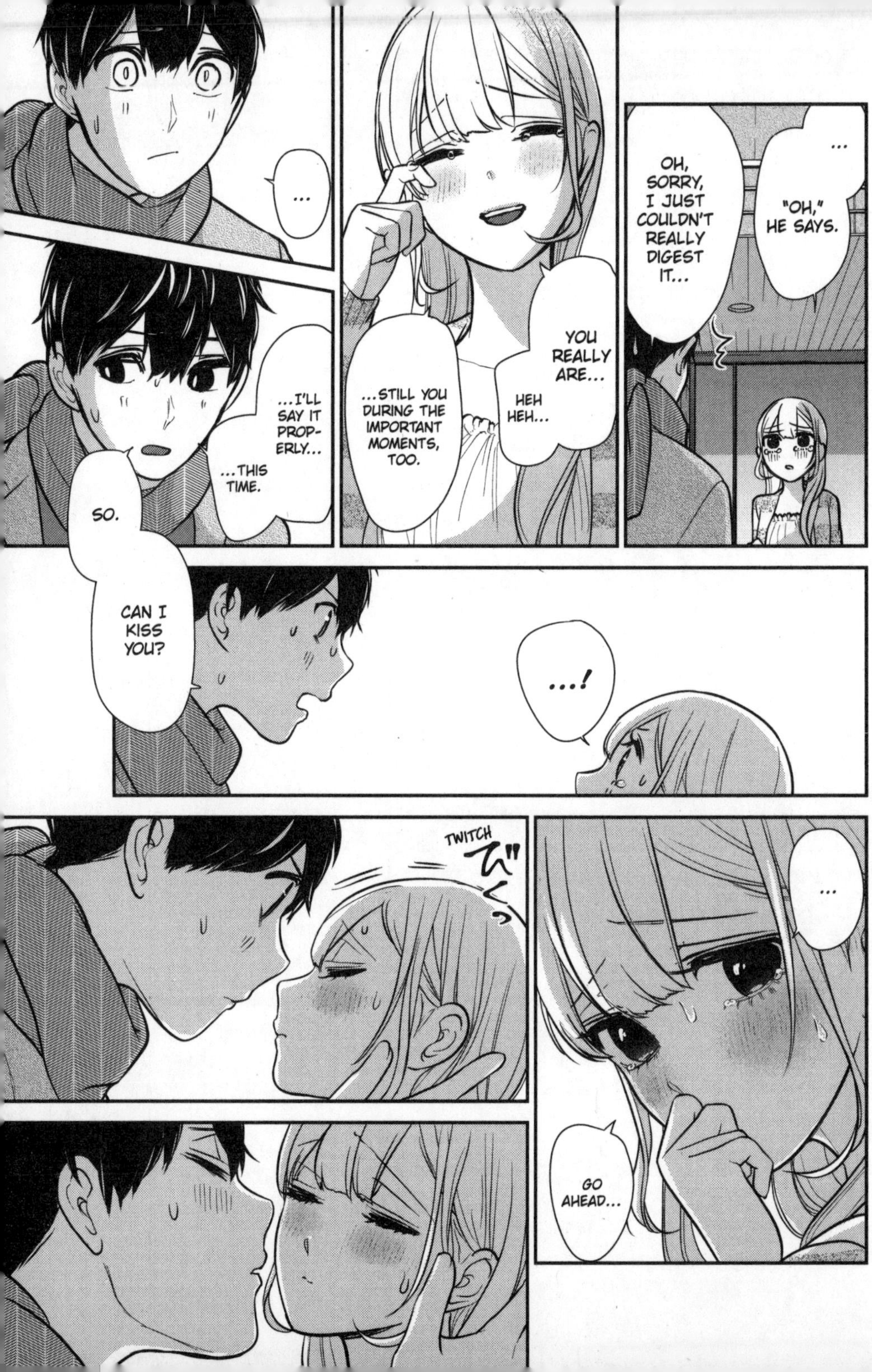
...
"OH," HE SAYS.
OH, SORRY, I JUST COULDN'T REALLY DIGEST IT...
YOU REALLY ARE...
HEH HEH...
...STILL YOU DURING THE IMPORTANT MOMENTS, TOO.
...
...I'LL SAY IT PROPERLY...
...THIS TIME.
SO.
...!
CAN I KISS YOU?
...
GO AHEAD...
TWITCH
びくっ

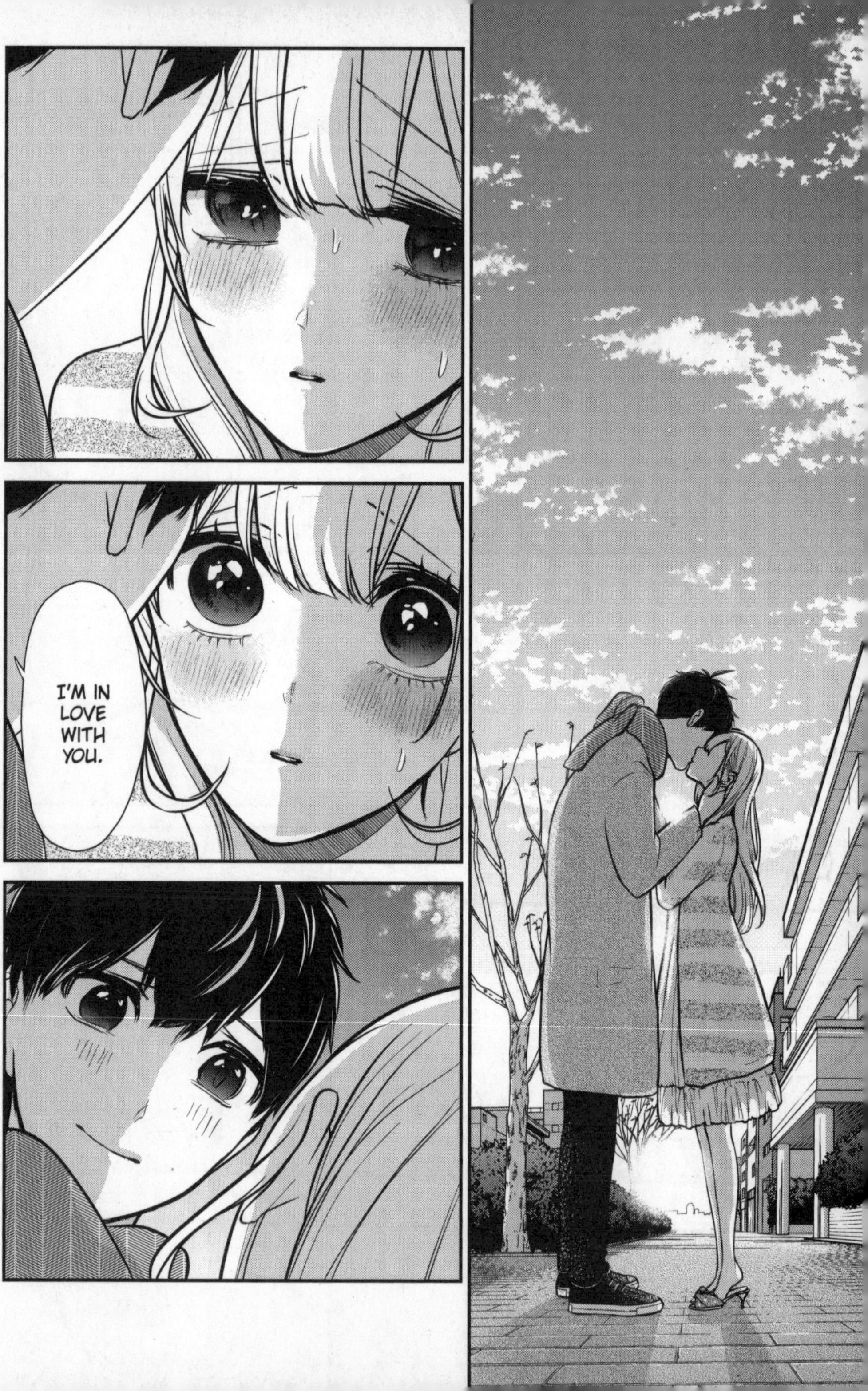
I'M IN LOVE WITH YOU.

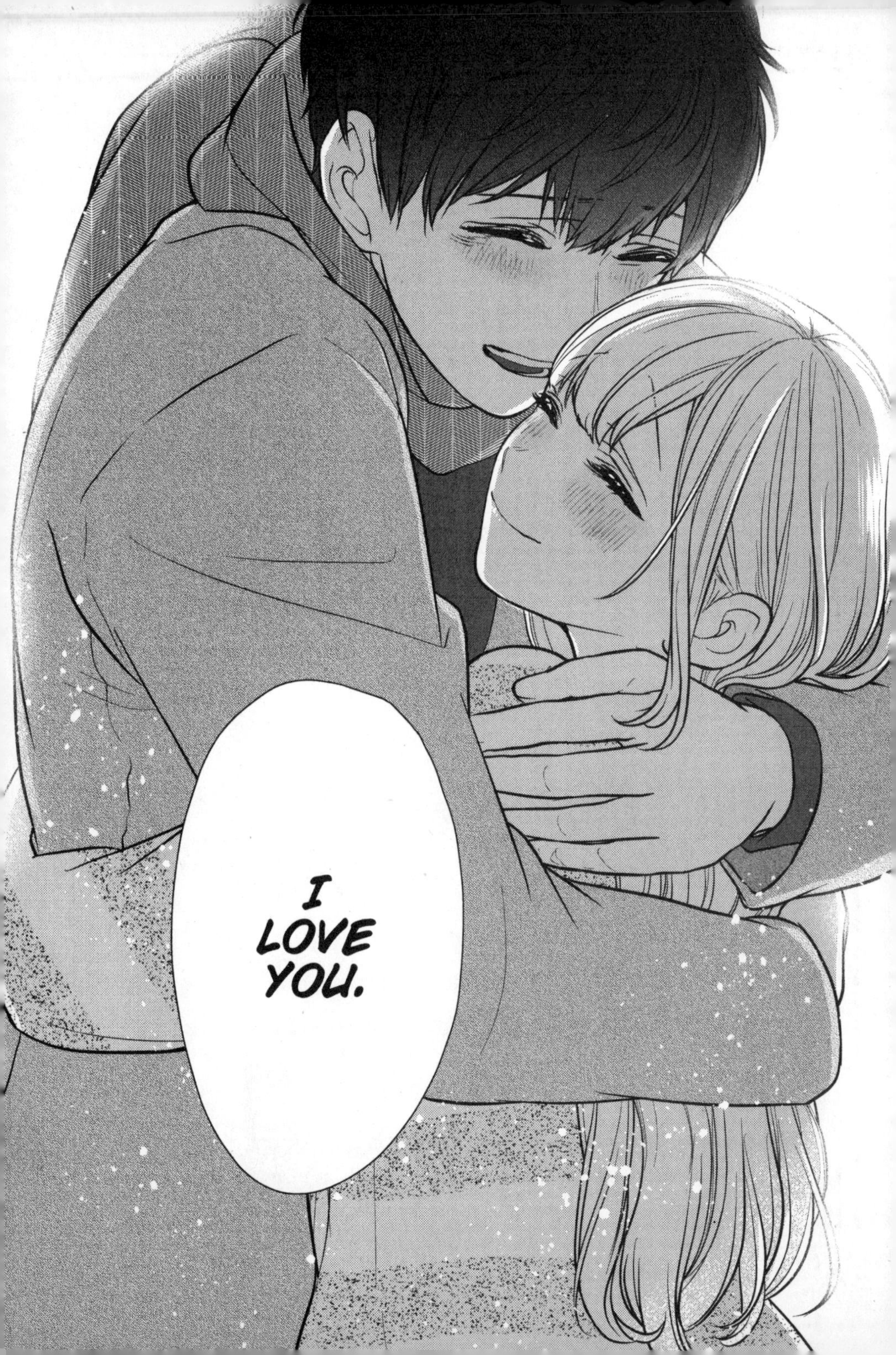
I LOVE YOU.

★ SPECIAL THANKS ★

TAKANAGA-SAMA

YOSHIMURA-SAMA

ISHIKAWA-SAMA

SHINOHARA-SAMA   BOKU-SAMA

MANARU AMAGAWA-SAMA   FUKU-SAMA   KOUSUKE KOMATSU-SAMA
YUTAKA TACHIBANA-SAMA   KATSURAGI-SAMA   SHIDOU   HIDEKI-SAMA

WEEKLY SHONEN MAGAZINE EDITORIAL
EVERYONE FROM PROOFREADING, SALES, ADVERTISING, RIGHTS
AND MANGABOX

SHINDO KEISHODO KK   FUTABA KIKAKU KK
ALL THE BOOKSTORES ACROSS THE COUNTRY
EVERYONE INVOLVED WITH THE ANIME

COVER DESIGN
HIVE-SAMA

ALL MY FRIENDS
EVERYONE IN MY FAMILY

☆ AND ☆

ALL OF MY READERS

I WAS ALWAYS PUSHING MY LIMITS TRYING TO MAKE THIS MANGA AS GOOD AS IT COULD BE,
SO I STUMBLED A LOT, AND EVERY TIME, MY EDITORS SUPPORTED ME AND KEPT ME GOING.

THANKS AS WELL TO THE BOOKSELLERS WHO SHIPPED OFF THIS MANGA I WORKED ON,
AND ALL OF THE READERS WHO PICKED THEM UP. WITH THIS STORY, I WAS ABLE TO
REACH PLACES THAT I WOULD NEVER HAVE IMAGINED BEFORE THIS SERIALIZATION BEGAN.

THANK YOU VERY MUCH FOR ALWAYS STAYING WITH ME AS I'VE DONE MY BEST TO PUSH MYSELF.
I HOPE NEXT TIME I CAN SHOW YOU EVEN GREATER GROWTH!

MUSAWO

Final Chapter : At the End of the Red String

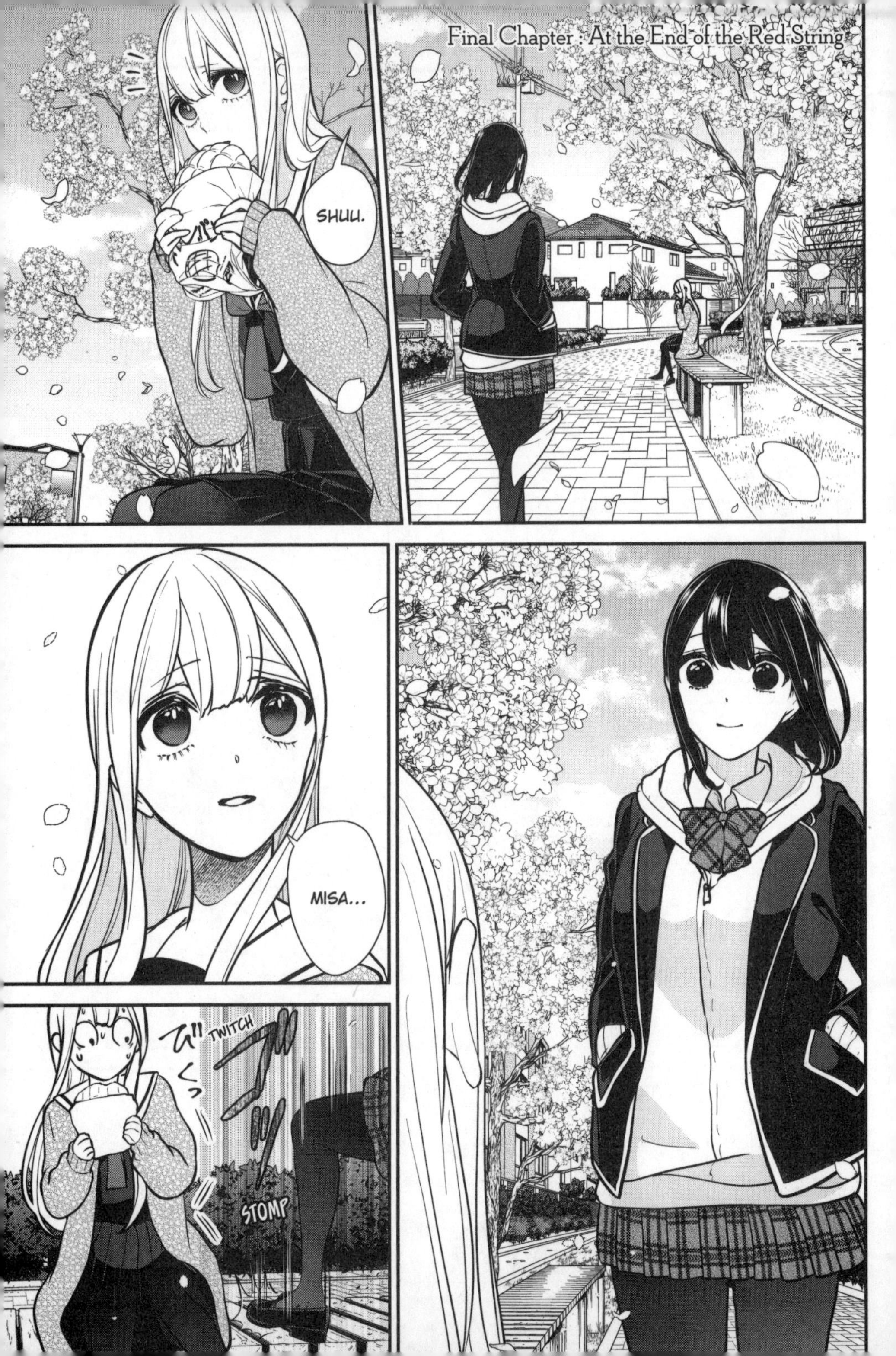
SHUU.
MISA...
TWITCH
STOMP

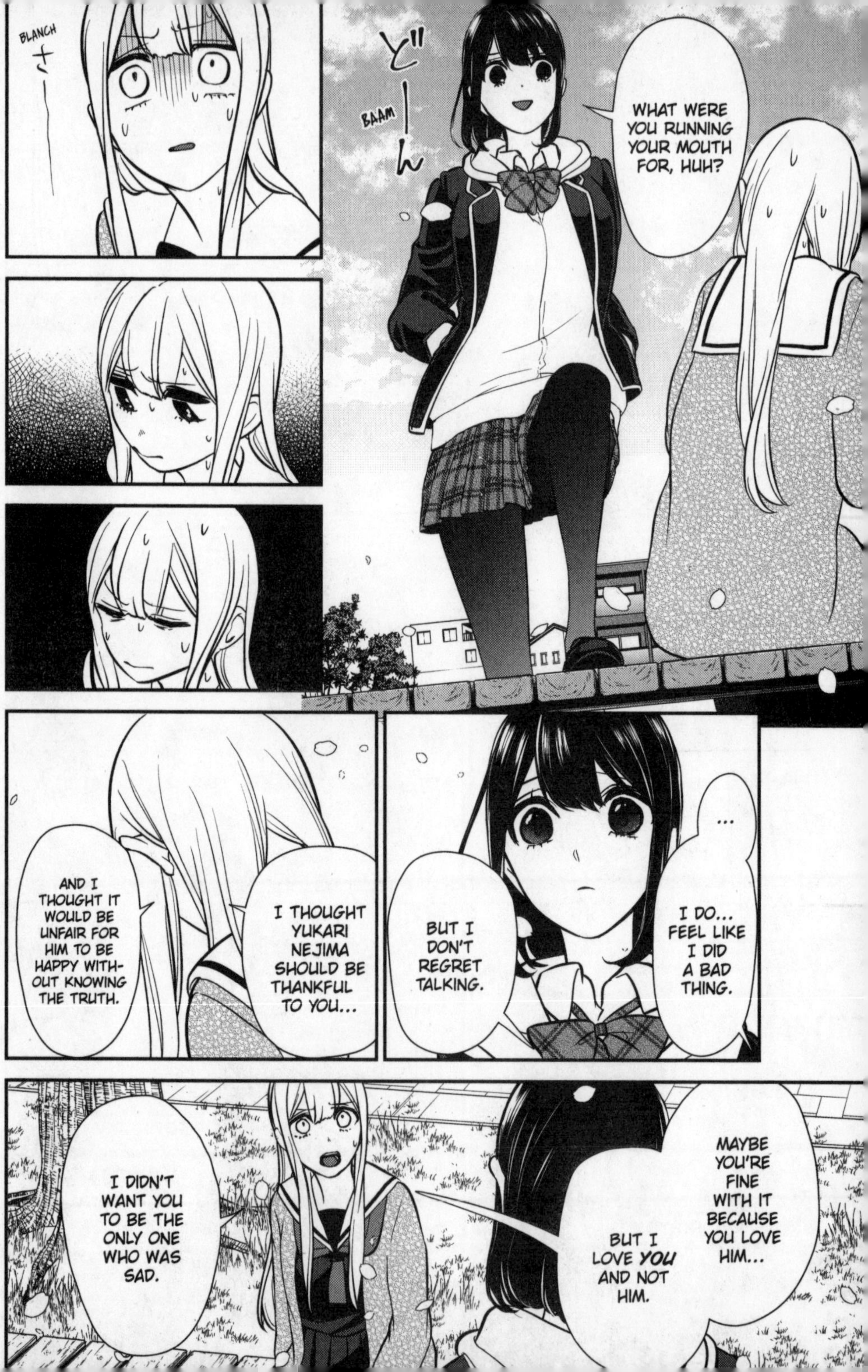
どーん
BAAM
WHAT WERE YOU RUNNING YOUR MOUTH FOR, HUH?
さー
BLANCH
...
I DO... FEEL LIKE I DID A BAD THING.
BUT I DON'T REGRET TALKING.
I THOUGHT YUKARI NEJIMA SHOULD BE THANKFUL TO YOU...
AND I THOUGHT IT WOULD BE UNFAIR FOR HIM TO BE HAPPY WITH-OUT KNOWING THE TRUTH.
MAYBE YOU'RE FINE WITH IT BECAUSE YOU LOVE HIM...
BUT I LOVE *YOU* AND NOT HIM.
I DIDN'T WANT YOU TO BE THE ONLY ONE WHO WAS SAD.

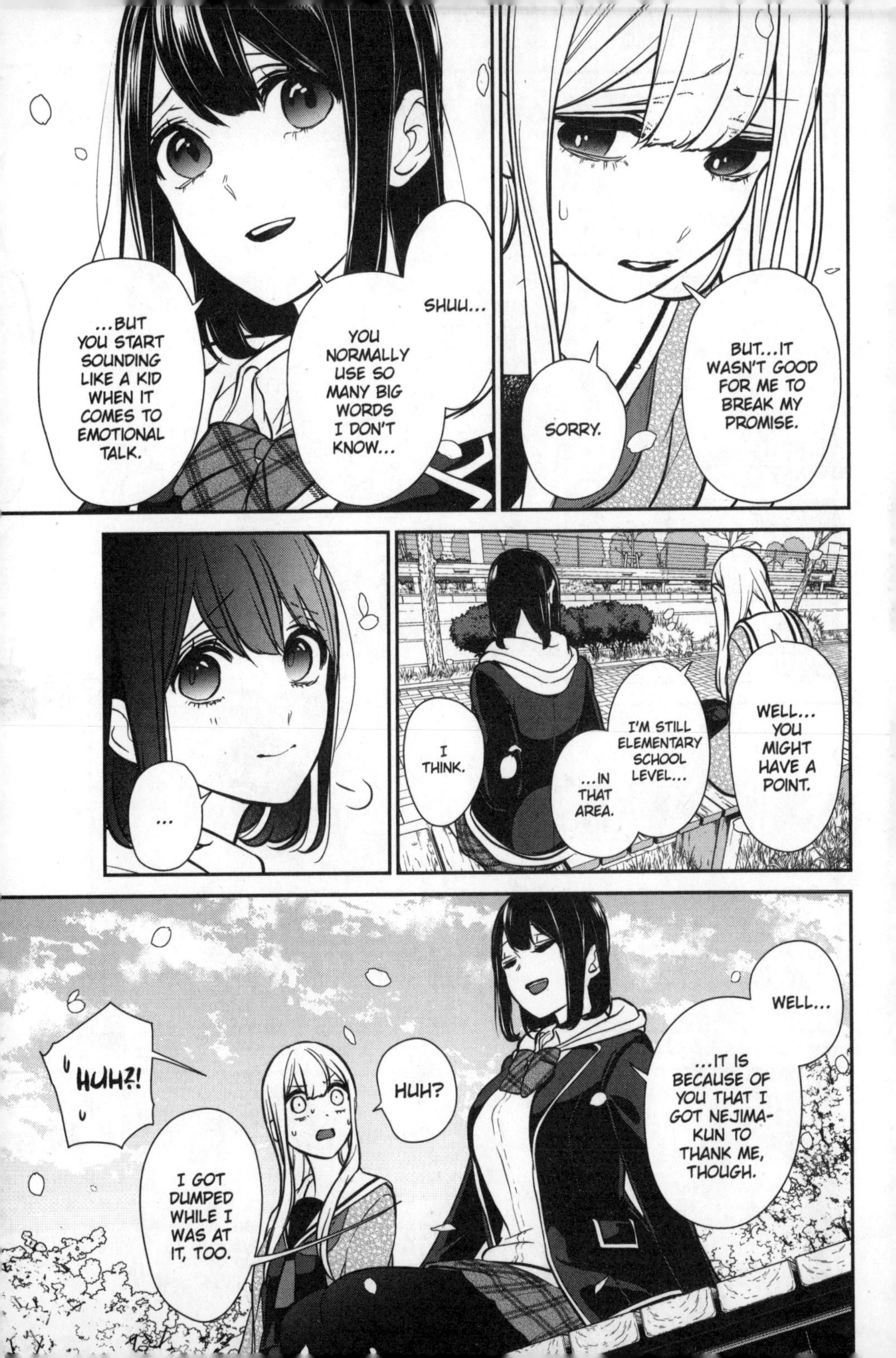
BUT...IT WASN'T GOOD FOR ME TO BREAK MY PROMISE.
SORRY.
SHUU...
YOU NORMALLY USE SO MANY BIG WORDS I DON'T KNOW...
...BUT YOU START SOUNDING LIKE A KID WHEN IT COMES TO EMOTIONAL TALK.
WELL... YOU MIGHT HAVE A POINT.
I'M STILL ELEMENTARY SCHOOL LEVEL...
...IN THAT AREA.
I THINK.
...
WELL...
...IT IS BECAUSE OF YOU THAT I GOT NEJIMA-KUN TO THANK ME, THOUGH.
HUH?
I GOT DUMPED WHILE I WAS AT IT, TOO.
HUH?!

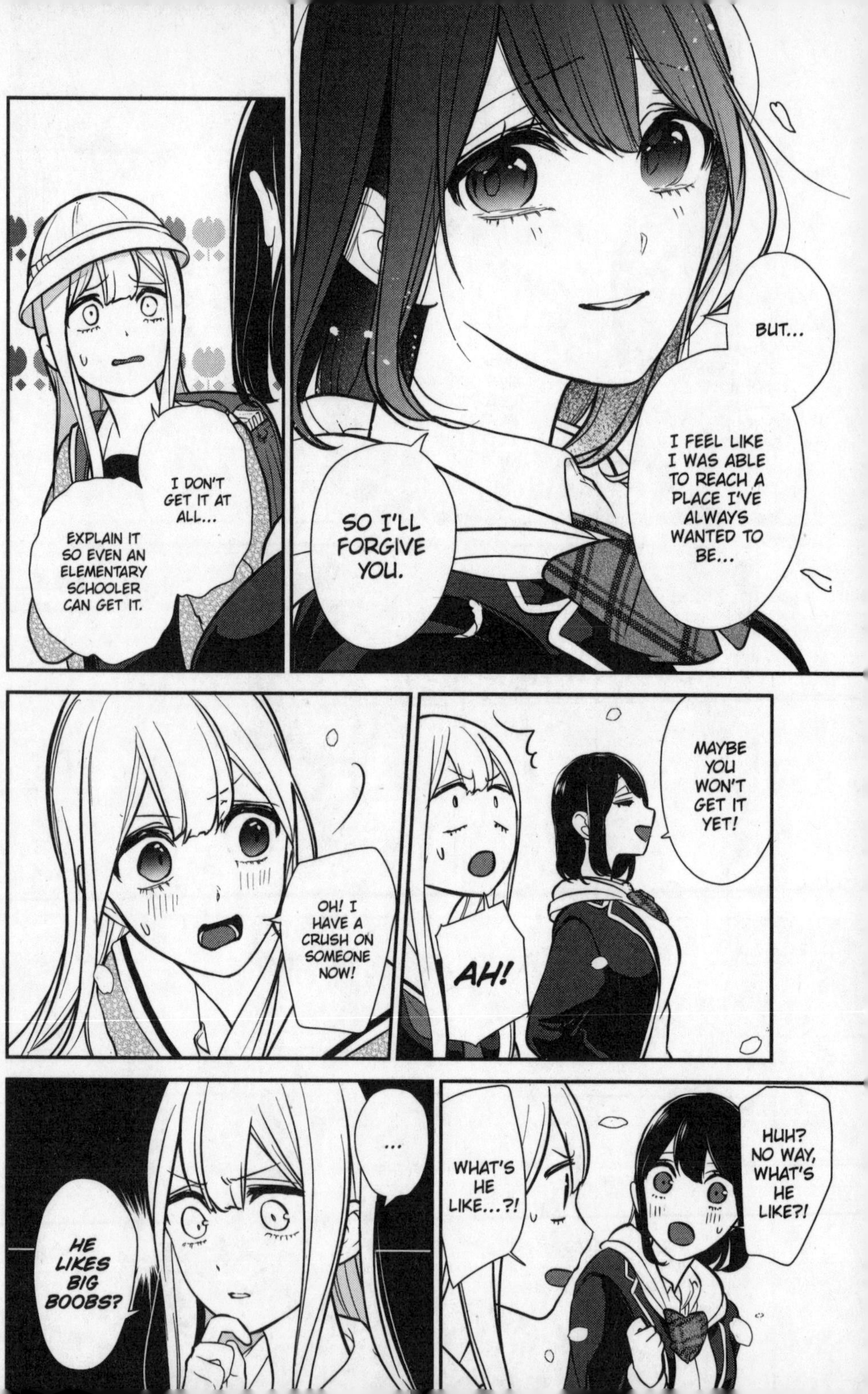
BUT...
I FEEL LIKE I WAS ABLE TO REACH A PLACE I'VE ALWAYS WANTED TO BE...
SO I'LL FORGIVE YOU.
I DON'T GET IT AT ALL...
EXPLAIN IT SO EVEN AN ELEMENTARY SCHOOLER CAN GET IT.
MAYBE YOU WON'T GET IT YET!
AH!
OH! I HAVE A CRUSH ON SOMEONE NOW!
HUH? NO WAY, WHAT'S HE LIKE?!
WHAT'S HE LIKE...?!
...
HE LIKES BIG BOOBS?

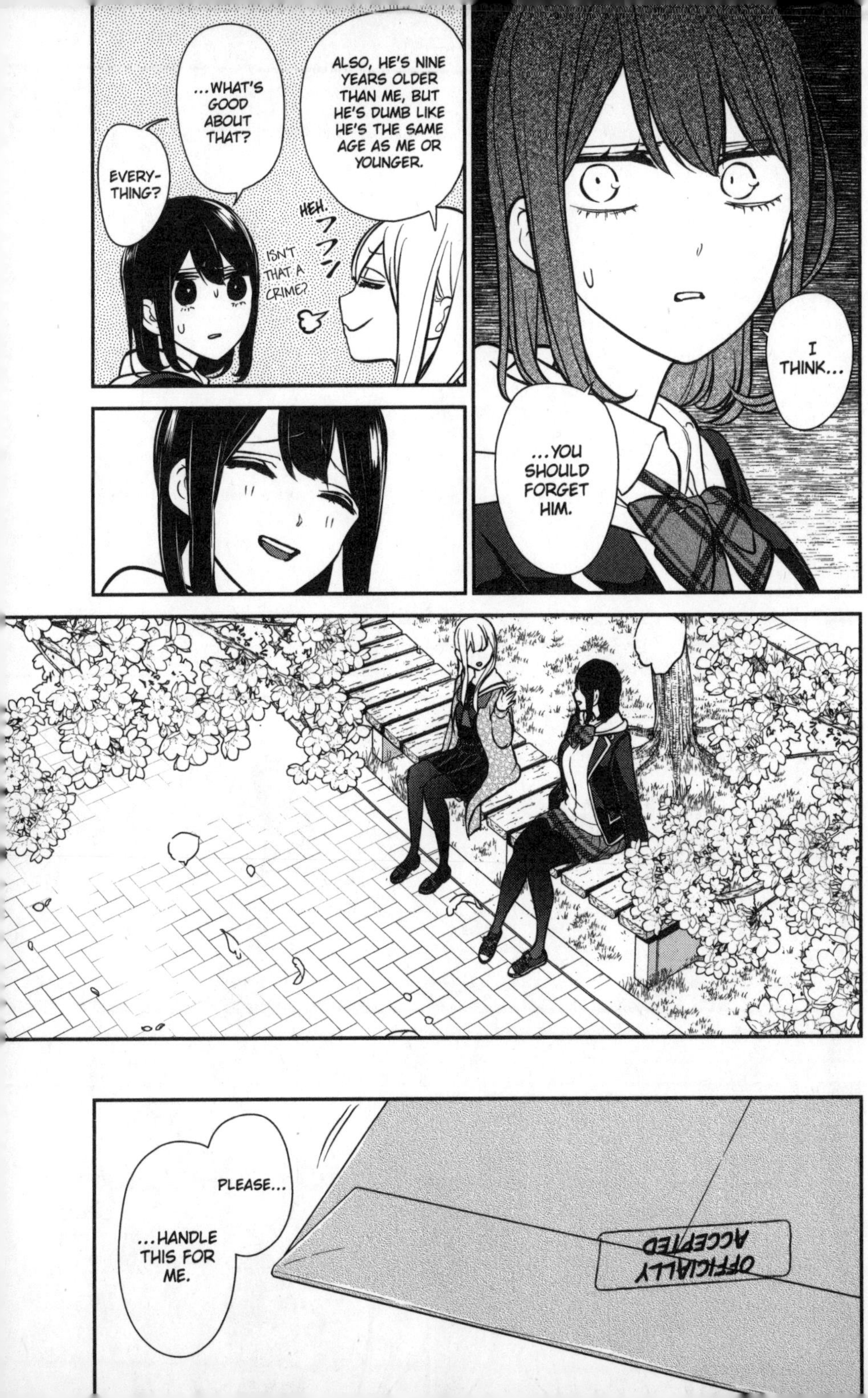
I THINK...
...YOU SHOULD FORGET HIM.
ALSO, HE'S NINE YEARS OLDER THAN ME, BUT HE'S DUMB LIKE HE'S THE SAME AGE AS ME OR YOUNGER.
HEH.
...WHAT'S GOOD ABOUT THAT?
ISN'T THAT A CRIME?
EVERY-THING?
PLEASE...
...HANDLE THIS FOR ME.
OFFICIALLY ACCEPTED

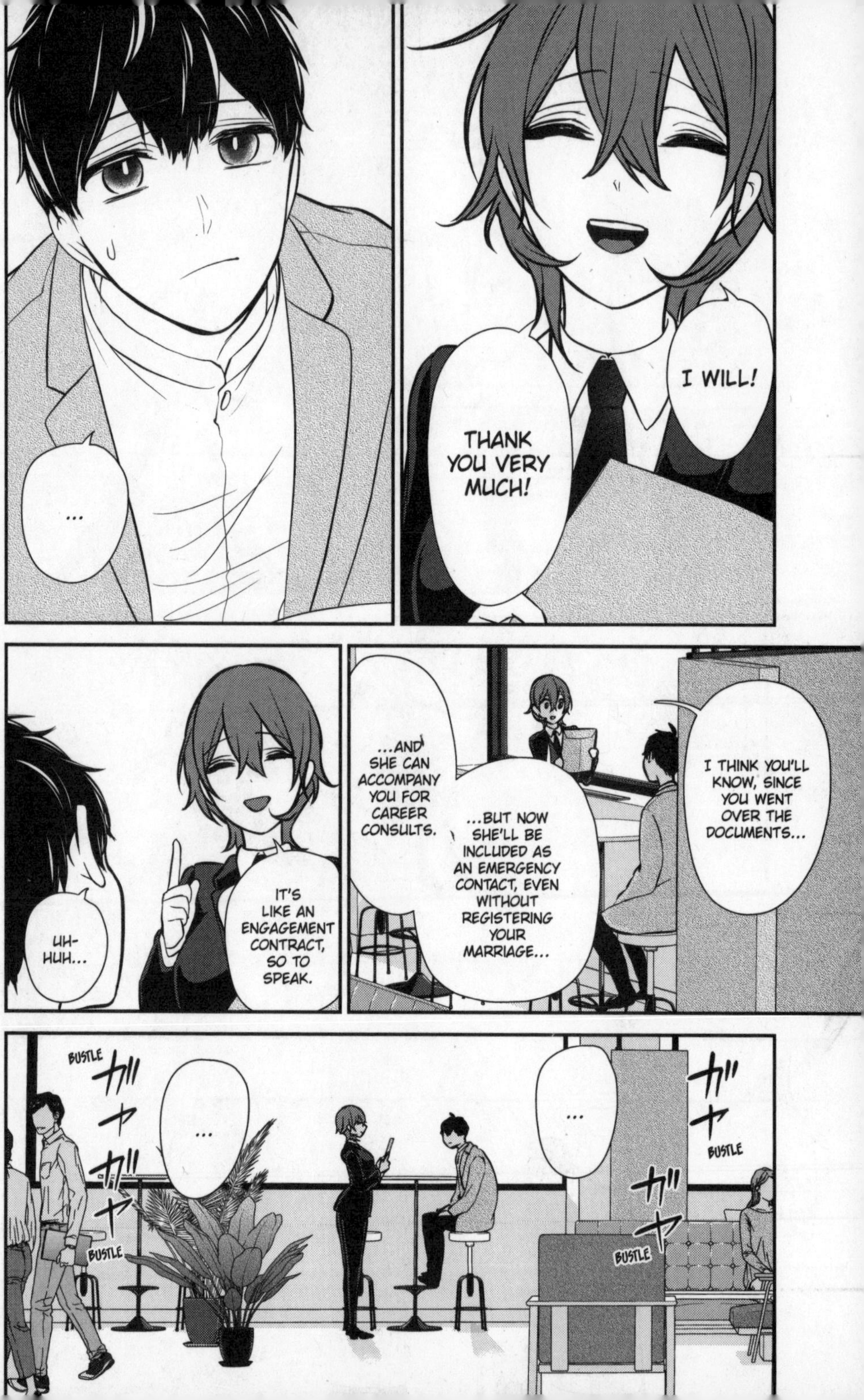
I WILL!
THANK YOU VERY MUCH!
...
I THINK YOU'LL KNOW, SINCE YOU WENT OVER THE DOCUMENTS...
...BUT NOW SHE'LL BE INCLUDED AS AN EMERGENCY CONTACT, EVEN WITHOUT REGISTERING YOUR MARRIAGE...
...AND SHE CAN ACCOMPANY YOU FOR CAREER CONSULTS.
IT'S LIKE AN ENGAGEMENT CONTRACT, SO TO SPEAK.
UH-HUH...
BUSTLE
BUSTLE
...
...
BUSTLE
BUSTLE

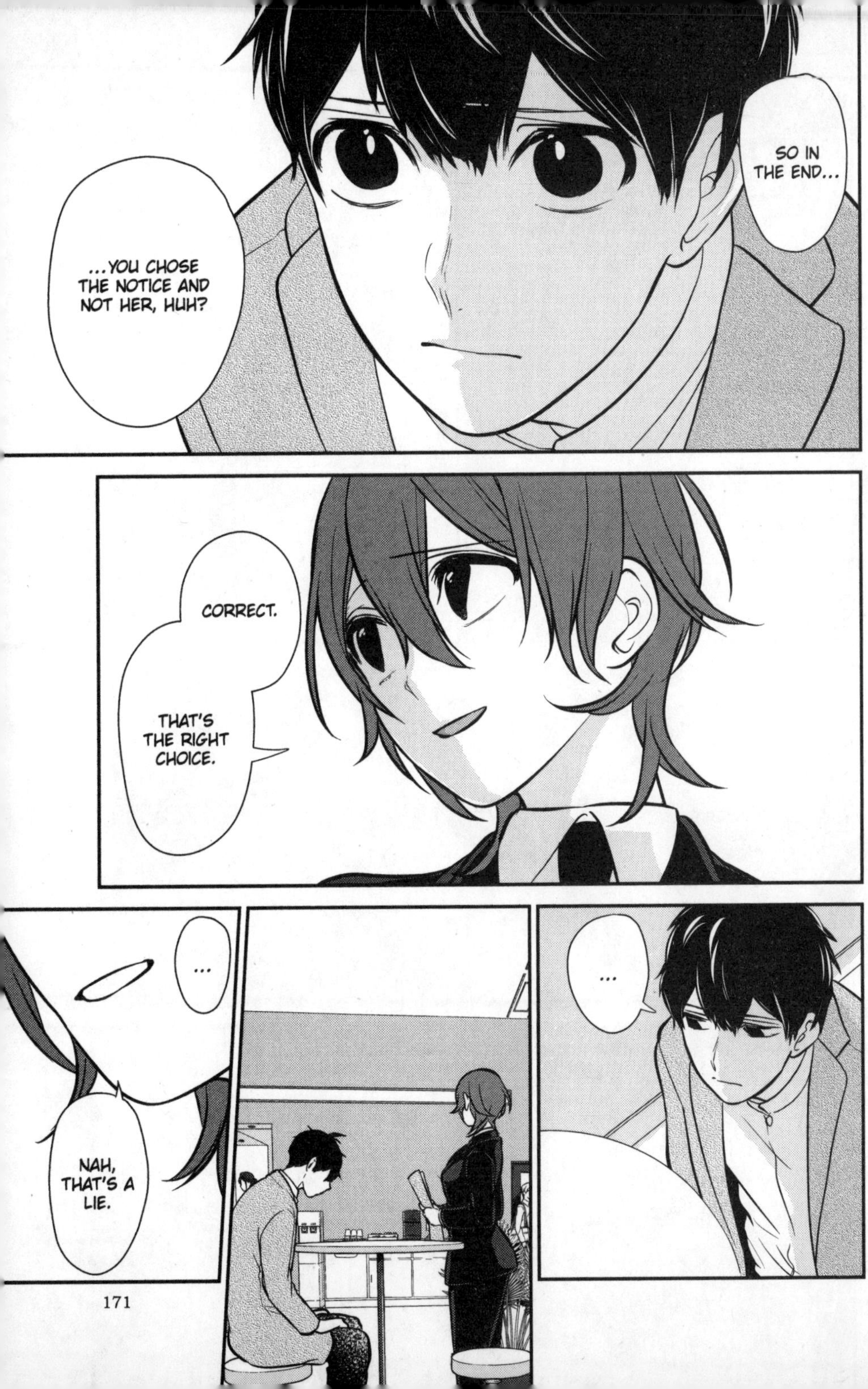
SO IN THE END...
...YOU CHOSE THE NOTICE AND NOT HER, HUH?
CORRECT.
THAT'S THE RIGHT CHOICE.
...
...
NAH, THAT'S A LIE.

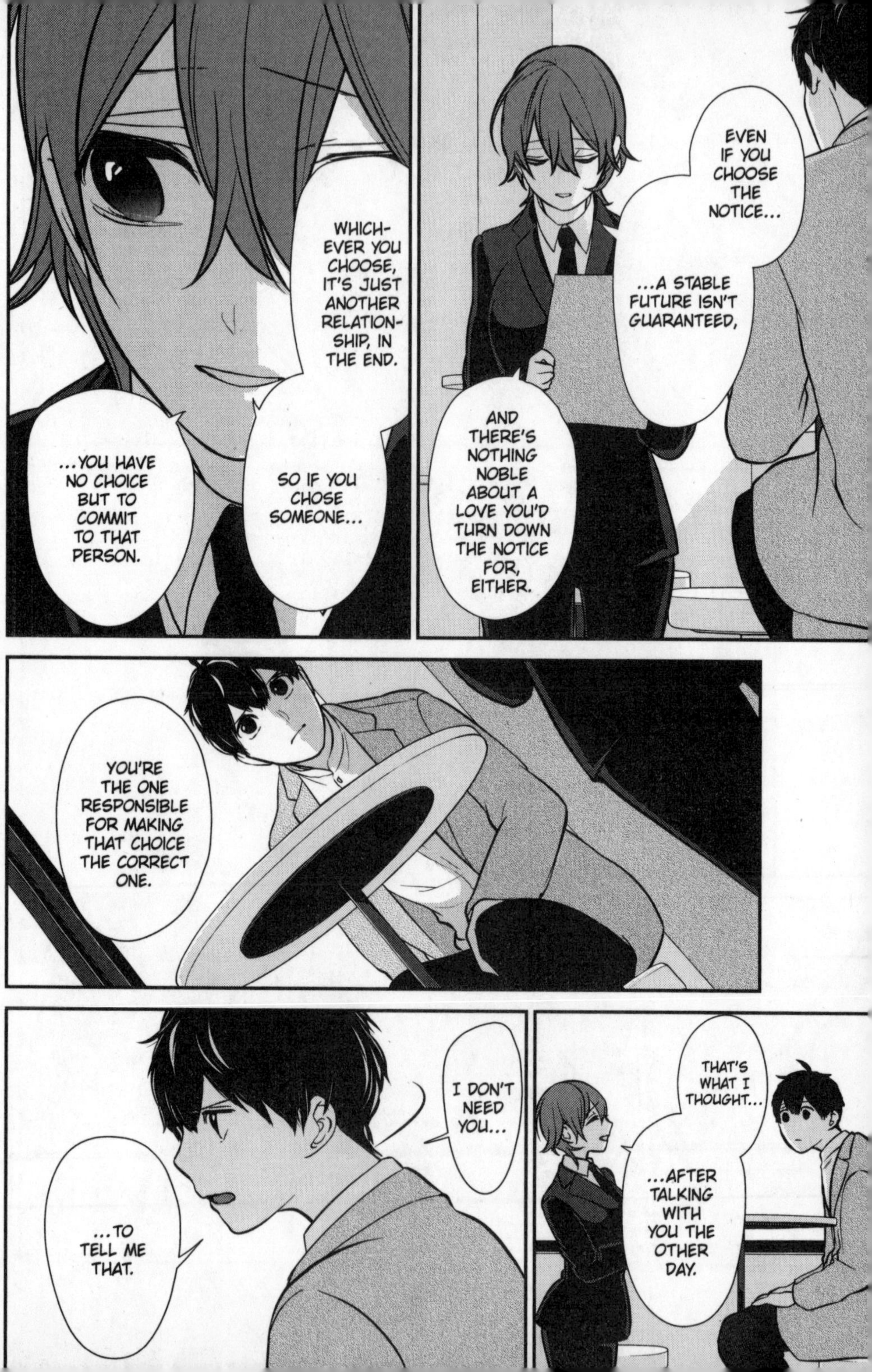
EVEN IF YOU CHOOSE THE NOTICE...
...A STABLE FUTURE ISN'T GUARANTEED,
AND THERE'S NOTHING NOBLE ABOUT A LOVE YOU'D TURN DOWN THE NOTICE FOR, EITHER.
WHICH-EVER YOU CHOOSE, IT'S JUST ANOTHER RELATION-SHIP, IN THE END.
SO IF YOU CHOSE SOMEONE...
...YOU HAVE NO CHOICE BUT TO COMMIT TO THAT PERSON.
YOU'RE THE ONE RESPONSIBLE FOR MAKING THAT CHOICE THE CORRECT ONE.
THAT'S WHAT I THOUGHT...
...AFTER TALKING WITH YOU THE OTHER DAY.
I DON'T NEED YOU...
...TO TELL ME THAT.

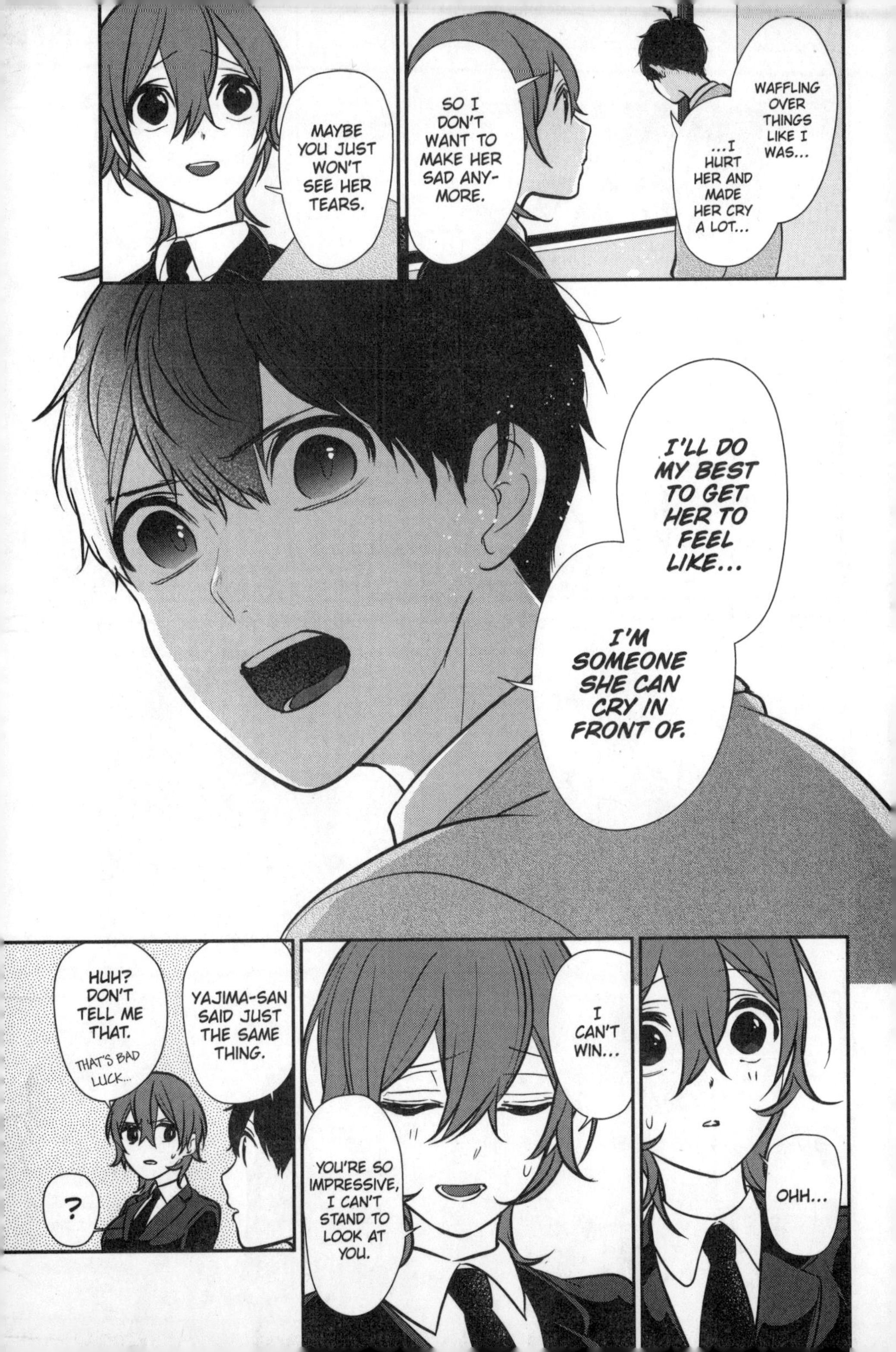

WAFFLING OVER THINGS LIKE I WAS...
...I HURT HER AND MADE HER CRY A LOT...
SO I DON'T WANT TO MAKE HER SAD ANY-MORE.
MAYBE YOU JUST WON'T SEE HER TEARS.
I'LL DO MY BEST TO GET HER TO FEEL LIKE...
I'M SOMEONE SHE CAN CRY IN FRONT OF.
OHH...
I CAN'T WIN...
YOU'RE SO IMPRESSIVE, I CAN'T STAND TO LOOK AT YOU.
YAJIMA-SAN SAID JUST THE SAME THING.
HUH? DON'T TELL ME THAT.
THAT'S BAD LUCK...
?

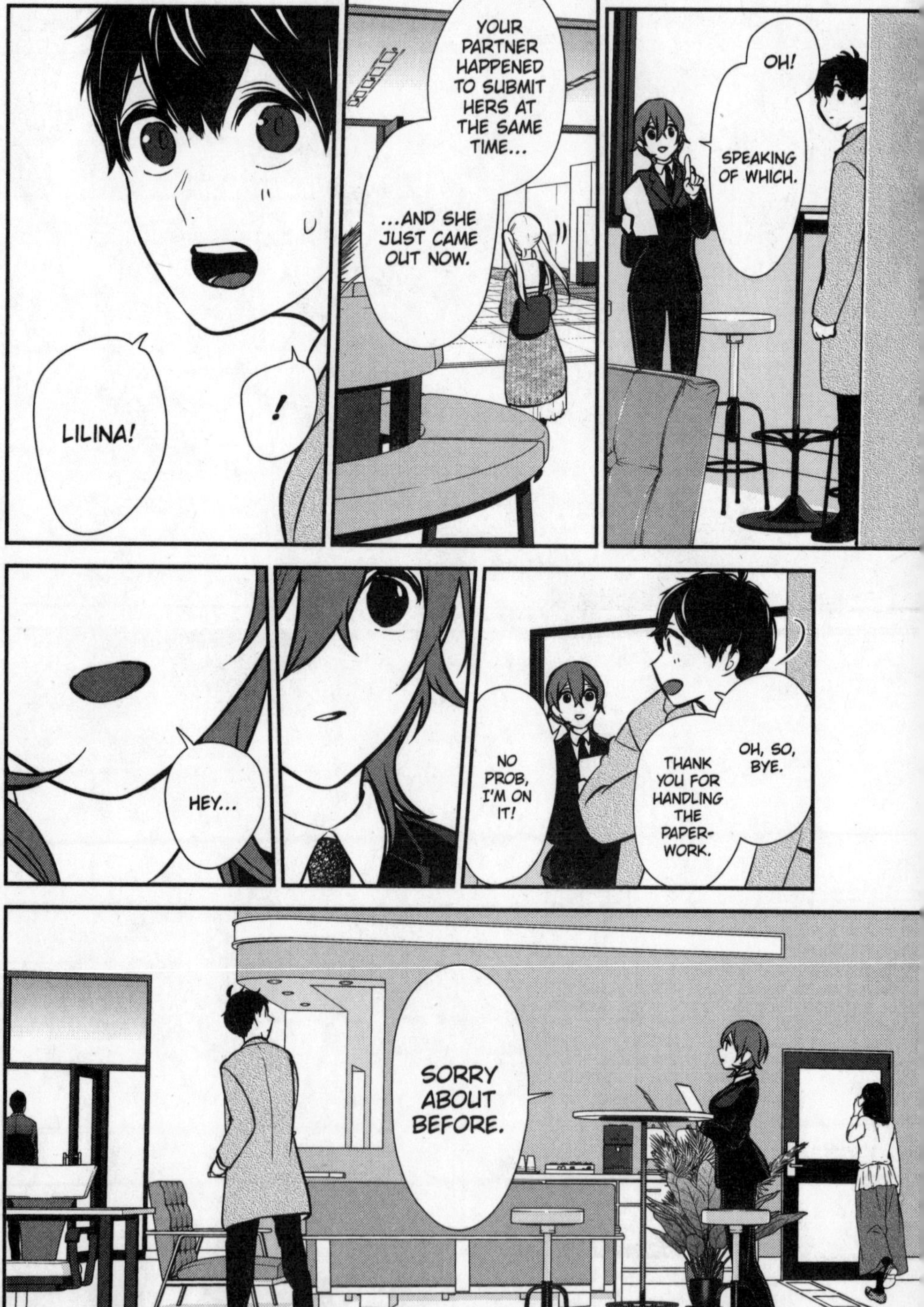
OH!
SPEAKING OF WHICH.
YOUR PARTNER HAPPENED TO SUBMIT HERS AT THE SAME TIME...
...AND SHE JUST CAME OUT NOW.
!
LILINA!
OH, SO, BYE.
THANK YOU FOR HANDLING THE PAPER-WORK.
NO PROB, I'M ON IT!
HEY...
SORRY ABOUT BEFORE.

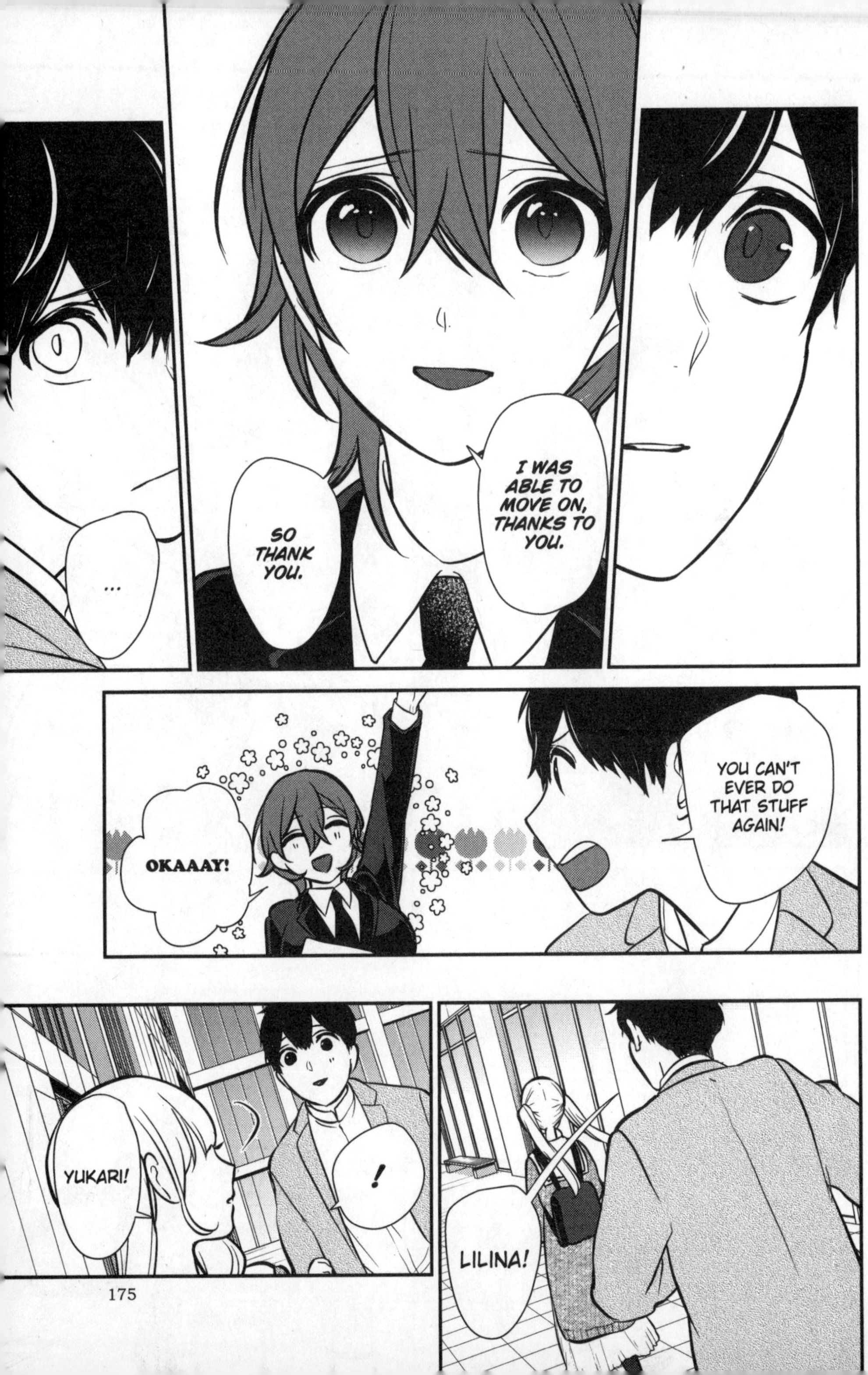

I WAS ABLE TO MOVE ON, THANKS TO YOU.
SO THANK YOU.
...
YOU CAN'T EVER DO THAT STUFF AGAIN!
OKAAAY!
LILINA!
!
YUKARI!

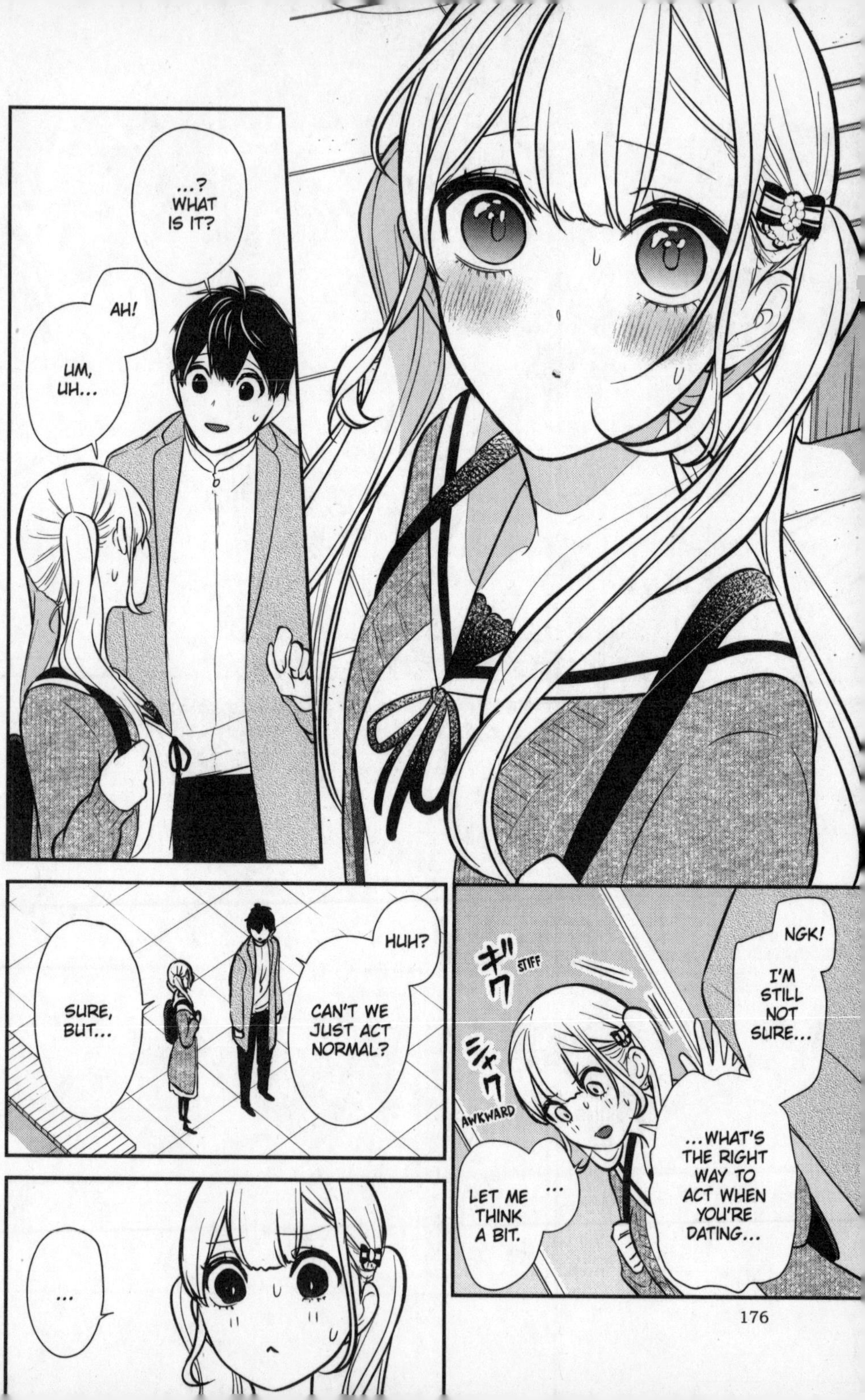
...? WHAT IS IT?
AH!
UM, UH...
NGK!
I'M STILL NOT SURE...
ギク STIFF
ギクシャク AWKWARD
...WHAT'S THE RIGHT WAY TO ACT WHEN YOU'RE DATING...
...
LET ME THINK A BIT.
HUH?
CAN'T WE JUST ACT NORMAL?
SURE, BUT...
...

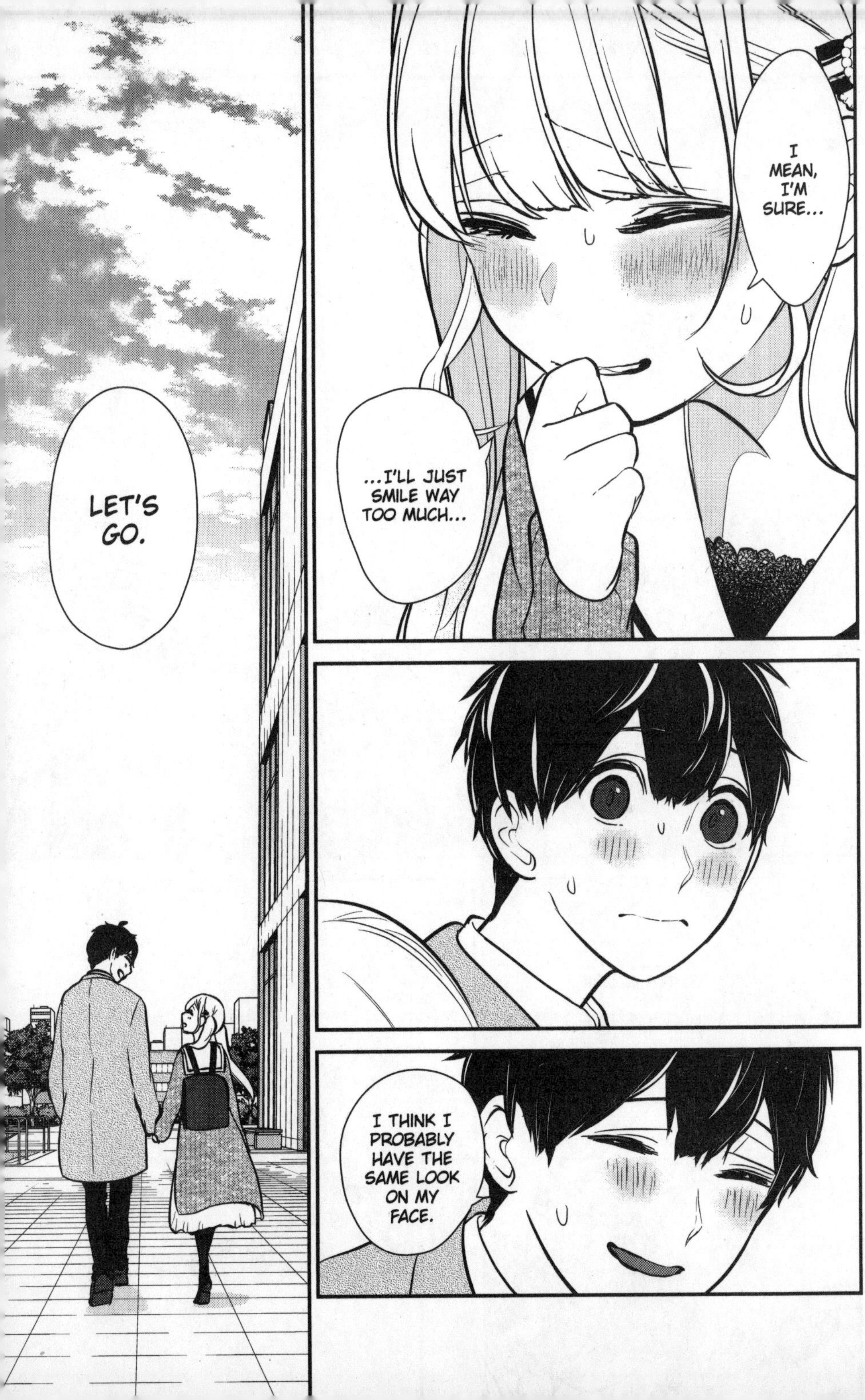
I MEAN, I'M SURE...
...I'LL JUST SMILE WAY TOO MUCH...
I THINK I PROBABLY HAVE THE SAME LOOK ON MY FACE.
LET'S GO.

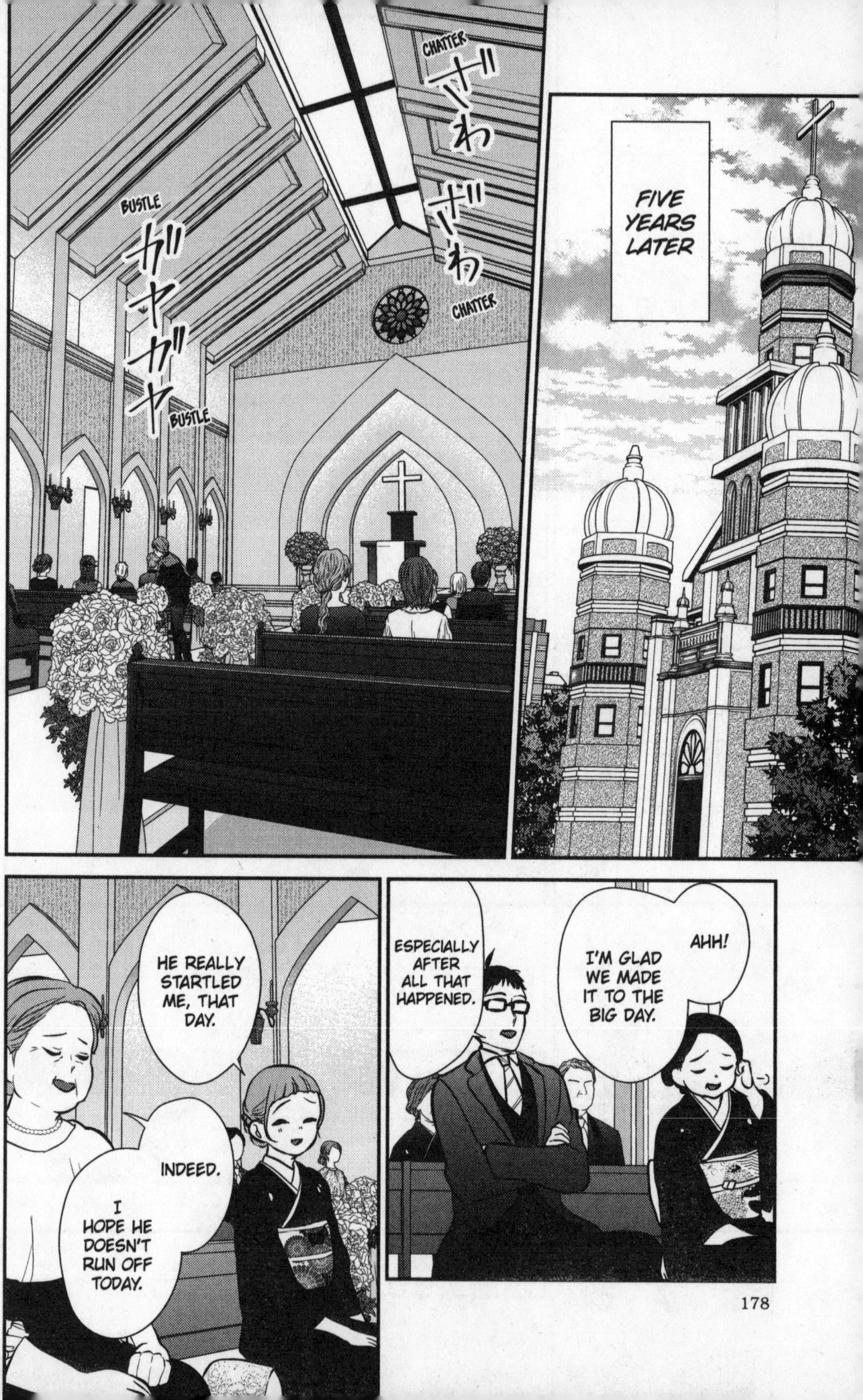
FIVE YEARS LATER
ざわ ざわ
CHATTER
CHATTER
ガヤガヤ
BUSTLE
BUSTLE
AHH!
I'M GLAD WE MADE IT TO THE BIG DAY.
ESPECIALLY AFTER ALL THAT HAPPENED.
HE REALLY STARTLED ME, THAT DAY.
INDEED.
I HOPE HE DOESN'T RUN OFF TODAY.

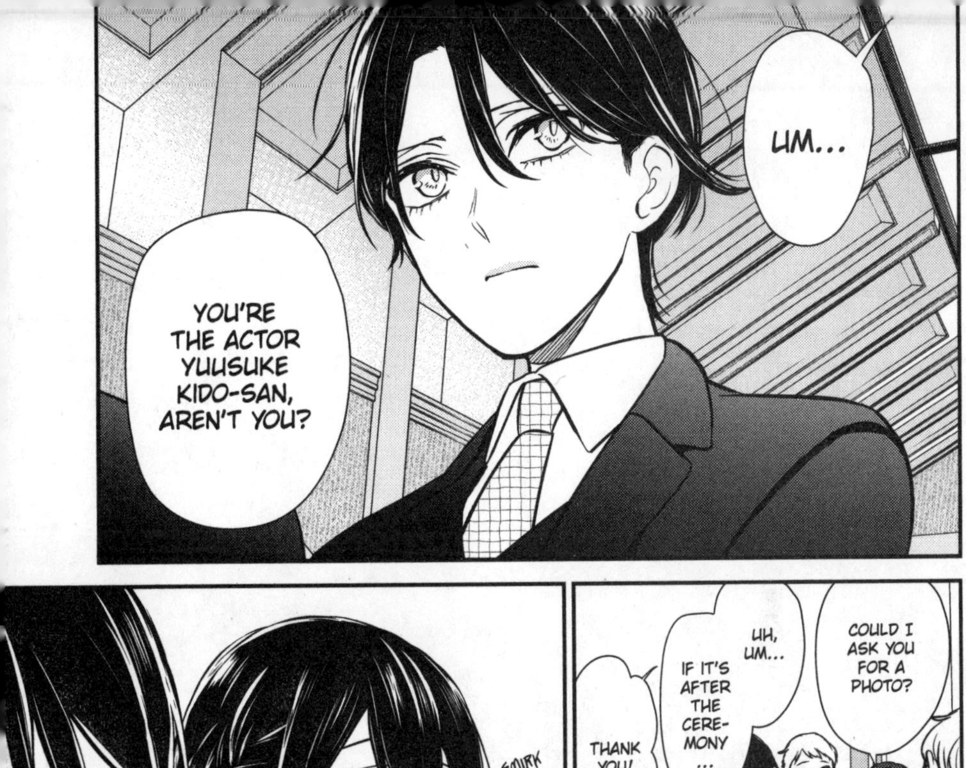
UM...
YOU'RE THE ACTOR YUUSUKE KIDO-SAN, AREN'T YOU?
COULD I ASK YOU FOR A PHOTO?
UH, UM... IF IT'S AFTER THE CERE-MONY...
THANK YOU!
SMIRK ニヤニヤ SMIRK
IT'S TOUGH BEING POPULAR, HUH?
...

*A TSUCHINOKO IS A MYTHICAL ANIMAL THAT LOOKS LIKE A FAT SNAKE.

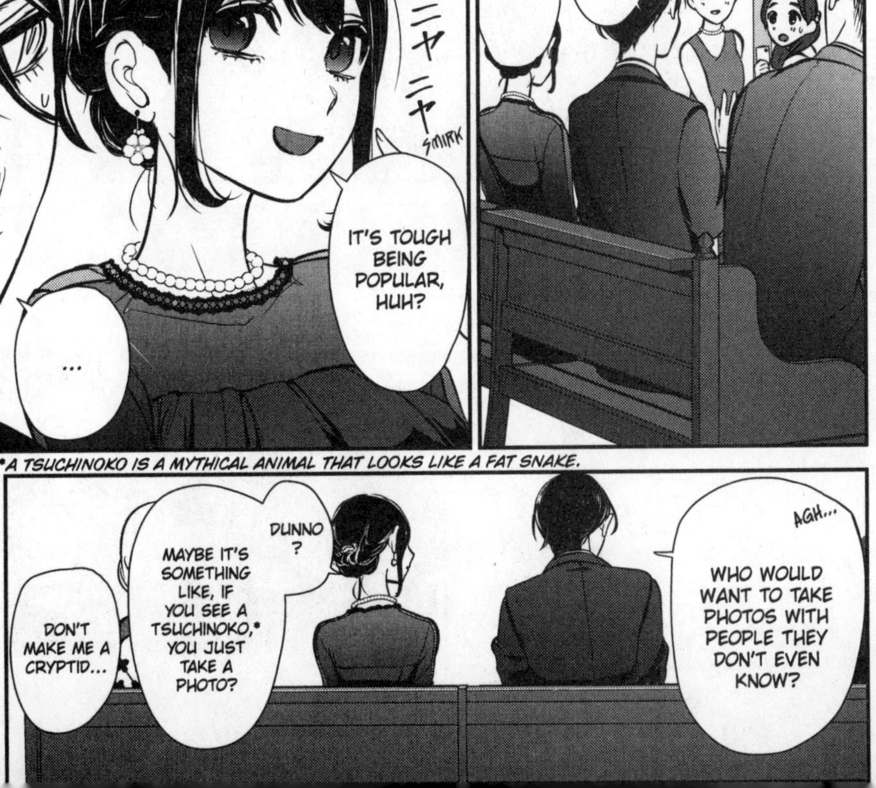
AGH...
WHO WOULD WANT TO TAKE PHOTOS WITH PEOPLE THEY DON'T EVEN KNOW?
DUNNO?
MAYBE IT'S SOMETHING LIKE, IF YOU SEE A TSUCHINOKO,* YOU JUST TAKE A PHOTO?
DON'T MAKE ME A CRYPTID...

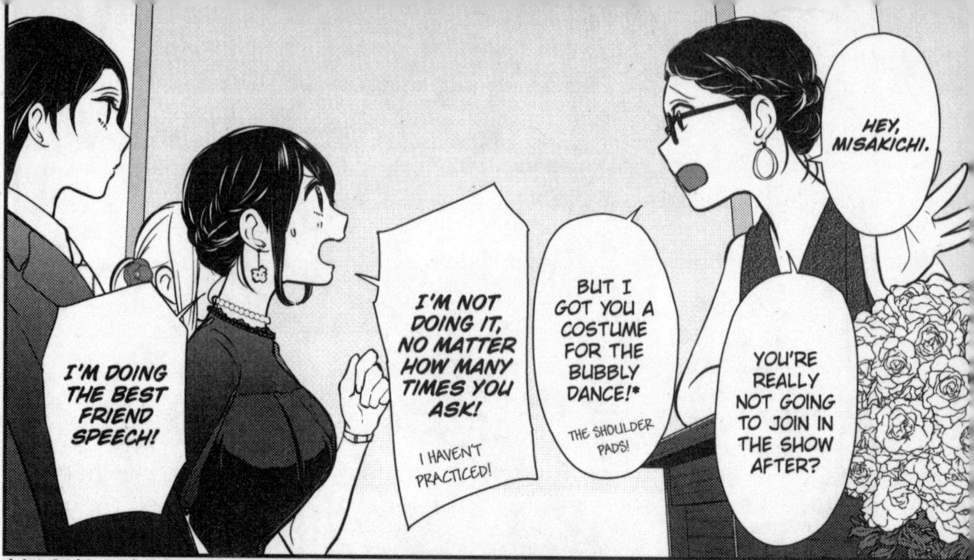
HEY, MISAKICHI.
YOU'RE REALLY NOT GOING TO JOIN IN THE SHOW AFTER?
BUT I GOT YOU A COSTUME FOR THE BUBBLY DANCE!*
THE SHOULDER PADS!
I'M NOT DOING IT, NO MATTER HOW MANY TIMES YOU ASK!
I HAVEN'T PRACTICED!
I'M DOING THE BEST FRIEND SPEECH!

*AN 80'S STYLE DANCE NUMBER THAT BECAME POPULAR FROM A 2017 VIRAL VIDEO.

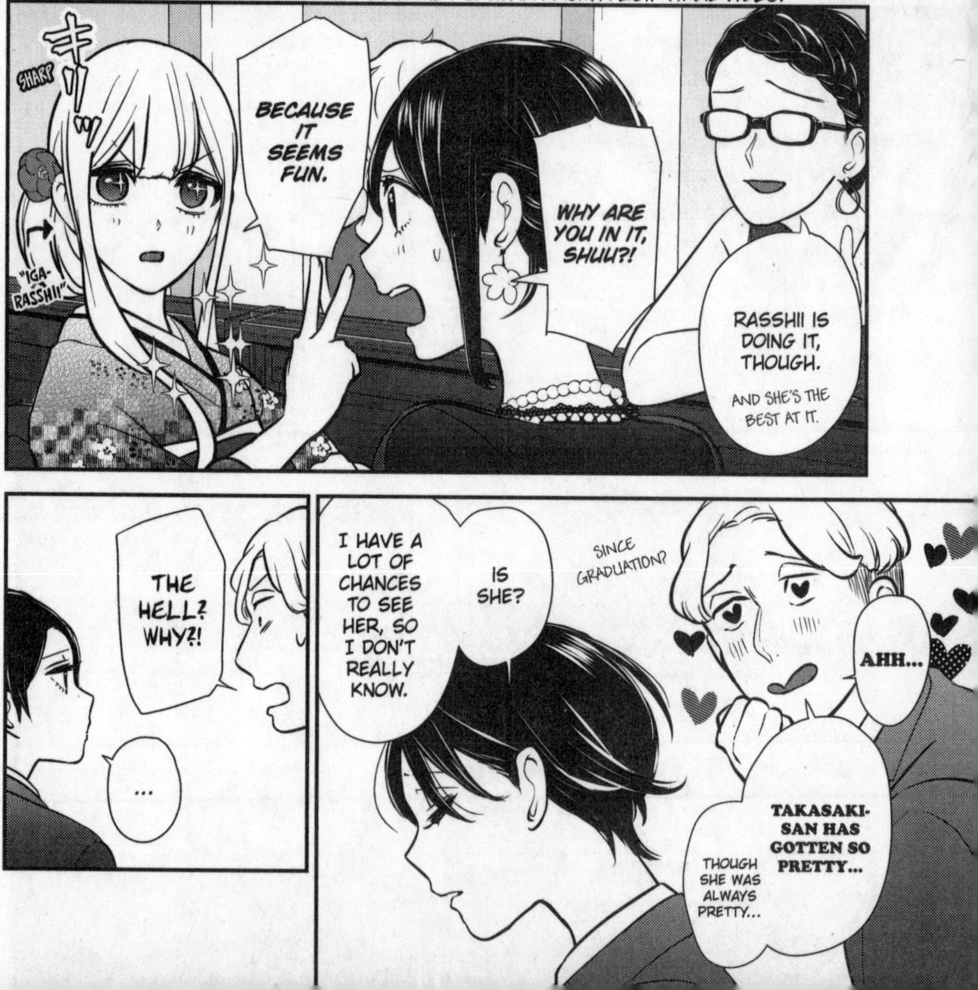
RASSHII IS DOING IT, THOUGH.
AND SHE'S THE BEST AT IT.
WHY ARE YOU IN IT, SHUU?!
BECAUSE IT SEEMS FUN.
SHARP
"IGA-RASSHII"
AHH...
TAKASAKI-SAN HAS GOTTEN SO PRETTY...
THOUGH SHE WAS ALWAYS PRETTY...
SINCE GRADUATION?
IS SHE?
I HAVE A LOT OF CHANCES TO SEE HER, SO I DON'T REALLY KNOW.
THE HELL? WHY?!
...

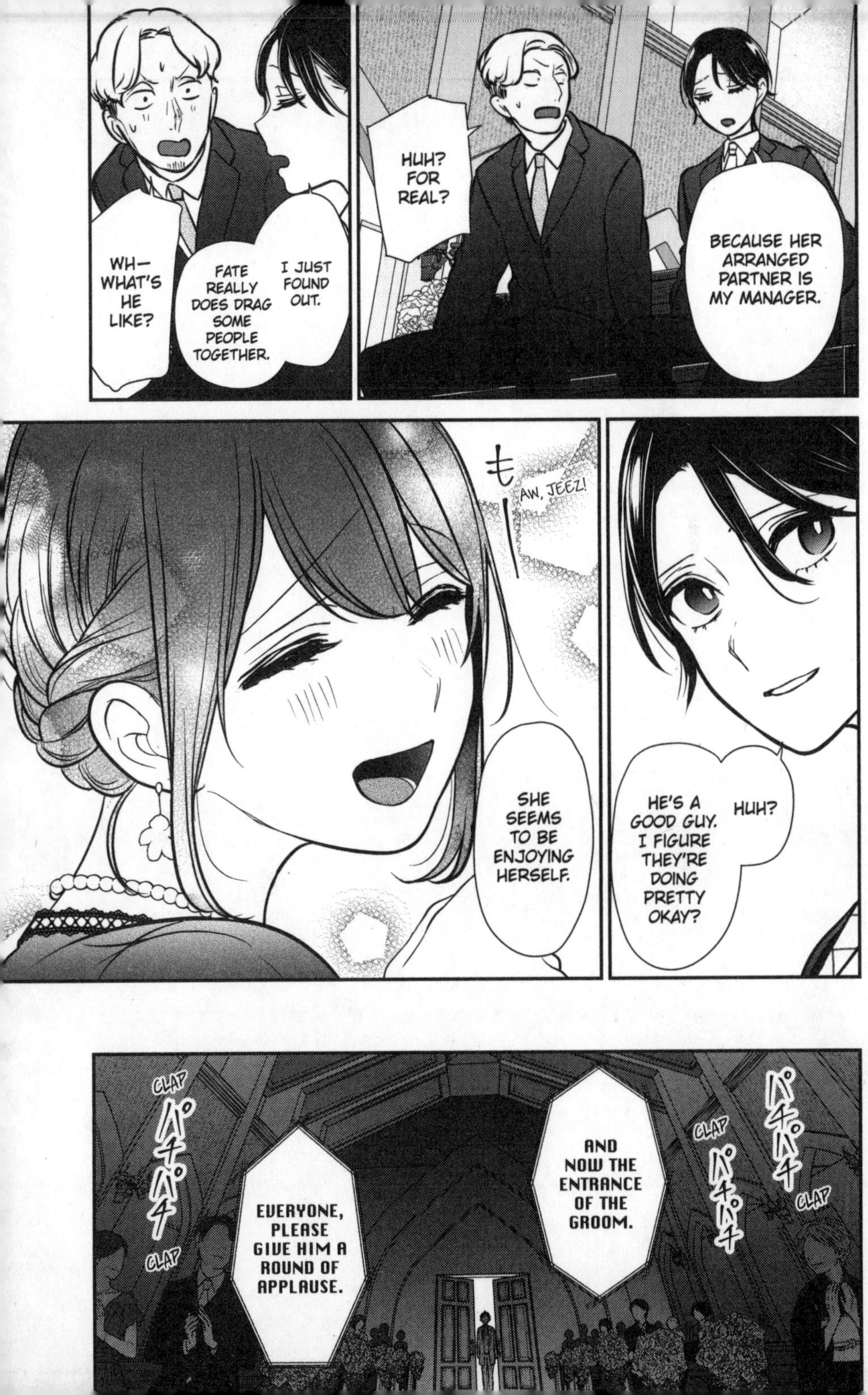
BECAUSE HER ARRANGED PARTNER IS MY MANAGER.
HUH? FOR REAL?
I JUST FOUND OUT.
FATE REALLY DOES DRAG SOME PEOPLE TOGETHER.
WH— WHAT'S HE LIKE?
HUH?
HE'S A GOOD GUY. I FIGURE THEY'RE DOING PRETTY OKAY?
もー
AW, JEEZ!
SHE SEEMS TO BE ENJOYING HERSELF.
パチパチ
CLAP
パチパチ
CLAP
AND NOW THE ENTRANCE OF THE GROOM.
EVERYONE, PLEASE GIVE HIM A ROUND OF APPLAUSE.
CLAP
パチパチ
CLAP

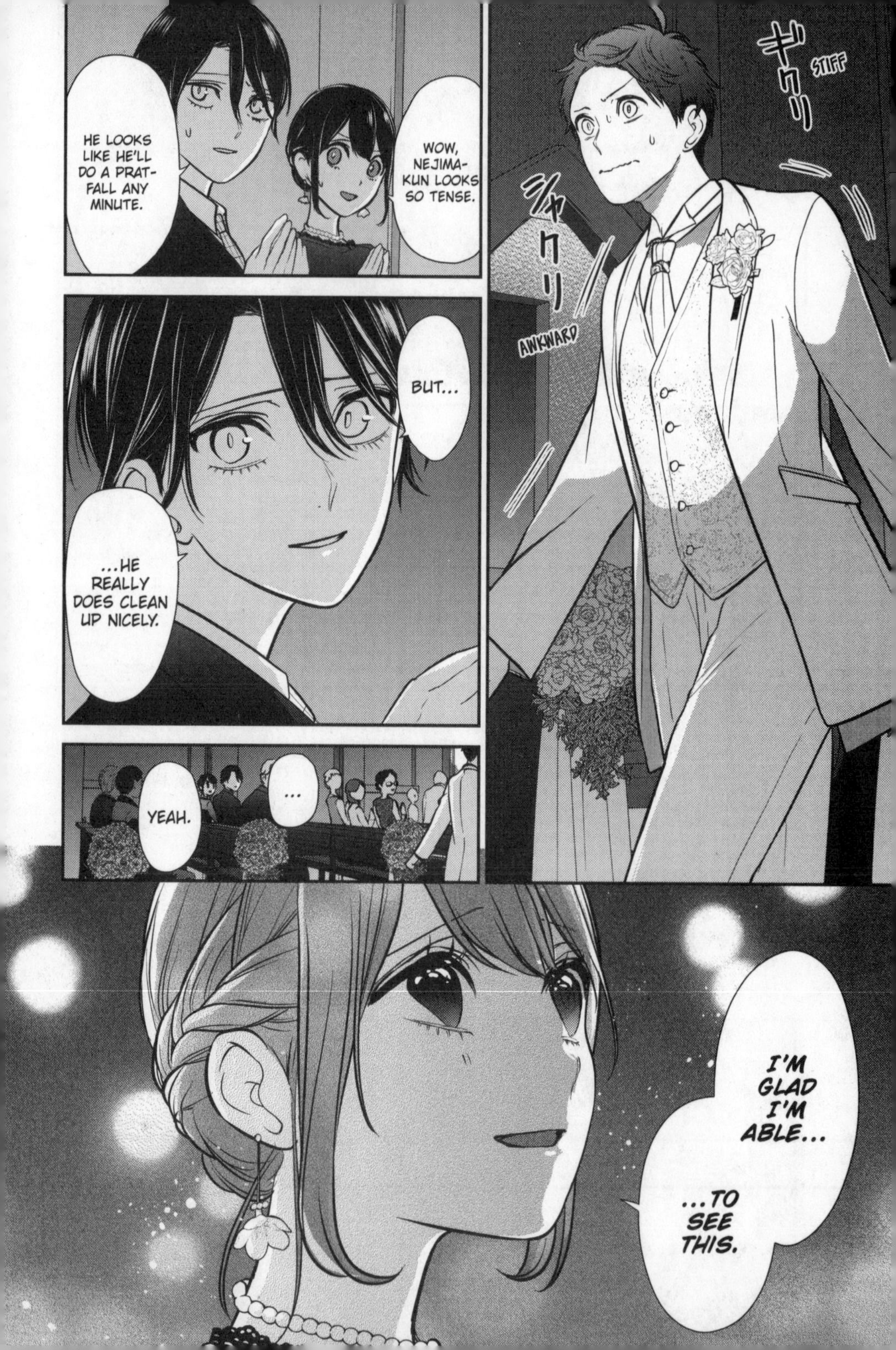
STIFF
AWKWARD
WOW, NEJIMA-KUN LOOKS SO TENSE.
HE LOOKS LIKE HE'LL DO A PRAT-FALL ANY MINUTE.
BUT...
...HE REALLY DOES CLEAN UP NICELY.
...
YEAH.
I'M GLAD I'M ABLE...
...TO SEE THIS.

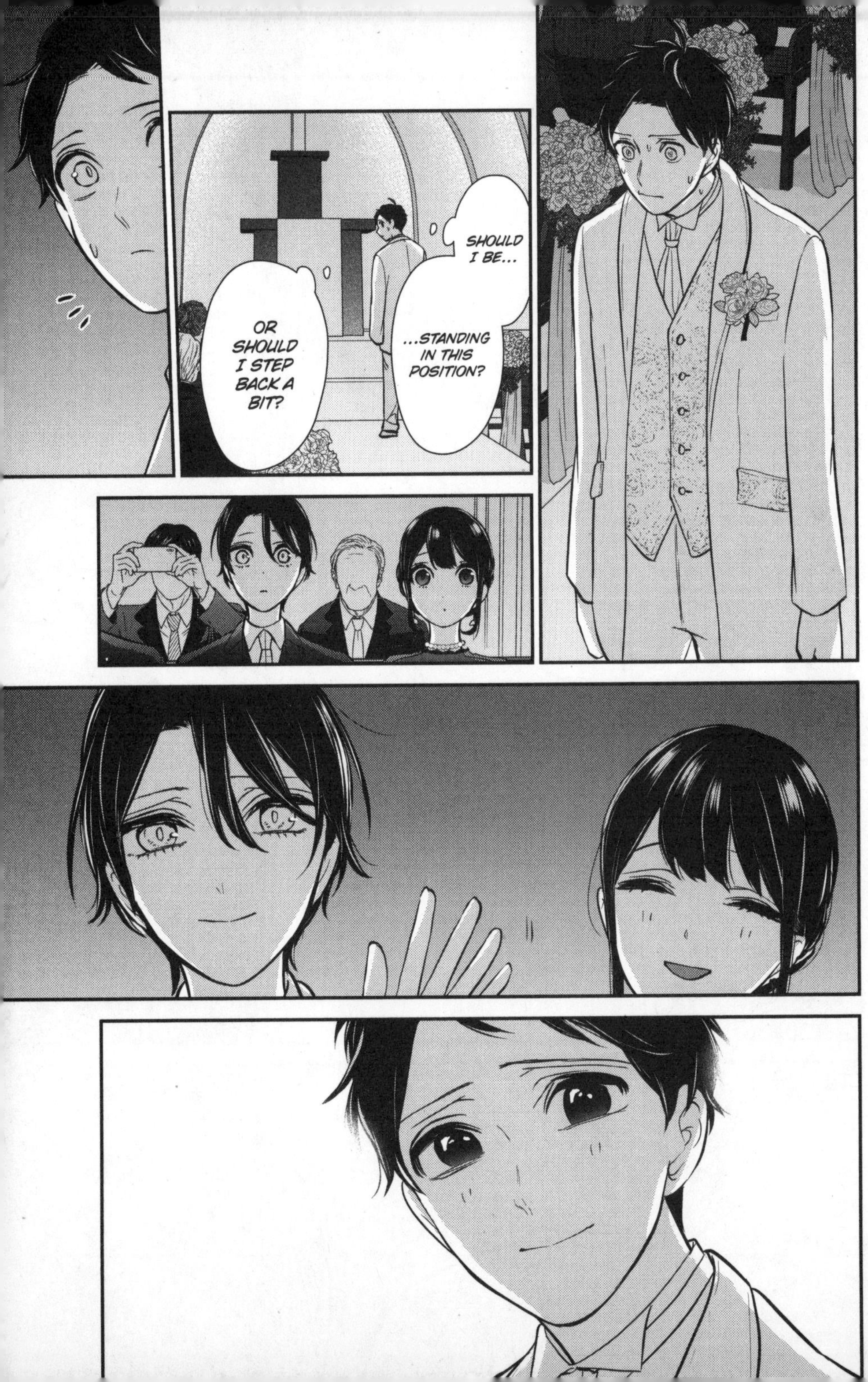
SHOULD I BE…
…STANDING IN THIS POSITION?
OR SHOULD I STEP BACK A BIT?

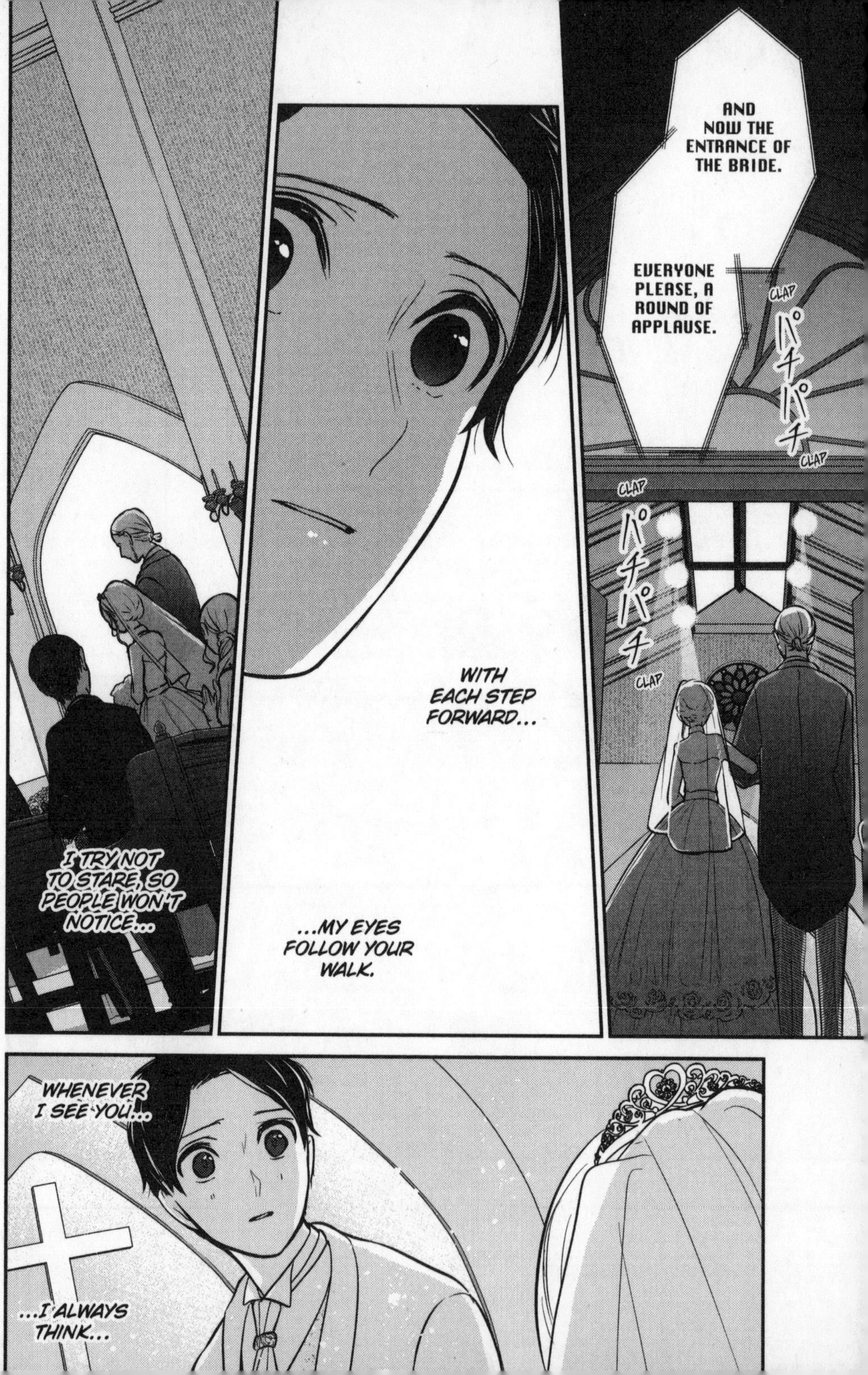
AND NOW THE ENTRANCE OF THE BRIDE.
EVERYONE PLEASE, A ROUND OF APPLAUSE.
CLAP
パチパチ
CLAP
CLAP
パチパチ
CLAP
WITH EACH STEP FORWARD...
...MY EYES FOLLOW YOUR WALK.
I TRY NOT TO STARE, SO PEOPLE WON'T NOTICE...
WHENEVER I SEE YOU...
...I ALWAYS THINK...

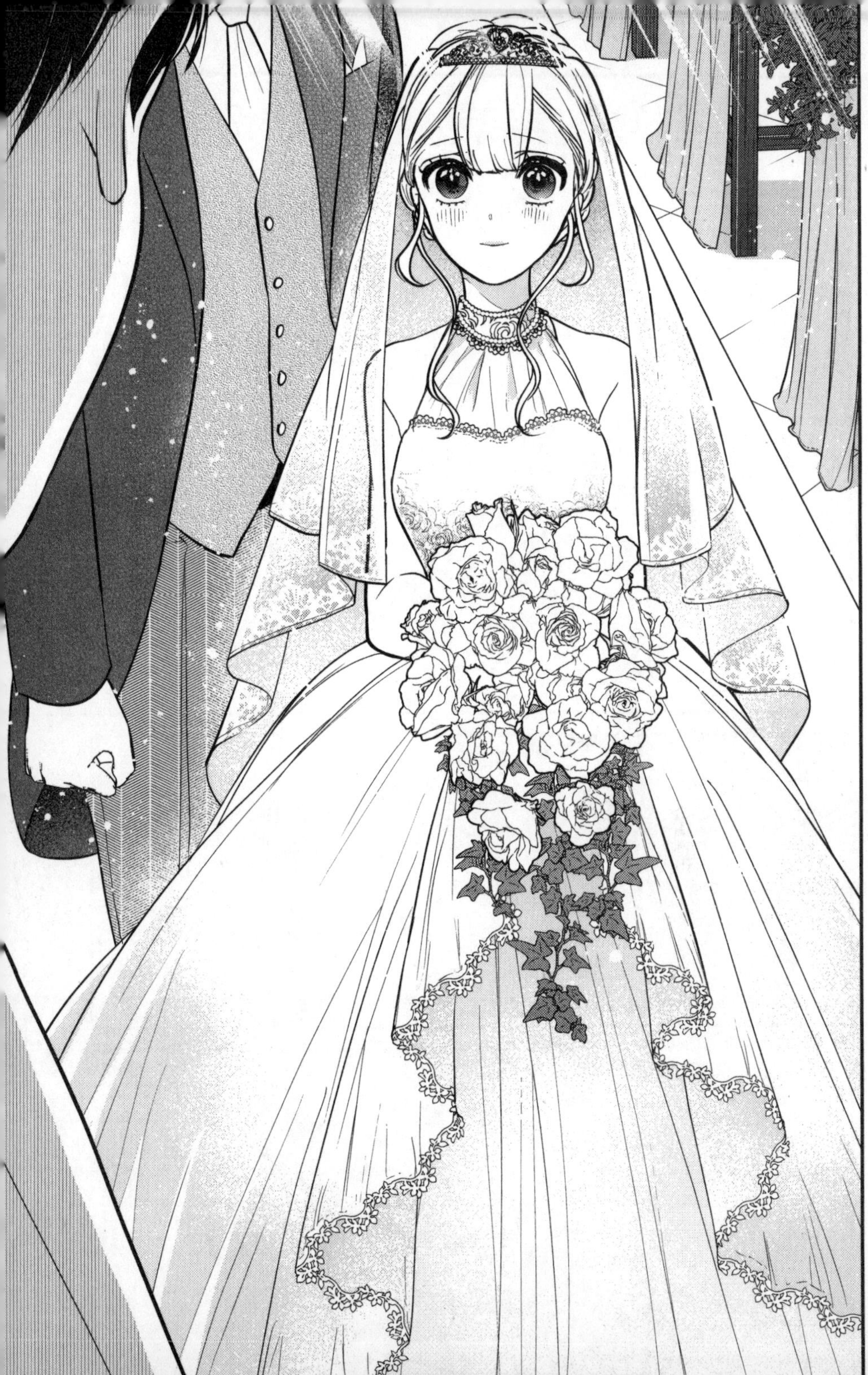

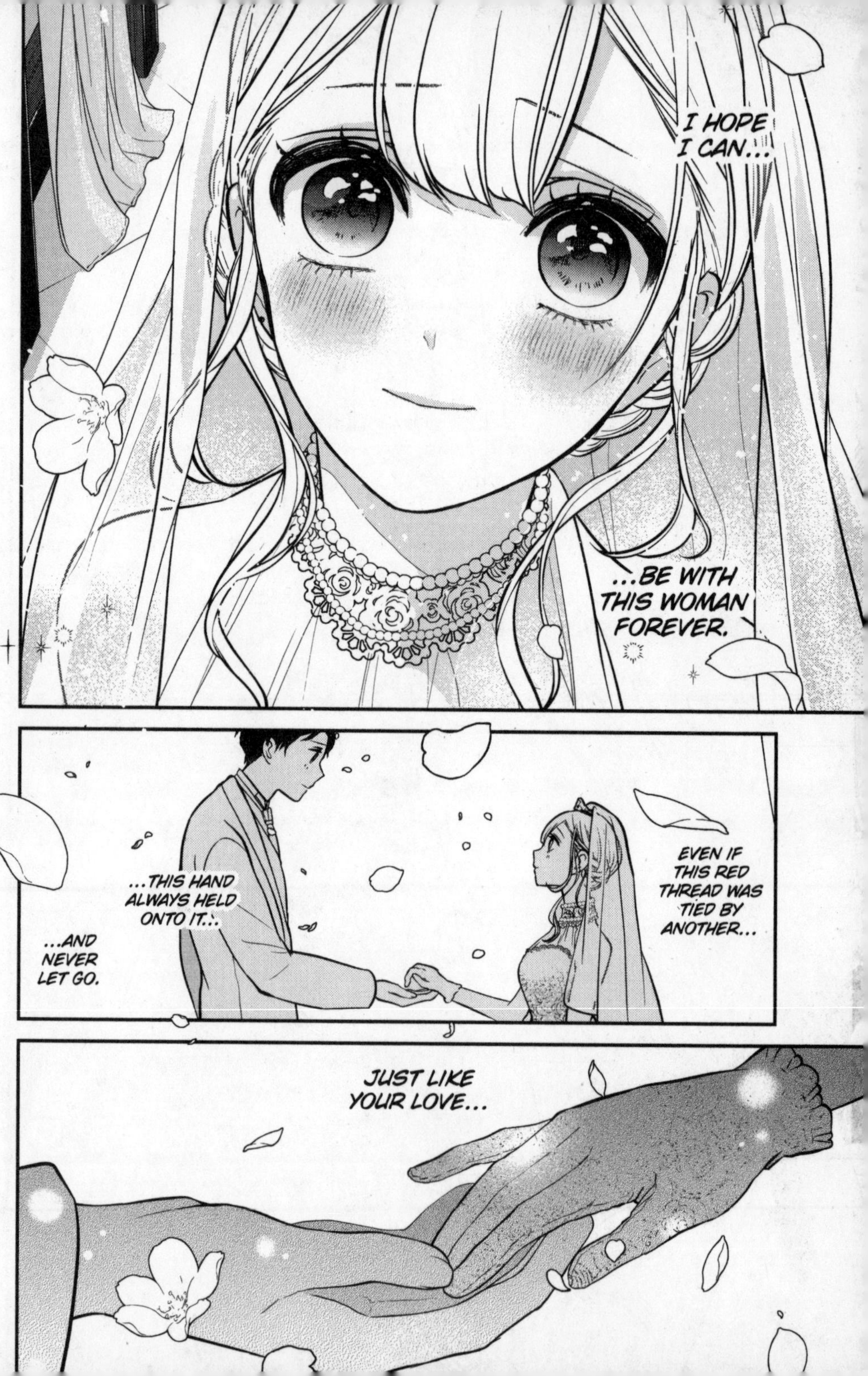
I HOPE I CAN...
...BE WITH THIS WOMAN FOREVER.
EVEN IF THIS RED THREAD WAS TIED BY ANOTHER...
...THIS HAND ALWAYS HELD ONTO IT...
...AND NEVER LET GO.
JUST LIKE YOUR LOVE...

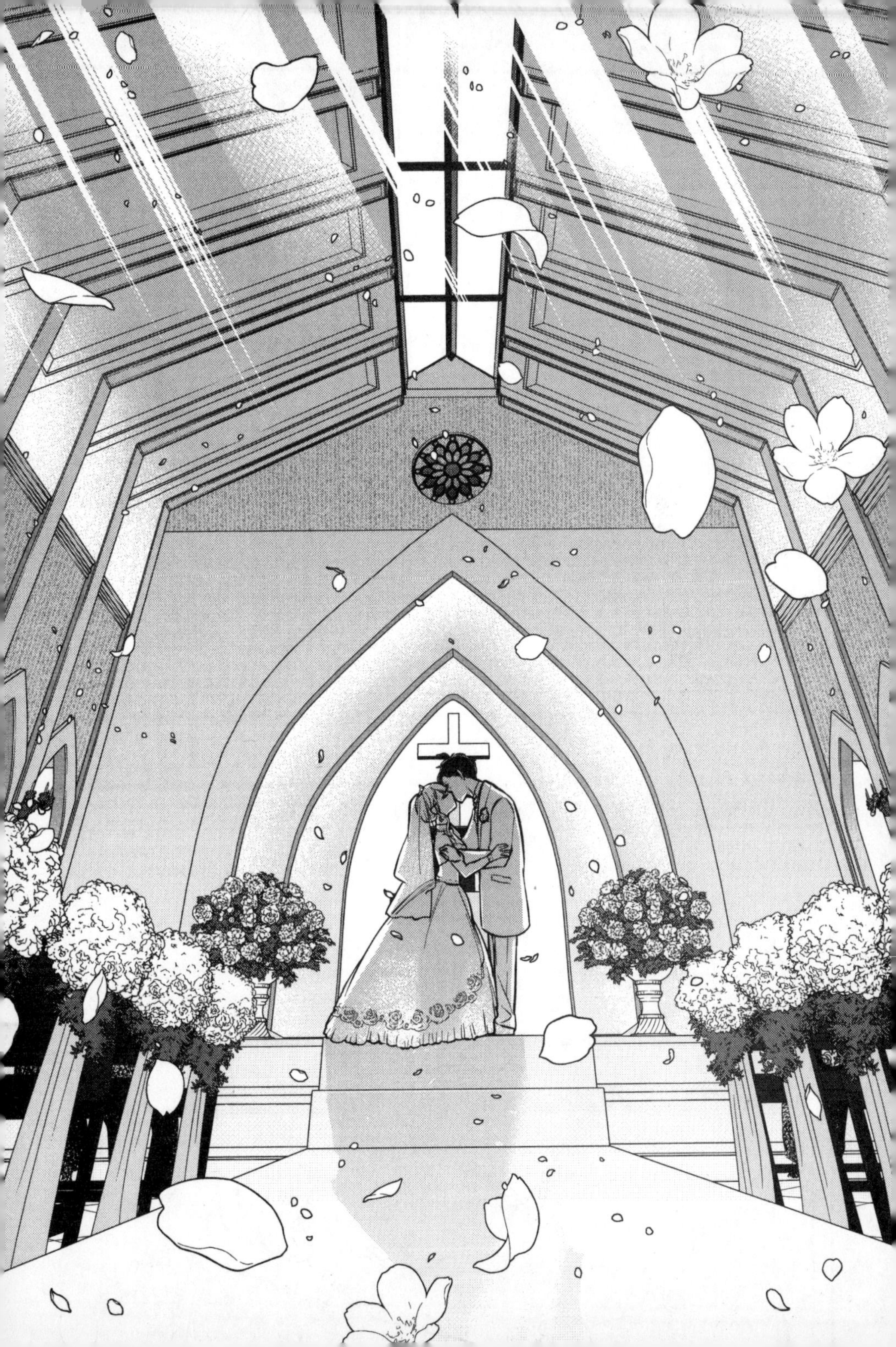

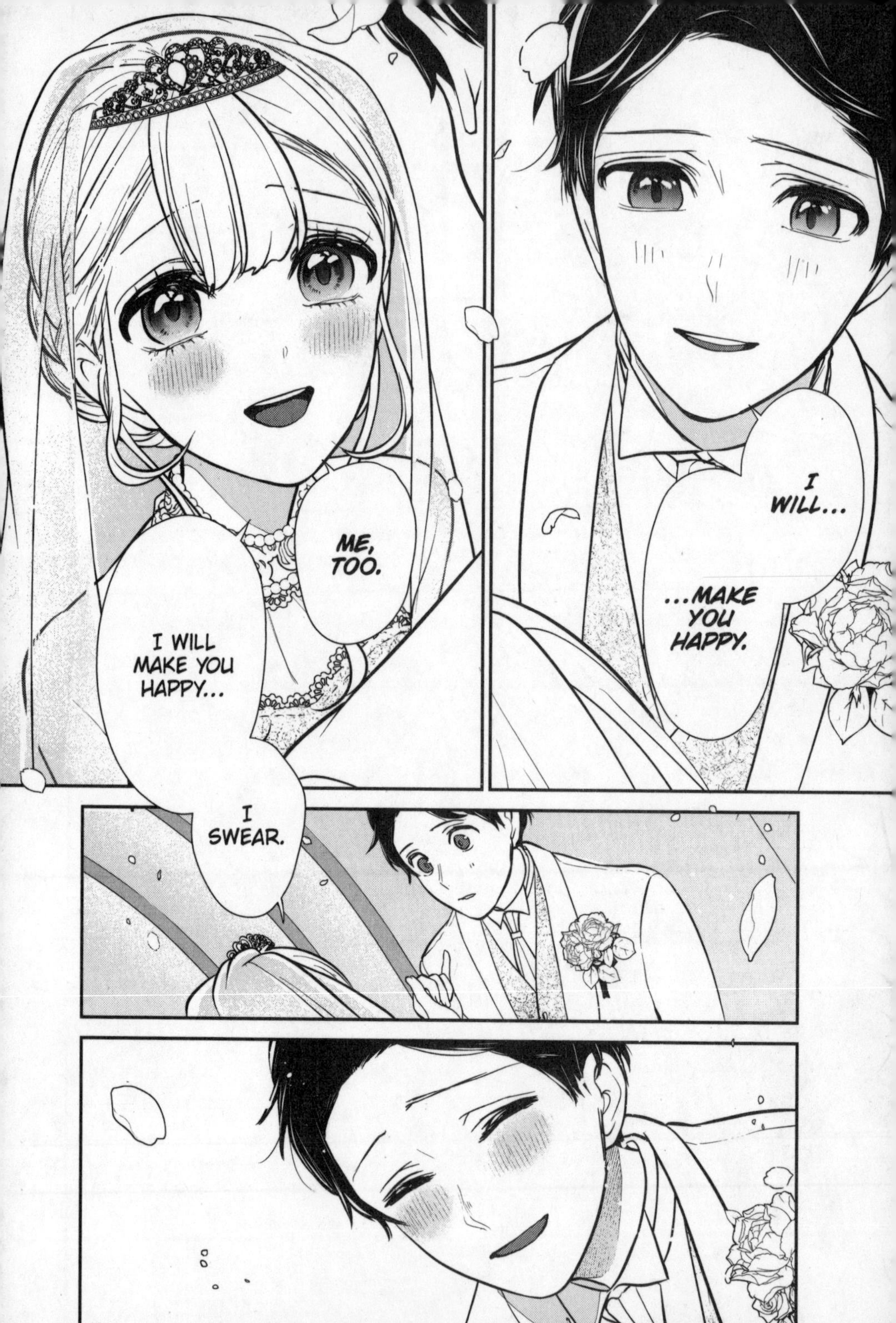
I WILL...
...MAKE YOU HAPPY.
ME, TOO.
I WILL MAKE YOU HAPPY...
I SWEAR.

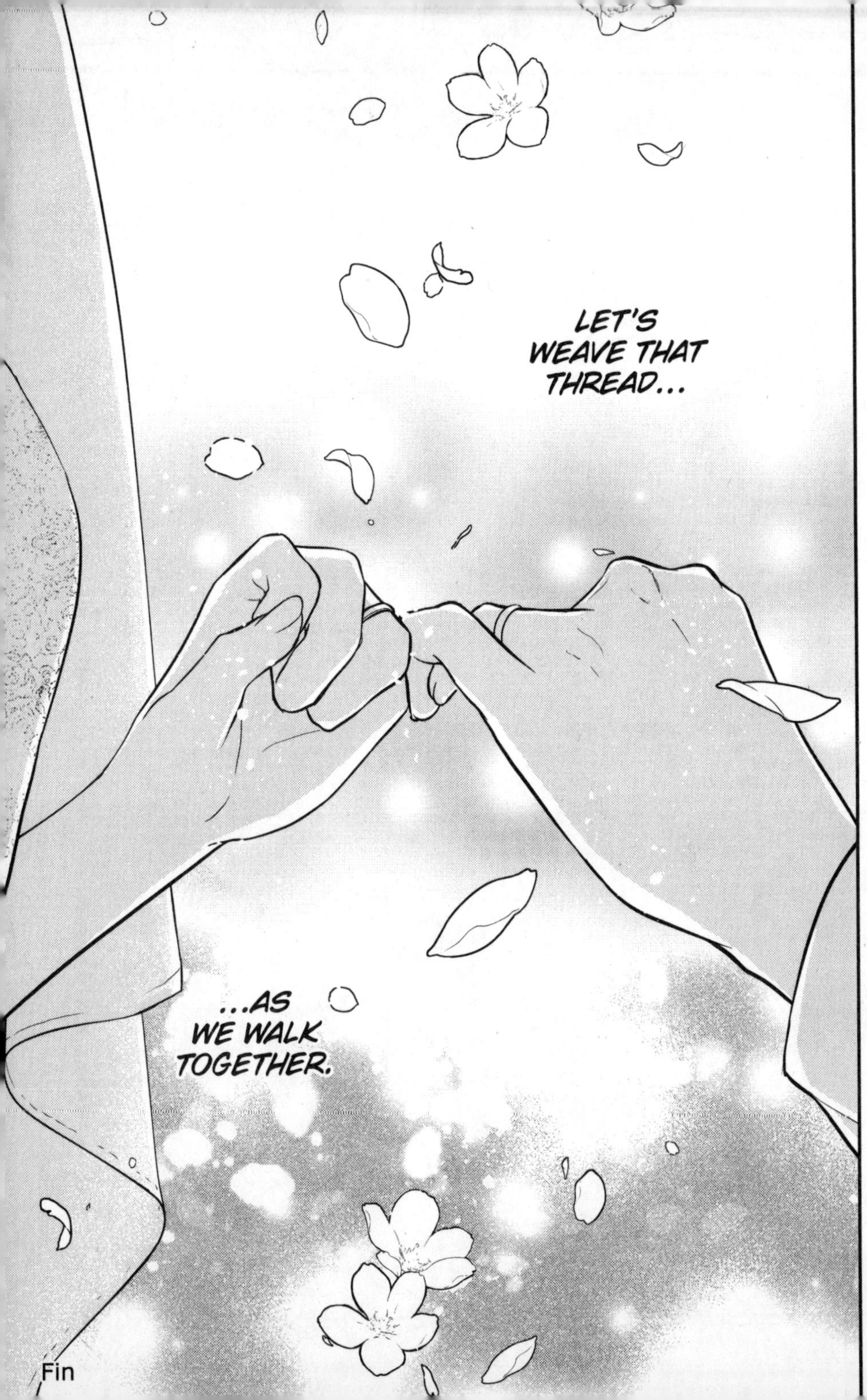
LET'S WEAVE THAT THREAD...
...AS WE WALK TOGETHER.
Fin

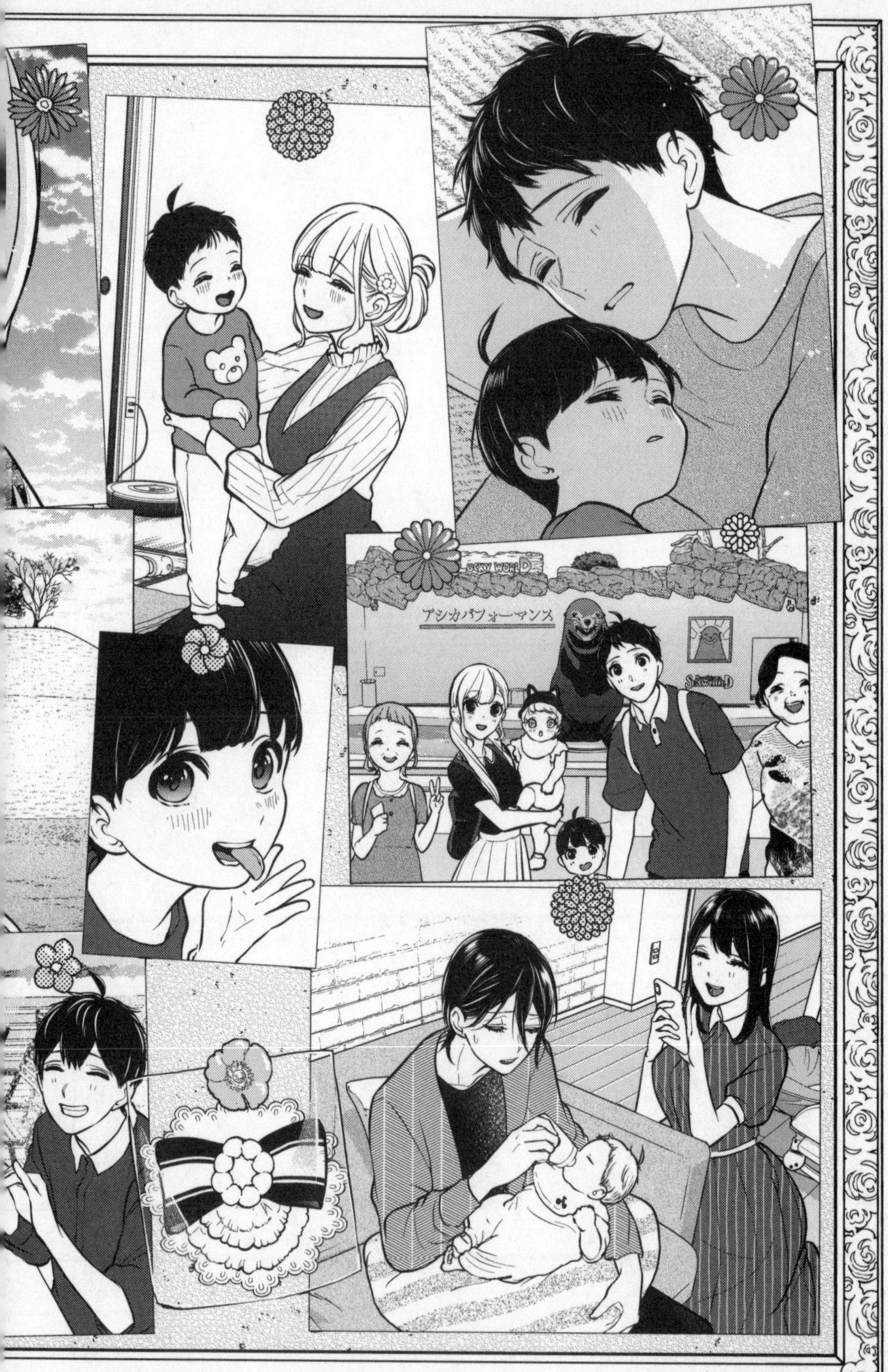
アシカパフォーマンス

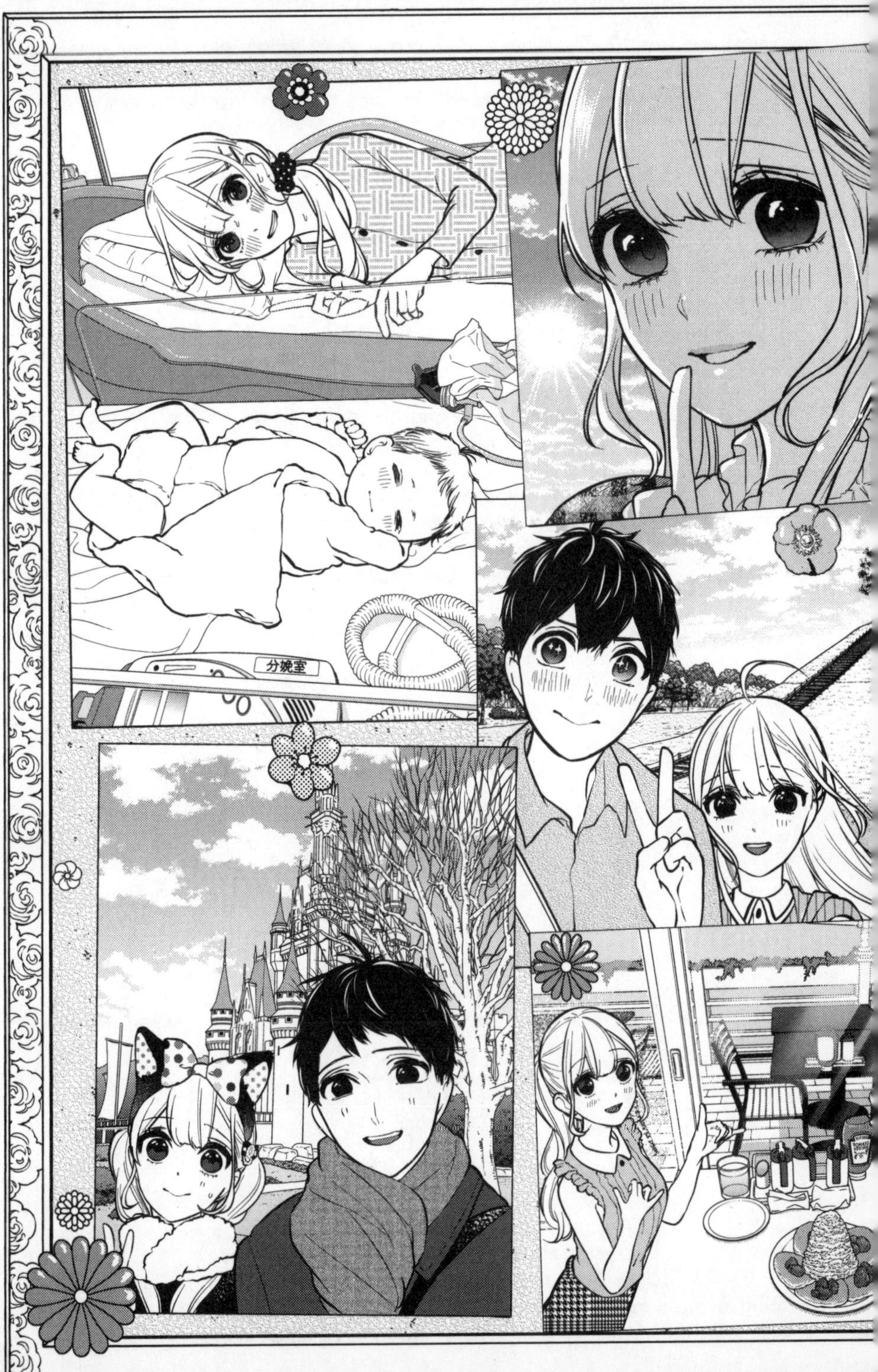
分娩室

A Kodansha Comics Trade Paperback Original
Love and Lies 12: *The Lilina Ending* copyright © 2022 Musawo
English translation copyright © 2022 Musawo

Published in the United States by Kodansha Comics, an imprint of
Kodansha USA Publishing, LLC, New York.

Publication rights for this English edition arranged through
Kodansha Ltd., Tokyo.

First published in Japan in 2022 by Kodansha Ltd., Tokyo
as *Koi to uso*, volume 12, Ririna ver.

ISBN 978-1-64651-313-0

Original cover design by Tadashi Hisamochi (hive & co., Ltd.)

Printed in the United States of America.

www.kodansha.us

1st Printing

Translation: Jennifer Ward
Lettering: Daniel CY
Editing: Aimee Zink
Kodansha Comics edition cover design by Phil Balsman

Publisher: Kiichiro Sugawara

Director of publishing services: Ben Applegate
Director of publishing operations: Dave Barrett
Associate director of publishing operations: Stephen Pakula
Publishing services managing editors: Alanna Ruse, Madison Salters, with Grace Chen
Senior production manager: Angela Zurlo